D0202797

RED STARS

RED STARS

PERSONALITY AND THE SOVIET POPULAR SONG
1955–1991

DAVID MacFADYEN

McGill-Queen's University Press
Montreal & Kingston · London · Ithaca

Legal deposit second quarter 2001
Bibliothèque nationale du Québec

Printed in Canada on acid-free paper

This book has been published with the help of
a grant from the Humanities and Social
Sciences Federation of Canada, using funds
provided by the Social Sciences and
Humanities Research Council of Canada.

McGill-Queen's University Press acknowledges
the financial support of the Government of
Canada through the Book Publishing Industry
Development Program (BPIDP) for its
activities. It also acknowledges the support of
the Canada Council for the Arts for
its publishing program.

Canadian Cataloguing in Publication Data

MacFadyen, David, 1964–
Red Stars : personality and the Soviet
popular song, 1955–1991
Includes bibliographical references and index.
ISBN 0-7735-2106-2
1. Popular music – Soviet Union – History
and criticism. 2. Popular music – Social
aspects – Soviet Union. I. Title.
ML3497.M143 2001   782.42164'0947'0904
C00-901683-X

Typeset in New Baskerville 10/12
by Caractéra inc., Quebec City

Once again for my parents, brother, and sister

CONTENTS

CONTENTS

INTRODUCTION

This is the first of three books designed to investigate a subject virtually passed over by English-language scholarship, and very rarely researched in Russia: the performers and texts of the Soviet popular song. Here I have in mind not the two specialized fields of jazz and the so-called bards, both of which have enjoyed serious attention. Instead I mean those considerably more influential and widely disseminated songs broadcast every day on Soviet radio for decades, on occasion garnering sales figures in the hundreds of millions. Songs so frequently broadcast and purchased had a profound social significance in the Soviet Union, yet remain unstudied, save their occasional inclusion in some broader studies of Soviet popular culture as a whole. Hoping to do justice to that significance, I have divided my research into three books concerning three periods: 1900–54, 1955–91 (this volume), and 1991 to the present.

Since all of the performers I discuss will no doubt be unfamiliar to my readers, I have chosen to focus on a small number of representative performers rather than taking an exhaustive, encyclopedic approach, listing hundreds of strangers and their work. This book, therefore, considers seven of the most famous singers in the Soviet Union, from the death of Stalin to the fall of the ideology he embodied. Biographies of each performer make them more credible as personalities and help to show how they became so famous. Discussing these singers in chronological order, we can also see how the notion of fame changed over the period in question. How famous could a singer afford to be in the Soviet Union? How did that personal renown express itself in the songs that made these people celebrities? As we will see, the answers to these questions change with the singers.

The evolution that took place in the world of Soviet popular songs not only reflects political and cultural shifts: the nature of fame in Russia after the mid-1950s allowed these songs to *create* change. They helped to alter Soviet society, all within the restrictive framework that financed, supported, and propagated them. The subtlest of games is played over several decades between public or "civic" vocal music and its gentler, "lyric" counterpart. Within an impersonal political system, the artist finds some room for personal expression – without disrupting a state-sponsored art form.

Approved by the state or not, these works would mean absolutely nothing in the long run if nobody *liked* them. As a result, I pay much attention to the way that both the Soviet press and its readers reacted to the growing dimensions of fame, to the impressive dimensions of a "star" and his or her work in a socialist society. By looking at what Soviet audiences liked (and dismissed), we can also help to define their outlook and desires. Performers, of course, anticipate those desires, and a culturally vital dialogue between stage and audience begins, based upon mutual sympathy rather than politics.

I begin this sentimental journey with an introduction to what the small stage of variety performances meant in Russia prior to the 1950s. I then offer an equivalent background to the notions I have touched upon here of "civic" and "lyric," so that we may understand the efforts of our performers to express subjective experience in an objectifying society. In order to place those efforts within the broadest possible definition of a shifting worldview across Eastern Europe, I also suggest how tendencies in Soviet philosophy of this period scribe a parallel path to that taken by the popular song. My hypotheses are followed by seven portraits of seven singers, their lives, and common craft. The various cultural and philosophical problems or tendencies outlined in my initial chapters shift and evolve throughout these careers, leading us little by little to what constitutes Russian popular culture today.

In closing, I hope with this book and the two that will follow to bring a remarkable and woefully underestimated aspect of Russian culture to the attention of English-speaking readers. Political generalizations and elitist attitudes have stopped us so often from asking perhaps the most important question of all in this field: "What did Russians *like*?" My hope is that these pages go some way towards an answer to that question.

In tracing these preferences across several continents, I must express my own thanks to an audience of sorts, those who observed this project taking shape. In St Petersburg, Russia, where most of the work took place, I made considerable use of the National Library on Ostrovskii

Square, and I would like to thank Natalia Kraineva once again for her help and guidance, together with Anna Ostrovskaia of External Services and the eternally jolly Alla Lapidus. (To study estrada and frown is impossible.) In that same building, Rob Romanchuk and Lisa Wakamiya also helped by endorsing and encouraging some initial concepts. On the Fontanka, I was greatly assisted by the Music Division, in particular the very obliging Vasilii Zvariichuk.

Elsewhere in the city I relied upon the wonderful Nadezhda Kavarina as research continued in various archives, museums, libraries, and academies devoted to theatre arts. Her colleagues Vladimir Bychkovskii and Slava Guretskii offered priceless advice and services in the hunting of archival sound recordings and photographic materials. Things rarer still were found in the archives of Vera Metlitskaia and Valerii Safoshkin, before whom a deep bow of gratitude is due. As ever, the hospitality and understanding of my friends Elena and Iosif made this entire process a most enjoyable one.

In Canada, the support of my colleagues was much appreciated: John Barnstead, Marina Glazov, Norman Pereira, and Ieva Vitins. The university's Document Delivery service allowed me to import the most exotic and elusive materials to this side of the Atlantic with great frequency and rapidity, for which I am very grateful. Also in Canada, the suggestions and first-hand knowledge of Olga Aleinikova and Dima Sikalskiy (the "Singing Chef") were a substantial comfort.

Between the two frosty locales of Halifax and Petersburg, my parents in Scotland, together with my brother and sister, helped to invest this project with the good cheer that it deserves and demands, so that, in the words of Alla Pugacheva, "Today we won't talk about the bad stuff. We'll only talk about happy things."

Red Stars

Maybe our songs will still be heard in 2001.

"We Sing Songs" (*My pesni poem*),
performed by Lev Leshchenko

Even the most hopeless ideology chooses
the most talented people for its prophets.

Lev Leshchenko, *Komsomol'skaia pravda,* 1994

PROLOGUE

"Buy some tickets! Come on in! Enjoy yourself, honourable ladies and gentlemen! You'll be amazed! The more you pay, the more you'll see!"

This brash invitation rang out on sunny Ukrainian fairgrounds a few years before the Russian Revolution. Inside, in the big top, moustachioed acrobats flew above strongmen, drawing gasps of amazement from tightly corseted young ladies and their earnest suitors. Outside, gypsy musicians strolled across the grass, serenading the crowds with their guitars for the price of a few coins. And at fairs and circuses very much like this, a young man by the name of Leonid Utesov honed both his theatrical and musical skills, going on to become the most famous bandleader in Ukraine and Russia.

Over the years the popular songs of strolling, seasonal musicians also moved indoors. The nostalgic tang of canvas and sawdust was replaced by clouds of tobacco smoke and the smells of beer and spirits, as taverns and bars hosted impromptu concerts. To the accompaniment of a gypsy guitar or a poorly tuned piano, tales were sung of love lost and found. If the compering skills of the landlord were not equal to the task, one could go instead to the music halls of the big towns and cities, where the same kind of songs were interspersed with comic skits, all loudly applauded by the finest members of society.

That resonant laughter ended in 1917, but the music continued, in the front-line tents and ditches of the Civil War, on both sides of the conflict. On agit-trains, songs or satirical sketches soothed the wounded going home and inspired zeal in those on their way to the fields of battle.

Music halls lived on for a while, but in the 1940s armed combat again thrust song into the strangest of settings. In the dank fields and trenches of World War II, artists cheered the Red Army with romances, waltzes, foxtrots, tangos, and folk numbers. When there was enough room, they were even joined by acrobats and jugglers. There and at home, at the front and in the rear, millions of men and women listened to sentimental songs and just for a moment forgot the horrors of battle.

In the quieter decades that followed, Soviet performers mixed these songs with theatre, while comperes used wit and whimsy in popular mélanges of vocal music, comedy, and poetry. This tradition, born before the Revolution, had outlasted all forms of international butchery. It still rolls on today with relative ease, surviving even the demise of socialism.

Let us now cross continents and seas to join the audience at Roy Thompson Hall in Toronto, where on 20 February 2000 the most famous woman in Russia has come to sing, bringing that same colourful and multigeneric heritage with her. As the lights dim, an instrumental prelude heralds the grand presence. Alla Pugacheva makes an entrance only after her venerable musicians, who sport t-shirts bearing the logo of Russian designer Valentin Yudashkin. She strides across the stage, her long hair a vivid russet, a voluminous dress of black silk billowing in her wake. In Moscow this show began with a dancer performing alone to the same music. Tonight there is no dancer, only the small ensemble and one artist, playing many roles. Just as in war, so in the rigours of the modern marketplace mobility and adaptation are key.

A few props stand in readiness on either side of the stage: a chair draped in the many folds of a white shawl, a low table with a mirror, powder-puff, wine glass, and a candle waiting to be lit. As the singer moves through the evening's program, she both plays the part of compere and transforms herself constantly, changing with the heroines and the emotions of each number. The shifting genres and skills of an Odessa fairground almost a century ago are absorbed in the artistry of one woman.

Caught in a tight circle of light upon the stage, Pugacheva adopts yet another persona. "I lived ..." She stops and confides, "I can't stand the past tense." She begins again: "She lived, she was, she sang ..."

Again she interrupts herself. "I don't want the past – and I'm afraid of the future. What's wrong with me? It's neither fatigue nor disappointment. It's some kind of death ... from joy. It's the feeling that you have something that others don't. You have that place, a holy place where you're never lonely ... Because I know that in this darkness, this

4

terrible darkness, you are all out there somewhere. You, the people who chose me, and chose these songs, the songs that helped me live ... I can never see you because of the bright lights, I can only hear you.

"This is happiness! It's a road, the long road of a creative life. It's strange, with its twists, turns and stopping-places, with farewells and chance meetings, with friendship and love – sometimes with disappointments ... What gives someone the strength to travel that road? I know that it's precisely this road that leads to a temple, to the temple of your hearts. They're all so varied, half-broken, resurrected with the strength of your spirit, both dark and radiant ... so very varied. May that road never end ... May it go on for as long as possible ... somewhere or other ..."

At this point her words turn to song. In her performance the philosophies of emotional maximalism, audible change, audience involvement, and endless role-playing in the present tense all find expression. The songs change, as do the roles, voices, and props.

Later Pugacheva offers a little more explanation of their rationale, to the delight of her audience – émigrés, nouveaux riches, Russo-Canadians, many themselves with much experience of social metamorphoses. She hears the audience applaud, and she interjects: "I should be the one shouting 'Bravo!' – to you, your lives, and all the things you've done, to all your remarkable characters. That's what has allowed me to create my heroines. Well, of course you thought I'm the one who's just like this or that heroine..."

She laughs. "No! Maybe I'm nobody in particular, so that it's easier for me to play any woman at all ... I change with pleasure from one woman into another ... But there's something about this one [in this song] ... She's different each and every time, because I just can't capture her. She's truly remarkable. A brightly made-up blond, full-bosomed, full-figured, always cheerful. Got a gold tooth, too. Didn't want a porcelain one. She thought, 'What's all that, then? Porcelain? Let 'em see I'm not poor!' You can talk about absolutely anything with her, but it's better to just shut up. All she has to do is ask, 'How are things with what's-his-name?' 'With who?' I say. 'Why do you even ask?' 'You forgot or something?' she says. 'I warned you – all men are sons of bitches ...'"

So begins another heroine, another song.

1
THE SOVIET POPULAR SONG AFTER STALIN

> The best of our popular singers today offer
> something new; they do so by embracing
> a tradition bequeathed by the masters of their
> chosen genre. Today's performers bring us
> their own understanding and view of the world,
> the suggestions and symbols of their
> generation. Their task lies not only in the
> propagation of Soviet songs, the propagation of
> our views; it lies also in struggling against an
> emotional drought. It's the struggle to promote
> good taste. The struggle to make one's listener
> or viewer brighter, better and purer. Basically,
> it's a struggle to cultivate feelings.[1]

In a tiny Soviet school in the late 1960s, a young teacher was having problems controlling her music class. As the boys and girls fled the room en masse, only her shouts that everybody had been awarded the lowest grade – one out of a possible five – stopped the exodus. Mercifully, she gave the students a chance to redeem themselves. Each was called to the front of the room to sing a popular song by Èdita P'ekha, entitled "The Boundless Sky." Those who sang well were now awarded four out of five; those who sang horribly were offered the same grade to shut up. The teacher was unable to offer a higher bribe, since a "1" cannot be altered to look like anything else except a "4," and she had no desire to explain her unorthodox tactics to her superiors.

Both the teacher, known to her class as Miss Pugacheva, and Èdita P'ekha would go on (at different times) to become perhaps the two most famous women in the Soviet Union. The following pages tell their stories and those of five other singers. Their songs in turn tell the story of Soviet popular culture since the death of Joseph Stalin in 1953. In order of seniority these performers are: Èdita P'ekha (born July 1937), Iosif Kobzon (six weeks later), Lev Leshchenko (1942), Sofiia Rotaru (1947), Valerii Leont'ev (March 1949), Alla Pugacheva (the following month), and Irina Ponarovskaia (1953). If the reader has any doubts as to the ability of this brief list to represent a political space equivalent to one-sixth of the earth's surface, I should note that recent estimates for the career sales of Alla Pugacheva's songs alone easily excede 200,000,000. The long-term disregard for copyright laws in Russia has undoubtedly been responsible for suppressing even this phenomenal statistic. Only cinema remained more popular in the Soviet Union than the type of song under investigation here.[2]

All the above performers were born into the Soviet Union of Joseph Stalin, Irina Ponarovskaia in the month of his death. Collectively, all seven embody the efforts of a generation to fashion a qualitatively different worldview after the waning of a philosophy prevalent since the end of 1927. At that time Stalin's star had risen, and with it the principal metaphor of an omniscient, ubiquitous presence that could unify all political and aesthetic phenomena. The sudden absence of that unity on 5 March 1953 ushered in two years of haggling amongst potential successors: Beria (for as long as political manoeuvring would allow), Malenkov, Molotov. The eventual victor, Khrushchev, enjoyed true ascendancy in February 1955. There he remained until 1964, ceding only to the corrupt and protracted term of Brezhnev's "Stagnation." Given – eventually – the market woes and concomitant Machiavellian eroding of Yeltsin's powers by wily oligarchs in the last few years of the twentieth century, it is not surprising that there is emerging today with Putin a powerful if not mythic nostalgia for an earlier order: "Empires have never been happily lost, and the mourning that follows is a natural response, a form of aesthetics and a form of politics."[3]

Popular entertainment today in Russia feels that loss deeply as it is swamped by "foreign" product and by the absence of any singular guiding principle, be it vaguely moral or specifically social. In film, for example, nothing has replaced something. Withstanding this vacuum, the most significant and stubborn champion of old-style Russian movie-making has been Nikita Mikhalkov, who won an Oscar for Best Foreign Film in 1994 with *Burned by the Sun*. Mikhalkov laments the loss of great Russian cinema, but as one critic has it, that sense of bereavement has been so pervasive for so long that any attempt to resurrect past traditions – no matter how honourable – seems hopelessly outmoded.

Mikhalkov makes the cinema of status, which must in some way be big in its staging; it must be a grandiose product. He is the recipient of a most Russian tradition, when the artist felt himself distinguished by a higher mission. All the same, though, an artist *is* just an artist and when he starts in all earnest to solve world problems, it can only be at the expense of what he does. Probably Mikhalkov has more right to do this than anybody else; he *does* make real cinema. [Yet] by doing so he stands outside of what we might call the current of modern culture, no matter how good or attractive his camera-work.

This, incidentally, is the fate of many great people; at some moment or other they step to one side and continue to make good films, but they're simply not in the spirit of the time.[4]

Columnist Iurii Gladil'shchikov's extension of this critique is germane: "Europe keeps on struggling with zero success against Hollywood expansionism. Many of our directors demand the same [stance ... but a] culturally defensive ideology, designed to protect [Russian] originality, will rarely stop expansionism and moreover leads merely to provincialism."[5] These two complementary attitudes to the lapsing of an ideology prompt the suspicion that to some degree rosy-spectacled retrospection is involuntary, either for one's youth, or for a finalized (and therefore riskless) past, in this case that of Russian culture's erstwhile high ethical standards.

Soviet culture drew often upon the ethical authority of a nineteenth-century realist tradition, as Joseph Brodsky noted in one essay: "From time to time in the course of our [twentieth] century, here and there one could hear voices nominating this or that [Soviet] writer for the status of the Great Russian Writer, purveyor of the [pre-revolutionary] tradition. These voices were coming from the critical establishment and from Soviet officialdom, as well as from the intelligentsia itself, with a frequency of roughly two great writers per decade."[6] In the great movies of the 1980s and during perestroika, this emphasis shifted from the politically moral to the morally political; the ethical art born of Soviet ideology began to criticize its parents. As recently as 1992 the film historian Anna Lawton wrote of the status quo in Russian filmmaking: "Today no filmmaker would dare release a film that does not include at least a sprinkle (and more often, an avalanche) of 'sharp social issues' – [of] organized crime, rackets, drugs, prostitution, youth violence, suicide, rape, corruption, alcoholism, shortages of housing and food, speculation, blackmail."[7]

Such social critiques have evanesced, however, as the very problems listed here became as widespread as they are today. Ironically, freedom of speech has meant that the number of people voicing what they feel will be heeded (or even heard) lessens constantly, to the point where the spoken hope for a better future becomes quiet yearning for a better past. Nabokov makes the same point in his own paean to Mnemosyne, *Speak Memory*, albeit with a sharper pen: "I found in the neighborhood [of Lausanne] quite a colony of old Swiss governesses. Huddled together in a constant seething of competitive reminiscences, they formed a small island in an environment that had grown alien to them ... One is always at home in one's past, which partly explains those pathetic ladies' posthumous love for a remote and, to be perfectly frank, rather appalling country [Russia], which they had never really known – and in which none of them had ever been very content."[8]

This chapter looks at a similar competition of love and grimness in Russian popular songs from the years following Stalin's death until the present. The newer names that have arisen in this genre over the last few years are to be the subject of a future study; here I concentrate on the experiences of seven established singers, all alive, working, and successful today. I follow their plans, creativity, and reputations over three decades relative to the two contradictory forces suggested in these initial pages: the moral integrity of the past versus the risk or transgression of novelty. This dynamic is closely linked to *lichnost'*, the notion of person(ality) or individuality emerging amongst the youth who flourished in the wake of the cult of personality.

Stalin's aura once made him "a man of magnetic power, distinguished by some kind of extraordinary biological or psychological qualities. Something akin to a born leader. Absolutely convinced of his destiny and able to convince all others of the same: those around him, a crowd, the nation."[9] Any social shift opposed to this type of *lichnost'* would have to involve either an inversion of the relationship between imperial subject and venerated, lofty object or a careful disassembling of that relationship altogether. It is the latter process, the gradual lessening of distance between high style and lowly consumer, which will be the focus of our attention. Petr Vail' and Aleksandr Genis describe that distance prior to 1953, and later dramatic changes:

Stalinist culture propagated works of the high genres. In movie theatres plays by the Moscow Academic Arts Theatre (MKhAT) predominated, symphonic music rang out from the radio, odes in both poetry and prose constituted literature ... This kind of art, emanating from above, had something of a sacral demeanor; but any kind of [opposing] art from the people [*narod*] would demand relations of equal status. An equalizing of artist and consumer would be needed .... [and so] the newly opened frontiers [of the Thaw] let in foreign art. The accessibility of its images, as is always the case, did not qualitatively improve social consumption; it merely worsened a type of imitation. Thus in the [resulting] eclecticism of the 1960s there arose Soviet mass culture: guitar songs, intimate poetry, fashionable clothing, youth slang, *Little Blue Light* [a New Year's Eve television show], lighter furniture. And then there was the most important thing – variety performances [*estrada*] ... The biggest role here was played by Èdita P'ekha.[10]

Who is Èdita P'ekha and why is she so important in the development of a post-Stalinist worldview? How did the singers who followed in her

9

elegant footsteps contribute to that view? The socio-political term "Thaw" is most commonly referenced through literature, through prose and poetry; but what about songs, the sung poetry heard by broad swathes of Soviet society on the radio? The songs of P'ekha, Pugacheva, et al. were so widespread that they fostered a new subjectivity, as we will see; but within the confines of a communist society (and especially given the manner in which personality or *lichnost'* is fashioned by popular music) to what degree could any of these performers afford to become famous? The attention given to their careers in the Soviet press documents how private renown can (or cannot) be fostered in a society of public philosophies. The story of these singers in fact affords an insight into the workings of self-realization in any modern society.

Before we start, however, the genre of the Russian popular song demands an introduction. Here I mean neither folk song nor even the better-known "bards" or guitar-poets of the 1960s. I mean – purely and simply – the *truly* popular, modern Soviet songs played to tens of millions of people every single day on the radio.

ESTRADA: SOME DEFINITIONS

It's always pleasant to see an injection of new
strength into the art of estrada, which is truly
a popular art-form, loved by our entire
[national] audience. It has merited this
affection over many years, having travelled the
glorious roads of both the first Five Year Plans
and the rapid construction work conducted
by the Communist Youth League. It has made
this journey together with the Soviet people.
How many bright memories are preserved
in the way songs instilled strength,
determination, and courage in the hearts of
our soldiers; they did so with a bold quip,
a fervent dance, witty folk songs [*chastushki*],
satirical ballads – all of which ridiculed
the enemy ... All of this lays a particular
responsibility upon the artists and singers of
Soviet estrada [today], it places certain
demands before them. The main one is
to be a worthy successor to the glorious
traditions of the Soviet song.[11]

Iosif Kobzon

Documenting the early tradition that enabled the "glorious" Soviet genre lauded here by Iosif Kobzon is a task that deserves a separate volume. Here my emphasis is directed towards the second half of the twentieth century, to provide a sketch of the pre-Thaw decades and then show their evolution in a post-Stalinist form of expression. Throughout this time estrada had often been on the defensive, struggling against accusations of triviality or, worse still, decadent maximalism. A late (1988) Soviet overview of the genre, puzzlingly titled *Estrada: What? Where? Why?*, summarizes the problem: "Estrada is rightly abused for its low taste, its absence of spirituality, the predominance of spectacle at the expense of content. All the same, this 'light,' 'second-rate' art-form, as the champions of high spirituality would have it, has entered firmly into social consciousness, into our daily lives, and has become an indispensable participant in all our holidays, at grand youth conferences and festivals. Its infectiousness and general accessibility help to bring people together."[12] But what *is* it?

The term came to the Russian language – if one casts a glance back far enough – from the French "estrade" or Spanish "estrado," meaning platform and stage; both definitions have been preserved in the Russian. A modern dictionary might offer the English equivalent, "variety," a term that perhaps carries overtones of Victorian music-halls. The most authoritative Soviet history of estrada and its development up to 1977 admits there is no muse of estrada,[13] an easily reached conclusion when one considers the following categories appropriate to a full definition of the term: theatre (of a light or comic nature), literary readings, feuilletons, satirical songs, comic stories, parody, compering, puppets, popular songs, folk music, vocal ensembles, dance, and finally (as if the bag were not mixed enough), circus.

The Soviet scholar E. Kuznetsov manages to see common ground among such diverse phenomena: forms of estrada expression adapt with little effort to various loci of public performance; they do not last long, they support a bold conception of the performer's individuality, and they tend towards the quotidian for their material, to the "living word," so that an emphasis falls often upon a contemporary socio-political thematic, on humour, satire, and publicistic intent.[14] One senses here an attempt to metamorphose traditional or pre-revolutionary arts into harbingers of something socialist. Richard Stites, in his broad investigation of all forms of Russian popular culture across this century, looks back to older, genuinely traditional amusements that might conceivably have prompted or promoted modern forms of light entertainment. He finds that estrada's origins are rooted in "rural and traditional outdoor shows … *Narodnoe guliane*, meaning carnival, folk fair or folk festival, was a traditional seasonal event with deep roots in pagan and Christian rites, minstrel companies and folk games. It offered fair-booth satire, sleigh rides, dancing bears, carousels and swings, ice hill sledding, food stalls, and general drinking and merrymaking. In the last years of the old regime, folk fairs were organized on designated grounds or indoors by private enterprise, government, and civic societies who hoped to woo people away from politics or the tavern. Their ban on drinking and stringent rules [over many years] marked a shift from spontaneous popular festival to greater social control."[15]

Here we have the crux of the matter: what was once a supposedly spontaneous or private form of expression becomes useful for a public purpose. This shift has been accompanied by a filtering of history so that Soviet histories of estrada song prior to 1917 are often derisive or prudishly disapproving, as in the following: "There was indeed a time (which we recall with a smile) when on the Russian pre-revolutionary estrada heart-rending romances were popular. They had a somewhat 'harsh' intonation, as in the pseudo-gypsy or pseudo-Russian songs 'My Heart Is Broken,' 'Booze-Up, What a Booze-Up,' 'Marusia Got Poisoned' and so on. During the First World War the bourgeois public also loved salon songs about refined feelings, exoticism, and eroticism: 'I'm Tired of Life,' 'Lady Coke-Head,' 'Kitty Dear' and others. Performers sang these works with a languid limpness."[16]

AN INTRODUCTION
TO POST-REVOLUTIONARY ESTRADA

> We took the baton from the hands of the
> famed masters: Klavdiia Shul'zhenko, Leonid
> Utesov ... We are obliged to preserve the best
> traditions of the Soviet song, which "people
> need like a bird needs wings to fly," as Utesov
> once sang. Not only to preserve them, but to
> multiply them and then with dignity hand
> the baton over to young performers
> as they come to replace us.[17]
>
> Lev Leshchenko

What the Revolution did to song in Russia has been neatly expressed by the nation's greatest bandleader, Leonid Utesov: "The Soviet song is a new genre. It is neither a romance, nor an urban pre-revolutionary song. It is a form born of the Revolution, reflecting its forward movement, its struggle for a new life, for a *new person*."[18] The pan-generic, almost carnivalesque manner in which the Revolution swept across all forms of artistic expression was in harmony with estrada, given its links with the chaotic, messy theatricality of circus: "The mutual connections between estrada and the circus have deep historical roots. In Russia these roots stretch back to the work of the *skomorokhi* [errant comic minstrels], who offered a truly syncretic estrada or circus type of performance. Around the puppet-fairs there later appeared gymnasts and dancers, acrobats and storytellers, athletes and impersonators, magicians and singers."[19] One of our chosen singers, Valerii Leont'ev, in 1988 noted several points of contact or similar means of expression between estrada and the circus arts: "Both arts demand exaggeration, the grotesque, the strong expression of feelings. Last of all, they both use tricks or stunts (*triuki*). Estrada and the circus combine well. Even though circus doesn't look that good in the framework of a stage's wings, estrada adapts well within the big top."[20] Circus is a muddled, multigeneric performance, paralleling all that estrada offers.

Like the circus, which is both unified and offered directly to the audience by a ringmaster, estrada has the equivalent in a compere, who acts as a form of semantic control, creating a meaningful whole from the initially disparate acts and intentions of any estrada show. He also exemplifies the audience-oriented nature of the performance, as opposed to the voyeuristic stance of a typical theatre audience. For unlike theatre, estrada is performed directly at an audience; that direction is emphasized by the compere's frequent addressing of those seated before him.

This direct address of performer to spectators was echoed by those writers who took advantage of the small stage to read their works, in particular the Futurist Vladimir Maiakovskii (1893–1930) during the 1920s. Maiakovskii's confrontational, agitational style was well suited to the degree of audience contact traditionally expected by an estrada audience. Just as variety performers travelled with their respective genres to the front-line Red troops during the Civil War of 1918–20, so Maiakovskii – ever the mobile rhetorician – moved to find his audience, giving more than two hundred performances in over fifty cities across the incipient union. He conducted these extended searches for an audience "perhaps because he was unsatisfied by the [already huge] runs of his published works, believing that he was not yet reaching a [truly] wide audience. He wanted to present himself to young people, to workers, to the new intelligentsia, to teach them how to understand his poetry. But there is another reason, of which Maiakovskii himself once spoke. He wrote his poetry to be perceived aurally, poetry to be read aloud from the estrada."[21] This, no doubt, is why his verse was prized by some later variety performers such as Alla Pugacheva: "I still love Shklovskii's memoirs of Maiakovskii. That's the kind of book that's dear to me even now. It means more to me than just literature."[22] Aleksandr Bronevitskii, the creative force behind Èdita P'ekha's ensemble, was also an admirer of the poet,[23] and Iosif Kobzon has read Maiakovskii's verse between songs of the same period at his concerts.[24] Even Kobzon's aesthetic opposite, the younger Valerii Leont'ev, has been likened to the young, extroverted Maiakovskii and his dramatic "creative personality (*lichnost'*)."[25]

Maiakovskii transformed the quiet and intimate literary readings by the Symbolist poets prior to the Revolution into those which were large, loud, and accessible. "Shunning all intermediaries, he used the estrada to make contact directly with the masses and read them his verse, to toss [revolutionary] slogans into the auditorium and put a philistine in his place – yet in a lyrical piece he could also read what was most precious to him. His estrada performances were in fact talented one-man shows; he read, played compere, answered audience notes, presented improvisational monologues, and in moments of heckling could stun his opponent with a biting, precise come-back."[26] Working in music-halls, Maiakovskii lamented on one occasion how "theatre has forgotten it's a spectacle," and so he made up for it – with the help of his audience.[27]

This new, democratic form of stage-floor relationship in Maiakovskii's career, the levelling of contact between performer and audience, is shown by the fact that between 1926 and 1930 some 20,000 notes were passed to him from the rows of viewers.[28] Fostering a novel dialogue such as this was no doubt a great struggle for early Soviet performers. Lenin's New Economic Policy (NEP) through most of the 1920s allowed for the solace – horror of horrors – of private enterprise. Troubled by peasant outrage at the state's seizure of their harvests, Lenin opted quickly for a system of taxes that would calm the peasantry and allow them to sell their excess in the autumn or to make a profit. Filthy lucre could be smelled everywhere, in all forms of art, "but estrada in particular. There arose legal or semi-legal private enterprise, a cynically commercial stance towards estrada presentations, which were run by administrators or businessmen on the make. They attracted hack-work, vulgarity, and began pandering to the common tastes of NEP's public. Estrada wandered between restaurants and bars. From the boards there once again sounded low-grade satirical ballads and songs, some of which were far from being ideologically inoffensive."[29]

One aesthetic response to such offensiveness is the subject of a 1924 tract by Maiakovskii's publisher, Osip Brik. The book *Estrada for Dining Tables* concerns one of the best-known and influential variety theatre groups after the Revolution, the Blue Blouse (Siniaia Bluza). They performed many works by Maiakovskii, inspired by his status as a poet "both mobilized and summoned by the Revolution."[30] Like their mentor and sometime playwright, the Blue Blouse also travelled the Soviet Union offering a new audience a new aesthetic: "political topicality, a combination of revolutionary pathos and biting satire ... In its finest shows it was truly a 'live newspaper,' responding to current events with the vivid directness and primitivism of its chosen artistic forms."[31] Such "live" press used songs together with dramatized news items, all in mockery of anti-revolutionary elements.[32] Their wardrobe was meagre: a shield might represent a Red soldier, an apron and head scarf a peasant woman, or a top-hat would symbolize a diplomat.[33] The Blue Blouse worked together in this manner for about ten years, thanks to their constant ability to answer the "urgent call of the times," said Brik. "Their earliest programs were artistically pretty hopeless, but you could already see a hint of how to unify serious agitational content with an investigation into vivid forms of estrada."

Brik's study refers to worries amongst some members of Siniaia Bluza that variety was perhaps not a genre able to support the long-term, increasingly serious concerns of agit-entertainment; estrada would "spoil their dignity." Nevertheless, as they continually resorted to dramatic crudity and immediateness, the actors would ultimately capitulate yet do nothing more than play with semantics: they re-named themselves a "polit-cabaret." Even so, nobody knew exactly what kind of language the cabaret repertoire would be composed of: old or new, "literary" or journalistic? "Where's the text? [Because] the repertoire's the main thing."[34] The success of ideological Soviet estrada depended on language, on words to unify the various parts into a whole. Brik observes, "an estrada number is only possible where all its elements, beginning with make-up and ending with the *text*, are uni-fied in an organic whole. The insufficiency of any one element will ruin the entire number."

Brik uses his experiences with the renowned troupe to champion the cause of topical, journalistic, and transient estrada as a prime Soviet genre: "The opinion exists – and not for nothing – that permanent theatres with their so-called major forms exist here in the Soviet Union as leftovers of another [earlier] culture. There is also the [similar] opinion that any monumental form of Soviet theatre is destined to fail, since our age and culture are not monumental but transitional. In this transitional time culture moves not in grand forms, but those that change quickly, are mobile and small."[35] Brik makes a case for estrada as *the* Soviet form of cultural expression, the one that both reflects and meets the needs of daily socialist life better than anything else: "Soviet theatre cannot build itself upon a rift between that [old] theatre and the present political situation. No matter how hard stationary theatres try to give their productions a political character, it'll never work. By

their very nature they are completely obliged to fall behind – far
behind – the problems of life today. Only estrada can keep in step with
the political calendar. There's absolutely no doubt whatsoever that
when the time comes for battle once again, estrada will be the one and
only theatrical genre that'll be able to step – there and then – into the
workings of widespread, revolutionary labour."

ESTRADA IN WARTIME

> The words to P'ekha's song "There Will Never
> Be War" are felt as the vow of a woman
> and mother for whom nothing is dearer than
> a peaceful world. After all, both her daughter
> Ilona and grandson Stasik will live in that
> world. P'ekha sings like a citizen of
> her country, one who has known both
> the awful years of World War II and
> the threatening skies of Afghanistan.[36]

Variety after the Revolution emphasized dialogue with its audience and
the resulting ability to both show and fashion contemporary reality. I
have already mentioned that performers, bearing the new agitational
thematic in their songs, travelled to the Red Army's front lines. There
they discovered that the revolutionary public on the firing line was
not especially enamoured of heroic, public arias. One Soviet historian
notes the dogged persistence of "intimate songs," "mood-songs," and
gypsy romances. Again Lenin's New Economic Policy is viewed as
responsible for this obsolete, yet fondly fostered subjectivity.

Having survived the Civil War without great losses, these types of songs
acquired full strength during NEP. "Intimate songs" found support among a
certain section of the population after the Revolution. They created an illu-
sionary world of isolation, estrangement from the stormy onslaught of a new,
unclear world. Gypsy romances were accepted even more willingly by a wide
audience. It was their accessibility that attracted the most untrained of listeners
– one could even perform them to a guitar accompaniment. They had a
simple, usually primitive content, the heightened emotionality that is common
to any such song, and a shifting of emotions towards either melancholy or a
furious, heady ecstasy. All of this pleased, charmed, and excited its audience
and was therefore happily embraced.[37]

In the late 1920s, no doubt as an organized response to such
stubborn decadence, music-halls were funded by the state in major

Soviet cities including Moscow, Leningrad, Gor'kii, Rostov-on-Don, and Taganrog.[38] The capital's music-hall opened in 1926, and for ten years until its closure (when it was handed over to a folk troupe) it offered variety shows, unified both ideologically and aesthetically by a resident company. One of its last artistic directors, Nikolai Akimov, strove to separate estrada from the classical, purer genres by insisting upon a synthetic aesthetic, mixing drama, opera, ballet, operetta, songs, and circus.[39] The Kremlin was unimpressed. Despite having been a generous sponsor for an entire decade, the state was now asking whether estrada was by its very nature unavoidably bourgeois and fit for extinction, natural or otherwise. Certainly some tendencies within the lighter genres were very much at odds with the officially endorsed aesthetic of Socialist Realism: "Music-hall with its inclination towards the grotesque, eccentricity, and patent showiness, with its wide use of circus numbers (some of which were *foreign*), brought more and more attacks upon itself. Many critics were scared by music-hall's movement towards satire, [but] without satire, music-hall cannot get by; it is the very essence of its being." The Moscow Music Hall closed, and Leningrad's equivalent suffered the same fate.

Even outside of such establishments, topical songs suffered. Given the new, grandiose leanings of Stalinist art after the 1920s, the subjective interpretation of satire or love songs was outmoded, to say the least. Singers moved into the genre of (non-satirical) feuilletons for the sake of safe, political clarity and a "more meaningful content." Others organized and conducted estrada orchestras. A few tried to stay true to their songs, yet "they could only do so by adopting a more declamatory air or a spirit of crude time-serving." The result was unfortunate, as "pathos looks rather silly when the melody of a gypsy romance is used for songs about industrialization and collectivization."[40] In general, songs between the 1920s and '30s reflect a lessening of the performer's significance and an increase in a given song's integral (textual) importance, as idiosyncratic estrada is squeezed out of the big cities.[41] It matters less *who* is singing than *what* is being sung. Politics matter more than personality, because public life is more important than private.

This tendency towards homogenization is marked further still by the formation in 1931 of the State Union of Music, Estrada and Circus (GOMÈTs). In an initial survey GOMÈTs found that the standards – as defined by the state – of many estrada performers left much to be desired. One year after the creation of the Soviet Union's officially endorsed aesthetic of Socialist Realism, a call went out for the Writers' Union to help estrada out of its ideological doldrums.[42] The announcement was further testament to an ongoing disparity between big Stalinist aesthetics and the little art forms of estrada. Even in 1940, when a large exhibition was held to celebrate the achievements of Soviet variety, suspicion persisted as to its applicability for a socialist society. It came under constant fire for being excessively "light" or entertaining (*razvlekatel'nyi*). "The ability to entertain was often perceived as 'scoffing' [at Soviet mores], as satire of the everyday which had become mere 'pettiness.'"[43]

The one highly entertaining male voice sounding clearer than any other through the monumental greyness of Stalinist culture is that of Leonid Utesov. That voice is both a symbol of (sung) subjectivity under Stalin and a harbinger of the braver estrada under Khrushchev. Utesov's female counterpart is Klavdiia Shul'zhenko. These performers – both Ukrainians, incidentally – are frequently referred to by the singers in this book as their two greatest mentors from Soviet traditions of previous decades.

LEONID UTESOV

> For me Kobzon is singer number one on
> today's estrada. Why is he so dear to me?
> I remember how he started; at that time I had
> dispatched a great deal of criticism (mentally,
> not openly!) in his direction. I wondered why
> nature had given him such a beautiful voice,
> so surprising in its timbre, just so he could sing
> with that voice alone and not his heart? I was
> convinced he'd snap – and do so in a really
> petty fashion. You can't imagine how happy
> I was to find that he had eventually got to
> grips with his surroundings, sensed life and
> figured out his role in art. Edith Piaf once
> said: "You think we've got lots of people who
> know how to sing songs – and indeed there are
> thousands of them. But give me *a personality!*"
> And here's Kobzon, who in my view has
> become just such a personality in his art.
> Leonid Utesov, 1978[44]

Utesov (whose real name was Lazar' Vaisbein) was born in Ukraine in 1895. By the age of fifteen he had already begun his career in estrada. Though he sang on occasion at Jewish weddings, he gave his real energy to a circus troupe. He moved on to provincial operettas and then concentrated upon songs alone, beginning with those of his native Odessa, performed to a guitar accompaniment. This city, founded by Russia in the late eighteenth century as the hub of its southern trade, was naturally a cosmopolitan centre, and family links to the port were surely a reason why Utesov, when he turned his hand to literary readings, performed the tales of fellow townsman Isaak Babel (1894–1941). Babel's tales, set in the cruelly pragmatic Jewish underworld of Odessa or the morally ambiguous chaos of the Civil War, did not lend themselves to didactic manipulation. Utesov also read the Leningrad satires of Mikhail Zoshchenko, born in 1895, again Ukrainian and yet another writer whose work confused the authorities by blurring the thin line between instructive and destructive mockery. (The year of 1946, however, proved to be a humourless one when Stalinism, in the form of A.A. Zhdanov, had Zoshchenko expelled from the Writers' Union.) Similar questions of ambiguity arose early in Utesov's history. Something of an individualist, he was expelled from school for abusing the theology master and smearing his own clothes with ink. Quite *why* he did so remains a mystery.

After his schooling, neither World War I nor the Revolution resulted in military postings far from home, so his family life and his professional career were uninterrupted. He managed to extend his dramatic skills to silent movies after a bold move to Petrograd (St Petersburg) in 1922. Over the next few years, showing no preference for any one genre, he gained a reputation as a singer. By the time he cut his first Moscow recording in January 1930, questions were being asked about the apoliticism of his work, performed to a happy mélange of upbeat, artless jazz, and gypsy violins. "In this talented artist's songs of the 1920s, people of the urban netherworld and self-centred philistines settle into their free and easy ways ... [Take, for example,] the good-natured cynic, grown languid beside the samovar with his girlfriend Masha who promises so much. It goes without saying that when performing such a repertoire, Utesov presented that cynic ironically. But 'Nevsky [Prospekt, in Petrograd] and its tasteful public' were not going to judge anybody in its hunger for fun. They embraced all this with leniency and – no doubt – great sympathy. That Petrograd public loved the exoticism of the underworld. The critics [however] were right to criticize Utesov for the insufficiencies of his repertoire."[45]

The song referred to here is "By the Samovar," recorded in the winter of 1933 when Utesov was heavily influenced by British and American jazz musicians such as Jack Hylton and Ted Lewis. The simmering samovar is used as an extended sexual simile, and indeed, as the Soviet critics harped, there is no socially redeeming aspect to this song. Here, instead, perhaps as a result, is the joy of Utesov's music. The song begins with a slow, melancholy trumpet and the

Utesov with some of the band members who helped him
institute the idiosyncratic, theatrical traditions of Soviet jazz
after the late 1920s

plaintive call of a gypsy violin, straight from a pre-revolutionary
romance. Together they become a stately tango – but suddenly the
tempo doubles, and cheerful syncopation breaks out from the piano.
With a banjo playing rhythm and a horn section playing bass, we move
faster and faster.

У самовара я и моя Маша,
А на дворе совсем уже темно.
Как в самоваре, так кипит страсть наша.
Смеется месяц весело в окно.

Маша чай мне наливает,
И взор ее так много обещает.
У самовара я и моя Маша –
Вприкуску чай пить будем до утра!

[My Masha and I sit by the samovar; it's already pitch-black in the
courtyard. Our passion is bubbling like the samovar. The moon looks
merrily through the window. Masha pours me some tea, and her look

promises so much. My Masha and I sit by the samovar – we'll drink tea with sugar until dawn!][46]

This introspective world is just as small in the early recording "Bye!" (Poka!). Utesov directs his words towards those at the concert hearing the song, a cheeky farewell to his band members or their paying clientele. The two vowels of the title are repeatedly drawn out in each chorus as he plays the pseudo-crooner. Jazzy piano and horns are mixed down to allow for rhythmic games by the percussion section. Here we have minimum music and maximum croon: the effect is deliberately silly.

А теперь, когда, ребята,
Отзвучал наш джаз,
Вы домой скорее отправляйтесь!
И, прощаясь, вам скажу,
Как приятно сейчас –
Ни привет, ни до свиданья,
Ни прощайте, а ...

Пока! Пока!
Уж ночь недалека.
Пока! Пока!
Вы нас не забывайте!
И намекну я вам пока –
Вы надоели нам слегка!
Пока! Пока!
Уж ночь недалека.

[Lads, now that our jazz has played, get off home sharpish! And, seeing you off, I'll say how good it feels right now – not a "Hi!" nor a "Til we meet," not "Farewell," but ... Bye! Bye! Night's not far off. Bye! Bye! Don't you forget us! For now I'll let you know that we're a little bored with you! Bye! Bye! Night's not far off.[47]]

The animated relationship of Utesov to what "is important and dear to *him*, to that without which he'd have no life,"[48] was also embodied in the form of his ensemble, its "theatricalized jazz" (*tea-dzhaz* for short). "Utesov would appear as singer, dancer, violinist, play on strange instruments and act as compere ... The music was not an independent element of the program, more an aid to what was happening on stage. The orchestra turned into a troupe of actors, playing musical instruments ... Thus from the very first attempt to use jazz for a staged program of songs, the original talent of Soviet estrada's undisputed master stood out, together with the lyricism and optimism of his art."[49] Some archival shots of Utesov's *tea-dzhaz* were used in the 1986 film *How to Become a Star* (discussed in a later chapter) and are undoubtedly hinted at in the Soviet perestroika comedy of 1983, *Jazzmen* (*My iz dzhaza*), which tells how American ragtime was slowly weeded from the repertoire of young Soviet musicians.

Utesov's attraction for audiences lay in his stubborn insistence upon lyricism, upon the private importance of individualized Odessa under-world characters in his songs. "Perhaps in these numbers, as in no others, listeners sensed a freedom limited by no one, a freedom lacking both in their own lives and in all the compositions which had been edited or constrained by warnings from 'above,' the [edited] work of composers and poets who were scared of a minor key, of decadence, of a descent into intimacy."[50]

Not only the way he performed brought Utesov fame: his strong good looks were undoubtedly a factor. Years of working on the docks in Odessa had given him a sinewy, muscular physique. He wore his dark hair combed or lacquered back without a parting, but energeti-cally directing the band, he was often caught on film with that hair falling rakishly across his brow. "He had masses of female admirers whose love for him neared fanaticism. Once during a concert Utesov fell through the gridirons and was badly bumped about. A rumour reached Odessa that he had died; one of his female fans shot her-self."[51] The way he lived was of great interest, in particular his extra-marital affairs. Despite fifty years of wedlock, his multitudes of female followers made temptation too great.

The accusations of decadence or simply "sticking out" too much come when the lyricism of these songs (or the ensemble that performs them) is transferred to one man, in this case Utesov himself. Take for example a 1929 review of the busy, jolly *tea-dzhaz* and its front-man, more of a gentle raconteur than a gifted singer: "If the 'family atmo-sphere' of this matter [the concert] was expressed in the liveliness of the performance alone, that'd be a plus and not a minus. But when *between* the numbers the tireless Utesov starts telling his old Odessa stories, that 'cheapens the brand name,' it makes the whole idea vulgar. *Tea-dzhaz* clearly lacks the hand and careful editing of an experienced director."[52]

Utesov was accused even in 1932 of perpetuating the vulgar tradi-tions of NEP, three years after the policy had passed into obscurity.[53] He had frequent troubles with the authorities but was saved by Stalin's peculiar fondness for some of his songs written in criminal slang. One memoir records a pre-war concert at the Kremlin when Utesov was approached behind the scenes by a master of ceremonies in military uniform. He told the bandleader to play "From an Odessa Lock-Up" (*S odesskogo kichmana*), about a dying prisoner on the run who begs his partner to tell a lie: "Comrade, comrade, / Tell my mother / That her son died at his post / With a sword in one hand, / A rifle in the other / And a jolly song on his lips."[54] "I'm not allowed to play that stuff," replied Utesov. "*He* asked for it," said the MC and gestured over his shoulder through a gap in the curtain to where Stalin sat among some military cadets.[55]

The formalist critic Viktor Shklovskii, writing about Utesov in 1946, described the charm of these modest songs which reached all the way to the Kremlin. "We're all very interested in the quotidian song because it uses the material people think with, it's sung on the streets, people are brought up with it. The words of a romance dictate how lovers talk to each other. Kids sing movie songs on the street. We're all deep in an ocean of songs."[56] That combination of familiarity, private concerns, and nationwide popularity let the authorities overlook their dislike for Utesov as an individual, especially during wartime, when his band financed several planes, christened "The Happy Guys" (*Veselye rebiata*) after the 1934 musical of the same name. The movie had been a huge success, and in fact starred Utesov in the role of a shepherd who becomes a bandleader; it did nothing to increase the distance between his actual and artistic personae, between actuality and art. In the film he plays an eternally naive yet honest young man, heartlessly shunned at a southern resort by an audience longing for western notions of cultivation. By contrast, he soon becomes a huge success in an ingenuous (and often violently chaotic) jazz ensemble. Testament to the film's lasting influence on future estrada stars is a remark by Alla Pugacheva in 1985: "I dream of helping to create the kind of films like *Circus* [1936] or *The Happy Guys*."[57]

The front-line success in Utesov's repertoire was "Mick from Odessa" (*Odessit Mishka*), a song whose social significance or patriotism was once again relayed by his friendly warble so that it had a wholly private resonance. Others had sung it before, but "it was wholly indebted for its success to Utesov's performance. He brought it alive with his personal touch, enriched its musical and lyrical content." The bandleader's own memoirs tell of receiving 423 letters in 1942 from other "Micks" at the front. Wrote one soldier, "That song's about me … I'll kill more of the scum with it than I have already. I'll get back at them for our beautiful Odessa"[58] (a rather violent response to a lazy, jazzy song, one might think).

The song has four similar verses, beginning with a description of Odessa's "broad estuaries and green chestnut trees." In four scenes

Mick experiences the stages of the city's wartime metamorphosis: the town of his youth, then under enemy fire, left in retreat, and finally won back in triumph. Despite his rapid changes in fortune, Mishka is "from Odessa and that means / Neither woe nor misfortune scare you. / You're a sailor, Mick, sailors don't cry / Or ever lose their cheery spirit." His mother tells him so in his youth, he tells himself on duty, and a commissar reminds him in battle of his southern duty to be happy. But the return to his beloved city is too much for his emotions to handle, and there Mick lets the tears flow.

The ensemble's music for this song is in no way melancholy. The gracefully harmonized horn section crafts unhurried, stylish melodies, more than a little reminiscent of Glen Miller. Despite the serene, American-style solos, nevertheless the musicians pause on several occasions for Utesov to play the southern fool, dramatize a character, or draw out another vowel or two, in a comic turn of mock pathos.

Широкие лиманы, цветущие каштаны
Услышали вновь шелест развернутых знамен,
Когда вошел обратно походкою чеканной
В красавицу Одессу гвардейский батальон.
И, уронив на землю розы,
В знак возвращенья своего
Наш Мишка не сдержал вдруг слезы,
Но тут никто не молвил ничего.

Хоть одессит, Мишка, а это значит,
Что не страшны ему ни горе, ни беда.
Ведь ты моряк, Мишка, моряк не плачет –
Но в этот раз поплакать, право, не беда!

[Broad estuaries and blossoming chestnuts heard once again the rustle of unfurled banners, when the guards' battalion came back with a precise gait into beautiful Odessa. And, having dropped a rose on the ground as a sign of his return, our Mick suddenly let his tears slip, but here nobody said anything about it. Mick's from Odessa, and that means that neither woe nor misfortune frighten him. You're a sailor, Mick, and sailors don't cry – but this time, you're right, it's not so bad to cry!][59]

The war – to official surprise – allowed Utesov's persona to flourish, in both song and in person, and he was awarded the Order of the Workers' Red Banner. When it came to the Stalin Prize, however, the degree to which his extravagance could be officially recognized had reached its limit. Stalin crossed his name from the list of candidates,

Utesov was rarely seen without a smile,
but towards the end of his life he was
profoundly troubled by family illnesses
that only the stubborn joy of his music
could begin to counter.

asking: "What Utesov is that? The one who sings those ditties? But he
hasn't got any kind of voice, it's all just wheezing!"[60] To Utesov's initial
distancing from public life by this political disapproval was added the
personal blow of his wife's death in 1962. Feeling alone, he moved to
live with his daughter, Èdit, whose perky, juvenile voice brightens many
of his songs. Under Khrushchev until 1965 the atmosphere was more
conducive to Utesov's individuality, and he was awarded the title
People's Artist of the U.S.S.R. But once the transient atmosphere of
the Thaw had evanesced, his troubles reappeared, and faceless bureaucrats again crossed him off a candidates' list in the mid-'70s, this time
for Hero of Socialist Labour.

Longevity made Utesov a sombre witness to his son-in-law's death
and then that of Èdit herself from leukemia in 1981. That was the
last year he performed on stage, admitting that his family's private
woes had left him an orphan.[61] The following year, two months after
a twilight marriage, he passed away. The event was marked with
typical Soviet posthumous posturing and the glossing-over of past
mistreatment. "Friends wanted to bury him at the Vagan'kovskoe

cemetery where there was public access. The Soviet government, however, decided otherwise and saw that the People's Artist was buried in the prestigious Novodevich'e cemetery – which was promptly closed off."[62]

KLAVDIIA SHUL'ZHENKO

Listen to me carefully – sing about *love*.
That's always needed …
Your strength is in tenderness, in love.
Do all that you can to protect that.[63]
Klavdiia Shul'zhenko

A forgiving Soviet overview of Utesov's work four years before his death described the quintessential hero of his songs, "a simple, sincere man of labour and considerable achievement. Utesov shows him not in a ceremonial setting, but tells of his inner world, his commonplace yet outstanding deeds. In many songs sung by Utesov people saw their own biography and the way it was connected with the country as a whole. In these numbers the 'personal' was so close to the 'public' that within them lived the entire age that those people had engendered." [64] The suggestion here of singing for the good of the Soviets is a touch excessive. Although Utesov at times waxed patriotic and made attempts to forge a "Georgian, Armenian, or Ukrainian" version of American jazz, his devotion to public Russia was questioned often enough to make credible a rumour of the 1930s that he had fled the Soviet Union. What makes the story odd is that he was supposed to have left behind Soviet shores in an inner tube, floating slowly across the Black Sea to Turkey.[65]

Like Utesov, Klavdiia Shul'zhenko (1906–84) attempted to combine Russian with "foreign" elements, private with public. Nine years Utesov's junior, she too was born on the edge of an empire, in fact, not in Russia at all but in Ukraine. Over the years she would enter little by little into Russian-language variety, so that in retrospect Soviet historians would be able to say that "her story reflects the beginning and formation of all Soviet estrada, in particular the vocal genre."[66] Her quiet ballads, waltzes, and romances, sung to piano or modest string accompaniments, are indeed hugely important.

Shul'zhenko was born in Kharkov and learned Ukrainian folk songs from her father, an accountant for the local railways. Her first taste of public performance came in the form of children's plays, dramatized fairy tales staged to a guitar accompaniment in a courtyard. "These plays created an awful amount of interest not only in our building,

Shul'zhenko, the darling of troops
in World War II, displaying the
sentimentality so prevalent in Russian
light entertainment

but neighbouring ones, too," she recalled. "Viewers came with their chairs, stools, and benches. Some were smart enough to bring an armchair or the kind of rocking-chairs that were everywhere at the time. At the 'entrance' to our theatre there stood a mug on a little table. People threw into it whatever they could afford. A small sign lay next to it, telling everybody that our collections were simply in order to justify any expenditures on the play."[67]

It was at the prompting of her parents that Klavdiia went to the Kharkov Conservatory, where a professor noticed the quality of her voice. More serious studies ensued, but it was when she went with a friend in 1923 to a local theatre on the off-chance of an audition that her career was decided. The regular rehearsal of a play was grudgingly interrupted to allow the two young women a chance to prove themselves with a couple of songs. Klavdiia was accepted by the theatre on the spot and remained associated with the "big" stage until 1928, when estrada beckoned. Her decision in the late 1920s to embrace the lighter genres, given the association of variety with NEP and other nastiness, cannot have been considered without risk. Simply to earn a

basic living, estrada performers were often obliged to form troupes
and beg for alms after concerts deep in the provinces. Unemployment
was high even in the cities, and earnings – scraped together in bars
and restaurants – were irregular. "To be blunt, it is hard to imagine
what was even meant then by the term 'estrada art.' More often than
not it was equated with [things like] circus, with a genre designed
purely to entertain and from which it would be rather awkward to
expect anything serious. Usually estrada artists performed in bars and
played to the tastes of the clientele. Even in official documents one
would see specific references to 'bar estrada.'"[68]

Shul'zhenko found work singing in the movie theatres of Leningrad
before the main feature. Eventually a tour was offered around the
music-halls of Moscow, Nizhnii-Novgorod, and as far south as Kiev,[69]
while subsequent work in the Leningrad Music Hall brought her
together with Leonid Utesov in one production. These tantalizing
brushes with fame took on greater substance with her "Brick Factory
Song" (*Pesnia o kirpichnom zavode*) known more commonly as "Little
Bricks" (*Kirpichiki*).

The song became so popular that Shul'zhenko came to loathe it.
"'Kirpichiki' soon became odious; it really had no musical or poetic
virtues to help it stand out. The composer, Kruchinin, reworked the
melody of a well-known waltz for me, one you could almost consider
a folk tune. You'd hear it in the circus, in the puppet fair, organ-
grinders would play it. I even heard it in my youth. At home we had
a gramophone, and among the many records was a waltz called 'Two
Doggies,' which I recalled as soon as I heard Kruchinin's new song.
Don't think we're talking about deliberate plagiarism. No, in fact …
he sought a melody for ages that would be easily recognized, easily
memorized, accessible. The song's text was just as accessible, and
hardly differed from the songs you'd hear in city outskirts, very widespread at the start of the century. Some of them, for example, 'Marusia
Got Poisoned,' were sung into the Twenties."[70]

The song inspired many factory workers, touched by the work's
relevance to their lives, to ask Shul'zhenko to copy down the words.
Written by Pavel German in 1924, they are related by an unnamed
girl and concern her beloved, Sen'ka. Raised in a poor family, she is
taken on for fifteen years in a local brick factory. The work is hard
but nevertheless offers the "happy roar" of massed effort. Every day,
at the factory whistle, the girl runs off to see Sen'ka. Then pre-
revolutionary unemployment strikes the couple, together with a hundred friends. The "bourgeois war" [World War I] seals the factory's
fate for good, bringing resentment and the building's destruction.
Only after the Revolution do the couple return:

Там нашла я вновь счастье старое,
На ремонт поистративши год,
По советскому, по кирпичику
Возродили мы с Сенькой завод.

Запыхтел завод, загудел гудок,
Как бывало по-прежнему, он.
Стал директором-управляющим
На заводе товарищ Семен.

... Так любовь мою и семью мою
Укрепила от всяких невзгод
Я фундаментом из кирпичика,
Что прессует советский завод.

[There I found again my old joy. A year spent on all the repairs, brick by brick; in Soviet fashion Sen'ka and I gave birth to the factory. The factory puffed, the whistle screeched, and everything was the way it used to be. Comrade Sen'ka became the factory's managing director. Thus I fortified my love and family against all sorts of misfortunes with a foundation of bricks made in a Soviet factory.[71]]

The personal celebrated as an important, if not the most important, vigorous element of social processes made Shul'zhenko a hugely popular wartime singer: "In those tragic days anything [such as her songs] which had a direct relation to peacetime acquired a special significance. The warmth of a family, the hands of a loved one, the smell of springtime, the quiet of night, the blue of the sky: they were all valued as if anew."[72] Such significance was indeed heard "as if anew," because the early 1930s had seen an official objection to introspective lyricism, which might "demoralize" the masses with maudlin ramblings on "love, separation, the woes and joys of the human heart."[73] (The same thing would happen in the early 1950s, when personal themes were considered "petty and vulgar.") Desperate for the haven of such pettiness, Soviet soldiers in World War II were treated to record numbers of concerts by Shul'zhenko, for which she was awarded the Order of the Red Star. Her graceful figure and her smiles and winks spoke to millions of soldiers of home and domesticity.

She also had a reputation for individualism, for headstrong action, as a couple of anecdotes attest.[74] One concerns a meeting, scheduled in later years with the Soviet minister of Culture, Ekaterina Furtseva, which proved to be especially difficult to arrange. (Furtseva, who died in 1974, was the only woman ever to get into the Politburo.)

The reception was constantly postponed due to the minister's busy schedule. When a day was finally agreed upon, Shul'zhenko arrived punctually, only to be told that the minister's arrival was imminent. As the minutes dragged on and became hours, Shul'zhenko's temper rose to the point where the danger of rudeness to a high-ranking official was forgotten. She stood up and stormed out, telling Furtseva's secretary: "Please inform the minister that she was *very* poorly brought up."

Such proud individualism was celebrated in song as well as in the vestibules of high-ranking ministers. One of Shul'zhenko's most popular numbers, "Mine No. 3," tells of the proud, private sacrifice needed to keep the shafts working. Here are the two stanzas with pre- and post-revolutionary scenarios.

1

Пришла весна, а с нею Оля,
Проснулась крепкая любовь,
По вечерам тянуло в поле,
И горячей бурлила кровь ...
Манил простор. Рябины куст,
Забор, скамья и свежесть уст,
Тогда ...

Многое видала,
Многое слыхала,
Многое узнала
Шахта номер три.

....

2

Уж много лет советской власти.
Заводы крепнут с каждым днем,
Шахтера кровь скрепила части
Живою памятью о нем.
Спасая свой родной Донбасс,
Погиб шахтер, но шахту спас ...

[1. Spring came and with it Olga; a strong love awoke. She felt the fields' pull at night, and her blood rushed warmer than ever ... The expanses beckoned. Rowanberry bush, a fence, a bench, and lips so fresh ... Back then Mine No. 3 saw so much, heard so much, found out so much ...
2. Soviet power's been here for quite some years. The factories strengthen every day, the blood of a miner strengthened their depots in

living memory. In saving his native Don Basin, that miner died. He died, yet saved the mine ...[75]]

Shul'zhenko's identification with the "strong love" and introspection found in poetic figures like Olga far from the Stalinist social hubbub could have cost her dearly, as a second anecdote makes evident. It takes place just after the war, on New Year's Eve, 1945, and begins with the ring of a telephone. Despite plans to spend the evening with friends, Shul'zhenko and a young woman suddenly found themselves invited to a party by Stalin's son. The singer explained that she had already promised to meet some acquaintances; a little prior warning would have made a change of plans possible. "I can't come," she said, and hung up. The friend was horrified at Shul'zhenko's audacity, but amazingly neither woman had to answer in the next few days for such an arrogant refusal, for putting friends before politics.

By the time she was made a People's Artist of the Soviet Union in May 1971, this type of pride was officially tolerated, and Shul'zhenko had inspired a whole generation of female singers (including Èdita P'ekha, to whom chapter 4 is dedicated). As one reviewer of the 1966 Soviet Estrada Festival wrote, "Everything good here was tied closely to the traditions of Soviet estrada, to the art of recognized masters Leonid Utesov and Klavdiia Shul'zhenko, who opened the festival with huge success."[76] P'ekha and her group Druzhba appeared at the festival; in an interview she remembered how she had by chance been at a Shul'zhenko concert of the late 1950s and then realized: "I have to sing lyrical, spiritual, and intelligent songs."[77] As for Utesov, he inspired P'ekha through the silver screen in Poland: "There was a minuscule movie theatre in the little town where the P'ekha family lived in the postwar years. Èdita and her girlfriends would sit for hours without coming out of the theatre, despite its crumbling plaster-work. Entranced, they watched their idols: Liubov' Orlova, Leonid Utesov ... Then they returned home, singing the songs they loved and imagining themselves to be real artistes."[78] Even in an interview of 1993, P'ekha's wartime heroines persist as she lists Shul'zhenko and Edith Piaf as her favourites.[79]

In the years before Shul'zhenko's death in 1984, other stars of Soviet estrada, for example, Alla Pugacheva, spoke of how they felt themselves indebted to her: "Pugacheva remembered how Shul'zhenko [at an advanced age] would often forget where things were at home. Knowing that Shul'zhenko had a tiny pension, Pugacheva would frequently leave some money in the former's apartment, hiding it under various objects. It was not possible to leave it in the open because she was such a proud woman."[80]

FROM UTESOV AND SHUL'ZHENKO
TO THE THAW

I think I've been surprisingly lucky in life.
I was witness to the Klavdiia Shul'zhenko "era,"
took part in the "era" of Leonid Utesov
and have become a contemporary
of the Iosif Kobzon "era" as well.[81]

Without any doubt I can say that Iosif Kobzon
is one more star in the constellation of those
Soviet estrada masters such as Klavdiia
Shul'zhenko and Leonid Utesov.[82]

Leonid Utesov and Klavdiia Shul'zhenko are only two of many names that fuelled the post-Stalinist song in the Soviet Union. But who they were and what they sang of became inexorably intertwined with the private lives and thoughts of their respective (and often common) audiences. What these people meant as personalities is therefore intertwined with the notion of personality itself. Their examples have shown how problematic it was being a celebrity in Stalin's Russia. The following pages will show that although "personality" within the popular song underwent great changes in the 1950s, those changes were nevertheless informed by several traditional notions. The first of these is the distinction in sung thematics between "lyrical" and "civic" (*liricheskaia ili grazhdanskaia tematika*), a distinction of more than passing relevance to the development of both Utesov and Shul'zhenko. The second is how any *lichnost'* or *lirichnost'* might be informed by reference to the time-honoured estrada practice of genre-mixing, in this case between songs and circus. As the mass market of Soviet songs moves from the stage to television, "theatricality" becomes an enormously important element of personality and its expression through song, even more so in the 1970s than in the first few years of the Thaw. These combined traditional notions lead us to a few broad, philosophical observations on the claim for space, both staged and spoken, in new songs after the death of Joseph Vissarionovich.

2
LYRIC OR CIVIC:
PERSONALITY AND THEATRICALITY

Fact: a star expresses not only talent, but the
highest professionalism, an ability to voice the
moods of the masses and satisfy their spiritual
needs. A star expresses the objective position
of an artist within a system of socialist culture.
And here in order to be a recognized leader
one must answer to the specific demands of
those who guarantee that recognition. The
main thing in Alla Pugacheva's songs is the
inner world of an often lonely personality
[*lichnost'*], one that keenly senses reality. That
personality is internally divided; it strives for
happiness but in attaining that happiness it
runs up against insurmountable obstacles.[1]

The Russian word *lichnost'* has the same dual significance as its
English counterpart, both "nature or character of self" and "celebrity." It appears with surprising frequency after the late 1950s in
interviews with Soviet singers and critical articles devoted to those
performers. What is interesting, however, is not the frequency but the
manner of its usage. The word is debated more than stated; its
significance is unsure yet potentially great, because the singers discussed here are operating in a socialist society that continuously
invests their songs with (ostensible) moral significance. Soviet songs
are to be good and useful, pure and simple. The popularity of those
songs will create a *lichnost'* in the sense of a "star," but that does not
mean for a second that the singer's audience embraces the morally
laudable intent in a socially utilitarian, melodious message. Despite
the often woeful lack of variety in Soviet variety, its audience is not
made of dullards. The singers in Russia who truly did become stars
had private significance for each of their individual radio listeners or
concert-goers. Within the impersonal, social schema of "socialism," a
lichnost' (star) only rose when that star had a personality (*lichnost'*) of
interest, formed in the confused space between what singers sang and
who they "really" were.

People emulate their favourite stars; by looking at singers in Russia we can thus infer who the Russian public wished to be. Soviet stardom, like any form of renown, was based on the rise of an individual to widespread recognition. An examination of its workings can show how much Soviet society – and the conduits of information that maintained that political structure – was willing to accept in terms of difference, idiosyncrasy, and other fundamental aspects of an individual's *raison d'être*.

I am interested not in the grinding tedium of popular music as a vehicle of social protest but in songs embraced – even with faint enthusiasm – by a Soviet government, those that were expressions of a gentle, slowly growing subjectivity after Stalin. Later on, especially in the so-called "stagnation" (*zastoi*) of Brezhnev's reform-wary, conservative '70s, those songs were often received with greater enthusiasm by their audiences than by the bureaucracies that approved their release. These revered expressions of *lichnost'*, awkward at times for the state, were nevertheless not repressed: "Soviet leaders during the Brezhnev period were sensitive about appearing to be heavy-handed and insensitive enemies of art and literature."[2] As a result, we see that audience tastes and their degree of support begin increasingly to *dictate* the repertoire of an artist. A dialogue of sorts ensues. The very word "dialogue" (*dialog* in Russian also) as a definition of how audience participation creates *lichnost'* is very common in post-Stalinist media. Personality for a singer is not so much discussed in terms of something engendered between a performer and the society of his or her workplace, say, but is instead a spoken, fundamentally emotional entity, one forged between singer and audience (who *like* each other) and between new and old songs, current and recognized repertoires of past *lichnosti* (who are *liked*). The language or diction of materialist philosophy is soon used to foster an idealist aim!

An enormous part of the shifting between the material and ideal, private and public, comes from endless discussions in newspapers, radio, and television of the relationship between two genres of the popular song: lyric and civic. Their differences are outlined in this chapter; subsequent chapters will show how songs of the Thaw and beyond began harmoniously (and with minimum upset) to merge the two. One of the most important bridges between them is "the staging" or theatricality of a song, a notion referred to at times in discussions of Utesov and Shul'zhenko, but which in fact goes back to the pre-revolutionary traditions of estrada and stretches forward far enough to dictate the presentation of songs on Russian television today.

LICHNOST' ACCORDING TO IOSIF KOBZON
AND ALLA PUGACHEVA

> See those photos on the wall?
> They're pictures of people who are dear
> to me but no longer among us:
> Iurii Gagarin, Leonid Utesov ...[3]

To introduce the notion of *lichnost'*, two of our seven exponents of post-Stalinist personality, one man and one woman, Iosif Kobzon and Alla Pugacheva, suit our purposes admirably. The former is more traditional, the latter more innovatory. The manner in which they see connections between individuality and genre, and then again between individuality and fame, will tell us much about the changing notion of "self" in popular culture and the masses that *make* it popular.

When Iosif Kobzon decided in 1997 at the age of sixty to step no more upon the estrada, one Russian newspaper drew parallels between the strength of his persona and the spatial and temporal fields that made the Soviet Union:

Kobzon was one of those very few artists for whom differences in age or geography did not exist ... He got the same welcome in Moscow, Alma-Alta, Vladivostok, [the Jewish autonomous region of] Birobidzhan, Yerevan, Baku ... Our neighbour in the communal apartment, an elderly lady of gentrified origin, even forgave him for being a Jew (an exceptional case for her) ... It was clear that you'd get nowhere without Kobzon when the troubled years of perestroika came around. An enormous number of people got lost: singers, actors, directors, all blessed by the old powers no less than Kobzon had been. Some of them vanished forever and now, ten years later, try to return to active existence. Through all those years, Kobzon kept singing – stubbornly ... The greatest exit along with Kobzon will be the political geography of the U.S.S.R. It'll simply cease to exist ... If even a great internationalist like Kobzon is clearly saying that there cannot be any return to the Soviet bosom, then there really won't be. And that means we'll all breathe a little easier. All the same, though, I'll really miss your songs, Iosif Davydovich.[4]

Kobzon sings the reality of Soviet cohesion into being; he stops singing and it dissipates. The personality of the singer and that of the nation are unified in a strange form of lyricism. Kobzon himself talks about the nature of this connection: "A performer must absolutely know for whom he is working, to whom a song is addressed, for whom the image [*obraz*] he has created is intended. Only with those kinds of precise considerations will the viewer feel himself a participant in what his – or any other – song is about; then a reverse connection arises [from audience to performer], so important in any art, but especially in estrada. Today's viewer, today's listener – as we know – himself becomes a personality [*lichnost'*]. One must be worthy of answering the spiritual needs of that personality."[5]

Elsewhere we read that the auditorium "returns what Kobzon has given it – strength, passion, lyricism."[6] Dialogue between the singer and listener fuels the significance of both singer as socially valid and the social unit (the hall) as made of individually discrete units. In Kobzon's songs, the ideal personality that strikes this mutual chord is a bold one. A concert review of the early 1970s calls it "masterful": "Here we're talking about the quintessential idea of a concert – about what Stanislavskii called the 'hypertask' – the assertion of a modern hero, a personality [*lichnost'*], a fighter overcoming difficult obstacles. When one considers the massed nature of estrada and the essentially youthful audience, the importance of those such as Kobzon is clear, those who bring bright socialist ideals to the concert hall and do so masterfully, radiantly, and with talent."[7]

The notion of "socialist ideals" suggests singularity across multiplicity; the notion of *lichnost'* does the same for generic disparity because a personality unifies various disparate genres. From the pre-revolutionary polytheism of estrada a more monologic intent arises as a consequent step: one Soviet singer also comes to embody the one idea that will bridge multiple genres. As time goes on, though, the one idea designed to unify the individuals in an audience is gradually undermined by those viewers' private ideas and perceptions of the songs within supposed homogeneity. A dialogue of stage and multifarious audience becomes more important than that of singer and state (or, come to that, audience and state). The thousands of newspaper articles read for this book also stress the *live* contact of performer over record sales, bureaucratic appeal, or other forms of validated discourse.

A late Soviet definition of Kobzon as personality implicitly places two such audiences at loggerheads: those who love him and those who do not.

Iosif Kobzon is an independent state on the Planet Estrada because he fawned neither before the passing years, nor before the listeners. He wanted to sing what he *liked* personally (*lichno*). That's the way it always was. The Russian romance or the song of youth, the ultramodern rhythm and the smooth expanse of Russian folklore are all [potentially] within Kobzon's ability. That's because Iosif Kobzon is not only a beautiful singer whom nature granted a gorgeous voice, but also a personality (*lichnost'*), an artist of wide range and considerable, singular culture. He gives voice to our time and does not fear what others think of him. Perhaps this explains his constant ascent to the heights of art.[8]

Kobzon has *his* public. This is not a political division but one based upon varied reactions to his personality. Maybe his audience sympathizes with the politics of his songs, maybe not. It is actually not that important, as the idea of this man in particular offering something *special* and being of private, emotional significance to a viewer or listener means more. Personality, initially used as a vehicle for politics, soon supercedes dogma but becomes itself "political" as a consequence in that a politic of sentimental difference grows out of and beside one of sameness. Such was the state of affairs in 1987, when the words above were published.

The quote also shows that Kobzon's odd position as Soviet singer nurturing a growing sense of self is – paradoxically – bolstered by another group (Kobzon's non-audience) considering him *less* significant. Many people see private meaning in his personality during the 1970s, but Kobzon's classic style goes slowly out of fashion, which sidelines him a little from the mainstream. His stage/hall dialogue, composed of Soviet songs, fosters a sense of self under the Soviets; when that regime fades during perestroika, new types of music emerge. Both the singer and his audience, having engendered an expression of some subjectivity within social processes, are outpaced by newer, supremely private and socially noncommital songs. He sings (and causes a philosophy) of minor private difference but is soon outrun by its effects. Kobzon's early audience felt a sense of self relative to their contemporaries and thus took a wilful step towards difference; now that audience is shoved further into obsolescence – by the next generation. As a result, although Kobzon sings the same songs, the audience metamorphoses and his *lichnost'*, formed in the audience/artist dialogue of the Thaw, is projected into the "romantic" isolation of outmodedness in the late 1980s. The author of the above words is a member of that early audience; hence the negative reference here to younger, more fickle "listeners" of a post-Kobzonian audience as the U.S.S.R. wanes. One senses a proud defeat in the face of inevitable fashion.

Within the supposedly limited lexicon of state-lauded songs, while he was simultaneously embraced by the state as the finest exponent of socialist ideals, there had been room for *self*-development, and Kobzon found it. The artist in 1973 provided yet another definition of self and its realization in song: "Personality (*lichnost'*) within art is composed of talent, a sense of measure, a bright expression of individuality, an inimitable intonation and – of course – a very great love for people, for life, for your work."[9] Nothing here is surprising except the appeal for measure or moderation. The movement, philosophical or otherwise, of self-realization goes hand in hand with an equal and opposite reaction, one of self-restraint. Somehow "inimitability" and "a sense of measure" (which itself requires a common, quantifiably determined norm by which to define itself) are compatible.

A November 1980 issue of *Soviet Estrada and Circus* announced both Kobzon's receipt of the title "People's Artist of the Russian Federation" and Alla Pugacheva's of "Honoured Artiste of the Russian Federation." Kobzon, the bulletin briefly noted, "belongs among the leading performers of the Soviet song. The completeness of his craft and the multifaceted nature of his repertoire distinguish this extremely talented singer."[10] Once again synonymy exists between disparate genres and a measured, if not "completed" (*zavershennyi*) reigning in of self. Kobzon's restraint was in fact sometimes seen as excessive, even for a Soviet audience in the early 1970s; perhaps as an embodiment of Soviet ideology, dare I suggest it, the estrada multiplicity of genres is in Kobzon unified, even levelled in one person, acting himself as one tiny idea (perhaps socialist, perhaps not). Here *lichnost'* does not so much create itself through songs, existentially, as it makes songs conform to itself. One man sings lots of songs and his personality unifies them; he becomes a personality (star) and that personal significance radiates back out into the songs. The bigger the personality and the more he sings, the more of a personal trace he leaves on a public song. A song is associated with one person, with what that person means.

Kobzon personally, however, could only mean so much. Even in 1970 a writer noted the failure of this early personality: "Kobzon sang a lot. It seemed he could sing endlessly. Composers brought him their songs. He took them. Songs of lyricism. Heroism. Pathos. Lyrico-heroic songs. Heroic songs of pathos. Serious and comical songs. Sad and happy songs. Tender, spiritual songs. His voice sounded as good as ever. But suddenly something happened. Songs appeared that seemed faceless. It was as if the living, intelligent, passionate heart had vanished ... In many songs the singer became somehow worse than himself. Worse than he could or should have been."[11] Kobzon's career marks the early stage of post-Stalinist repertoires; he unifies different songs with his one personality but perhaps values restraint too highly to create any radically different meaning, star though he is.

Now for the second announcement of state honours, Alla Pugacheva's becoming an Honoured Artiste of the Russian Federation. Pugacheva, another leading light of the same generation, "possesses striking vocal and artistic abilities, a sparkling temperament, a rich arsenal of expressive means and places high demands upon her own creativity." Whether or not this type of description is in some manner gender-determined, nevertheless we see a different perception of a sung personality than Kobzon's unifying of genres. He represents the harmonizing of old estrada traditions before they truly regain or reinvent their pre-revolutionary multifariousness. Kobzon works in many genres, but adapts them all to his one personality which generally operates in harmony with the status quo; Pugacheva's plural "vocal and artistic abilities," her "expressive means," meet each genre of estrada on its own terms. A circus piece demands circus skills, for example. Estrada remains multigeneric and must be respected as such. If one person is to perform several genres, he or she must be willing to play several roles. Difference from state ideology must even intensify to the point of difference within oneself. Here the key is the conjunction in the phrase "vocal *and* artistic abilities." An estrada singer increasingly needs (and becomes socially esteemed for) something other than singing. Kobzon's traditional craft is finally unsuitable for the full expression of *lichnost'*, yet his Soviet popular songs, even in the most patriotic forms, laid the groundwork for a sense of lasting, variegated subjectivity both among *and with the help of* his listeners. Pugacheva's personality is negotiated with her audience, often – though not always – separately from the dictates of established ideology. She builds upon the understanding of particularity laid down by, among others, Kobzon.

Iosif Kobzon talked in 1996 about his relationship with Pugacheva over the years. Though he speaks with some coolness here, this is a tale of an earlier compatibility (Pugacheva has indeed spoken with gratitude of Kobzon's assistance).[12]

Q: Iosif Davydovich, it's generally considered that you and Alla Borisovna [Pugacheva] are the two most authoritative artists in Russian estrada. One hears not infrequently about your complicated relations …

KOBZON: I must say that Alla Borisovna got her first award – a third prize! – at the All-Union contest, and that was thanks to my ardent support. I saw her for the first time when she was brought into a radio studio for the program *Good Morning!* She was sixteen, covered in freckles, wearing braids and had skinny little legs! I also remember how she bowled everybody over with the song "Arlekino" [1975, her first major success] at the Golden Orpheus [competition held in Bulgaria]. To a considerable degree she got there by chance, since Alla replaced the main [Soviet] contender at the last moment. At that time Leonid Utesov – with whom I was very friendly – told me: "Listen, did you watch TV yesterday? That trollopy redhead is doing some amazing, crazy stuff!" That very same redheaded wonder became a crazy artiste, one who has beaten out the rest of us and kept us interested all these years. I really don't think it's our business keeping up with her affairs or what she does in bed. Alla and I have had differing relations; she at times allowed herself all kinds of liberties, but I always helped her. I helped her get divorced after her first marriage, get an apartment, get an award, in fact a lot of things. When she was ill she would always come to my dacha ... I'm ready to help her now, too, I always stand up for her, I'll never say a bad word about her, although we're not close friends now and don't visit each other's houses.[13]

A look at how Pugacheva once viewed *lichnost'* can provide us with an introduction to how the (fairly) smooth and mutually agreeable transition from Kobzon to her took place. In chapter 1 Utesov saw in the work of Iosif Kobzon a successful response to Edith Piaf's demand for personality. On the television program *Musical Ring* in 1989 Pugacheva was asked how she related to Piaf's view. "I agree," she replied, "*lichnost'* is necessary."[14]

In this "trollopy redhead" of "striking vocal and artistic abilities" a "sparkling, temperamental" and spoken *lichnost'* attempts to re-create (or differentiate itself from) quotidian reality. Personality, all the way from Utesov to Pugacheva, is a necessary form of spoken or sung difference. "Difference from *what?*" is a question, however, that changes with each generation.

Here there emerge contradictions which acquire their full representation in Pugacheva's songs. In essence this is the contradiction between the free self-realization of her *lichnost'* and that objective reality granted her by nature. One wants so much to be young, beautiful, loved ... Nevertheless the "antique clock" [a 1981 song by Pugacheva] doesn't tire; together with fame and recognition comes the sense of their transience, their finiteness. Alla Pugacheva tries to view all of reality's manifestations through the prism of her inner world, the prism of her "soul." Everything she sings about in her songs is exactly that kind of reaction [to the world], whether it's a simple lyric, various forms of reminiscences, everyday sketches, or worries over the fate of peace in our generation. And here there are no contradictions.[15]

Beyond the jab at Pugacheva's desire to remain youthful, a serious point is being made. Impressions of the material world are received by the individual or, more explicitly, matter is impinging upon the "soul." The journalist's use of quotation marks with such a concept here displays a Soviet materialist emphasis, yet observations such as these bear more than a passing resemblance to an older, Lockean view of human development, to matter's impression of its qualities upon our senses. That English philosopher's views were of huge importance in defining Russia's cultural comprehension of sentiment. In the 1987 article quoted above we can perhaps see Locke's distinction between primary and secondary qualities, between reality and appearance. Reality *is*, but what it means is also what it *appears* to be. The former is given, the latter empirically determined in a dialogue with that given. What exactly this "soul" is, if we can reduce the hyperbole of the journalist's metaphor a little, is what *lichnost'* is (the "prism" of her subjectivity) – and the way in which Pugacheva offers a multifarious alternative in place of Kobzon's unified "socialist ideals."

Another journalist in 1991 offers further definition of how individuality relates to materialism: "The seething hordes of performers huddled at the microphone today do not strive for what distinguished pop music ten years ago: the romantic flood of feeling. Those feelings made the *lichnost'* played by an estrada singer stand out from the crowd."[16] Emotion, as the portraits of Pugacheva will show, is the spoken and ideal response to reality. The (initially civic and later lonely) romantic hero of Kobzon moves out into the world to make it all his own, to unite it with a long-held Soviet conviction or worldview. Pugacheva's songs offer a different and more literal ideal in response to intransigent matter, as the epigraph to this chapter suggests. She defines her subjectivity not by subjecting reality to a social ideal but by offering a spoken, motley response to numerous phenomena of Soviet existence. Kobzon's philosophy is centrifugal, Pugacheva's centripetal; his is basically social, hers basically private. He is *the* Soviet singer, she is *a* Soviet singer. Though both have claim to the epithet "sentimental," Kobzon is more "reasonable" (mental) and Pugacheva more "sensual" (sentient). The similarity and difference between the two performers is hinted at in the 1991 reference above to *lichnost'* being "played" and the success of that play defining one's difference. Not only, by implication, is personality given but it is made; it is created from the intent or desires of both performer *and* audience. A major role in that creation is played by the genre of a song. The fundamental difference in songs mentioned throughout our study of seven singers will be whether such texts are "civic" or "lyric."

CENTRIFUGAL AND CENTRIPETAL, CIVIC AND LYRIC

Q: Are you interested in stressing the civic direction of Russian estrada?

PUGACHEVA: Absolutely! The civic song impinges upon our age, our type of person. My worldview must be reflected in it,

my obeisance before Russia, before the Soviet
nation. But it also has to be a good song,
equal, for example, to "Victory Day"
[by D. Tukhmanov and V. Kharitonov]. If only
I had a song like that! I sing for Russia and
together with other performers try to raise the
authority of Russian estrada. How can that not
be a civic matter? Besides, one can perform
passionate, light-hearted or lyrical songs for
one's nation. My father said that the soldiers
listened to lyric songs at the Front. "They
remembered their home, and understood what
they might have to lay their head down for ..."
That's the kind of approach we need today.
One should sing about what needs to be
protected from nuclear murderers: children,
love, work, laughter, beauty, friendship. I want
people to see life as beautiful and to look
after it.[17]

In their study of spoken estrada, such as comedy and compering, Iu. Dmitriev and O. Kuznetsova comment on the "enormous significance" of individuality on the stage, "since it alone defines the genre in which an artist works. A bad artist remains in the power of his repertoire. He looks for the kind of material which in and of itself will produce laughs and applause. He'll use anything, even crude and vulgar material, just to be successful in the auditorium."[18] Genre is chosen to amplify an incipient personality. Utesov, for example, has been schematized in histories of estrada as instigator of the search to find the right genre for *lichnost'* to flourish. The bold humour of his "social," ensemble-based pieces has been termed "centrifugal," as distinct from Shul'zhenko's "centripetal" lyricism;[19] a word or two about the way in which the two of them performed will clarify matters.

A 1929 review of Utesov's *tea-dzhaz* in an open-air concert describes a merry philosophy uniting all the songs with one social notion: "'The orchestra will dance!' announces the conductor [Utesov]. The musicians do indeed start to shuffle on command, to paw the ground. They stand up and sit down together. They turn around and sit down again. It's not yet a genuine dance-number, but the elements are there." Utesov's orchestra leaves everybody happy. "Two thousand faces dissolve into one beaming grin. The ticket-collectors don't bother checking tickets. Even the organizers have smiling faces. It seems that given a minute more, they'd treat the gate-crashers to mineral water after they'd snuck into the park."[20]

Compare the massed grins of Utesov's leaping jazzmen with this description of a Shul'zhenko concert: "Shul'zhenko comes out onto the stage without looking out into the auditorium. She is concentrating as if deep 'within herself' ... It is as if she walls off a certain space for herself in order to enliven it, spend a little while there and fill it with her joy and her sadness. This space barely reaches the proscenium, so the viewer stays outside it, outside of its transparent but impenetrable wall."[21] Shul'zhenko on stage left an entirely different impression from Utesov, based upon "the education of feelings through the poetry of an enamoured human heart."

These differences will allow us, perhaps, to differentiate between the men and women: Utesov/Kobzon, Shul'zhenko/Pugacheva, but the distinctions between them go beyond gender. In terms of their chosen genres both Utesov and Shul'zhenko are in essence lyrical, not civic artists. Utesov's centrifugalism is across a stage; Kobzon's is across an empire, and the theatricality of *tea-dzhaz* is in fact much closer to Pugacheva. We can sort the matter out by renaming the opposition; instead of "centrifugal" and "centripetal," let us try "realist" and "romantic." In an opposition suggested from within Soviet studies,[22] "realist" means alignment with a materialist worldview (concurrence with the nature of ostensible Soviet reality), while "romantic" here recalls the Soviet distinction in discussions of nineteenth-century literature between so-called active and passive romanticism, used to manage the generic wanderings in the work of long-lived poets such as Vasilii Zhukovskii (1783–1852). On this model Utesov, Shul'zhenko, Kobzon, and Pugacheva are *all* romantic in their search for something beyond the limits of official materialism. Within that group all four show occasional tendencies towards either activity or passivity. The difference between the tendencies lies in their intensity and longevity.

But what exactly do "active" and "passive" mean? Active romanticism desires to alter the world, to employ the lonely rigours of individual effort for future, general good. Passive romanticism is more immobile in social spaces, tending as it does towards reverie or a yearning for the past. Given that I am inclined in subsequent pages towards an analogy of post-Soviet estrada with sentimentalism, the romantic connection between Utesov, Shul'zhenko, Kobzon, and Pugacheva will ultimately be more useful than the centripetal/centrifugal position, if for no other reason than it references concrete traditions, rather than the vagaries of psychology, as do the singers themselves. Every one of the performers in this book has something romantic with which to counter, even if at times not noticeably, the wholly objective nature of materialism. Sometimes it is active, sometimes passive. The ideal of *lichnost'* in varying forms is heard in all of their work. In the songs of Russian estrada's greatest exponents, civic or lyric songs are rarely entirely so.

So what are the lyric or civic extremes of sung genres between which estrada tries gracefully to orient itself from either a realist or a romantic tendency? How does this romanticism express itself? Perhaps the clearest evaluation of lyric and civic has been in the work of Tat'iana Cherednichenko. Here she writes of estrada under Stalin, in the period prior to this study and prior to the emergence of a new form of singularity.

Civic songs (*grazhdanstvennye pesni*) praised leaders, the party, the army, *komsomol* [youth organization], the Pioneer organization [akin to the Scouts], the Revolution, the achievements of labour, in fact labour in general – so the addressees of such toasts merged into some kind of abstract victorious "we." This strength was expressed in the hyperbole of the text ... a vocal style oriented towards crushing volume. In a number of songs this abstract "we" came to mean the listener as "us" in an everyday setting (workers "of our factory" ...) and a glass was raised to lyricism, albeit of a certain type. Here the warmth of another person was equivalent to the comfort of communality ... [As for] lyrical estrada, it was moved by the ordinariness of its heroes. A condition of love was a person's ordinariness, and consequently his utter integration into the massed whole. "We" were so much higher and important than "I" that the latter could only sing in an intentionally diminished and domestic voice, as if testifying to the absence of any pretensions towards lofty self-evaluation. From Utesov and Shul'zhenko [until the 1960s] a lyric vocal would tend towards unassuming delivery. Therein lay its charm. The more mundane the delivery, the further the song was from "red army" officialdom ... The modest estrada, rejecting everything big (including great passion) and falling sentimentally into the transparent expanse of the heroes' inner world, was orchestrated around the main lyric theme – love ... [But] the myth that fed the classic Soviet songs had a mobilizing character, it "summoned and led." In this lies the difference from the myth of western estrada, which neither summons nor leads. It simply colours everyday existence with a dream of festivity and comfort. In an amazing manner, though, that comfort was in our sung forms of mobilization, too. Its goal, the "bright tomorrow," in its own way justified the necessity for intensive effort and informed it with the joy of an already attained happiness.[23]

This rather dreary scenario, lit on occasion by the rare lyrical moments of Utesov and Shul'zhenko, is the background to our story. We begin where this description ends. Civic songs pure and simple (either before or after 1953), being utterly formulaic in nature, are not of interest to us here. Instead we need civic songs that have lyric moments together with lyric songs of a civic hue, since they will allow us to chart the quiet shifts from public to private genres via the move from realist to romantic philosophies. Two names come to mind immediately: Robert Rozhdestvenskii and Il'ia Reznik, two of the Soviet Union's most important lyricists after the 1950s.

CIVIC LYRICS AND THE STAGE/HALL DIALOGUE

Я так хочу,
Чтобы лето не кончалось,
Чтоб оно за мною мчалось,
За мною вслед.
Я так хочу,
Чтобы маленьким и взрослым
Удивительные звезды
Дарили свет!

[I want so much for summer not to end,
for it to rush behind me. I want so much
for remarkable stars to bless young
and old alike with light!][24]

Robert Rozhdestvenskii was born in 1932 in the Altai region of southern Siberia, making him part of a generation to graduate from university at the outset of the Thaw (1956). Widespread success with several volumes of romantic poetry, in many ways typical of the 1960s' post-Stalinist swagger, led to the prestigious Komsomol award for literature in 1972. It is, however, Rozhdestvenskii's lyrics for many popular songs that attract our attention as an interplay between Soviet "active," socially committed romanticism and its "passive" variant which would inform the popular song in later years. Il'ia Reznik, our second poet, is perhaps the greatest songwriter of this latter tendency. He was born in 1938 in Leningrad, a "blockade baby," during the 900 days when the city was under siege. He is to this day extremely well known for his contribution to the most influential songs of Russian popular culture in the 1970s. Working for several years with the Latvian composer Raimonds Pauls, he created a large number of hugely successful songs, often for Alla Pugacheva. A brief comparison of Rozhdestvenskii and Reznik will help both to show the differences between civic and lyric Soviet songs and to suggest that truly popular vocal music was neither entirely public nor entirely private. Rozhdestvenskii begins his own treatise on song-writing with a quote claiming the ideal work to be both lyric *and* civic;[25] both he and Reznik's long-term partner Pauls have independently said that hearing one's words sung on the street as "public" property is the highest praise of all.[26]

In Soviet estrada the words or "poetry" of a song are often seen as a separate task from the music – hence the usual trio of poet-composer-performer. The text is held in the highest regard. Iosif Kobzon noted with incredulity in March 1983 that "there was a time when we used to have 'poet-songwriters' ... But can you really use the term 'songwriter' to describe such great poets as Robert Rozhdestvenskii? Great music is born of great poetry."[27] (In return, Rozhdestvenskii has said many kind words about Kobzon.[28]) This poet's greatness has been assessed rarely and roughly in the West in order to show, through negative comparison, the *non*-conformism of bards such as Vysotskii (1938–80), Okudzhava (1924–97), or Galich (1918–77). Scholar Gerald Smith writes: "He tends to be the poet with whose work Party-minded Soviet youth identified most closely as an expression of their ideals ... The idealism that permeates Rozhdestvenskii's songs at times becomes indistinguishable from religious mysticism, which is the case with many official songs about the destiny of the individual ... Rozhdestvenskii is an accomplished poet with a sincere and questing intellect. Even his most orthodox songs contain what might be seen as the seed of their own destruction in their persistent leaning toward sadness and mysticism."[29]

True, there is much in Rozhdestvenskii's orthodox songs to please the powers that be. Nevertheless, what is here termed "the seed of destruction," or melancholy musing upon individuality, is perhaps the incipient stage of a different theme: the troubling responsibility of self-realization, increasingly independent from ideology. Sentiment, I will argue, is a major conduit for this sense of self. Since I am stressing in these pages that self-realization was a dialogue between singer and auditorium, then audience emotion or reaction should also be of interest to us. In May 1975 the director of the Moscow Theatre of Estrada spoke of the "emotional intensity" evoked by hearing Iosif Kobzon sing a Rozhdestvenskii song about the rigours of war. (Rozhdestvenskii has himself written on the lyric hue given many civic songs during the war, all a consequence of *personal* suffering or loss.[30])

I had remarkable feelings sitting in the auditorium; [both] those of a soldier ... and a professional director, experienced in the intricacies of how to stage or act in a work. Kobzon's performance left a great impression and deserves the highest marks, from both points of view! High marks for Rozhdestvenskii's composition, which is dramatically complete and romantically elevated so that it answers to the *Zeitgeist*. High marks for the masterful performance by the artist Iosif Kobzon, winning us over with his emotional intensity, with his internal – not external – expressiveness, his profound comprehension of each song in the program (and there were thirty-eight of them) … Fidelity to vital themes, to his theme of individualistic performance, his high professionalism which is increasingly evident against the backdrop of growing estrada dilettantism, the musical completeness of each number – all of this distinguishes Iosif Kobzon's creative manner.[31]

The relation of romantic yet public songs to private, "internal expressiveness" is best seen through the example of one song by Rozhdestvenskii, "For That Lad" (*Za togo parnia*). The music begins with a small, shimmering string section, scarcely marked out rhythmically by a cymbal. The song thus far is not at all strident. Only with a reference to beating rain do we hear the martial pride of trumpets and a discernible drum. Moments of retrospection and talk of "youthful winds" are bolstered with a wave of violins. An electric bass and modern rhythm section give the song added verve and a contemporary significance as the text turns to issues of duty and burden:

Я сегодня до зари встану.
По широкому пройду полю.
Что-то с памятью моей стало:
все, что было не со мной, помню.
Бьют дождинки по щекам впалым.
Для вселенной двадцать лет – мало.
Даже не был я знаком с парнем,
обещавшим: «Я вернусь, мама!»

А степная трава пахнет горечью.
Молодые ветра зелены.
Просыпаемся мы –
И грохочет над полночью
то ли гроза, то ли эхо прошедшей войны.

Обещает быть весна долгой.
Ждет отборного зерна пашня.
И живу я на земле доброй
за себя и за того парня.
Я от тяжести такой горблюсь.
Но иначе жить нельзя, если
все зовет меня его голос,
все звучит во мне его песня.

А степная трава пахнет горечью.
Молодые ветра зелены.

Просыпаемся мы –
И грохочет над полночью
то ли гроза, то ли эхо прошедшей войны.

[Today I'll rise before the dawn. I'll go across the spreading field.
Something's happened to my memory: I recall what did not happen to
me. Rain beats down on sunken cheeks. Twenty years is not enough for
the universe. I didn't even know the lad who promised: "Mother, I'll
return!" The grass of the steppe smells of grief, the youthful winds are
green. We awake at midnight to the roar of thunder or war's erstwhile
echo. Spring promises to be long. Fields wait for select seeds. I live on
this bountiful earth for myself and that lad. I'm bent double from that
burden. But I must live that way if his voice calls me and his song sounds
within me. The grass of the steppe smells of bitterness, the youthful
winds are green. We awake to the roar at midnight of thunder or war's
erstwhile echo.[32]]

Of all our seven singers, this song is associated most with Lev
Leshchenko, who along with Kobzon has been the brightest champion of the civic song. (It is Leshchenko's music described above.)
He calls Rozhdestvenkii's work a celebration of "human courage
commensurate with great deeds, [of] the extreme emotional strength
inherent in great works of art."[33] This song became significant for
Leshchenko when he chose to perform it at an important competition
in 1972, held in the Polish city of Sopot. To overcome the language
barrier, he decided that a "more emotional, dynamic" treatment
would help the Polish audience, yet rehearsals led him to believe that
the song could survive either a stadium-oriented treatment or a
smaller, "chamber" arrangement. He was worried, however, that such
a serious song, which filled him with a sense of "civic responsibility,"
might not be well received amidst the competition's "light-hearted
festivity." Only when he saw the faces in his Polish audience did he
realize their approval; they were gripped, in fact "electrified." He won
the competition and was congratulated afterwards by a group of
Polish admirers expressing their gratitude for such songs that could
"win viewers' hearts."[34]

The emotional significance of this text, realized only in direct contact with the audience, was great. Leshchenko says about "Za togo
parnia" that although it was a "song reflecting a certain period, it
actually *became* that period's main symbol." The strong emotional
perception of a song by an audience returns the text to its performer
with a changed, increased significance. "Za togo parnia" does not

sound terribly lyrical; instead Leshchenko interprets the song's "private" appeal in terms of its respectful continuance of many other, earlier Soviet songs – one modern text acquires its significance as part of (and thanks to) the company of a massed canon. "The Soviet song is a type of annalist or chronicler ... All heroic pages in our history, wishes, thoughts, hopes, victories are printed upon its sung leaves." It does not, though, as "Za togo parnia" in Sopot shows, just record history, but makes it all dependent on whether anybody actually *likes* it! A Polish audience determined what the song meant; Leshchenko had no idea before he went on stage and could not even decide if it should be tailored for a stadium or a parlour. By 1983 he concluded that in Soviet songs "there's a kind of dialectic: the viewer forms us and we form the viewer. I'd imagine that's what art consists of."[35]

The success of a Soviet song appears to depend on the audience discerning a private significance within its performer and performance. An outside opinion of the Polish competition supports such a view: "When Lev Leshchenko sang 'For That Lad' in Sopot there arose among many people a common opinion. In the face of the Soviet performer were indissolubly merged [not only] the features of that boy who had given his life for his country, [but] also of our contemporary, of the young man living today for the sake of that lad."[36] Leshchenko's public song is seen as privately relevant, and there is no gap between the singer's identity and that of his song's heroes. This confusion of identification will prove to be most consequential as the years pass and other performers emerge.

A union of singer and Rozhdestvenskii's hero is therefore born of the sentimental dialogue of stage and auditorium, because again from among the audience at Sopot, and somewhat to our surprise, we hear that "content, figurativeness, and *emotionality* are the three most important things in a singer's art – and that's the performer's own opinion, too. They are needed by a singer who respects [us,] his listeners, and believes in his ability to see a song as something more than entertainment." Elsewhere in the same audience we hear that "there's a happy coincidence of the song's feelings and thoughts with the singer's character."[37] Seven years after this performance in an interview of 1979 Leshchenko seems to agree; he has adopted his *audience's* interpretation of the song. It was offered to an audience and now has more of a lyrical than a civic resonance: "'Za togo parnia' was built upon the marriage of a lyric confession and a courageous vow by the living to that lad, left to lie in the earth."[38]

Just as with the confusion of private and stage personae, so the frequency of lyrical moments or even full-blown confessions [*ispovedi*] will grow over the years in consequence. Rozhdestvenskii's name will appear in several chapters that document that growth, since his songs have been performed with varying designs by disparate artists. Those artists draw out latent lyricism as his poems are sung over the years. Although Rozhdestvenskii's texts have their fair share of an "actively" romantic striving through time (to a wonderful "tomorrow") or space ("beyond the horizon"), such grand dimensions are often described relative to the more attractive and modest importance assigned a friend, be it human, animal, or even a familiar song. The "very worst thing of all" is to lose that immediate, proximal, and private relationship.[39]

In a schema of post-Stalinist popular songs in Russia, Il'ia Reznik would stand at the opposite end of a thematic scale from Rozhdestvenskii, at the pole marking just such proximal and private concerns to the exclusion of almost everything else. As an example of how the public/private dichotomy is switched, Reznik said in an interview of 1988 that a "mass song is not what is sung in chorus but a song that you want to sing to a lot of people."[40] The individual moves out from, not into, a crowd as a prerequisite for self-expression. Reznik is best known for his work with Pugacheva, whose persona he sees as "a master of transformations ... with a sincere, confessional (*ispovedal'naia*) intonation ... [whose songs as] monologues are directed straight into the auditorium ... an extraordinary personality (*lichnost'*), generously gifted, both unexpected and attractive in her staged incarnations."[41]

Confessional lyricism and dramatized songs are key elements of the manner in which subjectivity truly manifests itself after the civic tendencies that Rozhdestvenskii personifies. Reznik can perhaps therefore be defined as the quintessential 1970s songwriter, making Rozhdestvenskii the essence of the 1960s. Rather than lean on such divisions too heavily, I should note instead the opinion that much of Pugacheva's persona, reliant as it is upon Reznik's texts, is nevertheless indebted to the Thaw for its worldview. That 1960s worldview, even a decade later, is stuck between the desire and ability to realize itself in full: "A desperate yearning, a rush towards comprehension, a virtually physical hunger for love – and some kind of delicate tenderness ... This emotional split was a particular sign of an age [the mid-1970s] which still remembered the hopes of the Thaw, but had come to terms with their unrealizability."[42] Reznik's significance endures well beyond the years of this "split," as the newspaper *Moskovskii komsomolets* reminded its readers in 1995: "The poet Reznik is a truly historic figure not only in the fate of Alla Pugacheva but in all our popular music. It's impossible to calculate the number of immortal lines from his pen in songs that became genuinely national."[43] Elsewhere we read that Reznik's texts together created "the biography of an artiste who had decided to fix her fate in a song. He became her confessor, hearing her secret admissions and then returning them to her in a kind of edited translation."[44]

Reznik's lyrics for Pugacheva have warranted at least a couple of published collections.[45] A review in 1981 serves as a good indication of the Soviet press's reaction: "This poet has the ability to enter the performer's world. [Conversely,] the life of the poet's soul, having become the subject of the poems, also defines their intonation and content. True, the poet's own voice sometimes suffers from a dearth of original lines or views, a lack of measure or taste. The poems, being both private and touching, seem at times to be banal, since the poet makes such an impression with his chosen image [in songs written for or concerning Pugacheva] that he forgets about himself. That would appear to be the reason why a few lines also lack ... their own intonation."[46]

A good example of Reznik's "touching banality" – one that acts as a counterpart to Rozhdestvenskii – would be "Maestro" (*Maèstro*). Written with Raimonds Pauls, the song helped to create part of what Reznik refers to in retrospect as the "peak" of his career. If Reznik's words are banal (a rather cruel assessment) in their simplicity, Pauls also has been accused of somehow tailoring his music to Pugacheva's *lichnost'* without doing that personality full justice. Pauls, it was said, "restrains" Pugacheva and therefore makes her more "elegant," given her real-life tendency to "scheme and concoct some scandal or other." Pauls himself wittily remembers this contradiction between a new, maximally confrontational *lichnost'* and the restraint of traditional estrada. When "Maèstro" was performed live on television, Pugacheva wished mid-song to sit beside the composer, accompanying her at the piano. Because the piano stool was rather small, she asked if he "couldn't move his rear-end over a little. But she said it more crudely than that, in true Russian fashion, such that I almost fell off the stool. That was her style."[47]

However, Pugacheva is not singing to Pauls but to the audience, and here in the 1970s we see an even greater significance attached to the singer/auditorium dialogue as the prime regulator of meaning. I have mentioned Reznik's definition of Pugacheva's metamorphoses; any changes in her repertoire are responses to positive audience reaction (an increase or intensification of what those people like) and at the same time something of a guess, a presumption of what that intensification might be (one does not know until the next encounter with that audience). These points are foremost in a joint interview by Pauls and Pugacheva given in 1982:

PAULS: Earlier, when I was very young, I used to think that there's no point in writing for a wide audience, since it doesn't accept everything, so you have to try and foist your understanding of music upon it. Gradually, though, I understood that our only judge or evaluator (*tsenitel'*), the person for whom we perform, is the people.

Q: What do you consider the main thing in your work?

PUGACHEVA: The ability to improvise. Improvisation brings genuineness into an actor's art. After all, words and music – that's by no means everything in the creation of a song. The process is completed by intimate contact with your viewer in the auditorium.[48]

Intimate though this contact is, moments of civic resonance are sometimes heard even in Reznik's texts – not necessarily those sung by Pugacheva, but poems elsewhere in his collected works. In his cycle *Nostalgia for Russia*, in particular a text entitled "White Moscow" (*Belaia Moskva*), the entire nation's future existence is guaranteed by the power of song, which means "we'll survive."[49] The pronoun "we," though, is more likely to mean "we two" rather than "two million" or any other massed figure. Reznik draws upon the bravado of Maiakovskii in his cycle *Life Is Passing* (*Zhizn' prokhodit*) or, more accurately, upon a poem he wrote to reject the life-negation of the suicide of a fellow poet, Sergei Esenin, in 1925. Maiakovskii suggested that life is difficult, yet dignified by its usefulness to others. Esenin, in his final poem and day of life, had complained that neither dying nor living were especially meaningful. Reznik attests he "loves this life terribly. / By the way, such axioms are nothing new. / But I'll repeat them once again. / Sorry for my immodesty."[50] Reznik sides with the life-affirming Maiakovskii but does so in a quiet, private manner redolent of Esenin, and thus the energy of civic verse is put to lyric ends. (The distance between public verse and Reznik's songs is perhaps clearest in the remarkable number of references in his work to flight, escape or – to steal the title of an entire cycle of Pugachevian songs – the need to "rise above [worldly] vanity" [*podnimis' nad suetoi*].)

Reznik's self-effacing tendency can be further seen in his epigrams. The one written for Rozhdestvenskii plants the poet firmly on the ground, far from Reznik's frequent flights of fancy. This is a writer of materialism, writing about matter: "He's simple and real. / The way he seems to our eyes. / He's documentary ... The pen's like a chisel in the poet's hands. / As a sculptor from granite blocks / He excises his essence."[51] In a similarly earnest manner the epigram to Kobzon tells of a singer whose individual songs are unified, often by one socialist aim. International or thematic diversity is subsumed by the aims of internationalist socialism. All the same, Reznik sees in Kobzon's use of folk songs (laments in particular) both the essence of the modern "confessional" lyric and the "spiritual" abstractions that would also inhabit the more private songs of the 1970s.

С давних пор песня русская исповедальна.
И покой в ней найдешь. И грозу.
Все, что истинно, то интернационально.
Вне таможен и прочих цензур.
...
Про мужицкую Русь и про бабьи обиды,
Про святую, земную любовь
Спойте песню простую, Иосиф Давидыч,
И заплачет душа моя вновь.[52]

[The Russian song has for ages been confessional. You'll find peace within it. And thunder. All that is true is international, beyond customs officials and other censors ... Sing of peasants' ancient Russia and women's grudges, of holy and earthbound love. Sing a simple song, Iosif Davydovych – and my soul will cry again.]

This request of listener to performer lies at the foundation of Reznik's previously mentioned 1980 song "Maèstro," which is a "confession," a lyric counterweight to either Kobzon or Rozhdestvenskii.[53] The text is a monologue, directed from the eighth row of the parterre to a beloved performer on stage. The female viewer calls the performer her teacher, one who may even be her saviour (*spasitel'*). The eight rows leave them as far apart as "yes" and "no," but she "dreams, sitting in this hall, of being together with you on stage to serve music!" The songs create a link that would be utterly absent in silence. The somewhat asymmetrical positions of teacher and pupil are eradicated when it becomes clear that the song's present tense, the voice from the auditorium, is in fact a dramatized memory of somebody who has herself become a *lichnost'* and sings to the maestro, who is now taking his turn in the auditorium to be an audience member. On the other hand, this may be pure audience fantasy.

That fantasy changes radically in its musical expression over the course of the song. The jazz tradition of those such as Utesov is felt in the opening jangle of lone rhythm guitar and hi-hat. Electric bass and organ, however, soon replace double bass and piano in a light-hearted series of dreamy improvisations. Over the course of several minutes Pugacheva's voice and musical accompaniment grow in both volume and drama. As the lines quoted below are heard, a small orchestra suddenly powers forth with strings and horns in a dramatic punch that, strange though it may seem, appears to be taken straight from a James Bond soundtrack.

Я для вас была
Лишь тенью.
А сейчас я вырвалась
Из плена.
Прочь тревоги!
Прочь сомненья!
Я теперь стою
На этой сцене!

В зал, смотрю я в зал
И вижу
Взгляд ваш бесконечно
Удивленный.
Столько лет прошло.
Но ближе
Стали вы, Маэстро,
Мне с тех пор!

Он пришел, мой час!
Мой звездный час.
Играю я для вас,
Маэстро!
Вы в восьмом ряду,
В восьмом ряду.
И тот же зал,
И то же место.

[I for you was just a shadow. But now I've burst from confinement. No more worries! No more doubts! Now *I'm* standing upon that stage! I look into the hall and see your endlessly surprised gaze. Years have passed, but you're nearer now, Maestro, since that moment! My hour has come in the limelight! I play for you, Maestro! You're in the eighth row, the eighth row. The hall's the same and so's the seat.]

The expression of speaker/hearer or singer/audience dialogue is so strong here that a slightly closer look is warranted at what Pugacheva says on the matter, because as Leshchenko's memories of "Za togo parnia" showed us, the fashioning of semantics between stage and hall is *the* means by which singers become the heroes of their songs and Rozhdestvenskii becomes Reznik.

STAGE AND HALL (1):
PUGACHEVA AND THE CHANGING SIGNIFICANCE
OF INTIMATE RELATIONS

> We have to remember our best
> achievements, the best estrada music of
> years gone by, and give it airtime. That
> old tradition, though, must also be
> developed, enriched, just as we must create
> music in harmony with our own times.[54]

In the article quoted above, Raimonds Pauls insists that "there really must be a serious attempt to understand the phenomenon of popularity." The major performer of his songs, Alla Pugacheva, has herself constantly made reference to the intimate, dialogic manner in which Pauls' work is performed or perceived to then constitute a popular *lichnost'* in the sense of both an artist's self-perception and the way that artist is viewed by the public, as a "star." In an article of 1976, she looks back over the ten formative years since her first recordings, such as "Robot" (1965). Already she is able to formulate the give-and-take involved with a Soviet audience of the Thaw and beyond. True to Soviet aesthetics, though, ethical concerns are never far behind: "Ten years I've been looking out at people sitting in the auditorium, looking at how they have changed, together with their attitudes to a [given] artist. I remember the type of viewer who would come to a concert as if to visit ... The artist was like a cordial host. Now people don't come to visit us; we go to them as guests! Now the viewer prefers other songs. He has become more refined, more demanding and sensitive. In order that he not lose that sensitivity, it must be cultivated. Good songs are those which help him do that. They must both respond to a certain sense of [good] taste *and* develop it."[55]

The following year in the Estonian capital of Tallinn Pugacheva worries about the lack of feedback she will receive from a musically knowledgeable but emotionally restrained Baltic audience, "though I'm sure that nonetheless our personalities (*kharaktery*) will come together."[56] The hint here at a split between the performer's singular personality and the diverse nature of the audience sounds louder in 1977: "Different kinds of people are sitting in the hall, so if I'm going to compose a repertoire based upon the taste of one individual or other, everybody else will find it boring. Therefore I sing basically songs that are close to me and with which I can reach the listener. And then it's his business whether or not to accept them. Usually, though, the viewer will accept any song that's free from artificiality."[57]

This note of slight doubt over the harmony between stage and hall remains, as here in 1978: "I'm overjoyed when children understand me, since they are listeners with spontaneous, direct perception. You might say I direct my work towards them and flatter myself with the thought that when they're adults they'll value and love estrada – real, profound songs. Their sympathy is a clear sign that as an artist you haven't lost your sincerity and haven't substituted mere images for their feelings."[58]

In another article of the same year, voicing her distaste for any artist's haughtiness on stage, she admits to varying the program out of ignorance of her typical viewer.[59] By 1980 these doubts have been countered with a proud, confrontational air. "It's all the same to me who's in the hall ... Of course I can't aim to please absolutely every-body ... Once you're out on that stage, just do all that you can, convince people you're right. And stay yourself."[60] Perhaps as a result, in 1981 she admits to preferring the eye-to-eye contact of little halls.[61] In 1983, right after praising Shul'zhenko and her ability to sing of love and bring people closer during wartime, she remarks: "Human relations and love are two notions very dear to me. I dream of a stage program where these two ideas merge, where there's a direct dialogue with the viewer. Sometimes like the contact of like-minded people, sometimes like a duel of protagonists."[62] This antagonistic air can be rather prounounced; on one occasion she says directly to the audi-ence: "This is really hard for me. Your eyes are like ice. But I have to win you over, and I'll do it, too. Just watch me."[63]

Whether or not Pugacheva acquiesces to, fears, or confronts her audience, the interaction has gradually changed in Russia between the Thaw and perestroika and acquired huge cultural consequence. Take, for example, this wonderful letter sent by a reader to the journal *Teatr* in 1985. The dialogue of Pugacheva and audience alters in turn the dialogue of that audience with itself and others:

Things often go very wrong for me, for some reason I'm often unlucky, but when I put on a record of her songs, they sound sincere; it seems she's talking to me: "Don't be upset, it'll all go away, it'll all be OK" ... And I believe what she says about the future, I believe her words *because* they're sincere. When I come home from work tired, I sit on the sofa to rest a little and look at her picture hanging in my room; my tiredness suddenly vanishes. Each new performance by Alla Pugacheva is for me personally an ocean of emotions and experiences. I can't live without that. I need a genuine and dear person in my life, one who cries and laughs like I do, one who'll talk about my sadness and happiness. That person is exactly the same as me, yet stronger and brighter. That's why Pugacheva's songs have more than just a musical influence on me and my friends.[64]

The significance of this mutual musical influence, of estrada and its audience, is an enduring one. As recently as 1994 the singer spoke of the audience's increasing confidence when she referred to her songs as "a defence" before the public, without which she is nothing. In looking at the workings of the stage/hall dialogue, the final point we need to address in brief is how that defence or mask is put up, the mask that would finally grow to fit the face. The reader may have noticed thus far how often the word "viewer" is used when our masked singers are referring to their addressees in the auditorium. A primary reason for this is the importance of an idea called "theatricalization" or "staging."

STAGE AND HALL (2): "TEATRALIZATSIIA"

> I didn't want the hero [of my song "Arlekino"]
> to be a traditional court jester, but a clown.
> That's where the elements of circus music
> in the arrangement come from. Not the light,
> waltz-type music you could walk a dog to,
> but something from a parade, something
> festive that rings out as soon as the artist goes
> out on stage.[65]

This term "*teatralizatsiia*" became so widespread in Russian estrada that by 1987 Valerii Leont'ev had a rather curt response when asked what he thought about it. "You know, I start feeling sick when I read in some interview or other with an artist that he or she is 'striving to stage a song,' that 'each song is a little play.' Those clichés already set my teeth on edge."[66] So how did we get from a novel idea to an idea used *ad nauseam*? We could of course trace the stagey origins of estrada back to the folk, fairground roots of popular entertainment; but rather than develop such culturally involved parallels,[67] a glance cast once again in the direction of Utesov and Shul'zhenko will serve us better to help explain the origins of post-Stalinist *teatralizatsiia*.

One direct influence in the development of staged songs was a trip taken by Utesov to Paris in 1927, where he saw Ted Lewis perform.[68] The clarinetist was a vital figure in the development of Dixieland and remains famous for both his wacky behaviour on stage as well as the phrase that defined the mood of his program: "Is everybody happy?"

He inspired Utesov to mix both physical and musical performance; on 8 March 1928 Soviet *tea-dzhaz* was premiered in Leningrad. The result, in the words of one Soviet historian, was that Utesov had "destroyed the static nature of the ensemble by joining all the performers, the soloists, and all the accompanying musicians, in one dramatic goal. Together they staged each and every song." The massed jumping and swaying of the ensemble did nothing to undermine Utesov's happy lyricism. "Keeping estrada's particular and direct address by the artist to the hall, he established his own type of delivery as a sung conversation."[69] But as the rhythmic movement of band members became more adventurous to the point of including tap-dancing pantomime horses, Utesov himself by the early 1930s was concerned that theatrical extravagance was overshadowing, if not displacing, the private intent of his songs.

A related but different understanding of staged songs was proposed by Shul'zhenko. She used the quietest, most unobtrusive means to dramatize the themes and heroines of her texts. Her typical heroine was "a passionate, timid woman who is capable of an elevated love while restrained in the expression of her emotions." The space she occupied on stage created a domestic haven; it was "filled [by her songs, with] the smell of roses and a quiver in the air, wicker fences and tiny roofs, it illumined table-lamps and conjured up a pile of old books or letters. This was all done simply through gestures, intonations, or a single glance from her bright, shining eyes." Such movements were not contingent upon the rhythm of the song.[70]

Shul'zhenko's motion was not confined to gesture; she flew in the face of traditions that frowned upon movement around the stage during the song. She "allowed herself to command the entire dramatic space" and move as she sang.[71] Together she, Utesov, and other performers helped to institute a combined sense of staged or theatricalized songs. One of the most important performers of our period, Mark Bernes (1911–69) defined the ingredients of the ideal estrada song in a way that shows how entrenched the notion of staging eventually became:

1 Thought: An intellectual song, able to touch both heart and mind
2 Dramatic talent: The ability to find and engender one's artistic and human image
3 Dramatic mastery [the skill to fully develop no. 2]
4 Absolute musicality: This is to be bolstered by absolute rhythmic freedom
5 Voice, vocal gift: A wealth of intimation, warmth, spiritual sincerity and clear originality of sound.[72]

Not surprisingly, perhaps, we will encounter *teatralizatsiia* more in our discussion of lyric songs than civic. Dramatized civic works exist,[73] but they pale in comparison with, say, Pugacheva, who is hugely responsible for reinstituting the staged song. An article of 1975 complains that "there are enough singers [on today's estrada], but the genre has almost no actresses. Alla Pugacheva [however] *is* an actress of songs." Describing how she performs her hit "Arlekino" "is a thankless task. But everything leaves an extraordinarily strong impression – all the way from her severe black dress and her tired eyes, directed out into the hall, to her rather sinister laughter at the end of the song."[74] In fact Pugacheva used to stand for this song like a broken puppet with her arms dangling from the elbow, because "the words could not say everything."[75] By 1977 she was calling herself a "musical actress" and receiving training from professional clowns.[76]

The notion of a "theatre of song" is deemed widely "popular" by a leading thespian publication in the following year,[77] but is already starting to worry a few critics: "Remember the guitar solo in the song 'Come to Me' [*Priezhai*] and Pugacheva [who wrote the song] under a beam of light as she moves about in a rhythmic illustration? And what if she just stood still, kept quiet, and looked at the musician? Wouldn't the impression be stronger?"[78]

During the 1970s, Pugacheva often appeared in a voluminous, diaphanous dress. Despite many jibes at its sack-like appearance, the singer held that its ample fabric allowed her to adopt the various personae or moods of her songs. It "heightened expressiveness" so much that by the end of the decade it was deemed "not a cliché, but something utterly natural, an expression of her 'I' – sometimes to excess, but never in imitation. The singer [with that self-expression] stubbornly asserts herself on stage, and at times clearly demonstrates her difference from everybody else, her absolute freedom from canons."[79]

Freedom from canons is a position unlikely to meet with rousing endorsement from Soviet critics, and indeed, as with Utesov, the big, staged persona of Pugacheva often bumps loudly against the boundaries of official tolerance. As Utesov experienced with his pantomime horses, that kind of persona tries to stage itself in a big way but can easily gallop too far. This happened in 1985 when Pugacheva organized a huge solo concert for Moscow's Olympic stadium. "The singer was unable to keep the attention of the thousands of people in the audience all the way to the end of her show. The reasons, of course, were that the setting itself was poorly suited for such an event, the distance was too great separating the auditorium from the performer. But that's not all. Even though it's not pleasant to hear it, Alla

Pugacheva the theatre director inhibits Alla Pugacheva the singer. The abundance of gear filling the stage, the enormous number of dancers, circus acts, a full-blown light show, waves of mist or smoke that envelop the boards, and a small car bearing the singer along endless footlights" were too distracting.[80] The growth of dramatized performance from a broken puppet-show to an Olympic stadium marks the beginning and end of Pugacheva's Soviet story, the limit of her personality, inspired to such dimensions on stage by the urging of her audience.

Drama and gesture are an important part of this story. In opposition to Soviet classically static "poses" embodied by the immobile civic singer, an estrada performance will gradually become what Iurii Lotman has termed a nonchalant, *"careless* pose, a touching motion, the ostentatious rejection of [public] signification."[81] A singer's gesture is expressed spatially, as a response to the static status of Stalinist classicism, and that gesture is used as an expression of self, of idiosyncrasy. The more movement, the more gesturing, or the greater expanse of the stage claimed, the louder expression of *lichnost'*, until we start running around an Olympic stadium (a little ironic, when we consider the imperial politic and aesthetic for which that stadium was built).

Lotman, in writing about the type of signification embodied in theatre, positions stagecraft "between the nondiscrete flow of life and its segmentation ... we are presented with a series of discrete, immanently ordered pictures capable of instantaneous change from one pictorial realization to another." If we draw a parallel between a dramatic episode and a song, since episodes are linked to form plays and songs are linked to form concerts, then we have a mode of private expression which is positioned between stasis and movement, public and private, itself given significance by the positioning between stage and auditorium, singer and audience, "I" and "us" (or "them" or any other plural pronoun).

A 1990 article about Pugacheva positions her between the persisting thingness of Soviet life and an attempt to reclaim things, to make the tangible world one's own, not to escape it in abstractions or mysticism (of which we will see very little in this book). "Today we're coming to the conclusion that it's not one's daily life (*byt*) that destroys the spiritual in a person, but its very absence. We see [now] that a battle with 'things' led to the destruction of individuality."[82] "Things" here means the horrors of a greedy, materialistic worldview. Shul'zhenko's songs were an initial and opposing step across the stage to claim some space for herself:

Dreaminess is not really Shul'zhenko's element. Her element is something tangible, such that one could visibly draw not just the concrete event [of a song], but the surrounding things and where it takes place. We always see the keys of a piano with hands fleeting above them, the dusk of a train carriage, the smoke of a soldier's roll-up, a provincial railway stop where those soldiers met, bound for the front, little umbrellas, scarves and handbags that were lost in a moment of thoughtlessness, flowers in the hands of an ideal husband whose virtue is worthy of a song, the old gramophone with its record starting to play, one's first wrinkles of age, the first grey locks of hair.[83]

As a modern counterpart, perhaps, to this creative, often sentimental reassessment of the material world, Il'ia Reznik has dedicated a poem to Pugacheva and "Talking Things" (*Govoriashchie veshchi*).[84] The objects around a woman's house, implicitly Pugacheva's apartment, complain of how they are misused. Their mistress has donned a green wig and stuck her tongue out at the mirror, a dining table is scratched from too many guests, the telephone is exhausted from too many calls, and slippers are offended at not being suitable for public display on stage! Only the piano is treated with care. Troubled by all this, the woman puts on her slippers, looks at herself kindly in the mirror, lays a tablecloth, turns off the phone, and "sits at the piano. To play. Until the morning." The sung calming or reclaiming of the material world, in order to fashion a private space with a private text, has some broader philosophical significances in the creation of personality. Those significances expand the importance of estrada songs far beyond the small or trivial sphere of cultural significance they are generally assumed to have.

3
WHY SING ESTRADA?
PHILOSOPHICAL CONTEXTS OF THE GENRE

> Everybody knows that for decades we lived on
> songs ennobling, glorifying, or appealing to the
> Homeland, Party, and Friendship. Despite their
> different titles, they could only be distinguished
> by degrees of some high-flown solemnity or
> generalizing. There was evident falseness in all
> that cantata-like, epoch-making creativity, so we
> tried instead to help to create the kind of
> lyrical songs where there'd be not only pathos
> but everything else too. They'd have to be
> oriented towards a concrete indivdual, neither
> to the masses nor a crowd. The [new] songs
> were not to leave that individual indifferent.
> They had to touch his soul.[1]
>
> Alla Pugacheva

In discussions of estrada in the post-Stalinist Soviet press, much is said
and written around the simplest of questions: Why sing? The responses
can be assessed in two ways, by looking at what singers say about their
craft, and at why they might talk thus in post-Stalinist Russia. The
second of these issues begs prior consideration; it will provide a broad
philosophical context against which we can view the smaller, more
private concerns of any one performer's worldview.

Estrada both fostered and reflected the cultural movement away
from Stalinism that began in February 1956 with Khrushchev's four-
hour denouncement of his predecessor at the Twentieth Party Congress. The political consequences of this address were felt all across
the Eastern Bloc, for example, in the increasingly "subversive" liberal-
ism of neighbouring Hungary and Poland. A suitable philosophical
context for this book, therefore, will be found in a similar sidestep or
initial motion away from the *Weltanschauung* of 1924–53. The gradual
and tentative steps taken towards tolerance after Stalin's death,
towards the exchange of ideas rather than unmediated projection of
state-sponsored notions, would suggest the now-modish Bakhtin as a
fitting prism through which to view the cultural tendencies of the day.

However, Bakhtin's torturous steps towards an established pedagogical position were taken in 1957 at the University of Saransk; such a radically provincial posting, despite its coincidence with the temporal boundaries of this study, cannot be presumed to be of direct consequence to the cultural milieu of either Moscow or Leningrad.

A POST-STALINIST THOUGHT OR TWO

> I don't have the ability to please bureaucrats.
> I don't know how to acquiesce to them,
> flatter them, or give them presents; they didn't
> let me travel overseas for ages. I was always
> being crossed off lists. After all, I didn't sing
> about the Party, but about love, friendship
> and the purity of human relationships.[2]
>
> Èdita P'ekha

Since this book concentrates not upon the sometimes consciously controversial bards such as Vysotskii or Galich but instead upon the delicate, often imperceptible deviations from a state-sponsored norm on national radio playlists, we need a philosopher closer than Bakhtin to the centre of a centralized system and to the middle of the road. Such a figure is Èval'd Il'enkov (1924–79). A brief look at Il'enkov's ideas as a tentative side-stepping of Soviet mainstream thought in the 1960s indicates the way in which an imperial philosophy after the death of Stalin was willing to accept, if only briefly, a voice of quiet difference. Il'enkov was born, educated, and employed in the capital, holding eventually a long-term position at the Moscow Institute of Philosophy. His previous post at Moscow State University had been curtailed as a consequence of tension with academic elders; the new ideas of Khrushchev's Thaw sometimes appeared faster than the new professors (who were willing to champion them) could find secure work. Il'enkov published a considerable amount before his death, but the struggles of working within the staid philosophical tenets of the age led to the lack of new (publishable) ideas in his 1974 credo, *Dialectical Logic*. Here, because of a very lengthy delay in its release, we see Il'enkov's worldview of the preceding decade, one with much in common with statements made to the Soviet press by our performers.

The best overview of Il'enkov's thought in English (and outside of Soviet dogma) is by David Bakhurst (1991), in research that explains the philosopher's investigation into the validity of non-material phenomena in a world of unyielding, official materialism.[3] Given the reinstituting of subjective concerns during the Thaw, of private beliefs or emotions once again being given some validity, a new definition of such non-material states would be of great use as an insight into the shifting Soviet worldview of the 1960s. For Il'enkov, these states are termed "the ideal" and discussed in a way that subtly challenges the "ban on anthropocentricity" marking Stalinist materialism. How, then, to squeeze the immaterial into a world that proclaims the undying primacy of the material? Bakhurst suggests that Il'enkov "offers a global response to the problem of the ideal: renounce the ban on anthropocentricity and attribute to humanity the power to endow the material world with a new class of properties that, though they owe our origin to us, acquire an enduring presence in objective reality, coming to exist independently of human individuals."[4]

How do these ideal, subjective properties get from us to an independent existence? Through activity, claims Il'enkov – in particular, socially determined activity that is acquired or learned from others. To take an initial and simple example, here is what Il'enkov says about the interaction of man and the substantial matter of clay. (Once again I note that *Dialectical Logic*, though published in 1974, "recapitulates positions Il'enkov forged a decade before ... He sought principally to find acceptance for an old message."[5])

The ideal is nothing else than the form of things, but existing outside things, namely in man, in the form of his active practice, i.e., it is *the socially determined form of the human being's activity*. In nature itself, including the nature of man as a biological creature, the ideal does not exist. As regards the natural, material organization of the human body, it has the same external character as it does in regard to the material in which it is realized and objectified in the form of a sensuously perceived thing. Thus the form of a jar growing under the hands of a potter does not form part either of the piece of clay or of the inborn, anatomical, physiological organization of the body of the individual functioning as potter. Only insofar as man trains and exercises the organs of his body on objects created by man for man does he become the bearer of the active forms of social man's activity that create the corresponding objects.[6]

The best and fullest exposition of Il'enkov's ideas comes when we transpose talk of matter or clay to that of language. For the philosopher, words are also things to be endowed with an ideal meaning. "The meaning of a word is an ideal form, acquired by a purely natural object through its incorporation into purposeful human activity. A word owes its significance to its use."[7] The use of words takes place in social interaction. As soon as the overcoming of objective reality becomes possible through the spoken use of words in a dialogic format, we start to hears echoes of Bakhtin, and christological ones at that. The supposedly objective or reified significance of a word gains a "non-fleshy," ideal state in the constant repetition of what Il'enkov calls the "closed cycle" of man's transformational activity upon word-artifacts: "thing → deed → word → deed → thing." A word in human dialogue comes briefly alive in a manner that improves upon its material, silent state; the ideal is *heard* in the word and needs to be constantly socially vivified.

Bakhtin noted in his work on Dostoevskii that Christ's entrance into the world and all his subsequent failings in fact gave Christianity a "living form" and saved it from the undiscussed dictates of "truth-as-formula, truth-as-proposition."[8] Christ's deeds took the form of words which in dialogue with the manifold characters of the New Testament were thus idealized. A secular version of this paean to discourse as the means by which Christ's ideal subjectivity was realized comes in Il'enkov's discussion of personality or individuality. No individual enters an idealized world; "the capacity to inhabit an idealized environment is not something that the human individual possesses by nature. Rather, children acquire this capacity as they are socialized by the adult members of the community into their practices. As they assimilate or internalize those practices, so they are transformed from epistemically inept masses of brute matter into thinking beings, subjects, personalities [*lichnosti*]."[9]

Both subjectivity and the ideal are born of inherited practices, of a give and take that turns things into words which are constantly negotiated with an "other," lest they fall back to an inert monologic state, to the "truth-as-formula" that seems such an apt definition of pre-Thaw Russia. In a post-Stalinist environment, however, Il'enkov is cleverly able to suggest "not only a universal scheme of subjective activity creatively transforming nature, but also at the same time a universal scheme of the changing of any natural or socio-historical material in which this activity is fulfilled."[10] The private is raised above the public and exclusively material, while still being of objective use to it; the private is raised above the social by *being* social and exercising culturally acquired skills. A full *lichnost'* is developed through the interactive processes of speech, the way in which the "deed" of speaking transforms the "things" of nature (even those thing-like words themselves) to reveal their ideal form.

The ability of thinking, culturally skilled individuals to enter into spoken dialogue with their material surroundings, to talk and think of them in a transformational manner, is to some degree determined by the nature of the environment in which those individuals happen to be. The material world itself is a mass of already accrued cultural significances that must be discussed and mulled over before they yield to an individual's subjective intent. Il'enkov leans upon Spinoza to draw an analogy between the unyielding material world and the attempts to refashion it. A successfully uttered thought or deed is akin to the mastery of matter shown by an accurate technical drawing:

With good reason he [Spinoza] linked adequate ideas, expressed in the words of a language, precisely with an ability to reproduce verbal forms in real space. It was just there that he drew the distinction between a determination expressing the essence of the matter, i.e., the ideal image of the object, and nominal, formal definitions that fixed a more or less accidentally chosen property of the object, its outward sign. A circle, for example, could be defined as a figure in which lines drawn from the circumference were equal. But such a definition did not quite express the essence of a circle, but only a given property of it, which was derivative and secondary. It was another matter when the definition included the proximate cause of the thing. Then a circle should be defined as a figure described by any line one end of which was fixed and the other moved. The definition provided the *mode of constructing the thing* in real space. Here the *nominal definition* arose *together* with the *real action of the thinking body along the spatial contour of the object of the idea.* In that case man also possessed an adequate idea, i.e., an ideal image, of the thing, and not just signs expressed in words. *That is also a materialist conception of the nature of the ideal.* The ideal exists where there is a capacity to recreate the object in space, relying on the word, on language, in combination with a need for the object, plus material provision of the act of creation.[11]

By active involvement in the social, inherited, or taught practices of speech, the individual describes or creates an object's "ideal being" from its "real being," to borrow Il'enkov's distinction. The ideal needs the real and vice versa, leading to the observation that "determination of the ideal is especially dialectical." The spoken mastery over matter is never complete (given the tendency of so-called "truth as proposition" to lapse from "deed" back into "thingness"), but with each spoken deed and discovery of the ideal in the real, objective reality is re-fashioned in a manner described here by Il'enkov (via Spinoza) as movement out and across space. The three-dimensional spaces of materialism are re-defined and idealized, one by one in the dialectic of real and ideal, of silent things and uttered words.

I have suggested that the better-known and more radically dialectical ideas of Mikhail Bakhtin have something of a conservative kin in those of Èval'd Il'enkov. Bakhtin's own writings question the stability and arrogance of any uninterrupted monologue's claim to control the world's significances by stressing the "dialogic" manner in which meaning is created; semantics are not the sole property of any speaker, since the intent of his or her words is filtered through the worldview of a listener, and those very words used to transmit a thought are themselves already imbued with centuries of older significances, accrued over years of long-forgotten conversations and debates. The struggle of any speaker's word with the "thingness" of silence or fossilized significances is also described by Bakhtin as movement through space. Both he and Il'enkov reinterpreted materialist thought as movement *through* matter, as if a speaker bumps and rubs against the solid significances of materialism in order to make the real into the ideal through the socially active "deeds" of language.

There are two possible ways of combining the outside world with a human being: from within a human being – as his horizon, and from outside him – as his environment. From within me myself, within the meaning-and-value context of my own life, an object stands over or against me as the object of my own (cognitive-ethical and practical) directedness in living my life; in this context, the object is a constituent of the unitary and unique open event of being, in which I partake as a participant who has an urgent interest in the outcome of that event ... The centre of gravity in this world is located in the future, in what is desired, in what ought to be, and not in the self-sufficient givenness of an object, in its being-on-hand, not in its present, its wholeness, its being-already-realized. My relationship to each object within my horizon is never a consummated relationship; rather, it is a relationship which is imposed on me as a task-to-be-accomplished, for the event of being, taken as a whole, is an open event; my situation must change at every moment – I cannot tarry and come to rest.[12]

Bakhtin here talks more explicitly of words as bearers of "cognitive-ethical and practical directedness" in an individual's thought-deeds and their application to material existence. By combining this ethical emphasis with Il'enkov's notion that "moral value should be treated as a species of significance that natural objects acquire by virtue of their incorporation into human practices,"[13] these two men together suggest that at the time of the Thaw an incipient philosophy was being heard in the (distant) classroom or read in the capital's libraries, which endowed the spoken word with an ethical or moral significance as crafter and conjurer of "ideal" properties in the natural world.

STALINISM AND MATTER

In the 1930s the ancient prototype "Praise be"
used earlier in hymnic or marching works
dedicated to the Revolution, Proletariat, Lenin,

and the Party, was now projected upon Stalin
... Any expression of gratitude and heartfelt
love was married to a voicing of glory ...
These types of social songs were coloured with
ceremonial sentimentalism. During the Thaw,
it was the sentimental foundation of such texts
that grew more evident.[14]

If there is one category associated in the common perception with Stalinist aesthetics, it is that of quantity, not quality: massive bureaucracy, agricultural collectivization, and vast labour camps born of sweeping and seemingly arbitrary prejudices. Metaphors for the might that fuelled such projects were found in power-stations (of the Urals), subway systems (Moscow), and inconceivably long canals (running south from the Baltic). A recent history of Russian culture notes Stalin's correspondingly grand artistic tastes:

[He] spent immense sums to subsidize huge murals, gigantic frescoes, massive friezes, and colossal mosaics, each and every one of which proclaimed that life was becoming gayer and better with every year that Russia lived under his leadership ... The Soviet masses were the audience for the monumental buildings with which the Bolsheviks proclaimed their superiority over nature and the societies of the modern world. Like the writers, painters, and film directors who had embraced Russia's Revolution in 1917, Bolshevik architects disdained their imperial past and sought to work with new concepts and materials. Only in that way could they design the massive subterranean People's Palaces through which Moscow subway trains carried millions of workers every day, and the gigantic factories and mills that armies of strong-backed proletarians raised up out of steel, brick, and concrete to become the new cathedrals of Bolshevism in the midst of the wilderness.[15]

Monumental structures reflected an age of monumental and inflexible dictates. One (little) presence amidst this marble bombast was the future Nobel laureate, the poet Joseph Brodsky (1940–96), who was not quite thirteen when Joseph Stalin passed away. In 1972 with the advantages of hindsight and the objectivity afforded by exile, Brodsky wrote that Stalinism had led to "the loss not only of an absolute but even a relative moral criterion." Brodsky's critique of his youthful milieu has remarkable parallels with the manner in which Il'enkov and Bakhtin differ from radical materialism by investing language with an ideal significance. The poet maintains that an emphasis upon utter substantiality had nasty consequences for both metaphysics and morality:

In the modern world approximately the same thing stands behind both good and evil: matter. Matter, as we know, does not have its own moral categories. In other words, both good and evil are in the same state as a stone. The tendency to the embodiment of the ideal, to its materialization, has gone too far – namely, to the idealization of material ... As a result of the secularization of consciousness that has taken place on a global scale, man's heritage from the Christianity he has renounced is a vocabulary that he does not know how to use, and therefore is forced to improvise. Absolute concepts [such as good and evil] have degenerated simply into words that have become objects of personal interpretation, if not mere questions of pronunciation. In other words, arbitrary categories at best. With the transformation of absolute concepts into arbitrary categories, little by little the idea of the arbitrariness of existence has taken root in our consciousness. This idea is very dear to human nature, for it excuses everyone and everything from any responsibility whatsoever. In this lies the reason for the success of totalitarian systems: they answer the basic need of the human race to be free of any responsibility ... [Stalin] took the first steps towards the embodiment of the new goal: moral non-existence.[16]

The Stalinist "embodiment of the ideal," if we draw a parallel with Il'enkov and Bakhtin, robs words and spoken "deeds" of their ability to perform an "ethical and practical" act upon the silent, real world such that they might realize their genuinely "ideal" state. The dimension of one's freely chosen, morally consequential, and socially developed attitude to the real world is erased, and matter not only triumphs but grows into the monumental façades of Stalinist public architecture. Matter simply *is*, and the potential for dialogue is lost.

RESPONSES TO STALINISM (1):
PRIVATE MATTERS

> Today you will hear her [P'ekha] perform
> your favourite songs, which over the course
> of many, many years warmed you,
> supported you in difficult times, and
> cheered you in moments of rest.[17]

In the all-embracing gloom of Brodsky's memoirs it is hard to find anything resembling a natural or gradual transition from the Stalinist heritage to the gentler years ushered in after 1953. Let us instead take heed of a recent observation by the historian Régine Robin in an essay on the nature of popular entertainment under Stalin: "We are victims of *ad hoc* categories, such the notion of totalitarianism, imposed on the entire field of Soviet Studies in the West at the time of the Cold

War."[18] If Robin is correct in her assumptions, then perhaps there are manifestations within the popular culture of Stalin's period in office that show a (latent, perhaps) harbouring of private matters in a time of publicly engendered materialism. Although I intend to prove in a subsequent study that subjectivity was cared for very successfully in the Soviet popular song before World War II, a lengthy monograph by Vera Dunham entitled *In Stalin's Time* has already shown that a careful examination of another realm, of popular reading habits under Stalin, in fact reveals a remarkable amount of private, subjective musing, none of it of particular use to grand social causes or five-year assaults upon the material world.

The inhuman energy and familial sacrifice embodied by the literary heroes immediately following the Revolution was hard if not impossible for Stalin to maintain after the ultimate sacrifice then made by so many during World War II. Mutual distrust was rife, especially amongst those who had fallen into enemy prison camps or been taken into the Soviet fold after wartime annexations (and then, as in the Baltics, been promptly ejected from their homeland). To such people and to many veterans the grand overtures of "we" in their choruses to "him" sounded empty, and so "I" staged a significant rejoinder in the Soviet literature people *liked* to read.

Yet even on a more official level, on the level of what the state presses would have liked the public to like, propaganda's purview had shrunk somewhat, since an army that had been officially driven by a proletarian, pan-continental impetus in the late '40s became by decree one driven by patriotism pure and simple. Russia, not the world, was now the centre of attention. The narratives of the time are correspondingly diminished, sometimes radically so: deep in the fabric of what we as western readers dismiss as the most monotone or uniform drone of state-inspired Socialist Realism there sounds the quiet and modest idiosyncrasy of the first-person pronoun. In the big stories of Stalinist Russia are the tiniest hints of something private:

[Stalinist heroism] clashed with the people's mourning. Although attempted by orthodox writers, the restoration of the clichés of the Thirties did not work. For one thing, the pronouns balked. Too much had happened in Soviet society to permit large retroactive movements, even in middlebrow fiction. For many reasons, the first pronoun singular would not give way, so the creation of the postwar public hero became a problem ... The regime's ambivalence towards the mythological legacy of the Twenties and Thirties, complicated by distrust of the [sceptical, world-weary] returning soldier, did not make it easy to work out clear directives for functional official postwar heroism. Nevertheless, official guidelines were issued soon enough. Inevitably, new ambiguities emerged with them. The postwar model was charged with keeping a balance in general and with balancing clashing traits in particular. For instance, simplicity and extraordinariness were to blend. A completely simple person, he was to be enraptured by that tidy row or two of private onions. At the same time, he was to perform inspiring deeds in the shop or field. But there too, he was to be a radiant achiever, not a brain-straining recluse. Avoiding any kind of exaggeration, his thinking, whether at home or work, had to be undercut in favor of dreaming. Yet dreaming was not to go wild. It was to be directed to one main channel: good things.[19]

In this awfully complicated hero we see some of the contradictions that are inherent in Stalin's cultural heritage, ones usually forgotten in sweeping generalizations about the grand and impersonal gestures of Socialist Realism. This was the name for the officially sanctioned and consolidated form of artistic expression after 1932, a term supposedly of Stalin's own suggestion. Leaning heavily on the realist traditions of nineteenth-century art, it was to be informed by the depiction not only of tangible, sensible reality but of the way in which that reality was progressing towards a revolutionary, socialist goal. Scenes of joyful social and national achievement predominated, be they in harvested fields, noisy factories, or packed conference halls.

Such enterprise was most famously cast in a literary form, as the maturation of a desire that had originally sounded in the years immediately after the Revolution, a tendency now referred to in retrospect as "Revolutionary Romanticism." What, then, is the difference between such works and the socially directed, spoken transformation or definition of reality proffered by Il'enkov or Bakhtin? The problem arises from the desire of Socialist Realism to show the revolutionary *development* of social man and his material context. Socialist Realism, by depicting not only what the material world is but what it should be, is in fact not realist at all. It does not reflect matter; it projects it into an assumed future state, one of centripetal allegiance to a centralized "state." Ideally any reader or viewer of a Socialist Realist work would be inspired to personal achievement only in an utterly social – and therefore anonymous – setting. Il'enkov suggests that personality is idealized by being social; Socialist Realism sells its ideal *to* a personality in order that personality recede into and therefore constitute society.

The idea of unique, idiosyncratic personality was erased to the point of strong, vital, but genderless heroes populating the typical Socialist Realist work.[20] Universality in gender was part of a general homogenization of space (not just corporeal) and time, such that the cherished desire of any empire, Soviet or Roman, be realized – to remain uniform and unassailable. Once again, Joseph Brodsky's work, as that of a Soviet citizen, has much to say on the spatio-temporal sameness of Soviet habitus: "The meaning of the Empire is in rendering space meaningless."[21] Il'enkov and Bakhtin both write of spoken definition or acquisition of the material world as a related movement through space, such that one's horizon comes to encompass more and more of the world. The goal, however, is not a public but a private condition gained and then monitored socially. Personality for the two philosophers is cultivated in a dialogue with matter, not defined *by* it. Personality is the spoken deed that momentarily de-reifies a thing and endows it with private, *meta*physical significance.

RESPONSES TO STALINISM (2): PUBLIC OR PRIVATE?

Q: What in your view are the ideal conditions
for an estrada concert?

P'EKHA: First of all the concert hall should be
a *hall*, and not a stadium! And in that hall
there should come together the kind of people
who listen with sympathy to a performer
and her songs ... People don't like being
passive listeners. They prefer songs that force
them to think, to feel deeply.[22]

Many an example of troubled labour upon the material world after World War II can be found in the poetry of Boris Slutskii (1919–86). Slutskii's verse, although firmly entrenched in the loud, material conflicts of wartime thematics, nevertheless demands serious academic attention as the moment when modern, subjective, and *Soviet* literature develops beside (or simply ignores) social dictates. A tiny Slutskian poem of the Thaw, "Khorosho, kogda khuliat i khvaliat," shows just such a move. The poet here celebrates a spoken conference with matter and a corresponding spatial movement, one that does not contradict the possibility of being "useful." The alternative to such a dialogue would be the absence of language altogether, here in what appears to be the form of a telegram from the front with a fallen soldier's name metaphorically cancelled out. Instead of such silent horrors, the poet asks that the pronoun or person called "I," although twisted like a piece of metal, be tenacious and sufficiently hardy to poke its way through to the future. A "non-crossed-out" word will, in its idiosyncratic, asymmetrical form, map out a modest step into a spatio-temporal expanse, a step not necessarily social in its application.

Хорошо, когда хулят и хвалят,
Превозносят или наземь валят,
Хорошо стыдиться и гордиться
И на что-нибудь годиться.
Не хочу быть вычеркнутым словом
В телеграмме – без него дойдет! –
А хочу быть вытянутым ломом,
В будущее продолбавшим ход.

[It's fine when they laud and lambaste, extol or drag one down to the ground, it's fine when one's proud or ashamed and there's something for which one is fit. I don't want to be like a word that's crossed out in a telegram – "It'll get through without him!" – I want to be like an elongated crowbar that has beaten a way through to the future.][23]

Here, as Vera Dunham notes in her book on the persistence of "middle-class" values even under Stalin, the first-person pronoun is stubbornly present. One might associate it with durability and a mis-shapen appearance, which by implication challenges the straighter lines and smoother surfaces of Stalinist classicism. A final word or two more about such pronouns and their aesthetic implications will help us to mark more clearly still the differences between, say, 1953 and 1963, between the rigidity redolent of Stalin and the relatively flexible, forgiving reforms under Khrushchev.

RESPONSES TO STALINISM (3): REFORM AS SENTIMENTALISM

I have my type of audience. It's neither loud
nor scandalous. It's attracted by beauty and
nobility. I am very glad that so many young
people come to my concerts. I think they are
from families where a love is fostered for
beautiful, refined music and refined human
relations, where children are not left without
care but raised upon cultural traditions. That's
what stops any rift between generations.[24]

Èdita P'ekha

The seemingly all-pervasive nature of Stalinism, the fact that it was so "big" and everywhere to be seen, together with its intent to not negotiate but *show* the desired state of the material world in the very near future, has led the writer Boris Groys to suggest that Socialist

Realism, far from being a "mere revival of kitschy realism" of the nineteenth century, was no less "projectile" in its movement towards a future than the preceding avant-garde: "It was realism in the sense of political realism, *realpolitik*. Avant-garde projects were rejected in the first place because they were unrealizable and neglected the reality of practical politics ... Socialist Realism, the art of the winners, wanted to take all reality inside itself, change it all, and bless it with Socialist ideals. In its planning for the future, then, Socialist Realism sought to base itself upon what has been built already, on the 'presence of the future in the present,' as the saying went."[25] The tension between what was promised and what was painfully apparent about the realizability of those promises led in some degree to the huge social resonance of popular songs, which propose a private dialectic, the chance for "me" to reflect the material world.

In an ideological[, sung] text, the singular or "mono-notion" may be expressed by a formula: "We + Them = Struggle." In its place the popular song offers: "I + You = Love." Both formulae indicate a state of happiness: the ideological one is in the future; the song's is in the present. In a quotidian fashion, the song realizes *every day* what official ideology [merely] promises. The actuality of a dance-oriented or lyrical happiness makes the ideological happiness worthless. This is exactly where ideology's long-lasting antipathy towards estrada comes from.[26]

Prior to the mid-1950s, however, the dominant form of cultural expression has precedence over all potentially subversive or deviant modes of interpretation. All other spoken deeds are muted, and thus Il'enkov's cycle of "thing → deed → word → deed → thing" often remains stuck in the first or last of its stages, that which either precedes or follows any deed and can be perpetuated indefinitely if nobody speaks up.

The style that corresponds to the greedy acquisition of all matter and rejects all twisted, Slutskian metal is, not surprisingly, smooth in its contours. "The social system was guaranteed by a style adequate to itself, that of Stalinist classicism which is – through a lack of under-standing – termed Socialist Realism. Its normative poetics unified culture on all levels, all the way from the epithet to architecture. Enemies of the people, the war, Stalin – all of this gave life a clearly heroic backdrop. Against this backdrop even the inflexible district committee secretary was defined. He entered into an ancient poetic system: Ajax, Achilles, Hector."[27]

Let us accept for a moment the analogical definition here of Stalin's grand marble unities as a latter-day classicism. If such parallels with past aesthetic phenomena are in any way instructive, then the reinstitution of an emphasis upon "me" after World War II, even within the ongoing limitations of Stalinism, may be akin to the fraying of Russian classicism in the eighteenth century. Such a suggestion has already been made by Mikhail Èpshtein in his assessment of what happened the moment Stalin's presence evanesced. "From the middle of the 1950s there begins a phase for which it is harder to find a better name than Socialist sentimentalism. There arose, as before, a critique of strict classical canons ... all to the advantage of moral approaches [to writing] as dictated by one's 'soul' or 'conscience.' At the centre of attention was the irrepeatable human personality (*lichnost'*)."[28]

Here, for example, are the hopes for an upcoming performance by Valerii Leont'ev from within the time frame of this study: "Let's hope that it'll be as merry as champagne. After all, isn't that an adult hope – sentimentalism and optimism? Let's grow up a little, see both the world and ourselves in a new light. One shouldn't stay in one place."[29] Or here, even, from the conservative "Nightingale of the Kremlin," Lev Leshchenko, is an explanation of how songs grow: "They arise as the result of a complicated and intensive search by composer, poet, and performer. Together they try to open the world of their feelings in song, to create an objective picture of modern life through an individual's perception of reality. A song is summoned forth not just to reflect but primarily to educate."[30] Such parallels as these are in need of justification. Exactly how valid is the rather loaded term "sentimental?" Can it be harmonized with the romanticism I suggested earlier as a possible epithet for our seven singers?

After the excessive rigidity of classicism, sentimentalism in the final third of the eighteenth century reinstated the validity of private experience, of empiricism fashioned by the gentle unpredictability of (a quiet) emotion. Nikolai Karamzin in his *Letters of a Russian Traveler* (1789–90) visits the homeland of the author of the hugely influential and prolix *Sentimental Journey through France and Italy* (1768), Laurence Sterne. In doing so he challenges classicism's insistence upon the universality of human nature, and sets off to experience (with heart more than head) the individuals who constitute the local colour of any given locale. With this emphasis upon smaller, private spaces, upon idylls, not empires, Karamzin is able to refashion London as a simple, clean city, where cows graze in St James Park. The surprisingly well-scrubbed cells of Newgate Prison, however, are inhabited by the unfortunate victims of ecstasy (an excessive emotion), who by the laws of nature have fallen to both melancholy and despair.

As Karamzin's prison inspection suggests, early sentimentalism had a marked element of didacticism, the social consequences of which were fed by the fraternal metaphors of burgeoning Freemasonry. This ethical commitment was managed aesthetically: good taste was ethically sound and guaranteed by the exercising of sentiment. One's very existence was guaranteed by that sentiment: subjective emotions, not objective society, were proof of actuality, as evidenced by Rousseau's aphoristic rebuttal to Descartes: *Je sens, donc je suis.*

The object of that feeling, the recipient of that spoken emotion, was a lot closer than the grand, often odic leanings of classicist discourse. A wonderful study of Karamzin's prose by Gitta Hammarberg has examined this new intimacy and most convincingly codified it in terms of pronouns: both the person to whom the author speaks and how they speak become quieter and more intimate, closer in both space and sentiment. She uses the grammatical category of deixis, or the tiny parts of speech used to define an utterance's spatio-temporal parameters: "Spatial adverbs, adverbial phrases, adjectives, adjectival phrases, and demonstrative pronouns (here, there, this, that, up, down, right, left, near, far) indicate the location of the narrator, narratee, or both, as a spatial reference point."[31] All these grammatical tools are ultimately used to persuade a listener or reader of a given proposition. The sentimental speaker feels s/he can say more to a person s/he trusts more, and thus the affection for one's audience ("My friends!" or "Gentle reader") allows for a preponderance of revealing first-person (rather than third-person) narration. "In sentimentalist fiction first person narration was particularly popular, owing to the personalization and fictionalization of 'author' and the influence of new literary genres, such as autobiographies, memoirs, confessions, diaries, and journals of various kinds where this form is natural."

PERSONALITY AND SENTIMENTAL EDUCATION: THE EXEMPLARY ÈDITA P'EKHA

> A romantic songstress – that's what they always
> say about Èdita Stanislavovna P'ekha. A singer
> with a timbre unlike any other: low and even
> a little muted in her singular, gentle way
> of performing. She does not assert her "I";
> it seems instead that she muses, dreams,
> and asks about herself.[32]

By drawing an analogy with the early flowering of sentimentalism in Russia and by talking of Russian songs in the late 1950s or early 1960s as a similar, rather callow process, I am bound twice over to examining the subject of *lichnost'* chronologically, as the growth or maturing of something. The first performer in my list of seven, by virtue of less than two months' seniority, is Èdita P'ekha, born not far from Paris in 1937. P'ekha returned to Poland after World War II with her mother and later arrived in Russia to study at Leningrad State University. Her story is told in full in the next chapter; here we are interested in how hindsight leads her to interpret that ("my") career: how she became who she is today, one of the country's most respected and influential figures in the world of so-called light vocal music.

In a 1979 article published in the newspaper *Sovetskaia Rossiia*, P'ekha assesses the current state of estrada and compares it to what should be – in other words, to that which it used to be. Her observations are a fine introduction to the ethical yet sentimental notion of *lichnost'* cultivated by singers during the early Thaw. What P'ekha says here defines a philosophy that was of seminal importance in the post-Stalinist shift from public to private, big to small, civic to lyric, Rozhdestvenskii to Reznik, objective to subjective – all *within* an officially embraced Soviet worldview.

Since the 1950s, says P'ekha, artists have become less demanding, less exacting of their craft, "of their expertise and what they offer to the masses … [And they are] less demanding of themselves, of their moral and ethical principles." Such talk might sound somewhat stuffy to western ears, but what surprises us even more is that P'ekha is "propagandizing" not politics, but beauty: "Any person who starts to advocate or propagandize the beautiful must first of all have himself the most completely defined moral and spiritual qualities. If not, then the artist has no *lichnost'*." The personality of the singer is defined not within the contexts of grandiose social plans but by the quiet parameters of private emotion. "The main criterion for me when I put together my repertoire is what I've felt, experienced, pondered. After all, if the song isn't clear to you yourself, then the public will stay cold and apathetic no matter how well you sing or what kind of vocal ability you have."

The public *makes* P'ekha's private sentiment public, if her song is heartfelt and "clear." She works towards that goal within a materialistic philosophy, by bringing spoken deeds to bear upon the real world around her in a manner very similar to that highlighted by Il'enkov. She herself is socialized into the spoken or sung ability to idealize the real by her mentor, Klavdiia Shul'zhenko, who talks of the sentimental drive behind any song's transformational potential. P'ekha herself mentions the "unusually hard work" involved in an artistic process, "in the creation or formation of the human soul. Art corrects nature," as Shul'zhenko had taught her. "On the stage one must be simple, natural, sincere, and everything must come from the soul. One time

I asked Klavdiia how to find the necessary, precise gesture, so that one might be a certain person in one song, and another person in a different song. She answered: 'When you sing with your heart, then your hands, eyes, and entire being will start to sing.'"[33]

As the next chapter will show, this transferal of subjective, emotional experience to the body, which then enters into a formative dialogue with a public sphere, has strong and telling philosophical parallels within the prevailing tendencies of materialist thought. "Materialism in this case does not consist at all in identifying the ideal with the material processes taking place in the head. Materialism is expressed here in understanding that the ideal, as a socially determined form of the activity of man creating an object in one form or another, is engendered and exists not in the head but with the help of the head in the real objective activity (activity on things) of man as the active agent of social production."[34] The social production here is both verbal and physical (i.e., on stage), the singing of songs that constitutes an "activity on things." That activity in turn creates an ideal image of things, a sentimental one inherited from and bequeathed to others. Both Il'enkov and Bakhtin define this activity as resulting in a new form or image (obraz); the same word, as we will see, emerges often in the different cultural environment of estrada as a "song-image," the union of the oral (song) and visually perceived physical (performance). Take, for example, one definition of Alla Pugacheva's importance: "She is a long-awaited phenomenon in our estrada music … Combining a vocal technique with an unusual dramatic principle, the songstress creates a song-image (pesnia-obraz)."[35] This image – and here we deviate from Bakhtin – acquires a universal, shared, and objectively recognized significance, one that allows for the image to have a commonly agreed-upon meaning and be pronounced either "good" or "bad." The private song creates (at times awkwardly) a public symbol. A "genuine estrada singer must always be himself, support his image, palette of colours and feelings. He must be an artist of his style, his theme … Today the art of the song is one of the most popular and this gives it a special responsibility. To assign it the role of a light, entertaining genre would be to lessen its true significance, to reject it as a most important and effective means of educating an individual. In such conditions the role of the artist on stage grows as a lichnost', as a person bringing to the masses the ideals of freedom, goodness, and love!"

The songs of Èdita P'ekha sit delicately in the dialogue between stage and audience, personal and public, real and ideal in their creation of obrazy: "A delicate musical sense, combined with a bright individuality and artistry, allows the songstress to create convincing artistic images (*obrazy*) in each song of her extensive repertoire; the leading place in that repertoire is occupied by Soviet composers."[36] The very name of P'ekha's bright ensemble, Druzhba (Friendship), is an extension of lyrical thematics to the level of implied international detente, of Soviet foreign policy.

Boris Groys in his essay on Stalinist aesthetics remarks that Soviet classicism "wanted to take all reality inside itself, change it all, and bless it with Socialist ideals." If all reality is claimed by the state, then perhaps no room is left for *druzhba*, for private definitions or a private ideal. Il'enkov's ideas begin to express that worry, if only by lamenting in metaphysical terms what might happen if matter is both legion and claimed by the state alone. Of the ideal as a symbol he writes:

The functional existence of a symbol consists precisely in its not representing *itself* but *another*, and in being a means, an instrument expressing the *essence of other sensuously perceived things*, i.e., their universal, socially human significance, their role and function within the social organism. In other words, the function of a symbol consists in its being just the body of the ideal image of the external thing, or rather the law of its existence, the law of the universal. A symbol removed from the real process of exchange of matter between social man and nature also ceases in general to be a symbol, the corporeal envelope of the ideal image. Its "soul" vanishes from its body because its "soul" is in fact the objective activity of social man effecting an exchange of matter between humanized and virgin nature.[37]

Popular songs in Russia after the death of Stalin make quiet claim to the material world, to a subjective interpretation of it. Here resides the ethically informed "soul" of which P'ekha speaks, the private symbol born of private interpretation of the world. What the Soviet Union, one-sixth of that global material mass, meant after the all-encompassing and semantically greedy culture of Stalinism vanished is both reflected and created by the songs which Soviet citizens waited to hear on their radios or watch performed on their television sets. The first of these stories, however, begins far from Russia, in a small mining village a few hours' drive from Paris, where Èdita P'ekha was born in 1937 – one of the saddest years in the history of Stalin's defilement of the material world. At this time the complicated and violent nature of European politics intensified as the Second World War drew nearer. But once that war ended, so the story goes, when the suffering soldiers who gave the lie to Stalin's materialist heroics began to head home, seven-year-old Èdita went out onto the streets of a French village to give her first public performance. To celebrate the cessation of hostilities, she broke into the *Marseillaise*.

4
ÈDITA P'EKHA:
GENTLE VOICE OF THE THAW

In the [1960s,] the decade of westernizing,
a non-Russian emphasis stretched across the
whole country; here's where Èdita P'ekha
played a special role. A Polish Jewess born in
France, she became leader of the Leningrad
ensemble Friendship (Druzhba) where she sang
[in Russian] with a [Polish] accent ... Charmed
by P'ekha's European gloss – and even more so
by her success across the U.S.S.R. – other Soviet
singers also began to sing with an accent,
hinting at their western standards.[1]

The quote above prompted this study. While working on the early
poetry of Joseph Brodsky, I came across this reference in a survey by
Petr Vail' and Aleksandr Genis of Soviet culture under Khrushchev. I
found it hard to imagine not only what P'ekha might sound like but
also that the result would become modish. (Several Russian journalists
have made attempts to transcribe her pronunciation.[2]) Subsequently,
gathering songs, articles, reviews, and books on Soviet estrada, I came
across an even clearer account of the extent to which her style caught
on, in a lengthy anecdote from the late 1960s. It takes place in a
chemical factory's amateur arts society: "A dress rehearsal for a concert is going on. People are singing and dancing – and out onto the
stage comes a very young woman from the packing department. She
breaks into a deepish voice and starts singing [the Rozhdestvenskii
song] 'Become the Man I Want' (*Stan' takim, kak ia khochu*). It's
pitifully out of tune and all with some kind of strange accent. 'What
on earth,' I ask her, 'are you doing to the words?' Absolutely everyone
around me is surprised and says: 'Don't you get it? She's singing like
P'ekha.' The young woman gets embarrassed, nods in agreement
[with her colleagues] and then announces in a surprisingly high
voice: 'I *really* like P'ekha!'"[3]

As the factory workers' surprise shows, to ask such questions in the
Soviet Union of 1969 indeed suggests a state of advanced unawareness.
Èdita P'ekha's popularity was great, working both as a reflection and

EDITA P'EKHA

An interesting image of P'ekha from 1981, since it demonstrates
the traditional significance of long, flowing gowns to which Pugacheva
gave such a radical reinterpretation

instigator of much that the Thaw represented: a post-Stalinist, "jolly
and internationalist spirit," one informed by "ease, liveliness, and
[personal] revelation."[4] That new spirit was worked out in the areas
highlighted in this book thus far, the competition between civic and
lyric songs, bridged with theatricality and/or an ideal sentimentality –
all within a healthy respect for tradition. In the work of Èdita P'ekha
and her ensemble Druzhba we find the groundwork for an entire
generation of post-Stalinist singers. Her work in the light genre has a
weighty significance.

THE COAL MINER'S DAUGHTER

> A song is the most direct path
> from one heart to another.[5]
>   Èdita P'ekha

81

Èdita was born to Polish parents in the coal-mining region of northern France, not far from Calais in Noyelles sous Lens on 31 July 1937. Poverty had forced her father to move and seek employment in France. Thus she began her life "in emigration," as she would later say, after her father had met, courted, and married a fellow exile. The young couple worked in the mines, he below ground, she above, sorting coal. That period of emigration would soon include World War II, which only Èdita and her mother would survive. Two family members died before the cessation of hostilities in 1945, her father at thirty-six from silicosis, her brother at seventeen from tuberculosis, brought on by a workload that forced him back to the mines the day after his father's burial.[6] Even when fatally ill, P'ekha's father had tried to keep himself busy and useful with days of tender care lavished upon his roses.[7] In such hard times, Èdita "kept on singing. Just to myself."[8]

Those difficult years of war she remembers clearly: "Evacuation, occupation, bombings, having to dig neighbours out from the ruins of their house ... Poverty, the shooting [by Germans] of miners who worked for the Resistance."[9] Elsewhere we read of the miseries of life in a mining town: "Èdita will not forget those sleepless nights and grey dawns when she and her mother stood with the wives and daughters of other miners. She always waited with a tremor in her heart to see whether her father would return today from the coal-face. The fat guards laughed from their greatcoats in the women's faces and found it amusing to scare them with machine guns."[10] If no member of a family was working in the shafts, housing had to be evacuated; thus Èdita's mother was forced by her husband's death into a loveless marriage to another miner, because looking for work in occupied France would have been an impossibility.

After the signing of the armistice, Èdita's stepfather was able at last to take everybody back to Poland.[11] The young P'ekha's love for music continued – she performed in a school choir – and earned her a nickname from her teacher and classmates: the "Singing Girl." Despite her popularity, Polish was not a language that she knew well and considerable effort was required to reach the magical desk at the front of her class. She dreamed of becoming a teacher and thanks to her diligence was indeed able in subsequent years to enter a pedagogical institute. When she graduated four years later, she did so with the highest honour, a gold medal.

Having completed an emergency class or two in Russian, she was awarded a place on a Communist Youth League study trip to Leningrad in 1955, the year the Warsaw Pact was formed. Her knowledge of Russian had been improved while still in Poland after a native speaker heard her sing and offered to help for a couple of hours each day.[12]

When exams were held to judge the cultural applicability of those wishing to go on the trip, P'ekha scored "a zero," she says, but was saved by her singing which allowed her dubious knowledge of Russian and history to be overlooked. She left with a generous passing grade.

In 1955 she entered the psychology faculty of Leningrad State University and soon after joined a choir made up of fellow Poles. It was directed by a student from the Leningrad Conservatory, Aleksandr Bronevitskii. From time to time some students from that conservatory would meet – as friends – and sing their favourite songs. They decided to prepare several numbers for a university ball, and although that evening was cancelled, the singers continued to practise together. It was Bronevitskii who invited P'ekha to join them, along with two new members, both German students. "Each member brought his own songs: Polish, French, Latvian, Estonian, German, Russian."[13] This multicultural atmosphere would always be part of Druzhba; by 1965, for example, it had members from Latvia, Armenia, Russia, Estonia, and Ukraine.[14]

The big breakthrough came in 1957 when Druzhba (as yet unsure of whether to keep its name) won first prize at the sixth World Festival of Youth and Students, held on this occasion in Moscow.[15] Such official acclaim negated the danger of the ensemble's international flavour being seen as "false exoticism [or] syncopated estrada stylization."[16] Many nationalities were represented linguistically in its repertoire, including Spanish and German, sometimes even splitting a song between two languages ("Dozhdik").

The fundamental novelty of the ensemble lay in its variation upon the typical and larger choral groups. As P'ekha subsequently put it – with some equivocation – "we were something between a choir and an ensemble, but closer to an ensemble." She felt that not only did the stage-shy youth of the day find it easier to express their new freedom in a group than alone but also that the same group could express a new "movement" in young Russia – in the cosmos (Iurii Gagarin had gone up in 1961), along the romantic Baikal-Amur Railway, BAM, or in agriculture and industry.[17] The influence of jazz is perceptible in Druzhba's expression of movement; here was an all-male group whose female singer first emerged to the accompaniment of a guitar, piano, and double bass[18] while managing, in the words of a Soviet writer, to exhibit "polyphony and naturally combined rhythmic, melodic, and harmonic phrasing."[19]

The members of Druzhba – the name suggests the bickering jazz ensemble in Utesov's comic musical *The Happy Guys* – share the microphone, especially in early recordings. When P'ekha is the vocalist, the male voices harmonize in a manner that may remind some western listeners of, say, the Inkspots aiding Doris Day. The elegant combination of organ or piano and double bass suggest what we might now term the backdrop for a "lounge" atmosphere, with the unintrusive use of brushes rather than drumsticks. More enthusiastic percussion is used at times, enough even to indicate the influence of skiffle. In time the modest yet predominant vocal harmonies of the early recordings are filled out by lush string accompaniments.

The group's first appearance was at a New Year's Eve party held in the conservatory's concert hall and ended with a quadruple encore by P'ekha singing a Polish folk song. Success led to closer relations between her and Bronevitskii; they married in 1958 and moved into a communal apartment. As P'ekha has said, "It was of course very flattering for a provincial girl to have the attention and respect of a man six years her senior with two conservatory qualifications. If he hadn't asked me to marry him we would still have been friends for many, many years."[20] This marital and professional partnership was to produce the Soviet Union's most famous ensemble of the early 1960s, thanks to qualities noted in perhaps their first national article, published in 1958. Their success "came first of all from a high quality of performance. When you listen to Druzhba, you clearly feel that the group's members came to the light genre only once they had mastered a wealth of serious music. Their harmonic and polyphonic ear is very keen; their voices sound extremely even and well integrated [P'ekha's own voice is a low mezzo-soprano]. The songs of many peoples, performed by the ensemble, express the fine, bright emotions of simple folk across the world. These songs are both close and clear to the listeners – and get a lively response."[21] The emphasis on emotion above all found strong yet simple expression in songs such as "It's Great!" (*Zdorovo!*) and "Good!" (*Khorosho!*) – "A man walks along and smiles, / Which means that man feels fine."

That reaction reached an ever-widening audience in the late 1950s and early '60s. Soviet variety and news broadcasts had for years been carried down telephone lines to domestic amplifiers, but in the 1950s production of fully fledged radio sets increased rapidly. Television was not far behind, and by the mid-1960s, Moscow programs were enjoyed all the way to the Urals. For radio the significance of music was great: in the early 1960s, 55 per cent of air time was given over to both estrada and classical works. On television in the same period 18 per cent was allocated to music, a high figure by contemporary western standards.[22] Druzhba's success on radio led to union-wide tours and performances abroad; by 1990 P'ekha would perform in nineteen countries.[23]

Fame, however, leads to envy, which can lead to robberies. The bad luck P'ekha has had with break-ins is a prime indicator of social conflict between Soviet personality and less personable have-nots. After Bronevitskii moved out of their communal apartment into a separate one in the late 1960s, burglars took equipment and personal belongings: "They cleaned us out of 5,000 rubles – which was a huge sum at that time – and left only the furniture. A pair of Japanese tape recorders (I was working on some songs) and fur coats disappeared." On tour in Hungary she was robbed of a stage dress, in Costa Rica a gold watch and bracelet, in Peru $100, in Leningrad her purse, in Cuba another stage dress, in Kamchatka more than 3,000 rubles from her dressing room – the deposit on a diamond ring. Another odd aspect to P'ekha's renown that spoke of official disapproval of her prominent personality was that in 1967 when she applied for Soviet citizenship she was turned down twice.[24]

This fame, inconvenient though it appeared at times to be, was extended by several experimental forays into the world of cinema. In the 1969 spy thriller *The Resident's Fate* (*Sud'ba rezidenta*) she played a small role in which her accent is explained away as Belgian. One of the scenes – all in French – involved an intimate if not erotic encounter as she seduces a young Soviet scientist. For P'ekha this was impossible to enact: "How can I get into bed with a person I don't even know? The scene seemed completely unworkable to me! Eventually I convinced the director."[25] The scene that appears in the film is nothing more than a kiss and embrace, but it is nonetheless used as compromising material to blackmail the scientist.

The tall, willowy singer would star in two further films: *The Incorrigible Liar* (*Neispravimyi lgun*) in 1972 and *Diamonds for the Dictatorship of the Proletariat* (*Brillianty dlia diktatury proletariata*), in 1974. In the latter film, her accent this time said to be Estonian, she plays a nightclub singer, deep in a Byzantine tale of illegal antique-smuggling four years after the Revolution. Her role includes a simple example of a staged song, performed with a single candle around the tables of the club.

In *The Incorrigible Liar* she plays herself, wearing a disconcertingly lurid dress (in sharp contrast to her usual fashion-conscious elegance). By accident she runs over an eternally tardy, forgetful barber who is crossing the road. She faints in horror and is taken back to his apartment, thus raising doubts about his fidelity to his wife, especially when the singer takes a shower after her ordeal. Sympathetic to the young man in his struggles against an employer who disbelieves the daily excuses for lateness, P'ekha smooths everything over with the wife and goes to the barbershop, championing the man's assertion that despite his amazing (yet entirely honest) excuses every morning, his stories are truer than the truth. She defends the individual against the crowd, the private verity against the less interesting, public version.

The films did much to bolster P'ekha's fame in the 1970s; the first two of this trio attracted 56.5 million viewers. Nevertheless, as Russian and Soviet spacecraft joined in the Soiuz-Apollo program in 1975, P'ekha made an opposite movement, since that year saw the end of her marriage to Bronevitskii. She had grown tired of his constant criticism, which was undermining her confidence: "People who knew Bronevitskii in passing considered him a scoundrel. Sure, he had a rather bitchy, despotic character; he'd stoop to anything for the sake of applause. All the same, he wasn't a scoundrel. By nature he was defenseless, but adopted the image of a despot long before our marriage … He would give both me and Druzhba a dressing-down. Knowing how it would infuriate me, he'd say: 'You're *so* unattractive!' I looked in magazines for photos of movie stars, compared myself, and thought: perhaps I should touch up my eyes like Sophia Loren? … Bronevitskii would say: 'You slouch. How can you walk around stage like that?' And I'd look to see how ballerinas 'float' … That's how Bronevitskii 'made' me … [But] I got tired of his endless 'must, must, must' and left him."[26]

Looking back from the early 1990s on the creative partnership between them, P'ekha drew a parallel with a more famous married couple: "I was like Krupskaia in Lenin's presence. The difference was that I was fighting not for leadership of the Soviets but for my own independence, my individuality. I didn't know a normal woman's happiness with him."[27] Bronevitskii's demanding standards for a stage performance are glimpsed at times in interviews, where he talks of both the technical and human elements to be attended to: acoustics, light, ventilation, mood. In the same conversation P'ekha says a performer needs above all a heart and [reasonable] head; Bronevitskii counters that with the need for talent, erudition, plus a good director to "observe and direct" the singer.[28]

Druzhba lasted only two years after P'ekha's departure as she set off on a solo career, beginning with victory at the 1976 All-Union Soviet Song Festival, held in the palm-lined southern resort of Sochi.[29] In the same year she was also awarded the title People's Artist of the Russian Federation, at which time her talents were officially summarized as "a delicate musicality combined with a bright individuality and artistry."[30]

P'ekha soon married again, this time to a KGB colonel seven years her junior. The arrangement lasted seven years until 1982. She herself has repeated for the press her second husband's complaints, "I'm tired of being Èdita P'ekha's husband, a wageless appendage to a famous artist. I want you to be my wife because it's not normal when the husband isn't the head of the family."[31] P'ekha had become in 1978 one of the first Soviet singers to appear in Afghanistan after the "April

Revolution"; once her second marriage was behind her, the rest of 1980s turned out to be equally adventurous. She embarked on long touring schedules and garnered a long list of official recognitions: the Order of the Red Banner of Labour, the Order of Peoples' Friendship, an award for "Strengthening the Art of Friendship" (France). She was also named "Dame of Song" in Cuba.

In 1988 she was made a People's Artist of the U.S.S.R. and organized an evening in honour of Bronevitskii, who had passed away in the same year. She used the occasion to lament in the Soviet press the sad discrepancy between her former husband's gift to estrada and his lack of official recognition.[32] P'ekha herself believed that she also waited an unduly long time for national honour.[33] Her complaint seems justified when we consider that by the start of the 1990s she had compiled a repertoire of more than four hundred famous songs.[34]

A three-year relationship with a man twenty years younger ended; it was not until 1993 – known by now as both the "Queen of Petersburg" and the "Grand Dame of Communist Leningrad"[35] – that she would marry again, this time to the man who is her current husband, Vladimir Poliakov. Poliakov had been a fan for a long time; he had kept a signed photo of her since 1963. When they were introduced in Moscow's Rossiia concert hall, the one-time journalist was working as assistant to the head of the Presidential Administration. Two years later the couple married.

In 1995 the St Petersburg firm Northern Lights (*Severnoe siianie*) created a perfume in P'ekha's honour (it would have been called "Anna Akhmatova," but the company failed to get the packaging ready for the poet's anniversary).[36] P'ekha had prepared for an anniversary of her own the next year: sixty years old and forty years on the stage. In an admirable moment of self-deprecating humour, she said the event would therefore mark her one hundredth birthday.[37] It was commemorated with a concert in St Petersburg's Palace Square, graced by the governor yet almost spoiled by a failed attempt to send her carriage, drawn by unruly horses, down the city's main thoroughfare.[38]

A 1996 story in the newspaper *Sobesednik* highlighted both the singer's fame and the ongoing price to be paid for it in a poor country. P'ekha has continued to be hounded by robberies: close to U.S.$25,000 was taken from her apartment, a huge sum for almost any Russian citizen. A locksmith entered her home while she was away on tour and took whatever he could carry, including many stage dresses. Realizing that these were of little use, he promptly dumped them in the Moika Canal.[39] Despite these unpleasant consequences of her fame, P'ekha still performs to great acclaim, still beautiful, accompanying the youngest and most popular of performers on nationally televised variety broadcasts. Birthdays and the New Year are marked in St Petersburg by her now-institutionalized concerts. The recent success of retro radio stations in Russia, "where one can hear not only Utesov but Shul'zhenko and P'ekha," guarantees her airtime and perhaps even a newer, younger audience.[40] Judging by an epigram in the magazine *Soviet Éstrada and Circus,* she is well suited to meet this audience: "Wrinkles born of woe and joy / We age through years and deeds ... / And only P'ekha will remain / Much younger now than once she was."[41] The essence of her lasting fame lies in her personality, in both senses of the word.

LICHNOST' AS DIALOGUE
BETWEEN STAGE AND HALL

Édita is the "Miss Elegance" of our estrada ...
She loves her viewers deeply and sincerely;
she literally overflows with love for the stage.
It's these sincere feelings and warmth
that have won her huge, undying
popularity with the public.[42]

Lev Leshchenko

In 1972 P'ekha talks of a "small emotional bridge" that forms between herself and the audience.[43] This dialogue is only part of a related yet more complicated interaction between herself and the heroine of a staged song.[44] The Soviet press had initially been reluctant to recognize the "staged" connection and was willing only to stress "self" as constructed *from* the stage rather than on it. Early descriptions of P'ekha promote this more evidently social singer/crowd relationship with the world rather than the introversion of performer/persona. She is discussed as a typical, social woman rather than someone privy to the emotions of a song's heroine: "P'ekha is a lyric singer. The individuality of how she performs does not arise from her access to another person's intimate or deeply personal experiences. It comes less from her singing as a dramatic personage than it does from her as a singer and woman." [45]

In 1983 she developed the same notion and wrote that concerts as a whole are an intimate, dialogic affair conducted *across* the footlights, not on one side of them. "I go out [on stage] to people in order to speak a little with them about life, love, and whatever bothers them ... The concert turns into a distinctive dialogue with a viewer."[46] The subsequent discovery of subjectivity on stage following that interaction is touched upon rarely by newspapers, as in an article of 1984: "With her soft manner of performing, P'ekha does not assert her 'I,' but seems instead to ponder about herself, dream and ask questions."[47]

More representative of the Soviet media response, prior to such pondering, is a 1981 article which retrospectively assesses P'ekha's personality as the result of two forms of "seeking": the search for a more Russian accent(!) and the desire to sing civic songs – to enter into the fold, as it were, to realize herself through membership in a selfless collective entity.[48] "There was a time when singing like P'ekha was a real craze amongst our amateur singers. Èdita, however, having chosen the path of a professional singer, spent many years in the language laboratory getting rid of that accent, which was so easy and tempting to imitate. She studied singing seriously and sought her repertoire, all the while defining with greater precision the civic stance in her work. Thus she avoided any simple, exotic tendencies in her generic range and became a *lichnost'*, the true phenomenon of Soviet estrada whose name is Èdita P'ekha."[49]

It goes without saying that the phenomenon of perceived "personality" in any singer – one watched by an audience – is due in part to how he or she looks. What P'ekha says in this early "social" stage of estrada's development of *lichnost'* hints at the "theatrical" tendencies that later charmed younger performers. The *Evening Leningrad* ran over several days a series of advice columns written by P'ekha and directed towards the women of her adopted city (and the children, too, since a Leningrad orphanage got her honorarium for the articles). What she says about beauty and how to cultivate it are entirely applicable to the theme of self. Talking of make-up, she says "the main thing is work out your own style and follow it through to the end."[50] The bodies physical and politic require similar attention.

The notion of "work" here can also do double duty, since the scarcity of consumer goods in Soviet daily life, the inability to simply buy what one needed, necessitated the processes of "making do." One transformed the most mundane of ingredients or actions into the guarantors of something hopefully beautiful and (to stretch a point) ideal. Thus P'ekha stresses the effort required for a woman in Soviet society to make herself attractive: "Beauty takes effort (*trud*), and serious effort at that. Truth is, ladies, we often forget about beauty! Afternoon – work; evening – more work, this time at home. So sometimes you get tired ... All the same I'm sure you can find twenty minutes for yourself. All you need is to really want to find that time."

At the mirror, when the "dialogue" of an incipient *lichnost'* is stripped of all outside intrusion, of social evaluation, one's personality is (blissfully) complete. The following lines must have sounded wonderful to Soviet women battling through the material world: "No matter what you feel like, no matter what mood you're in, sit down at the mirror as soon as a free minute presents itself: 'You're beautiful, beautiful, beautiful,' I tell myself – though the mirror tries to convince me otherwise. 'You are perfection itself,' I stubbornly assert and pick up my cream ..."

Here the discourse between singer and sung persona takes on its earliest, most domestic form; it is the interaction of who a singer is and who she would *like* to be. The fact that Soviet songs had virtually no negative heroes allowed for the transition of P'ekha's singer/mirror (at home) to the discourse of singer/heroine on stage. The private dialogue can create the better public person, just as the lyric song creates better civic relationships. Sweeping though that sounds, another article in the series makes exactly such an equation. A reader writes that she is extremely shy and feels that on crowded public transport she is the object of others' jokes. She asks how she can make herself "feel like a woman."[51] P'ekha suggests a version of her mirror therapy, plus the line "I'm better than the others," warning her fan that excessive shyness can result in a loss of both faith and interest in oneself. It is love that gives social "strength," love not only for oneself but of "profession, home and life." In an aside P'ekha notes that the modern woman, especially given the dearth of products in Soviet shops, should rely on the expertise accrued and tested by generations of grandmothers, who concocted wonderful creams from berries, sour cream, honey, and yoghurt.[52]

All of this effort to bolster one's self-esteem or to stand out finds strong expression in a song by Il'ia Reznik that P'ekha recorded fairly early: "I Won't Come Back to You" (*Ia k tebe ne vernus'*). In it we hear a little of the personality or the personal dialogue that would be a huge part of Alla Pugacheva's bolder individuality in the 1970s. P'ekha steps almost outside her gentle persona to hint at role-playing and give an idea of how her *lichnost'* might evolve in the work of subsequent singers. She begins by saying "my house is empty without you," but even an admission of guilt by her beloved will not let her go back to him: "I won't come back to you, / I'll laugh at you and myself." This bold, romantically ironic awareness of her chimerical desire is not really part of P'ekha's persona. As if to temper an awkwardly self-assured note, she then adds: "Oh, if only you knew how hard it is for me on my own!" This struggle with a latent, bolder personality is gaily orchestrated with a horn section worthy of Burt Bacharach and the type of jolly "Cuban" percussion that became modish amidst the romance of that tropical uprising.[53]

What P'ekha had to say about another uprising, closer to home and a lot less jolly, is most instructive about her worldview and the way in which her struggling, "private" philosophies dealt with the maximally public horrors of war.

AFGHANISTAN AND PUBLIC EXCESS

> I don't like the word "star."
> I much prefer "the public's sweetheart."[54]
>   Èdita P'ekha

The various attitudes of estrada to the Soviet experience of Afghanistan are telling. Èdita P'ekha and Iosif Kobzon are the two performers who make reference most often to the situation, the political background of which is as follows. In April 1978 an ugly uprising took place in that country and left a Marxist group in power (the People's Democratic Party), headed by Noor Mohammed Taraki. Internal strife, however, continued to the point where dozens of Soviets working in the country died during conflicts over the following year. A resulting shift in September 1979 to a more radical and now anti-Soviet Afghan leader, Haffizulah Amin, together with the murder of Taraki, led to an extreme decision by the Kremlin in December of the same year: remove Amin, install a sympathetic power structure (the pro-Moscow Babrak Karmal), and leave a major military Soviet presence in Afghanistan to guarantee calm. At the peak of Soviet involvement, over 100,000 soldiers were operating in the region, but never with long-term success against a smaller number of extremely able Afghan guerrillas. The Soviets had moved into a non-bloc nation and were paying a high price. The situation, inviting parallels with Vietnam, dragged on until Gorbachev began a withdrawal of troops that finally ended early in 1989, a year that only saw increased uprisings elsewhere, in Georgia and Uzbekistan.

In 1979, a few months prior to the overthrow of Taraki and the start of the Soviet headache, P'ekha was on tour in Kabul with what the newspaper *Leningradskaia pravda* called "a genuine display of friendship between peoples." During her work there she had kind words for the interest, refinement, and "cordiality, hospitality, and respect" showed by the locals towards their Soviet guests. She went on to express the conviction that "my tour will be one more step towards building and strengthening neighbourly relations between our countries, a guarantee of strong, brotherly love."[55] This was a Soviet artist turning the stage/hall dialogue into international detente.

Nine years later, the end of another tour was reported in *Sovetskaia Rossiia*.[56] P'ekha had been particularly touched by the opening of a new children's home and by government plans to reward parents financially for their children's good attendance at school. Russian language was at this time offered by the local education system, and the singer was made aware of a warmth and friendliness towards herself and all other Russian guests – although people were apparently somewhat bewildered that Soviet troops were being withdrawn. P'ekha performed in the hospitals for those Soviet soldiers, where she signed many autographs and made the promise to honour each autograph with a free ticket to any of her concerts in Russia: "I'd be more than happy to get together with these courageous people when they're back home." Singing for the troops – together with an Afghan audience – had been "a serious experience" for P'ekha; she hoped that "love" for her songs would overcome the complexities of the political situation.[57]

P'ekha's other visits to Afghanistan were made not in an atmosphere of overt politics but in the hope of a sentimental, virtuous stage/hall dialogue cultivating "Soviet-Afghan friendship."[58] In 1983, for example, she had spoken of her work in Kabul with the Union of Afghan Cultural Workers as "the nurturing of a new person," an ethical goal which "our concerts [here] have facilitated."[59] Her unending emphasis upon goodness over politics contributed to her receiving the Order of Peoples' Friendship from the president of Afghanistan. (In the same ceremony Kobzon was awarded the Order of the Red Banner.) The official proclamation lauded P'ekha's "strengthening of cultural links and Soviet-Afghan friendship."[60] It is indeed striking how the singer on the occasion stressed the suffering of mothers and sons, Russian or Afghan, over the vagaries of political detente.

The award came during the removal of Soviet troops, which P'ekha called "a complicated period, one of great responsibility." Her concerts at this time employed art's ability to "unify people, to bring them closer than anything else can." This utterly sincere sentiment is not so much contrary to the Soviet notion of space as alien to it. What matters to her is people more than place. P'ekha lacks the full-blown romantic stress on local colour, the nationalist leanings that a romantic writer might champion after the sentimentalist's enlightened insistence upon a person's inherent goodness, irrespective of ethnicity. P'ekha is at this point using the ideal connection engendered by the arduous stage/hall discourse not to bolster or complement Soviet detente but, in a strange way, to replace it. Yet not a word is said to turn such sentiment into political defiance. P'ekha is working consciously for, not against the status quo.

In one of her Rozhdestvenskii songs, "Clouds" (*Oblaka*), she sings: "I've fallen in love with the sun of these days and I've found happiness on my earth." The private spatio-temporal dimensions of where "you" and "I" happen to be today are the parameters within which happiness is conjured; anything bigger is simply inhuman. So what consequences does all this have for her choice of civic or lyric songs, especially given that she is a Soviet star?

THE PROBLEMS OF BUILDING A REPERTOIRE

> In my youth I adored Èdita for her "inner
> temperament." In years gone by one had
> to look very modest on stage, so I felt
> that there was something extraordinary
> in this stately, beautiful woman.[61]

An early article of 1960 praises P'ekha and Druzhba for their soft, lyrical air,[62] but even this apparent diffidence did not mean the abandonment of a public spirit. A 1965 column, for example, contains a quote by Bronevitskii that tersely defines the early aesthetic intent of the ensemble. Each song, he maintains, needs a recognizable context – or backdrop, to use his term – "of substantial heroic pathos, of substantial musings on life. That's the entire essence of the ensemble."[63] He voices a similar thought even eight years later, when he underlines a constant theme of Druzhba's work as "thinking about heroes."[64] The serious intent of the group is seconded by P'ekha: "I'm convinced that no modern rhythms or vocal expertise will save an artist if he has nothing to say to his listeners. Estrada long ago stopped being mere amusement. People come to our concerts to think together with us about something important, to dream a little, to smile, and perhaps to be even a little sad." Indeed the interviewer comments that Druzhba's songs cannot be light or frivolous if they are sung by millions of people – the same argument used by Reznik in later years to prove the civil consequence of a seemingly lyric song. Yet how can we tally all this with P'ekha's assertion in 1972 that "the main thing in a song is the expression of emotion: right from the heart, since that's the only place songs come from"?[65]

The combination of difference and duty appears in an old P'ekha and Reznik song which the lyricist was proud enough of even in 1997 to include on an album of his fourteen best works. "Land of Birches" (*Berezovyi krai*) is an emotional evocation of Russia, using that country's ancient name, Rus'. The song, though patriotic, has no concrete reference to the geography of the place. It defines Rus' in terms of the emotions it evokes in *me*: it recalls a tender, proud, or radiant song, a "handsome realm ... sincere and untrammelled." The lands of Rus' are in fact so abstracted that they lose all relevance to bounded space: "Land of Birches, land of Esenin ... limitless land." The reference here to Esenin opts into a major aspect of the poet's Soviet mythology, that of the wistful, blond country boy, and ignores, as ever, other aspects like his drunken, anti-Semitic tirades, homosexual leanings, or moments of suicidal depression.

Indeed, in the 1960s, when choosing a song to perform, even if its theme is a recognizably public one, emotion and private experience are of primary importance for P'ekha: "When I get to know a new song, the first thing I do is look into the text: what is it about, does its theme affect me, have I experienced something similar?"[66] A joint interview given by Bronevitskii and P'ekha in 1969 also stresses sympathy as a key to which songs are performed, creating a tight circle of mutual influence: "To some degree our songs answer questions that arise in the hearts and minds of those who love estrada ... [I look to see if] there is even a little bit of what my contemporary experiences."[67] A small article of 1965 in the newspaper *This Week* (*Nedelia*) seemingly contradicts Bronevitskii's "heroic" designs of the same year by praising P'ekha's intimate but never vulgar "salon refinement" that stops primitivism from swamping estrada. The writer even praises Bronevitskii for developing such intimacy in P'ekha's manner.[68]

The constant significance of intimacy and emotion in P'ekha's songs – civic or not – is something she admits in a 1993 interview. She believes herself to be out of step with today's estrada because of her fully fledged reliance upon "emotion and sentiment,"[69] and her conviction since the mid-1980s that the grand "Pugachevian" scale of entertainment is a little too much for her.[70] When she appears today on competition juries, she is sometimes upset by the lack of sentiment and a concomitant "lack of bright individualities" on stage.[71] "These people deceive not only the public but themselves too." Even back in 1979 she was complaining about the long, long wait required for a true *lichnost'* to appear on stage.[72] She is aware of personality as cultivated emotionally between two people, between stage and viewer, and even in a dialogue between generations of performers, yet she rejects the bolder steps of Pugacheva's individuality.

P'ekha cultivates the lyric song, but she uses "civic" notions to reign it in; hence her unflagging attention to public spirit. Ever the advocate of tasteful limits and a *reasonably* social *lichnost'*, she maintained in 1971 that "public spirit is the basic foundation of all the best folk and estrada songs. But you can't put an equal sign between them. Whether or not this sounds unlikely, an estrada song can touch – and even solve – universal human problems. Songs of a civic nature, for example, are especially close to me."[73] The 1970s see a continuation of songs about war, which journalists associate with her own wartime experiences and visits to the mass cemeteries of post-blockade Leningrad. This tendency was expressed in a 1972 interview: "The kind of songs that are attracting my attention more and more shouldn't be confused with any others. In absolute contradiction of estrada's 'levity,' these songs aim to talk about serious matters, about what's most important: loyalty to one's country, life and death, love and war, fidelity to one's human duty."[74] Can we perhaps find a term to designate this confusion of social and sentimental emphases?

At the end of the 1970s she suggests such a term while explaining that she works in many genres: patriotic, lyric, sometimes comic songs. "They seem very varied, but each and every one of them is a song of experience or feeling" (*pesnia-perezhivanie*).[75] Once again, P'ekha is the champion of lyric tendencies but refuses to see or discuss them in isolation from things civic. In a similar vein she talks of her role in singing for the Moscow Olympics; although public songs are closest to her, they should be tales of individuals – not crowds, battalions, or other forms of massed presence.[76] Those feelings she elsewhere describes as the property of "the hero of my songs who is subtly aware of the complexity of human relations and has an acute reaction to them. He is a person with his passions and weaknesses, he feels both happiness and suffering, knows how to be surprised by beauty and life's multifariousness; he sympathizes with any pain as if it were his own."[77] She thinks that, given such psychological complexity (and the generic complexity needed to depict it), not even twenty songs could do justice to that person's "spiritual world." In two interviews of 1978 the social potential of her songs is more clearly than ever filtered through lyricism: "Self-expression is inherent in people" and "a concert must enrich [its audience] emotionally." Nevertheless that emotion "develops the civic thematic ... and acts as the pivot of the artist's *lichnost'*."[78]

SONGS OF NOBLE SENTIMENT

> Есть любимая работа.
> Что же нужно нам еще?
> Но живешь и ждешь чего-то.
> Только не поймешь чего.
>
> [We have our beloved work.
> What else do we need?
> You live and wait for something,
> but you'll never know what.][79]

At the outset of the 1980s P'ekha's songs still refuse to be wholly private *or* public. The notion of being civically spirited has more of an ethical than a political hue: "I always think about the fact that a song inspires goodness, sincerity, and mutual understanding." In 1986, as Gorbachev and Reagan hold talks in Iceland to end the arms race, she calls "love the main theme of my work ... for love is so multifaceted. It can mean love for one's mother, one's children, one's country, or the beautiful town in which we live."[80] This expression of affection is one of the major ways in which P'ekha bridges the public and private, for example, singing for the mothers of war casualties on Victory Day[81] or drawing concrete parallels between the need for taste in songs and the effect they have on a child's upbringing.[82]

Perhaps the clearest expression of her maternal concerns is the song "Mother" (*Mama*). Here the general significance of everybody's mother is rejected in favour of what is private: *my* mother. A quietly spoken, if not whispered, introduction begins: "Today I got a letter, it was very short. 'How are you, daughter? Why don't you write? I can't wait to see you.' It was signed: 'Mama'" As the song begins, its privacy is made immediately clear, at the expense of the broad-shouldered, symbolic mothers of Soviet oration: "There are many songs about wonderful mothers, but I've composed my own. 'Mama' sounds like a poem, like a lyric; now I'll sing of my mother. Mother of mine, I know, I know, that you're far away and are waiting. If at times I forget to write, [I know] you'll forgive me, you'll understand." [83]

P'ekha has done much for Russian children's homes, prompted by the sympathy of a mother for those with impoverished childhoods similar to her own, when she was fatherless in France and Poland. She has special connections to what used to be Leningrad Children's Home (Detdom) No. 53, the number of her tiny house in Poland on a certain Stalin Street.[84] The power of parental sentiment is strong here:

I often think how hard it is to raise a person, to place within them a grain of goodness at the outset of youth, a sense of sympathy for a stranger. How hard that is when the first thing that a child senses is that he or she is not wanted by parents or their closest relatives. What kind of words can explain or justify that ...? What is happening to society when there are [in Russia] more than half a million "orphans" whose parents are still alive? Our moral foundations are wavering ... When I sing from the stage and look out into a huge hall, I want to talk to people about this, to get through to the heart of each person.[85]

Another source of P'ekha's emphasis upon the moral qualities of sentiment, she maintains, is gender. "I feel sorry for our women. There's an unhappiness in the family and disorder in society since women can quite literally tear themselves apart between work and home, dragging heavy bags around, standing in endless queues, and worrying constantly about where to get things and how to feed a family." In the 1970s, about two-thirds of divorces in the Soviet Union were at the wife's request. Primary reasons, male drinking aside, were the type of pressures P'ekha refers to. The wife was often better educated than her spouse, yet earned only 70 per cent of her husband's wage for similar skills.[86] As an indication in this decade of how early such stress began in a woman's life, for the first time in the century the average age of a woman starting her first real job dropped below twenty, to nineteen and a half years.[87] "All of this has an effect upon one's morals and, of course, upon children," P'ekha has said. Her own personal and long-term commitment to one particular children's home has attempted an atmosphere of morally beneficial, maternal sentiment that can be of use to future society: "Into Children's Home No. 53 with Èdita came beauty and music, an unusual femininity and elegance which forced girls to look at themselves in the mirror sometimes, and the boys to dress a little better … This very well-known person is a genuinely close, kind consultant and a friend, ready to fly to their aid at any time, irrespective of schedules or endless tours."

One of P'ekha's strongest expressions of this maternal sentiment occurred in 1976 near the town of Gor'kii. P'ekha was visiting student construction projects and judging a radio talent contest when she realized that buried nearby was a famous victim of the Leningrad blockade, a girl by the name of Tania Savicheva. She had kept the simplest of diaries, listing her family members as one by one they died around her from starvation. P'ekha was inspired to write a song asking for forgiveness that she had come to visit Tania "without flowers, but I want to leave a song here. Where there's forest all around."[88] She gave a concert in Savicheva's honour and donated her honorarium to a children's memorial, making a promise at the grave to return.[89]

Another related and important aspect of P'ekha's civic lyricism, so to speak, is evident in her depiction of Leningrad, Tania Savicheva's blockaded city. Any civic expression concerns a social group, and the logical reason to be civically minded is because that group happens to include the speaker: Muscovites are more likely to sing songs about Moscow than Surgut. P'ekha has lived for many years in Leningrad/ Petersburg, the city that educated her and gave her both a career and husband. She now thanks the Northern Venice with anniversary concerts and serenades the place with her older songs such as "White Night" (*Belaia noch'*) or the similarly titled "White Nights" (*Belye nochi*). The particularly severe atmosphere in Leningrad during the mid to late 1960s, its overly zealous and intolerant cultural mechanisms within the party structure, are not in evidence here. The first song talks not of Leningrad in summer but *my* Leningrad; anybody else's impressions are irrelevant. The city's bridges go up at night (to let shipping through until dawn), but the singer and her beloved cannot be parted. "White Nights" also links the lack of darkness in summer to sleeplessness and the quiet trials of love, of private matters. "The night flies above the [River] Neva, but I don't feel like sleeping. Can you really fall asleep when the night is so bright? If, since your childhood days, you have lived in Leningrad, then you'll understand me, my friend." The whole country shrinks to a city, which shrinks to *my* city, known only to me and my close friends (and even then with the heart, not the head). The minimal distance between speaker and hearer guarantees the maximum meaning. Lyricism and sentiment celebrate the city, but not with standard, social spirit (*grazhdanstvennost'*).

She goes on to sing that as a light drizzle falls, "I wander through puddles without a coat or my boots." Once again, only the closest of friends can sympathize. The pre-romantic scenario of the introvert, aimless wandering – on the fringes of society – as a means of discovering personality is celebrated in other leisurely, lushly orchestrated songs such as "I Bring Happiness" (*Ia schast'e nesu*) and "Winter Ditty" (*Zimniaia pesenka*). Both depict P'ekha wandering alone, in the former song along green boulevards: "Full of happiness, I smile to the spring; the sun shines and the rain laughs and the rainbow shines – all for me." Sentiment – a sung sentiment – transforms the world, or, more importantly, *my* world. That transformation is both noble and of positive benefit to a listener. Using such metamorphoses to locate and build an emotional home or find the desired other person will take some effort, and here P'ekha plays upon a fashionable metaphor of progression.

SEEKING

This quarter of a century [1956–81] has been
one of untiring creative seeking and fidelity
for Èdita P'ekha ... to her themes, to her style
on the estrada, to the great traditions of
Soviet songs and their classic performance.[90]

An article of 1958, the year that *Doktor Zhivago* was awarded the Nobel prize, concludes hopefully that the ensemble Druzhba will attract the attention of "elder comrades, of elder composers and musicians, all of whom will help such talented youth on the path towards genuine art."[91] The newspaper *Sovetskaia kul'tura* shortly afterwards conjures an even more declamatory turn of phrase: "Youth is on its way. Young people are searching!"[92] Such metaphors of investigation are sceptical towards their subject, defining in the most nebulous terms possible a "goal," the actual nature of which may be officially defined or refined at any moment. This tone continues even years later; the "romantic" musicians supporting P'ekha are said to embody all that excites Soviet youth: "distant roads, the subjugation and acquisition of new territories."[93] In an article of 1973 we are told that Druzhba has chosen the "most difficult but most reliable road in search of their listener: the road of friendship."[94]

The theme of a chosen way is clearest in the ensemble's early song entitled "The Road" (*Doroga*). Here, though, the road is not to an objective goal, the way to the wonderful tomorrow of Soviet teleology, but the path to one's true love. It does "not let us rest in this wide world. We were strictly taught from our youngest days that the harder the road, the truer it is." One cannot say "where or in what land you'll seal your destiny with love." Another song, "So Easy" (*Tak legko*), also talks of effort as something expended on the management of a subjective, not objective goal. P'ekha sings that it is easy to breathe with her beloved or to spin in a waltz, yet it is hard to say she loves him or to watch him dance with another girl. The song ends with her lamenting the difficulties of the simplest human intercourse, that of two people (not of two million on a grand social scale): "It's hard to find a good, true friend."

P'ekha's emphasis upon the (sociably) personal could cause her problems. In 1966 she was criticized for putting on a new dress just for the curtain call at a festival of Soviet songs. Surely, wrote her critic, "that characterizes precisely the direction in which the singer is doing her 'searching.'"[95] Other nasty criticism of her "wayward" seeking stressed her apparent provincialism and excessive frankness born of an irritating Polish naïveté.[96]

In 1973 we read that she "seeks and has always sought her theme in art, her unique creative signature, her style."[97] This remark comes after a little girl called Marina wrote to her asking how to become a "second P'ekha." The singer's advice was "don't be a second P'ekha, but the one and only Marina!" Here is the essential difference between the "seeking" lauded in writing about P'ekha and what the woman means herself. Soviet teleology clashes with an empirical sense of subjectivity; both need to be sought and are therefore situated in the future, but beyond that they have little more in common. (There is, however, a slight aspect of empiricism to the social, officially Soviet term, since singers at this time usually performed the songs of others and needed therefore to choose and compile their repertoire, rather than compose it.[98]) One year prior to Marina's question, P'ekha states

that her songs harbour private themes of noble sentiment (which in
turn are of implicit educational value to their audience):

[In my songs] there is the theme of that one [special] person I'm searching
for. The theme of a love that was not, but which should be. In other words,
the theme of what did not happen. There's no woman in my songs who has
seen everything, who knows everything. A woman who searches for her happiness, struggles for it, so that there'd be no evil in the world – that's the heroine
of my songs ... It seems to me that my first song where *my* theme could be
heard was Fliarkovskii's number, set to Rozhdestvenskii's words, "Become the
Man I Want." That's probably why it's one of my favourites even now.[99]

The song she refers to here (in Russian, *Stan' takim, kak ia khochu*)
indeed expresses a wholly lyrical seeking, one to counter the state-
sponsored "roads to tomorrow" and one, ironically, penned by a man
responsible for more than one paean to those roads. P'ekha first heard
it in the city of Rostov sung by another performer, Valentina Levko,
and decided on the spot, "That's my song, the one I've been looking
for so long." Once she had included the piece in her repertoire, she
felt that much rehearsing was required in order "to create the strong
and complete heroine who is striving for a love that's lofty, proud, and
beautiful. It wasn't at all easy to find the right intonation for the key
words, 'If I thought you up, then become the man I want.' For many
years the song was my favourite."[100] The music aiding that intonation,
especially in recent versions of this song, remains understated. A
faintly syncopated drum machine or the clicking of fingers gives this
very slow number a gentle, unassuming lilt. P'ekha's private musings,
more spoken than sung, are embellished with slight flourishes from
electric organ or, in another version, a saxophone.

P'ekha explains in another interview why the song had such great
significance in the search for her private and public *lichnost'*: "It was
the first song I performed on stage by a Soviet composer. Until that
point I had gone out onto the estrada with songs of my youth – French
and Polish ones. I was surprised by how precisely the song corre-
sponded to my mood at that time, to my need for a bright, lyrical
feeling. That's such a joy for a singer, when at the necessary moment
the right song turns up in your hands."[101] The text that inspired
P'ekha is as follows:

В этом мире, в этом городе,
там, где улицы грустят о лете,
ходит где-то самый сильный, самый гордый,
самый лучший человек на свете!

Вновь зима в лицо мне вьюгой дунула,
и навстречу вьюге я кричу:
«Если я тебя придумала,
стань таким, как я хочу!»

Ходит мимо в этом городе
и слова пока не слышит эти
самый умный, самый славный, самый гордый,
самый лучший человек на свете!

Знаю, скоро в этом городе
непременно встречусь в день желанный
с самым сильным, самым честным, самым гордым,
самым ласковым и самым славным!

Вновь зима в лицо мне вьюгой дунула,
и навстречу вьюге я кричу:
«Если я тебя придумала,
стань таким, как я хочу!»

[On this earth, in this town, where the streets mourn the summer, there walks somewhere the strongest, proudest, very best person in the world! Winter puffs in my face like a snowstorm again, and I answer that storm as it comes: "If I dreamed you up, become the man I want!" He walks by in this city and doesn't yet hear my words; the brightest, the finest, the proudest, very best person in the world! I know that soon in this city, on the desired day, I'll undoubtedly meet the strongest, proudest, most honest, the finest and most gentle man! Winter puffs in my face like a snowstorm again, and I answer that storm as it comes: "If I dreamed you up, become the man I want!"]

In the huge social expanses of the world is the *one* person that is meant for *me*. Yet what appears as a triumph of the private world over the public is a little more complicated. First of all, the "finest and most gentle person in the world" does not actually exist, or if he does, he is not here but in another space. The size and business of the material world has forced the singer to desire a change in its make-up. She effects such a change in two ways; she thinks and then says what she wants. Her ideal is an improved version of the material world, but one that is supremely – if not unnaturally – subjective.

Even these dreams or spoken orders to the material world are not shown here to have had any success. We hear a command to the dream-person to become the most perfect person, but we do not have

an answer. Maybe objective reality will defeat dreams. The other problem is that the singer actually believes that the best person in the world
exists and now tries to make dreams correspond to that actual person;
once again, reality wins out (with some difficulty) over private experience – but that does not mean that reality is better.

In these tentative steps to refashion or re-speak the spaces of tangible reality, to tentatively pronounce a lyric significance in a civic
framework, P'ekha also needs to refashion the very space upon which
she expresses those steps – the stage. Here begins the tale of post-
Stalinist "staging," the dramatization of songs.

TEATRALIZATSIIA

> You see, I never play the role of anybody ...
> I simply live the life I was given without
> representing anyone.[102]

Prior to Druzhba's union-wide success, Bronevitskii began to experiment with the idea of *teatralizatsiia*. An article of 1965 tells us that the
songs in P'ekha's repertoire are "theatrical miniatures" with all the
elements of a dramatic production:

That's why they're really emotional and exciting. P'ekha's success is shared by
her comrades in the ensemble Druzhba, which recently visited Moscow. Viewers in the capital greeted them warmly. The members of this young, talented
collective have fine voices, an original way of singing and of presenting Soviet
composers (who themselves have a great desire to write for the ensemble).
These Leningraders already have a long-standing friendship with the composers A. Pakhmutova, A. Petrov, and the poet R. Rozhdestvenskii. In P'ekha's
new program are a few works that belong to the leader of the ensemble, A.
Bronevitskii. They were written with P'ekha's voice in mind, her dramatic
abilities. The songs "Clouds" (*Oblaka*), "Mother" (*Mama*), and "Good!"
(*Khorosho*) enjoy great success.[103]

Another article of the same year lists the tools used by the ensemble
to achieve this success: words, music, lighting, colours, and action
upon the stage. All is done to realize the visual embodiment of the
song, its "musical image."[104] One example of Druzhba's staging of the
"Ballad of Bread" (*Ballada o khlebe*), with words by L. Palei, has been
recorded, and the story behind that staging deserves a brief digression.
Walking one day along the streets of Leningrad, P'ekha once found
a discarded piece of black bread. What troubled her was the careless-
ness behind the act, especially on the twenty-fifth anniversary of

Leningrad's freedom from German siege. "Before her eyes there arose a mental picture of all she had read, heard, and pondered: the 900 days of Leningraders' most awful suffering! Bread! How much tragic significance there was in that word! The life and death of Leningraders depended on that word. It was then that the singer had the idea to perform a song-requiem dedicated to the heroic defenders of the city."[105]

For P'ekha the song retains its relevance because the "pain of loss does not fade, nor does the excitement one feels at the courage and extraordinary fortitude among Leningraders."[106] To "uncover the idea" of this private song, several members of Druzhba were put to dramatic use on stage under a bright beam "recalling the type of searchlight that lit nocturnal Leningrad during the blockade. A triangle formed by the members of the ensemble depicted either the perspective of a street or the wing of an airplane. P'ekha stood at the head of the triangle in a light-blue dress with flared sleeves. The sculptural nature of her pose recalled an ancient goddess. The dark grey-blue backdrop of the stage and the pulsing beam of light around the frozen figures both concentrated the listener's attention on the content of the song."[107]

Despite the respectful, static nature of this staging, Bronevitskii said in a 1973 interview – the year that Brezhnev stepped out of the Kremlin to visit Washington – that the ensemble in general strove for movement on the stage.[108] P'ekha had said the same thing the year before,[109] and went further in a much later piece, claiming that "stillness is death and only in movement is there life."[110] The principles of a mobile *teatralizatsiia*, Bronevitskii declared, were "at the very foundation of our work. The ensemble's members have not only vocal but dramatic abilities too. That lets them perform expressive musical miniatures on stage that embody the content of a song in a mobile fashion."

Around this time the phrase "visible song" (*zrimaia pesnia*) appears in articles about Druzhba; it could well be applied to the staging of "Ballada o Khlebe." What is meant by this term is a degree of dramatic expressiveness, apparently insignificant but in actuality constituting the very heart of a performance. In a retrospective piece of 1997, P'ekha defined the principle behind these visible songs as "minimum props and maximum artistry."[111]

"THE BOUNDLESS SKY":
THE WORDS AND MUSIC OF A STAGED SONG

> Only while his memory lives does a man
> have the right to call himself such.[112]

The notion of minimum props and maximum artistry appears to have dictated the staging of the Rozhdestvenskii song "The Boundless Sky" (*Ogromnoe nebo*). A minimum of instruments was used, little more than organ and piano. All attention was on P'ekha, who would lay her microphone upon the proscenium as if it was a bouquet of flowers.[113] The reason for such a gesture was the song's theme, based upon a true story of two peacetime pilots whose plane cuts out over a densely populated area. To avoid the death of many civilians, they sacrifice their own lives by remaining in the plummeting aircraft long enough to reach a nearby forest.

P'ekha felt that by performing this song she was able to sidestep introspection and "give vent to many of my feelings and thoughts."[114] Elsewhere, and more exactly, she defines the song as a patriotic yet "anxious lyric monologue about heroes of our time."[115] Those feelings were experienced so keenly by the students of a Leningrad school that they staged an exhibition on classroom bookcases and walls; they wanted to express both their enthusiasm for the song and their admiration for the pilots' sacrifice.[116] "Ogromnoe nebo" had even more success among cosmonauts. The song was rumoured to be Iurii Gagarin's favourite; he and P'ekha knew each other well (a relationship that sparked some spousal jealousy). She sang "The Boundless Sky" on a radio link to other cosmonauts orbiting Earth, men who had already stocked up their space capsule with tapes of her songs.[117]

P'ekha performed this number at a 1973 concert in Rostov-on-Don, the home town of one of the two pilots. She was appearing with other artists and due to go on stage last of all, well after midnight. Nevertheless the hall remained full, and she sang "Ogromnoe nebo" to a standing ovation. After the event was over, some friends of the pilot telephoned P'ekha to thank her for "remembering us" and to tell her that nobody had any intention of leaving that auditorium before hearing the song.[118]

"The Boundless Sky" is structured so that it might well evoke strong emotions; it breaks towards the end for a percussive thump that dramatizes the crash of the aircraft. To emphasize the song's intent – to keep the pilots' memory alive – P'ekha invokes the social usefulness of that drama. "The main thing, I think, is to teach the public to listen, to catch the tiniest of its moods. You remember the song 'Ogromnoe nebo'? There's a pause in it, after the plane has crashed and the pilots have died. So the longer the pause, the tenser the silence in the auditorium and the more reason I have to assume that the song has cut people to the quick – and that no listener has been left indifferent."[119] The text is as follows:

Об этом, товарищ,
не вспомнить нельзя.
В одной эскадрилье
служили друзья.
И было на службе
и в сердце у них
огромное небо –
одно на двоих.

Летали, дружили
в небесной дали.
Рукою до звезд
дотянуться могли.
Беда подступила,
как слезы к глазам –
однажды в полете
мотор отказал.

И надо бы прыгать –
не вышел полет.
Но рухнет на город
пустой самолет!
Пройдет, не оставив
живого следа.
И тысячи жизней
прервутся тогда!

Мелькают кварталы,
и прыгать нельзя!
«Дотянем до леса –
решили друзья –
подальше от города
смерть унесем.
Пускай мы погибнем,
но город спасем …»

Стрела самолета
рванулась с небес!
И вздрогнул от взрыва
березовый лес! …
Не скоро поляны
травой зарастут …

А город подумал:
«Ученья идут …»

В могиле лежат
посреди тишины
отличные парни
отличной страны.
Светло и торжественно
смотрит на них
огромное небо –
одно на двоих.[120]

[You mustn't forget what I'll tell you, comrade. In one squadron served two friends. Both on duty and deep in their hearts was the boundless sky – entirely for the two of them. They flew, bound by friendship, into skies far away. Reaching out their hands they could just touch the stars. But sadness approached them, like tears in your eyes – on a regular flight the engine cut out. They should have ejected and stopped the flight short. But a pilotless aircraft would then crash in the town! If that happened there'd be no survivors at all. And thousands of lives would be severed at once. The apartments rush past them, but they mustn't jump out! "We can get to the forest," they decided as friends. "We can drag death a little further away from the town. We'll die if we have to, but the town will be saved." Like an arrow, the aircraft then tore from the skies! And surrounding birch forests shook as one from the blast! … Much later forest clearings would grow over with grass … and the townspeople thought, "That's the artillery school…" In two graves now together, now surrounded by calm lie a pair of young fellows from a land just as fine. Casting glances upon them, glances solemn yet bright – is the boundless sky, entirely for the two of them.]

The song begins with an organ alternating between two notes in a way that represents the hum of an airplane. On top of this sparse introduction, the first five lines are *spoken* as a male ensemble begins to harmonize. Before the song even starts, therefore, the listener is directly engaged and made aware of the text's moral weight. The rhythm changes to a waltz, suggesting the graceful circles of an aircraft around the sky, yet does nothing to hint at the impending tragedy. As P'ekha sings of the decision to overshoot the town and stay with the aircraft, she does so to the accompaniment of another organ effect, a swirling sound that grows in volume to represent the pilots' lack of control. The lines that describe the crash usher in some quick changes: P'ekha is replaced by the male voices; these sing en masse to what is now entirely a march with just drum and piano. With the mention of the explosion, a discordant note is heard in unison from all the instruments. A few seconds of silence are punctuated by a single, echoing bang on the drum. (More recent versions of the song have included an ominous drone from a synthesizer.)

To piano accompaniment alone – and much more slowly – P'ekha intones the description of how grass will cover the horrible crash in time ... and then, with the public's blissfully ignorant impression that the bang was artillery practice, the waltz reappears. Because of tragic sacrifice, normal private concerns (and misconceptions) may live on. The civic commitment guarantees the private life. Happiness is the final note in the text, but a sadness in the music constantly punctuates the song, to the point where the initial organ note becomes the last as well. Thus the joy of the present can never forget its debt to the sadness of the past, for lyricism (or subjectivity) is guaranteed only when framed by civic commitment.

Although songs such as "I'll Not Come Back to You" allow P'ekha (through Reznik's lyrics) a foretaste of the more confident *lichnost'* that will epitomize the 1970s through the work of Sofiia Rotaru and Alla Pugacheva, personality is here only cautiously establishing itself beyond the parameters of a wholly social existence. The songs of Druzhba and of P'ekha's solo career after the mid-'70s use the enlightened sentimentalism of morally committed emotions to harbour a quieter, less intrusive sense of self; personality is developed as a social phenomenon, either in a dialogue with a beloved "other" or in a lone performer's dialogue with her beloved audience. By the processes of *teatralizatsiia*, objective reality is to some extent reworked or altered in that dialogue so that an ideal, emotional alternative is fostered. That alternative in turn helps to foster an increasingly confident *lichnost'*. In other words, the smaller yet still social processes of these dialogues help personality to develop *away* from society.

There may be no better illustration of this quiet easing of self away from the centralized workings of society in P'ekha's songs than the heartbreakingly beautiful "That Means It's Love" (*Èto znachit liubov'*). It is based upon a series of oppositions – good and bad, bright and dark. The positive half of each pair cannot exist independently of the negative: "There's no morning without night, no joy without sadness, no life without death, no meeting without parting." The saving grace in this tight series of oppositions is a perfect Petersburgian metaphor for the Thaw, perhaps as a natural stage in a cyclical process of cold and warmth, restraint and release. "In early spring the ice-flows break up, and I believe in a limitless spring flood." Then, as the song moves

P'ekha in Petersburg early in 2000, showing her commitment to old-world elegance

on, after the melting of ice and hearts, the dark oppositions of the first verse turn around. "There's no sky without a sun, no bird without wings, no life without love."

This lavishly orchestrated celebration of an unfrozen, seasonally guaranteed subjectivity is effected, perhaps, at the expense of the social unit. It fell to Iosif Kobzon to balance the scales and sing out with greater volume in praise of that social cohesion, of deeds rather than dreams. Yet Kobzon in no way cancels what P'ekha has done, and in fact the two have often worked together with great mutual respect and admiration. He simply lays a different emphasis in the ongoing interaction of self and other, private and public, that undertakes to define the nature of personality after the death of Stalin.

5
IOSIF KOBZON AND THE CIVIC RESPONSE

Wave the microphone around all you want,
but sooner or later you have to put it
up to your mouth.[1]

Iosif Kobzon was born on 11 September in 1937, a year which for
most Russians is too mired in the horrors of the Purges to summon
any other associations. While Stalin went about the nightmarish business of arresting 5 per cent of his own people as "subversives," Kobzon
began his life in the small, yet busy Ukrainian town of Chasiv Yar. The
settlement is buried deep in the Donets (Donbas) coal basin, Eastern
Europe's industrial powerhouse. The region straddles Ukrainian and
Russian territory, and Russia did all it could soon after the Revolution
to incorporate that industry into its own economy, since local coal,
coke, iron, steel and other products could bolster state quotas hand-
somely. Manufacturing on this scale meant that the Donets basin was
affected by Stalin's purges and agricultural collectivization in a strange
way: people fled to it from the country in search of safer (and perhaps
anonymous) factory jobs far from the forced repossession of agricultural harvests, seeds, and stores.

In this area stolen from the Ukrainian people and overpopulated
as a result of Stalin's paranoia, Kobzon would grow up to be one of
the most famous and long-lived performers of Soviet songs. The jux-
taposition of his background and his career raises the question: why
did he specifically choose to sing Soviet songs – in Russian? What
significance does "Russian" have in the singer's repertoire? Kobzon
himself has said on several occasions that he performs civic (*grazhdanstvennye*) songs, yet insists that the word "civic" is not synonymous
with "political"; his supporters in the Soviet Union saw it as synonymous with "politically serious."[2] In this competition of meanings lies
the crux of Kobzon's entire career, reputation, and significance, especially after the Soviet Union ceased to exist in December 1991.

With his broad shoulders and booming voice Kobzon was the champion of civic song and the darling of Soviet estrada for several decades.
His songs are performed often at great volume to the accompaniment
of a small orchestra. The classical overtones of such an arrangement
lessen the influence of occasional slight syncopation by a rhythm
section of guitar or (unobtrusive) drums. They add, together with the

A photograph from early in Kobzon's career,
showing the conservative or classic attire
that has always been a trademark of his
performance

frequent strains of an accordion or balalaika, the stately lilt of many
a tango, waltz, or military musing on past adventures. What makes
these orchestrated numbers and Kobzon's biography so interesting is
how the man himself moves beyond the simple conflation of politics
and music. Firstly, not only was Kobzon born in Ukraine but he is also
Jewish. In a 1992 article in the newspaper *Moskovskii komsomolets* he
speaks openly about his Jewish roots. His stories range from the
charming to the unnerving. Into the former category falls a tale of his
daughter who was mocked at school as a "Jewess." When assured by
her parents that all was well, the little girl tried to use her new-found
exotic status to get out of eating the traditional Russian porridge or
kasha that her grandmother "stuffed" the family with every morning.[3]

This multifaceted and non-Russian cultural heritage has become
increasingly important for Kobzon and led to his serious support and
sponsorship of Jewish events on the post-Soviet stage.[4] Religious matters aside, the second complication within Kobzon's repertoire has
been his long-standing distinction between "civic" and "Soviet." It has

meant that while he has worked with the same (huge) repertoire both before and after 1991, "civic" has come to mean nostalgically patriotic rather than anything specifically communist. A third complexity comes from the fact that while Kobzon is today seen as a champion of Russian rather than Soviet songs, there have been persistent rumours that raise questions about his commitment to that idealized nation. By his own admission he has become a *very* successful businessman, and success in the new Russia cannot, sadly, escape talk of Mafia involvement. As a result, Kobzon has been the constant object of claims, in essence, that he has become wealthy through underworld connections amidst which he is a figure of some active importance. Kobzon says he feels like "a criminal who has committed no crime."[5] One particularly nasty article on such matters, published in the newspaper *Sovetskaia Rossiia*, led him to instigate legal proceedings. He won both his case and monetary compensation.[6]

The upshot of these cultural shifts and rumours is that the very definition of Russia Kobzon celebrates is up for grabs. He sings folk songs, together with wholly Soviet songs of factories and daring soldiers, and yet he is very much a man of the new capitalist Russia. His ability to bridge two periods and two ideologies, I will suggest, is in no way a consequence of political cynicism on his part. He sings of what one might call "traditionally" Russian civic traits, employed or even exploited by the Soviets and their notions of patriotism. Capitalism, appearing as it does after 1991, does not contradict that patriotism, for the positive, social aspects of "Russianness" that he has celebrated are not contingent upon the current political climate.[7] Those in Kobzon's audience who see no difference between civic and Soviet are troubled by (or perhaps the source of) the Mafia rumours and see his recent business ventures or his wildly successful political career as hypocrisy (if he keeps singing) or treason (if he does not). A problem as complex as this requires some contextual depth.

BIOGRAPHY AND BIG BUSINESS

> I'm not afraid of anything.
> I have my life behind me, three thousand
> recorded songs (they're not all equally good,
> but nobody in the world has recorded more),
> my work, family, and children.[8]
>
> Iosif Kobzon

Just before the Second World War Kobzon's family moved to Lviv. When hostilities broke out his father was drafted, while his mother (who worked as a farm labourer) was evacuated to Uzbekistan with the children and their grandmother in tow. More disruption followed, since Iosif's father later fell in love with another woman and settled for good in Moscow. When the evacuated family members returned home to Ukraine in 1944, the abandoned wife fell into a romance of her own and remarried. New stepbrothers and sisters meant that there were now six children in all. Iosif stood out as he began to rack up awards at school from singing competitions. In a 1978 interview he said, "I've been singing for as long as I remember. All the kids used to sing, and anyway it was wartime, with little in the way of entertainment. My brothers and I entertained ourselves, and of course we sang war songs. People are just made that way: if something painful runs through your childhood, it'll stay with you forever."[9] At the end of the 1940s the new extended family moved to Dnepropetrovsk. The other children, as Kobzon has recently said, today "all work in industry. Normal people."[10]

During what appears a rough-and-tumble childhood, he devoted much time to the sport of boxing, later becoming Ukrainian champion. By nineteen he was called into the army (1956) after studying at the Dnepropetrovsk Technical School of Mining. He served initially in Kazakhstan and later in Transcaucasia, where his evident vocal gifts landed him in the region's military song and dance ensemble. There he performed until returning home in 1959. The announcement to his mother that he planned to pursue a career on the Moscow stage left her unimpressed, but he took on part-time work as a laboratory assistant to save enough money for the trip north.

An impressive aspect of Kobzon's early career is that he managed on his first attempt to be accepted into three of the capital's most prestigious musical schools. (Even the briefest acquaintance with the biographies of the Soviet Union's other great singers quickly shows how very rare such first-time success is.) He chose the State Musical and Pedagogical Institute (*Gnesinka*), where his voice soon led professors to suggest he choose a career in opera.[11] It appears, though, that Kobzon's attraction for the estrada was too strong for that. Here, then, began a life-long relationship, since he now teaches at his old school and has been instrumental in the career of Valeriia, one of the two strongest female voices in today's estrada.

In 1959 as Khrushchev headed off to visit the United States and China, Kobzon was working part-time in the circus with a fellow student, singing at the opening and close of each performance. The then-famous composer Arkadii Ostrovskii came into the circus to work on some new compositions for a musical program; Kobzon saw the scores and begged Ostrovskii to be included in the songs' eventual staging under the big top. Surprised by the student's pushiness, Ostrovskii gave Kobzon his home telephone number. Kobzon called every day with the same request. Driven to distraction by both the constant telephone calls and his wife's irritation at answering them for him, Ostrovskii gave in.[12]

Such persistence earned the singer a position as soloist on national radio in the same year, and he was thus obliged to leave the musical institute. Rumour has it that Utesov heard Kobzon's voice in the early 1960s and was not impressed; but a rebuff from the key player in Soviet estrada only spurred the young man on to greater effort and triumphs. He started solo concerts in 1962, the year of the Cuban missile crisis and close to the time when television began to support estrada with its national New Year's Eve Blue Light variety shows (*Goluboi ogonek*).[13]

Solo concerts led to singular triumphs. The first of these was in 1964. As Khrushchev was removed from his post and his star plummeted, Kobzon's rose with that of Brezhnev. The singer triumphed at the international song festival in Sopot, Poland. The following year he took part in the lengthy "Friendship" contest held in six socialist nations; he won first prize in Warsaw, Berlin, and Budapest. Then he won the Golden Orpheus in Bulgaria. Not surprisingly, with this rapid ascent to international fame came the chance to make famous friends. I mentioned earlier that Èdita P'ekha knew Iurii Gagarin; so did Kobzon, well enough to refute claims that the cosmonaut in an angry moment threw a glass of champagne in Brezhnev's face.[14]

The early 1960s saw Kobzon's brief and unsuccessful marriage to the singer Veronika Kruglova, followed by a second attempt, this time with the very famous comic actress Liudmila Gurchenko, best known today for her work with the director Èl'dar Riazanov. Kobzon speaks of his marriage to Gurchenko with "enormous gratitude":

I think I got a great deal from our brief time together. Gurchenko's very talented as a woman and – excuse the personal details – she's not like anybody else. An individual in everything … We couldn't stay together, though, because besides attractions, besides love, there's life. Around that time my mother, father, and sister moved to Moscow and lived in my apartment on Peace Prospect; I lived with Liudmila. There was no way she wanted to mix with my parents. That wasn't, of course, the main reason for divorce. If only we had enjoyed similar creative interests or children together (she already had a daughter, Masha, who's a charming little girl), then …

But the way things were, she'd go off to her next shoot, and I on my next tour. Some wonderful people ratted on us about our adventures on the road, the fun had by all, the affairs. That created irritation on both sides. If we can step back from these trivialities in our lives, though, then in the big picture I'm very grateful to my fate that such a broad path was cast across it by Liudmila's *lichnost'*.[15]

Kobzon's private concerns cannot have been helped by the demands of his stage show, which often included more than forty songs. On occasion this led to accusations of a lack of respect for his audience: too many songs, no intermission, and no applause.[16] It was nonetheless at this time that journalists blessed him with what would perhaps be his longest-lived moniker: "The Plenipotentiary (*polpred*) of the Soviet Song." That bold metaphor is at times pushed further still to make Kobzon "the knight, singer-patriot, singer-citizen" of the U.S.S.R.[17] He kept this reputation by touring an average of eight months a year around the Soviet Union.[18]

He met his present wife at the start of the 1970s, at a party to which he was invited by friends. He asked a young lady there, Ninel', to show him Moscow, and their meetings grew more frequent; they married in November 1971. She gave up her employment and then a possible theatrical career in order to give birth in 1974 to the first of her two children.

In 1973 Kobzon met with great acclaim when he sang two songs in a long and very successful television series set among the intelligence networks of World War II, *Seventeen Moments of Spring*. (One of its songs is discussed below.) The same year he joined the Communist Party and was graced both as an Honoured Artist of the Russian Federation and recipient of the Lenin Komsomol Prize. Such awards came less as a result of his political affiliations than his chosen civic genre: "The genre I work in could never be popular on a mass scale. I worked with a civic thematic. It is often confused with a political one. The civic or patriotic thematic is the one that praises the people, their feats, and homeland." Indeed Kobzon's work is often defined by its refusal to create "hits" or *shliagery*.[19] But despite his modesty here, Kobzon and his songs were popular enough to warrant two or three concerts a day during the 1970s. Through effort and diligence he was able to earn a great deal by Soviet standards and purchase a prestigious country residence.[20] With his means, status, and fame all increasing in this fashion, Kobzon was blessed with the title People's Artist of the Russian Federation in 1980, while Moscow held the Olympics and Andrei Sakharov began his internal exile.

In the same year he went on what would be the first of several tours to Afghanistan. Claims that those trips were being used to smuggle silver, fur coats, and videos persisted; a recent biographical sketch records the most dramatic rumour of all, that on one occasion some form of contraband was indeed discovered. Kobzon was almost expelled from the Party and became deeply depressed.[21]

Rumours aside, what is true is that the singer was severely reprimanded for inviting on stage the head of the Israel–U.S.S.R. Friendship Society to sing a Jewish song. Kobzon himself had not long before been the first Soviet artist to visit Israel (1983), a country with which the U.S.S.R. had no diplomatic relations.[22] Somehow escaping long-term consequences for his acts, he was in the following year awarded the U.S.S.R.'s State Award. He also managed to tour in other countries such as America, Spain, Sweden, Germany, Greece, Finland, the Congo, Zaire, Angola, Nigeria, Costa Rica, Panama, Peru, Ecuador, Uruguay, Bolivia, Argentina, and Portugal[23] – a very grand tour for a Soviet artist.

One fascinating aspect of Kobzon's creativity and art is how they responded to perestroika and glasnost. The logical assumption would be that a public singer would oppose both types of reform. Kobzon himself refutes such a misunderstanding in a couple of tales that illustrate a mutual respect between himself, Gorbachev, and Yeltsin. When Yeltsin found himself ostracized after criticizing the sluggish speed of perestroika, Kobzon descended from a Kremlin stage following a concert and wished him "courage. I told him that if he needs my participation [in campaign work], I'll always be right there beside him."[24] As for Gorbachev, Kobzon helped him set up a possible concert on Red Square by Frank Sinatra. When, so the story goes, Sinatra wanted a personal air corridor and a red carpet from the private jet's exit to his accommodation (all formulated on a hand-written invitation from Gorbachev), Kobzon sent the arrogant American entertainer a letter, expressing his regret that he himself had ever been compared with Sinatra.[25]

When Gorbachev was on holiday in Yalta in 1991, Kobzon happened to be staying nearby and was asked to give a concert on 22 August. Since the so-called August Putsch occurred on the 19th, the planned event never took place. Kobzon, however, was mysteriously warned by an admiral (for whom he gave a concert on 18 August) that there would be interesting news in the morning. During the coup, the television coverage designed to smooth the troubled airwaves included a tape of Kobzon himself singing – "civic songs, of course." He managed to get through to the broadcast company and forced them to pull him from the air, having no desire to be an apparent participant in political intrigues.

The 1980s saw Kobzon involved in many business ventures, their success attracting perhaps more journalistic attention than that afforded "any other even vaguely renowned figure of Russian culture."

In 1990, for example, he formed his own private company Moskovit, part of a more prominent public presence that included becoming a People's Deputy of the U.S.S.R. Moskovit in its first year helped to support ailing artists, set up monuments to other (recently expired) performers, financed both children's and veterans' homes, held a congress of Jewish neurosurgeons, and gave large sums for a memorial to both Pushkin and Moscow's birthday.[26] Such generosity was funded by the company's operations in oil, metals, and other commodities.[27]

A *Washington Post* article of 6 March 1995 reported that Kobzon had been denied an entry visa into the United States. He promptly sued the U.S. government.[28] The Russian newspaper *Chas pik* (*Rush Hour*) claimed that the mayor of Moscow, Iurii Luzhkov (who was slandered in the article as a Mafioso), would in turn sue the *Post* and thereby raise "a few million" for the Church of the Saviour in his town.[29] (Kobzon in fact gave 855 million rubles to that cause himself.) "So what if Luzhkov does sue the Americans?" declared *Chas pik*. "That's one way of getting things done!"[30]

Kobzon and Luzhkov have been linked elsewhere in the western press, and never kindly.[31] Kobzon maintains that this bad press is concocted in order to spoil Luzhkov's political aspirations.[32] A lengthy and typical article of 1996 in the newspaper *Sobesednik* about Kobzon was subtitled "Sacred Cow." Readers no doubt expected little in the way of objective analysis from such a piece, written at the time of the singer's fifty-ninth birthday. "Look into his (reasonably) animate face," we are told. "Pendulous lips give an air of significance, of an utter absence of thought that comes from knowing everything about everything. His eyes are directed inwards, into his gut, where his eternal love for the Nation lives with undigested difficulty." [33]

Such awful press affected him "as both a businessman and an individual [who should] be free in the demonstration of his likes and dislikes."[34] Thus at the end of 1996 Kobzon announced that at the age of sixty he would leave estrada for good.[35] A huge tour was organized, over a hundred concerts – each four hours in length and consisting of fifty to sixty songs – all across the cities of the old Soviet Union. By July 1997 he had covered fourteen republics and fifty towns with a road crew of 240 people.[36] Only Uzbekistan caused a problem, since all state-run concert halls were undergoing major (though poorly funded) renovation at the time. As Kobzon himself said, "It's really hard for me to think that I won't be able to say goodbye to my public in Uzbekistan. They are especially dear to me. After all, it was an Uzbek family that took in me and my relatives during the war."[37]

In January 1997 Kobzon and his wife were unexpectedly held in custody at Ben-Gurion airport in Tel Aviv, reportedly in a cell with prostitutes.[38] It took the Russian ambassador Aleksandr Bovin and then-prime minister Shimon Peres to sort out the matter.[39] Kobzon flew home vowing never to return until an official apology was forthcoming. No apology was offered. As if the American visa situation were not bad enough, Australian officials delayed Kobzon's entrance papers for concerts late in 1997, even though he had sung there three times already.[40] Ignoring these problems with difficulty, the singer staged his farewell concert on 11 September 1997 in Moscow. It lasted a staggering ten hours, all the way through the night to 6 a.m. Russian state television carried the entire spectacle, with its glittering guest list which included the mayor of Moscow and Alla Pugacheva.[41]

But though the concert was designed to mark the end of Kobzon's career in estrada, articles in the press were talking of an entrance into opera soon, in the Krasnodar Palace of Arts.[42] And whether or not opera will beckon Kobzon after estrada, politics has done so already. In trying his hand at policy-making, he sees himself flying in the face of an unspoken attitude of government towards the entertainment world: "Keep busy doing what you want, deprave our youth with cheap pop music, put on some pornographic movies, but don't you *dare* move into politics."[43] In September 1997, three days after his official farewell, the announcement came of his election as State Duma deputy from the Agin-Buriat region, where he took 84 per cent of the vote.[44] No other candidate received more than 3 per cent.[45] This new and fervent activity was apparently welcomed by his wife, who said that she had awaited the song-less morning of 12 September "with horror."[46]

A letter by an elderly lady sent to a major Soviet newspaper about Kobzon's concerts speaks eloquently of his significance and the desolation many felt at the prospect of his absence from the stage:

I've been ill since my childhood and bound, tied, pinned – I don't know how else to express it – to my wheelchair. I live just outside Moscow in an old five-floor building without a lift. As a result I've hardly been outside for many years. Can you imagine what a trip to Moscow meant for me – all the more so in the evening *and* in a taxi. All these problems moved into the background, though, when the performer stepped out onto the stage. I heard both new numbers and those written long before I was born, together with songs of my childhood and youth. There was a wonderfully good-natured atmosphere during the entire concert. All the performer's songs brought light and hope, even his sad and tragic ones. I'd like to say lots more, but words won't let me express my feelings. I think you already know who I'm talking about ... Iosif Davydovich Kobzon! In talking with the auditorium, Kobzon let a phrase drop that made my heart ache. He said that his departure from the stage will depend upon his viewers and listeners. It's frightening for me to even think that he might leave the stage. His art gives me the strength to live.[47]

A FEW SAMPLE TEXTS

> Over the course of forty years, Iosif Kobzon's
> creative endeavours have promoted Soviet and
> Russian songs. The works of many composers
> were designed especially for him and he,
> of course, gave those works a start in life.[48]

The sense of life-giving song is very evident in a piece of 1964 entitled "Songs Stay with People" (*Pesnia ostaetsia s chelovekom*). Not only does it praise the staying power of music, but it is itself today best known as the theme song to the annual national celebration of the past year's variety. Called *Song '98* (*Pesnia 98*) – or whatever the year may be – it consists of two or three hours of recent hits, sung to the (apparent) accompaniment of a major television orchestra. The title song was written by the same Arkadii Ostrovskii that Kobzon hounded for a circus appearance; it speaks of how songs outlast even stars (here literally, in the television broadcast metaphorically). The music by L. Oshanin sets a mood of staid cheer that suits such programs. The few instruments of P'ekha's repertoire are here multiplied; a modish electric bass may be evident, but this song's fundamental structure is designed for a small orchestra.

Ночью звезды вдаль плывут по синим рекам,
Утром звезды гаснут без следа …
Только песня остается с человеком,
Песня лучший друг твой навсегда.

Через годы, через расстоянья,
По любой дороге, в стороне любой,
Песне ты не скажешь – До свиданья! –
Песня не прощается с тобой.

[Stars at nighttime float far off, down blue rivers, stars in daylight vanish without trace … Only songs stay with people, a song's your closest friend for evermore. Through the years and 'cross the greatest distance, along each highway and in every land, you cannot say goodbye to a song, a song will never leave you.][49]

Here, then, a song *per se* stands above its content, political or otherwise. The amity is what is important; we have a song about songs – and nothing else matters. Music is validated more than any potentially political content. If vocal music is inherently above politics or the "days and nights" that mark political movements, it is also above the geographical divisions by which those temporal divisions define themselves. Grand though that sounds, Kobzon has through other numbers touched upon various aspects of songs or poetry and their inherent connection to what is boundless – and coincidentally life-giving. He does so not only through the poetry of those such as Sergei Esenin ("Ia po pervomu snegu" or "Shaganè") but through the supposedly subversive aesthetic of the 1960s' bard Bulat Okudzhava, who died in 1997.

Okudzhava's studied, calm delivery of his songs to a single guitar is a quiet refusal to embrace loud, civic music. Kobzon has performed his 1957 song, "Midnight Trolleybus" (*Polnochnyi trolleibus*). In it Okudzhava tells of moments when he is overcome by sadness or misfortune. Without a note of Soviet fustian in his voice, he asks only to abandon himself to the aimless circles of a trolleybus and to enjoy others' silent (not noisily purposeful) company. Here Kobzon's orchestra is barely evident as he respects that quiet. A series of descending, overlapping chords fades into silence before his voice is heard. Then a lone piano marks the rhythmic emphases of the text during the first few lines. This modesty of presentation is challenged only by an understated electric guitar (replacing the bard's acoustic version) and a single accordion (to make the sound more locally specific).

Когда мне невмочь пересилить беду,
когда подступает отчаянье,
я в синий троллейбус сажусь на ходу,
в последний, случайный.
…
Я с ними не раз уходил от беды,
я к ним прикасался плечами.
Как много, представьте себе, доброты
в молчанье, в молчанье.

[When I cannot bear to overcome misfortune, when desperation approaches, I get on a navy-blue trolleybus on the move, the last one that happens to pass … Amongst your passengers more than once I've touched their shoulders and run from woe. Can you imagine how much goodness there is in silence, in silence?][50]

Other songs too have stressed the charm of the boundless, of that which lies beyond spatio-temporal limits. Kobzon draws at times not only upon Esenin or Okudzhava but Aleksandr Blok too. Blok (1880–1921), as one of the major poets of Russian Symbolism, saw the socio-political intent of the early Soviet Union in spiritual, at times specifically christological terms, as a cleansing fire or cathartic chaos that would purge the old world and give rise to a new. Needless to say, such ethereal emphases have little presence in songs from the land of materialism. Instead Kobzon sings Blok's paeans to the folkloric limit-lessness of Russia – poems that talk of space without limits, not (quite) of space's absence. (The supranational, ethereal emptiness is also downplayed by Kobzon recording his songs with the Academic Orchestra of Russian Folk Instruments.) In one land – or one woman from that land – there is *some* release from the limits of geography. Russia from one corner to another is unbroken "forest and fields, an embroidered headscarf upon a brow. The impossible is possible, the lengthy road is light, when in the distance of that road there shines beneath a scarf a fleeting glance."

Besides this text ("Rossiia") Kobzon calls upon related moments in Blok's repertoire. "I strive towards a luxurious fate, rush for the beautiful land where in the wide and pure field all is fine, like a miraculous dream" ("Ia stremlius' k roskoshnoi dole" [1898]). A momentary surrender to Blok's spiritual emphasis is heard in the poem of January 1907 which Kobzon sings: "Her Songs" (*Ee pesni*). The text tells of a passion so strong it allows for the words "love" and "destroy" to be rhymed (*liubliu/gubliu*). A call comes from the poem to surrender to a love "above the abyss" that both strangles with snow and deafens with laughter. Although this is an extreme example of Blok's response to the constraints of tangible space, we should nonetheless look in greater detail at one expression of geographical, political (i.e., spatio-temporal) dispute in the Soviet Union during Kobzon's career. That dispute will allow us to see whether the singer – supposedly the great champion of the *Soviet* song – comes down in favour either of policy or some older idea, something that is not temporally delimited.

AFGHANISTAN AND CHECHNYA

Здравствуй, мама, возвратились мы не все ...
Босиком бы пробежаться по росе ...
Пол-Европы прошагали, полземли –
Этот день мы приближали, как могли.

[Hello, Mother, we didn't all come back ...
To run barefoot across the dew would be
so fine ... We walked across one half of Europe,
half the world – we hastened that day, as best
we could.][51]

The 1979 invasion of Afghanistan was the first time that Soviet troops had stormed into territories outside of the Communist Bloc. In a 1989 article,[52] Kobzon looked back on the eight trips he had taken by then to that country; by 1994 he had made yet another.[53] His retrospection came at a time when doubts over the purpose of the entire operation could be expressed in the press. The singer wasted no time in stating his viewpoint: "After my initial trips to Afghanistan … I was tormented by the question: why do our lads in their field shirts have to fight beyond the boundaries of their homeland?" He admits that when he was first invited to perform in Afghanistan, he knew "virtually nothing about the war." He had gone at the invitation of the Afghan Ministry of Culture to celebrate the anniversary of the "April Revolution." The aim was for Soviet artists to play before an Afghan audience, not to spend time with the Soviet troops. From the indigenous audience he received "flowers, applause and awards";[54] he has in fact been graced five times with decorations by the Afghan people.[55]

Nevertheless Kobzon wanted to see his fellow countrymen as well, and he caused considerable headaches for the local Soviet command who were forced to bend protocol a little for the significant presence of an estrada star. The stories that Kobzon tells of his encounters with the soldiers radically change the manner in which that personality and the songs he brings with him are interpreted. Kobzon's audience at home – and the Soviet authorities – assumed a synonymy between his civic songs and state policy, between "Russian" and "Soviet" texts. In actuality the situation is simpler: Russian songs are Russian songs and a Russian artist is in Afghanistan to see Russian soldiers. What allows Kobzon to affect his (often wounded) military audience so strongly is something that, while Russian, is not exclusively Soviet. It must therefore be a notion older than twentieth-century politics, yet one that manages to exist beside those politics: patriotism. When he is with his fellow countrymen, the "problem of fathers and sons disappears."[56]

Kobzon's reports about Afghanistan, told in newspapers and television interviews, build to this conclusion slowly, with several honest and touching stories. He remembers a concert given to some paratroops, which was held in a hangar at a temperature of forty degrees Celsius. A huge, dove-blue curtain cast across the stage was sewn from the chutes of those who would never return home. On another occasion he came across a young man lying in a military ward, turned to the wall.

"What's the matter, son?"
He turned and whispered, barely audibly:
"It's cold and I've got the shivers."

I fixed his thin blanket, took off my jacket and laid it on top of the bedding. I sat down by his bunk and, taking his hand, began to sing softly. I don't even remember what it was that I sang. The melody came by itself. It seems that I didn't so much sing as just whisper him some words. The accordionist [with us on tour] gently picked up the melody. The lad turned to me and I saw that his eyes were full of tears. How do you think I felt? I kept singing, just for his sake. The boy's face grew brighter; you could sense that he was consciously listening and that the song had touched his spirit. The accordion fell silent. With a smile of sorts, the kid then said:

"Thank you."

Doubting that he would be able to perform before the calm, happy faces of an urban Soviet audience ever again, Kobzon falls to musing upon the differences between generations brought to his attention by the hospital visits. While the public with which he began his career, the workers at the myriad construction sites he visited, will still come to his concerts, he says, the younger generation has different tastes. "But there, far from home, in the Afghan lands burned by sun and fire, soldiers are [still] attracted by songs about their homeland, about their mothers. They are attracted by the melodies of the [Second World] War, by the type of song that excites the soul, that hurts, gladdens, and cleanses."

The plenipotentiary of the Soviet song is not doing a very good job. His songs evoke the desire to go home, back to the calm of childhood. His songs of war inspire a community of suffering rather than the orderliness of attack. He is calling upon ideas and sentiments older than most Soviet art, and thus – despite the differences in aesthetic and volume – there is much in common between the manner in which both Kobzon and P'ekha relate to Afghanistan. Both singers hold sympathy and private suffering or family loss higher than foreign policy. If, as the Soviet press itself contends, Kobzon's earliest songs are indeed closer to "reportage" than either the intrusion of private concerns (in Afghan hospitals) or the predominance of subjective philosophies, then we can say that from the 1960s onwards, Kobzon will slowly change his "reports." The dialogue of stage and hall, of singer and soldier, cultivates introvert tendencies in both parties; it fosters personality. As time goes on, Kobzon's audience starts to speak up, prompted simultaneously to a new and similar sense of self. Here is an example from 1988 of particular relevance to Afghanistan:

Last summer I was performing in Odessa. After one of the concerts a young, attractive woman came up on stage. She approached the microphone and presented herself [to the audience]: "I'm a medical worker, Nina Dvornik.

Not long ago I came back from Afghanistan. Mr Kobzon performed twice in our garrison with his ensemble. We really liked his songs, and that's why I came to the concert today."

I heard Nina's words and felt awkward. War is a man's business. The weaker sex shouldn't be sent into battle during peacetime. In Afghanistan there were quite a few Soviet women of various ages and professions who had gone there willingly. I felt like bowing before them, on behalf of all mothers and fathers whose sons they'd cared for in the hospitals, done laundry for, cooked for, fed ... Nobody forced these women to go where they'd be under fire. If they couldn't take it, they were free to come home at any time, but very few took advantage of that opportunity.

Moments such as these, either in Ukraine or in Afghanistan, left Kobzon with "a feeling of dissatisfaction that there was somebody I just wasn't singing for, somebody I really wasn't singing for." The impersonal Soviet performer did not suddenly begin stressing these private significances in the late '80s, during perestroika. The essence of Gorbachevian politics was always in Kobzon's songs; one simply has to look a little harder for it. What Kobzon encountered first hand in Afghanistan *in spite of*, not because of Soviet foreign policy, was a liberally inclined "fraternity ... a return to my [friendlier] youth." The social or civic intent of progressive Soviet society is met by the smaller, yet more significant public spirit of "familial" social units. This significance is even stronger a few years later when the conversation turns to problems that began in Chechnya close to Christmas 1994.

While Yeltsin's decision to invade the tiny southern territory was justified as the need to quash extreme criminal activity, to most outsiders it looked like one more (unsuccessful) attempt by a czar, dictator, or post-Soviet president to tame an unruly Caucasian people. Whether one sees that unruliness as admirable or infuriating is a big issue, since in Moscow the Chechens are at best looked upon as little more than grubby gypsy traders. Kobzon decided to hold a concert to help these people in the fall of 1996 in the strangest of surroundings, the ultra-fashionable Petersburg nightclub, Candyman. He had two aims: firstly, to see if such apparently unsuitable listeners could be won over (a personal challenge), and secondly, to raise money for young, innocent victims of war in Chechnya. Once again, as in Afghanistan, private loss took precedence over the "national" desire to regain the fractious republic.

In this regard Kobzon also uses the seemingly Soviet, enlightening "report-song" to the auditorium in order to convince them of his intent. He employs an old-fashioned approach to the hall to gain a modern consequence, that *they* approve of his intent and give both time (as attention) and money to support it. "I called the program 'Children of the Chechnian Front.' Official statistics claim that over two years of war, less than fifty children have suffered. That's a bare-faced lie, just as most sources of official information are! There's one woman by the name of Kryzhanovskaia who lost her son, and that prompted her to go to Chechnya where she found 138 children who had been crippled by the war."[57] To avoid the risks of official donations to faceless organizations, Kobzon opened up accounts for each individual child. He gave his substantial appearance fees from the Candy-man concert to the cause: "I'm a rich man ... believe me, I don't need the money."

Something else that Kobzon does not need is the horror of Chechnya. Three weeks after becoming a deputy in the State Duma, he was asked why he did not appear in Chechnya the way that he had done in Afghanistan years before. It appears that the sense of country, and its concomitant mores, that were in place during the Soviet Union have gone. Those mores were not *the* Soviet Union: they were synchronous with and encouraged by it. Today the situation is very different. Kobzon needs to be quoted in full here to do justice to his convincing viewpoint.

I decided that I'll go there [to sing] on one condition: if there'll be a cease-fire, a moratorium for ten days or so. Then I'll go there and perform before both sides. I won't sing for our lads alone. I've seen ... how they celebrate, how they cut off noses, ears and make themselves a collection. It's madness! Does anyone really benefit if they've hacked some people up ... and then I go to calm things down? What are they fighting for? When Shamil Basaev starts screaming that all Russians are guilty – the ones that fought, the ones that didn't fight, the ones that sympathized ... when he says they're all criminals, it's hard not to agree with him. After all, we did nothing to stop this war. I was very close to [Dzhokhar] Dudaev and to some degree influenced him. He asked for one thing only: an audience with the president. They killed Dudaev, they killed hundreds of thousands of people. The whole thing ended when, after all that, the president of Russia did accept the President of Chechnya.[58]

Kobzon has also spoken of the damage that the war in Afghanistan did to normal, familial processes. Here, however, he focuses less on civilians than on the soldiers themselves. "The Afghanistan veterans live by different moral standards. Coming home, they hold onto one another, because their atmosphere of noble military brotherhood is incompatible with the social deafness, careerism, and avarice which they come face to face with in peacetime existence."[59]

SONGS OF ADVENTURE
AS AN ALTERNATIVE TO JINGOISM

Взглянул в небо грозовое
Молодой трубач.
«Расстаемся мы с тобою:
Ты не плачь»

[A young bugler looked into the stormy sky.
"We're parting company; don't you cry."][60]

Kobzon's songs of adventure often express pure and lofty qualities. "Brotherhood" can be spoiled by nasty adult practices; one of his songs to touch upon a purer, pre-adult state of bold adventuring is an Ostrovskii number entitled "Boys" (*Mal'chishki*). Sung to the strident rhythms of a small, drum-driven orchestra, it tells at first of brave, energetic boys in winter. Once again the accordion adds an air of things Slavic, while the drama of strings, timpani, and martial horns combines with the spry sparkle of xylophones to connect the youngest of boys to the most adult of endeavours:

Рисует узоры
Мороз на оконном стекле,
Но нашим мальчишкам
Сидеть не по нраву в тепле.
Мальчишки, мальчишки,
Несутся по снежным горам.
Мальчишки, мальчишки,
Ну как не завидовать вам!

[On the window pane frost draws designs, but our boys cannot abide
to be stuck indoors where it's warm. Boys, boys, rush up hills of snow.
Boys, boys, how can we not envy you!]

They grow up and attend school dances, where the strains of an "energetic waltz" and pretty girls speed the heart. The boys are then shown stepping into an equally exciting, inspiring conflict with the enemy in wartime. By keeping their sense of adventure, purity, and brotherhood, they move outside of spatial constraints:

Плывут в океанах,
Летят высоко в небесах
Солидные люди

С мальчишеской искрой в глазах.
Мальчишки, мальчишки,
Пускай пролетают года,
Мальчишки, мальчишки,
Для нас вы мальчишки всегда!

[Respectable people sail out over oceans and fly high in the skies with
a boyish spark in their eyes. Boys, boys, may the years fly by. Boys, boys,
you'll always be boys for us!][61]

Hand in hand with all Kobzon's songs of adventure go what I might
call those of yearning, of a desire to return to a time or place now
lost. In his "Pre-War Waltz" (*Dovoennyi val's*) he sings fondly of
Leningrad's main street, Nevsky Prospekt, "when Utesov looked down
[at us] from a poster." This type of wistful retrospection starts to
explain why Kobzon reacts the way he does to the terrible sadness of
his countrymen stuck so far from home in uninspiring military conflict. Perhaps the most suitable song to explain this yearning is the
1972 song by Robert Rozhdestvenskii, "Song of a Distant Homeland"
(*Pesnia o dalekoi Rodine*). It is extremely well known, thanks not only
to Kobzon's performance but also to its key role in a wartime drama
of the 1970s, and has recently been re-recorded (then filmed) by two
popular singers of today, Leonid Agutin and Anzhelika Varum. Agutin
and Varum stress utterly the romantic side of the song, Kobzon the
civic. The ability to find both public and private meaning in one text
says much for Rozhdestvenskii's role as a transitional song-writer. A
double meaning is also possible because the "homeland" in fact is
represented by "my home [or house]" (*rodnoi dom*), a house of one's
youth, now gone forever. The air of timelessness surrounding this
song finds expression musically too, as there is no contemporary
electronic percussion present. Piano and violins rise and fall in waves
of emotion rather than demarcating the cruder rhythms of anything
specifically modern. The ballad takes on a classical elegance and
permanence.

Где-то далеко, очень далеко
Идут грибные дожди.
Прямо у реки, в маленьком саду
Созрели вишни, наклонясь до земли.
Где-то далеко, в памяти моей,
Сейчас, как в детстве, тепло.
Хоть память укрыта
Такими большими снегами.

[Somewhere far away, very far away, there are sun-showers. Beside the river, in a small garden, cherries have ripened and hang low. Somewhere far away, in my memory now, as in my youth, it is warm. All the same, my memory is covered by the deepest of snows.][62]

The wavering here is considerable between the homeland and *my* own home (where *my* mother or wife lives). Kobzon has been dismissed at times as a complete reflection of party policy, but songs such as "Pesni o dalekoi Rodine" suggest that a grave injustice has been done. One can, if diligent, find pro-Soviet proclamations in interviews with Kobzon, but on the whole the issues at hand are more complicated and help, once sorted out, to show how popular songs – although financed and broadcast by Soviet institutions – worked at times in subtle contrast to state intention. The crux of the matter, therefore, is the contrast between what Kobzon's manner was said to be (by the press) and what it was in reality.

REDEFINING THE CIVIC SONG AS ESSENTIALLY HISTORICAL

Today there's not a single major construction
project that I haven't been to, and I'm proud
of that. I travel to those sites not from
obligation ... not at all. I always felt myself
fulfilled when I came back from a site. It always
meant seeing one's contemporary, the person
who's making something new and beautiful.
When meeting that person, you feel as if you're
meeting the future. During [World War II]
artists went off to the front in order to help
soldiers in the hard work of battle. When
I travel to a site today, it gives me the feeling
that I'm on the front line, too.[63]

In a piece Kobzon himself wrote in 1983 as a jury member at the All-Union Estrada Artist Competition, he outlines all that is awry in the world of civic songs. Not only are "revolutionary, civic-patriotic" songs being ignored, he complains, but "the civic thematic at times is reduced to the style of posters or hymns," whereas there are in fact "many quiet, lyrical songs of civic intent that show it's possible to find one's own intonation."[64] This attempt to find (or put) the personal in the public is what defines Kobzon's choices or definition of genre. When he tried to include songs of both society *and* seclusion in a repertoire of 1969, the newspaper *Sovetskaia kul'tura* called it a "risky move."[65]

A few years later, in the early '70s as Pugacheva prepared to make her bold move onto the estrada, Soviet critics were looking at both pre-Kobzonian lyricism and current similar songs as somehow *wrong*, which raises a question. Is there *any* room for Kobzon's privately public spirit if mixing the two types of song is deemed "risky" and even when they are not mixed, the critics are lambasting the lyric style? "In the Fifties, when Kobzon began his artistic journey, a type of pseudo-lyric was evident in many estrada programs: the exaggerated wailings of one's spiritual woes, brought on by the exit of one's beloved. In keeping with that kind of content, genuine singing was often swapped for an intimate whispering into the microphone. Later on, very recently, in fact, that kind of performance was replaced by loud, rhythmic, cutting howls."[66] In terms of his stage personality, how does Kobzon manage to be socially committed, yet still personal, *and* avoid the pitfalls of introvert whispers or extrovert howls?

One starting point might be the way in which Soviet building sites or major points of construction were understood by Kobzon in the 1960s. The romantic wanderings out to such distant locales to build railways or dams have unkindly been equated with the rush of lemmings.[67] That observation is made in a book that notes the huge influence of "complicated and painful" existential authors entering Russia from the West at the same time.[68] Where is the common ground between existentialism and state-sponsored construction? How did Kobzon react to the result? An interview with one of the composers with whom he has often worked helps here.[69]

In the 1980s in the newspaper *Sovetskaia Rossiia* Aleksandra Pakhmutova spoke of Kobzon's connection with the romance of two decades before. For her one of the main symbols of the Thaw remains "young guys in plaid shirts with little volumes of Remarque in their rucksacks. They would tear off in one direction, to where there were important things to do, or in another direction where things would be tougher still." The big constructions of the '60s and the young people who helped build them were inspired by the same spirit. Remarque, however, is not likely to inspire sacrifice in the name of the state. Indeed, Pakhmutova speaks of places where Kobzon has sung, and she mixes projects of optimism with places of tragedy in the same sentence: Bratsk (the enormous hydroelectric plant), BAM, Afghanistan, Chernobyl'. (Kobzon by the mid-'70s had constructed entire concert repertoires around events such as the fiftieth anniversaries of the Revolution and the youth league or *komsomol*, Lenin's one-hundredth birthday, and the Twenty-Fourth Party Congress.[70])

The romance of the Baikal-Amur Railroad, for example, quickly evanesced in the '70s; by the '80s the custodian of the BAM museum
along its route complained that nobody cared any more and the whole
project had been forgotten. One worker, whose voluntary romantic
wandering eastward had been replaced by a forced wandering between
railroad settlements in search of ever-lessening work opportunities,
remarked: "I can't call this place home. I just can't. My heart doesn't
go out to the place, because my [initial optimistic] feelings were
nipped in the bud."[71]

With that in mind, let us consider an observation in 1967 from the
newspaper *Sovetskaia Moldaviia*, far from the centre of things: "What
does Iosif Kobzon sing about? Which songs work best for him? It's
hard to answer that question. It's hard, because his creative range is
very wide, his artistic interests are varied, his talent multifaceted. And
for each song in its brief embodiment, he finds his individual, unique,
and emotional tonality. However, it seems to me that closest of all to
Kobzon are those songs in which civic motifs are heard, songs replete
with heroic pathos or thoughts of people, of human fates."[72] A similar
remark is found in a 1983 review from Leningrad's October concert
hall: "Almost every song was like a full story of somebody's life, told
in a few minutes ... The performance was penetrated by an unusual
warmth, a loving relationship to the heroes of these tales."[73] Kobzon's
performance is implicitly seen as a narrative of private, not public
history. More than the stories of railways or hydroelectric stations
themselves, he tells the stories of people making homes and houses
far from Moscow. He sings not of things but of the people who make
or transform things. Hence the failure of BAM's romance is felt in
terms of its inability to be a "home" for the "heart" as Soviet economics
outdo the dream offered years before in songs like Kobzon's.

For the record, I should note that this "unusual warmth" of Kobzon's private histories can push public intent out of a song entirely.
Take, for example, the 1947 song "In a Town Garden" (*V gorodskom
sadu*) by A. Fat'ianov and M. Blanter. Here, just after the Second World
War but at the outset of the Cold War, a sailor sings of a woman he
sees sitting on a park bench. If Kobzon's supposedly societal songs
(such as "Mal'chishki" or "Pesnia o dalekoi Rodine") talk of Russia's
boundlessness, its oceanic fields, then his private songs talk of an
equally elusive "home," in the sense of the difficulties of finding one's
true love. His civic songs are often not civic (i.e., not *that* "Soviet"),
and his lyric songs talk of how obligations (such as war) to the state
have driven men far into the expanses of sea or Europe and have
therefore spoiled the idyll of personal life. Yet these songs were fostered by Soviet media, and all help to reveal Russian culture at the

time as more intricate and complicated than cold-war metaphors usually allow us to see. That complication is heard in the song's orchestration too, since it is a waltz, a form associated for millions of Russians with private emotions during public war. As Kobzon's vocal is supported by a small choir in moments of heightened emotion, the waltz becomes amplified by several voices; private issues are raised and muddled with the bolder sounds of public drama.

> Прошел чуть не полмира я –
> С такой, как ты, не встретился
> И думать не додумался,
> Что встречу я тебя.
>
> Знай, такой другой на свете
> Нет наверняка,
> Чтоб навеки покорила
> Сердце моряка.
> По морям и океанам
> Мне легко пройти,
> Но к такой, как ты, желанной,
> Видно, нет пути.

[I've crossed almost half the world – but never met anybody like you, and it never crossed my mind that I would meet you. You know that there's probably nobody on earth like you and that you've tamed the heart of a sailor forever. It's easy for me to cross the ocean and sea, but it seems there's no path to you, to the one I desire.][74]

The implicit relation here between one's desire and the search for it requires a little extra discussion. Moving to find what one wants is a process tied closely to our earlier discussions of *lichnost'* and movement. One claims space, be it large or small, and hopes to refashion it or make it one's own. That movement can be from one side of the stage to the other, or from the shores of the Baltic to those of the Pacific; it all happens within the Soviet Union in an attempt to fashion a sense of self.

LICHNOST' AND THE HERO'S (IM)MOBILITY ON STAGE

You want to give Iosif Kobzon a call? Be my guest – but don't call him at home, because he won't be there. You'd be better off calling

> Iuzhno-Sakhalinsk or Vladivostok; it may well
> be that he's there. If not, then call the
> diamond miners of Mirnyi or the concreters of
> the Zeiskaia Hydro-Electric Station ... Oh – it's
> entirely possible that he's performing now in
> Samotlor or in Naberezhnye Chelny ... Perhaps
> he's in Murmansk or Tselinograd ... But there's
> the Golden Orpheus going on in Varna, and
> then both in Zvezdnyi and near Moscow our
> cosmonauts are celebrating Iurii Gagarin's
> birthday. They probably invited Iosif Kobzon.[75]

In the spiteful *Sobesednik* article by Anton Bublikov discussed elsewhere in this chapter, the author claims – with some justification – that "the main feature of Kobzon's *lichnost'* is its inability to see itself together in all its mutually exclusive manifestations."[76] Here Bublikov lists Kobzon's patriotism, nationalism (be it Jewish or Soviet), friendships with political kingpins, sympathy for Russia's less fortunate citizens, and persistent calls for the increase of law and order, inspired by the "camaraderie between strong politicians and strong criminal authorities. And to all of this you can add his komsomol-revolutionary nostalgia." In this truly muddled and contradictory list lies all that Kobzon stands for and embodies in his *lichnost'*.

Russia's only substantial history of Soviet estrada defines Kobzon as a singer whose baritone "sounds ever more masculine with each stage program. He has chosen for himself a repertoire of significance and has been able to make the civic personal (*lichnyi*), to make it what he has endured or experienced, to make it his own." He does so with numerous songs each having a well-defined hero who is "courageous and tender, spiritually generous and open with people, ready to support, defend, and sympathize with others."[77] Elsewhere Kobzon's songs are described as the "affairs, feelings, and moods" of such a hero.[78]

Despite some cultivation of private moods in his lyrics, Kobzon is at times accused of an emotional paucity, of a lack of feeling, since the tendency to pomp in a flag-waving text – both in what it says and how it is performed – can displace anything personal. He is also, as mentioned earlier, upbraided for "reporting" rather than singing his repertoire.[79] The consequences of this upright delivery are felt squarely in the delicate dialogue of performer and stage. Kobzon would stand and give forth – nothing more and nothing less. The rigidity and length of his performances on occasion worked against his subjective lyrics, since he was seen by some as a severe presence on stage.

At a recent press conference, Kobzon manifests
the poise of a well-respected businessman and
politician.

A reviewer in 1985 characterized Kobzon's long program as
"unique generosity towards his listeners. In the first section of his
concert alone he sang thirty-one songs."[80] In his celebration of
Lenin's hundredth birthday, he sang close to fifty.[81] It is this expression of size, of expansiveness, that awes his audiences. Awe is not
something evoked by Èdita P'ekha's performances, and here is the
point where the dialogic construction of Kobzon's *lichnost'* deviates
from hers. Whereas Druzhba brought a happy novelty to estrada, a
testing of the new international, yet private waters of the 1960s
together with the audience, Kobzon's "other" is often in the past and
"seriously" respected as a result. Increasing ignorance of that past
"concerns" him.[82] Whereas P'ekha is at times the lonely, lyrical
dreamer, the more publically minded Kobzon talks much of the debt
a singer owes to the society or crowd of his predecessors on the stage.
That debt and the way it is (or is not) repaid sets the mark for the
"wholeness of character" lacking in modern performers. Kobzon lives
up to his predecessors – so much so that he says the entire notion of
"retro" is foreign to him[83] – and then reports to his audience; P'ekha
lives up to her audience since it has almost no direct predecessors.
The greater debt that Kobzon feels to an absent, deceased audience
gives an air of static severity to many concerts. He is less among
friends than is Druzhba.

Take, for example, this pointed observation from 1968 on how
Kobzon sang many songs in most concerts and did not like to be

interrupted by applause: "As soon as it was understood that there was no point looking in the program (you wouldn't understand anything), and that it was pointless clapping (Kobzon wouldn't stop), that you just had to sit and listen – then the auditorium surrendered and fell quiet. Although the singer left victorious, I must note that such a victory does not occur without losses. Kobzon placated the hall, but that took not only time, it took songs, as well, to which he could no longer return."[84]

A similar struggle ensued when Kobzon decided to play a Petersburg nightclub for a charity show in 1996 (see the section on Afghanistan). "As a sportsman [ex-boxer]," he said, "it is exciting and interesting for me to see what I can do with a nightclub audience. I'll either force them to respect me or they'll trample me underfoot."[85] Elsewhere this is termed his ability to "hold" an audience and not allow himself to "dilute the concert with an easier repertoire." [86] This head-on manner of telling, rather than a P'ekhian asking or suggesting, is associated with a different kind of post-Soviet transformation: his confrontational style is sometimes seen not as Soviet baggage but as the ultramodern, maverick mode of those such as the one-time presidential candidate, professional soldier, and governor of Krasnoyarsk, General Lebed'. A Soviet static pose looks tough as nails in the post-Soviet mêlée. "There was a time when Kobzon would go out on the stage and … well, he was basically your town council secretary. The haircut, suit, mannerisms, glances – they were all from the bureaucracy. Now the haircut, with the fringe hanging down, the mannerisms and squint all look like some 'Godfather,' some General Lebed' or other."[87]

Kobzon, we are told, is putting on an act, which ushers in our theme of "staging" or *teatralizatsiia*. Do Kobzon and his songs "stage" anything?

A CONCLUDING WORD ON KOBZON AND TEATRALIZATSIIA (OR THE LACK THEREOF)

> Severity and restraint combined with expression and the bold stamp of [a song's] form.[88]

> Dancers from Siberia and jazzmen from Latvia,
> singers from Belorus, Ukraine, and Georgia,
> musicians from Kazakhstan and Moldova …
> It's always pleasant for us [Kobzon and
> colleagues] as members of a jury to watch
> such waves of new energy.[89]

Kobzon was and is very restrained on stage[90] – in fact, he has been called a little chilly.[91] In a 1977 interview he argues his belief that too many gestures can undermine a song's effect:

I think that the singer mustn't under any conditions distract the listener from a song. If a gesture emphasizes the content, if it helps to create an image, some kind of generic sketch, then I'll all for it. Klavdiia Shul'zhenko used to do so – and by the way, she's my favourite singer. If it's all born of helplessness, if it's all just a "beautiful gesture," then I'm against it. In my civic and patriotic songs their meaning is so clearly expressed that I really don't have the moral right to add some kind of external effect. I work all the time on my diction – it has to be faultless. I carefully examine how correctly I stress the meaning – I do that in the most careful manner possible. It seems really important to me. But you can't swap or add to anything with a gesture – especially if there isn't enough thought and feeling, if you haven't felt the song with the very core of your being, if you haven't felt what the song's about together with the hero.[92]

That expression of feeling does not involve his moving around a great deal, but he dismisses criticisms that his performances are insufficiently theatrical.[93] "I sing Esenin, Blok, the very best poetry. They say that Kobzon's a static artist, but what am I supposed to do? Show [with gestures] how much Esenin loved birch trees, or something?"[94] The idea of a man as physically solid as Kobzon surrendering to wistfulness on stage and hugging an imagined tree does indeed sound silly. What Kobzon takes from Esenin – without acting it out – is the aforementioned sense of rustic boundlessness, one that uses the (political) geography of the area called Russia to cultivate distinctly non-civic sentiments. The poem Kobzon refers to here was written a month before Esenin's suicide and talks of his (drunken) affinity with lonely trees stuck in deep snow. It is an acutely sad text of extreme, nocturnal isolation. Nevertheless, it is at the same time a profound expression of love for the most Russian of trees, lost in the huge expanses of their homeland. Both Esenin and Kobzon celebrate their sense of self as something that is – ultimately – older and bigger than Soviet history or geography.

To talk about the boundlessness of a homeland, however, is contradictory. The homeland is defined by geographical borders. Although Kobzon is both Jewish and Ukrainian, only recently has he expressed those strong ethnic elements with great force in his interviews. We can learn a lot about the sense of self or Russianness during earlier periods of Soviet song by choosing an artist who also worked within elements of a folk repertoire but from the outset used a non-Russian background as central to a stage persona. The most suitable candidate is

Sofiia Rotaru. We will look at her songs together with those of another artist, one who is wholly Russian – Irina Ponarovskaia. Rotaru's art moves from the edges of the Soviet Union towards its Russian-speaking core; Ponarovskaia's story is a dramatic tale of how that supposed centre of fraternal relations, expressed in Soviet estrada and all its press releases, was in fact a cutthroat enterprise. Although she reached the inner circle of an international Soviet business, Ponarovskaia often wanted very much to get out. Together these two women reflect a heightened process of push and pull between notions of centre and periphery that are essential to one's sense of self as performer or supporter of Russian-language Soviet estrada.

6

IRINA PONAROVSKAIA AND SOFIIA ROTARU: IN AND OUT OF RUSSIA

> Even in moments of crisis [Ponarovskaia] never lost optimism, never walked away defeated by illnesses or circumstances.[1]

> [Rotaru] walked step for step behind Pugacheva. But Pugacheva wasn't worried by the breath on her neck. They worked upon differing auditoria, as if in differing spaces.[2]

Between the guiding lights of Èdita P'ekha and Alla Pugacheva in post-Stalinist estrada are several women who mark the growing importance and dimensions of personality. Two of the most important are Sofiia Rotaru and Irina Ponarovskaia. Rotaru has worked often with contemporary versions of folk songs, replete with the strings and horn sections of 1970s' production, Ponarovskaia in a more obviously modern, pop-oriented format. Rotaru was born in Ukraine, Ponarovskaia in Leningrad, and the great distances between these two places help to distinguish between two types of *lichnost'* and two attitudes towards the place where that personality is cultivated – the stage. Both women add to the lyrical emphases of P'ekha and Kobzon, while countering other elements, such as Kobzon's belief that *teatralizatsiia* and a public spirit are incompatible and when combined create nothing more than a muddled, ethically ineffectual personality on stage.

In essence, three factors help to distinguish how the notion of self is cultivated by these women: what they sing, what they say about themselves, and what is said about them. By looking at the rustic, even exotic Moldovan origins of Rotaru's self-perception and comparing them to the urban equivalent in Ponarovskaia, we can distil the essence of how personality was made by Soviet estrada in the 1970s. Given the fact that it is made on the stage, performers have first of all to get to that stage for anybody to be aware of their existence. Rotaru begins far away, Ponarovskaia close by. How they compose their personae for a "central" Muscovite audience is both a product and consequence of where they began in the Soviet Union, on the edge or in the centre. Through the sung genres, interviews, and movies of these women's careers we can see how the notion of "making it big" is constructed, and how that process of construction causes shifts in the dialectic of self and other, stage and audience.

SOFIIA ROTARU:
MOLDOVAN CHARM IN MOSCOW

Sofiia Rotaru was born at the outset of the Cold War on 7 August 1947, like Iosif Kobzon in Ukraine. Unlike her compatriot, however, she was raised not in an industrial region but a more rural one, amidst the arable farmland of the Carpathian Mountains. She grew up as one of six children in a village near the town of Novoselytsia, where "the houses, like little toys, are decorated with national, ornamental designs, all kinds of birds everywhere."[3] Even by 1990 this toy-town's population had not reached nine thousand. The surrounding region of Chernivtsi forms part of southwestern Ukraine, very close to both Romania and Moldova; Rotaru was in fact of Moldovan heritage. By 1980, 70 per cent of the population of her home region was Ukrainian, 19 per cent Romanian, almost 7 per cent Russian – even fewer were Moldovans. She learned both Russian and French at school and spoke Moldovan at home. Only when she later married a Ukrainian would she use the Ukrainian language regularly.[4]

Her singing career began early – in jest she has said that only a mouthful of pacifier stopped her singing while still in diapers.[5] At the age of twelve a series of successful singing competitions ended in a coveted trip to Moscow. She was inspired to study music seriously and at nineteen entered a musical school in the central town of Chernivtsi. Since there was no vocal faculty, she began to study conducting and choral work.[6] Continuing to enter contests, she was victorious in one which resulted in her photograph appearing on the front cover of the nationally distributed magazine *Ukraina*. One copy made it to the Urals, where twenty-year-old private Anatolii Evdokimenko was serving in the army. Rotaru's future husband cut out the picture and declared, "*Those* are the kind of beauties we have in Ukraine!"[7] (To this day he carries the picture with him.[8]) He would have to wait a considerable time for an actual rendezvous. He searched for Rotaru in vain in her home town, but met her only after he enrolled at a local university where she subsequently came to perform. After their initial meeting at the concert Evdokimenko courted her for two years, until she finally gave in and broke her mother's wish that she marry only a Moldovan.

Rotaru entered and won the folk-song contest at the Ninth World Youth Festival in Bulgaria in 1968 only a few months after her marriage, beating out over fifty contenders. Several newspapers used the

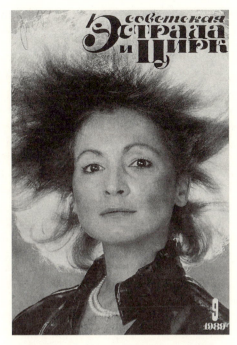

Rotaru wearing the pearls of a grande
dame but displaying both the abandon of
the 1980s and the whimsy of a performer
who had moved from her folk roots
to more overtly modern forms of
expression.

same headline: "Sofiia conquers Sofia!"[9] She sang a Moldovan pastoral, together with a Ukrainian military lament.[10] "The Vietnamese lads in the uniform of the defending People's Army understood the sense of the song without a translator – there were tears in their eyes."[11] The following year Rotaru entered the Moldovan State Institute for Arts. Her decision to stay home instead of heading for Moscow was endorsed (somewhat dramatically) in one early article: "Nothing enriches talent like proximity to one's native folk culture."[12]

It was in the year that Khrushchev died (1971), however, that the career for which Rotaru is known today truly took shape, with the formation of the ensemble Chervona Ruta. The name is Ukrainian for "red rue," a small flower not unlike a red buttercup. In one interview the soloist explained the origins of the collective's name: "Amongst the Carpathians we have a certain legend. In the hills there grows the yellow flower of the rue. Only once a year, exactly at midnight on

Midsummer's Night, the rue changes its yellow color to red, but only for a few minutes. If a girl is lucky enough to pluck the flower exactly at that moment of changing from yellow to red, she'll be able to charm any boy. They'll love each other and live in harmony … When people say '*Chervona ruta*', it's both a symbol of happiness and love."[13] In the group Evdokimenko had gathered together a number of suitable musicians, including himself as trumpeter. He would eventually join the band for good and abandon his career as an optical physicist.[14]

Chervona Ruta's success was sealed by a tour around the Soviet Union. One article describes how such contact with the "people" could have private, not just public consequence: "Rotaru's internal world widened and grew richer: she grew up, became more demanding of herself, her comrades, and her repertoire." The success came despite what she recalls as a tendency of state censors to "cut off the oxygen" to many creative ventures: "At that time you had to stick to a certain line, to sing optimistic songs. Something like 'Love, Komsomol and Spring.' And I sang 'The Enemy Burned Down My Hut' [already made famous by the performer Mark Bernes]. That didn't please the Ministry of Culture, so they cut the program."[15]

As perestroika appeared in the 1980s and Brezhnev passed away, criticism appeared of the so-called "stagnation" or *zastoi* of the preceding decade when Chervona Ruta had become famous. Ensembles popular during the period came in for censure. In Chervona Ruta's defence Rotaru insisted that "we always performed in the way we felt was necessary. It's another matter, though, when you run up against severe limitations placed upon your repertoire. They didn't let us, for example, perform songs that weren't written by members of the Soviet Composers' Union, even though you'd find really good works [elsewhere]. A Party ticket would decide a song's fate, not talent. Things could reach the ridiculous point where a song would come out on record, but they wouldn't let it on the TV, or if it was heard on the TV, then they'd drop it from the radio."[16] Such complaints were perhaps what led Rotaru in 1978 to ask that the Composers' Union create a special section for folk musicians, and therefore validate them officially.[17]

Along with such difficulties, there were less serious, more mundane ones: "A funny thing happened to us in Groznyi, when we appeared in a stadium. I went out onto the stage, elegant in a red, tight-fitting dress with a zip down the back. Right in the middle of the performance the zip broke. The audience noticed, of course. I'm holding the dress together with my hands so it doesn't fall off, when suddenly a kind-hearted citizen runs out on the stage with a huge safety-pin. He stands between me and the audience and saves me, to the great amusement of all concerned."[18]

One of the defining moments in Rotaru's decade of troubles with the Composers' Union and costume malfunction came in 1973, when she won the Zolotoi Orfei (Golden Orpheus) competition in Bulgaria and then a year later the International Festival of Estrada Songs in Sopot, Poland.[19] The first festival she won by a squeak; having just before lost her voice, she struggled with the tonality of her performance. But with such prestigious victories behind her, she had by 1976 become a People's Artist of Ukraine.

Counter to this success, however, ran constant rumours that she was sick, in particular with tuberculosis of the lungs, and her decision to move permanently to the southern resort of Yalta did little to allay such talk. The truth, however, was very different, as she explained years later. "I had one brother who had just served his time in the army and then another brother was also demobilized. New Years had come around, and the boys were still very young. Father had gone to sleep, and they managed to drag a big fir-tree out of the club and started to mess around with it. About 3 a.m. a car turned up at the house and Father was dragged off to the militia in what he was wearing. It was all caused by the rumour that he'd been taking part in some church service or other. Father, the first communist in the village, was turned out of the Party and my brother was kicked out of the komsomol. He had to leave the second year of the university there and then, since without the komsomol badge there was nothing to be done. It was a tragedy. I went to the First Secretary, who saw me and said: 'Do you really not understand that it's a crime? Go home and tell everyone not to do it any more.' I went home and found out that they'd also driven Father from his work – and he'd been head of a workers' team on the collective farm. We thought we'd lose him: he didn't sleep, he didn't eat, and started having some kind of attacks."[20] Thanks only to intervention from the director of the Crimean Philharmonia, whom Rotaru had met on tour, did word find its way through important channels to the ears of Brezhnev. As a result the head of the Ukrainian Communist Party offered the family an apartment in Yalta to escape local problems and prejudice.[21]

Since Rotaru has only been able to tell this tale in recent years, there was plenty of time for other stories to circulate, in particular one that her husband's greed had led her to perform concerts far in excess of a healthy norm. As a result, went the rumour, she was very often obliged to lip-sync at concerts and lost weight from subsequent stress. In an interview of 1978 she gives her heavy touring schedule as the reason for the need to move south and rest.[22]

It was, however, Rotaru's competition with Alla Pugacheva during the 1970s for the status of the Soviet Union's leading artist that fuelled the most gossip. On the heels of Pugacheva's record-breaking musical *A Woman Who Sings* (56.9 million viewers), Rotaru embarked on her own project, entitled *Soul (Dusha)* The film had begun as a vehicle for Pugacheva with her new husband, Aleksandr Stefanovich. Their marital problems during the filming brought the project to a standstill, and only then was Rotaru's name mentioned. "The idea pleased Stefanovich a great deal, since it was impossible to imagine better revenge against his [subsequent] ex-wife than to invite her prime and long-standing rival for the main role."[23]

The invitation to take part was a timely one for Rotaru, since she was recovering from the recent death of her friend and colleague, the Ukrainian composer Vladimir Ivasiuk, whom she had met when a student at the Chernivtsi Medical Institute.[24] Six weeks after he disappeared, last seen being driven off in a stranger's car, his body was found in a forest hanging from a tree. Officially the verdict was suicide, but Rotaru believes that either Ukrainian nationalists killed him, since he refused to write them a national anthem, or the KGB did the job. After Ivasiuk's death Rotaru sang less and less in Ukrainian.

Dusha gathered some of the biggest stars in Soviet music and cinema, all in a wonderfully mythologized premise: A singer, although warned of her increasingly serious illness, ignores her ailment, forms a new ensemble, and ventures forth onto the Soviet estrada.[25] Even though the film lagged behind Pugacheva's project, it was still a great success, with a fifth-place national showing in 1982 of 33.3 million viewers. The famous rock group Time Machine (*Mashina vremeni*) took part and contributed to Rotaru's development of a more youthful stage persona. One consequence was a strange influence of a stage *lichnost'* upon the real-world equivalent: as a result of the impression left by her role in *Dusha*, in the year Chernenko came to power – 1984 – Rotaru was held to have behaved too "provocatively" on tour in Canada and as a result lost the right to travel abroad for five years.

This did not stop her becoming a People's Artist of the Moldovan Soviet Socialist Republic in 1984 and in 1988 People's Artist of the U.S.S.R. But within a few years of her Soviet canonization, the notion of the U.S.S.R. as a centralized entity started to falter; certain nationalities along its edges began to voice ideas of independence with increasing volume. Because her fame was based on Russian-language songs, "things didn't look too rosy for Rotaru" in Ukraine or Moldova.[26] She was whistled and booed off the stage at a Lviv concert in 1989, only to watch Pugacheva come on afterwards with a blue and yellow Ukrainian flag to loud applause. Rotaru recalls, "I was very upset to see posters with the words: 'Sofiia, your punishment awaits you!' – But there were quite a few of my supporters too. It almost ended in fistfights. It was all so unpleasant … All the same I didn't hide my eyes from the hall. They're whistling, but I'm singing. I give them the finger! The TV crew are shouting at me: 'Get away from the spectator stands a bit further, don't taunt the geese …'"

In the early 1990s after Ukraine's independence, Rotaru found her performances dropped from Ukrainian TV line-ups and had to face numerous forms of provocation on stage. She was accused of not knowing the Ukrainian language and having sold out to Moscow. Even members of Chervona Ruta turned nasty. Rotaru, maintaining that she sang for all people, as long as they were prepared to respect one another,[27] disbanded the old ensemble and established a new one three weeks before an Australian tour. But even such speedy damage control could not outpace malicious nationalists who forwarded some Kievan newspaper clippings describing her as a Muscovite singer to a Ukrainian émigré newspaper in Sydney, which published them. As a result of such hassles, Rotaru swore never again to play in Ukraine. Only in 1996 when President Leonid Kravchuk asked her personally to break her vow did she go home to perform.

Within the Russian media, Rotaru has been part of a running story exciting enough to be worthy of Iosif Kobzon. It involves the purported Mafia kingpin Alimzhan Takhtakhunov, whom Rotaru met in 1972 during a Soviet tour. Takhtakhunov organized a huge feast for the singer in Uzbekistan. Rotaru has said that she was warned away from him in the mid-1980s by the Ministry of Internal Affairs, but the complete lack of evidence against him simply strengthened her resolve to continue their acquaintance. Pugacheva herself has said of Takhtakhunov, "Iosif Kobzon introduced me to him at the start of the 1980s … as Sofiia Rotaru's remarkable patron. When he told me that he helps her, I even envied her a little. These are the kind of sponsors you can count on one hand in the world of art, and to actually have one is a great joy … Any attention that he pays me is unforgettable, and I quite simply feel myself to be under the wings of a guardian angel."[28]

In recent years Rotaru's career has blossomed as she has released numerous recordings and continued to tour extensively. Her broad smile and brown eyes, clean, tanned features, and beautiful figure continue to disarm audiences as they have for decades. The glossy, chestnut hair falling straight from a central part has given way to more sculpted shapes fitting for a grand dame of the Soviet stage. She still lives in Yalta, despite a robbery in the summer of 1996 in which burglars climbed to the fifth floor, turned off the alarm, and took away as much in the way of technical items as possible. Notwithstanding this experience, she finds the peace and calm of Yalta a pleasant alternative to the high life of Moscow. "I don't like all the parties," she comments.

A photograph of Rotaru in concert in
the late 1990s shows the assurance of
a woman who has been acclaimed across
Eastern Europe for years.

"It seems to me that everything that goes on at them is insincere.
People party, figure out some scandal or other to get some exposure
on TV and get written about. I don't like that at all." Were she to live
in Moscow, however, she says she would "probably get together every
day with Irina Ponarovskaia."[29]

IRINA PONAROVSKAIA:
"PEOPLE CONSIDER ME A PATIENT WOMAN"

> If one follows your path through estrada, Irina,
> one gets the feeling that up until a certain
> point it was sprinkled with roses ... and then
> there's nothing but thorns.[30]

Nabokov once wrote that "to fix correctly, in terms of time, some of
my childhood recollections, I have to go by comets and eclipses, as
historians do when they tackle the fragments of a saga."[31] Nabokov

In the early 1990s Ponarovskaia,
evidently shown here during a
television performance, presented
a much more populist and less
glamorous image as conservatism
became a less determining factor
upon the estrada.

writes of salient moments in life which are then – retrospectively –
unified to create a sense of narrative. If we draw a parallel with the
plotting of a graph, itself conjured by the joining of such "comets" or
motley dots, then the very choice of these temporal signposts or points
of interest can determine a line's trajectory, bypassing many a lesser
moment. The more comets, the harder it is to draw a simple, straight
line across the sky.

Nabokov also maintains that "the following of ... thematic designs
through one's life should be the true purpose of biography."[32] If so,
there emerges something of a problem for the biographer of Soviet
popular culture. An individual's life in estrada, even though endorsed
and embraced by the Soviet media, tells a tale of constant struggle.
That embrace is never loving and often begrudging. Songs are played
and tours are staged, but only after enormous hassles, often of a
wholly bureaucratic nature. As each of our chosen singers' biographies

shows, the effort to get on stage, perform on stage, and then be allowed to advertise that stage was endlessly demanding. Whether a performer in relation to the Union was in some way confrontational or even fawning, the events of 1991 suddenly alter the situation and stakes enormously. There emerges a new need to plot different comets (to use Nabokov's terms). The state fostered a certain picture of a star, one available only through state-sponsored channels. Recently the free movement of information – cash permitting – has allowed for different events or eclipses to either be introduced for the first time (such as Rotaru's recent explanation of the move to Yalta), or to be replotted as part of a different trajectory. Into this second category fall incidents of a fundamentally "contrary" nature. Incidents of failure or loss at the hands of Soviet bureaucracy become early coordinates on a newly plotted line of (eventually) triumphant subversion; incidents of fawning are excused as necessary means of survival, acted out purely as ritual to allow the processes of real creativity to take place in a public arena.

Such a simplistic scheme, though, cannot hope to encompass the experience of every performer of the Soviet estrada, and indeed it is only intended as a rule of thumb. One fine exception is that of Irina Ponarovskaia. Although her plotting of eventful comets is clear in its intention, she nevertheless tells a story that does not allow the intricacies of human psychology to be reduced to political timetables. The year 1991 comes and goes, but the issues dealt with in Ponarovskaia's story are so entrenched in normal, quotidian Russian society that they stop us relying on the simple opposites of cold-war phraseology, on pre- and post-Soviet chronologies, and the concomitant notions of constraint and freedom. Ponarovskaia's biography, like that of Sofiia Rotaru, is acted out on a daily basis between the centre and periphery, between what I define in the title of this chapter as two positions, one "in" and the other "out" of Russia. This final dialectic is one much older than the crudities of Soviet politics. Whether the distinction between "in" and "out" is underwritten by gender, cultural condescension, or the ethnically coloured internal geography of the late Soviet Union is a matter to be decided over the next few pages.

Ponarovskaia was born in Leningrad, in March 1953 – just as Stalin died. She arrived two months prematurely, "although her mother did not particularly want her. She had tried to destroy the baby with quinine, vodka, hot baths, and had even danced around, all in order to cause a miscarriage – abortions were forbidden. The fetus held out. For some reason or other it had to."[33] Here we see comets being plotted far to one side of the night sky, before the woman herself has uttered a word.

The despair of Ponarovskaia's mother is understandable. Her father – Irina's grandfather – had been in Leningrad in 1941 while the Germans pounded it from the outskirts. In a moment of exhaustion, he wondered why it was even worth defending the place any more, especially since in the area he was stationed there was only one rifle for every ten men. Sadly, somebody heard this thought being uttered, and reported him. Thus began a chain of events that led, unbelievably, to a court case and a death sentence to be carried out by firing squad. At the last minute this was changed to ten years hard labour, but the man died of dysentery before he could be released.

Irina's mother became a celebrated pianist, often working as accompanist at major musical competitions. Irina's father was a jazz musician, playing the piano and accordion and singing in the restaurant of the Hotel Astoria which operates to this day. His musical career would be an influence of great future consequence; the hotel concerts were hugely popular in the Leningrad of the 1940s.[34] He had been overjoyed at the birth of his daughter, who quickly showed herself to be extremely stubborn, as her mother noted: "Ira even as a child decided everything herself. She learned exclusively through her own mistakes, never listening to advice or caution. She never surrendered to anybody. They'd say to her: Read – and she'd write. They'd say: Write – and she'd play on the piano. A demonstrative child – and that just emphasized her wilfulness."[35]

Ponarovskaia grew up on the Petrograd side of the city in a communal apartment, into which were squeezed two pianos, a double bass, a viola and a harp.[36] Given this context it is not surprising that she entered a musical school at the age of seven. When she later tried to get into a secondary school with affiliations to a conservatory, its standards were so competitive that only as she was bracing herself for a fourth attempt at entrance exams was she accepted to train on the harp. She had loved this instrument at home, but a harp presses hard on the player's chest and she had been advised because of a heart problem to move to the piano.

A prominent feature of Ponarovskaia's schoolday tales is her battle with her weight. "You're so fat," she was told, "boys'll never love you!" Her answer, in the form of a well-known Russian saying, was: "Men aren't dogs, they don't throw themselves at bones!" She began to lose weight after she started to sing. A vocal coach was found, and although her initial performances did little to impress her teacher, the young pupil was extremely persistent and diligent. Her father's work in the field of jazz had allow her to see some serious, rather tedious aspects of estrada, but that also did nothing to lessen her ardour. Her dreams of success were linked in her mind with being thin. Her mother found this worrying: "Irina's slimming was the cause of all my wrinkles. She'd either drink some tablets or simply not eat at all. When we all went off to the [resort of] Sochi, everyone at the hotel was amazed: her diet consisted each day of a glass of water and eggs. She refused bread all together."[37] A day's diet would be "tea or coffee, followed by fifty grams of cheese and an apple three hours later. After another three hours one hundred grams of meat, an egg-white, a cup of yoghurt, and that's the lot."[38] We see the pressures on an increasingly visible personality starting to tell on a young woman's psychology. (They intensify in Pugacheva's biography as she struggles with the same problems in the 1980s.)

Irina finished school accomplished on both harp and piano. In September 1971 as she began her conservatory studies, she was only two months away from going on stage for the first time with the Singing Guitars (*Poiushchie gitary*). The ensemble set off for Germany in the spring of 1972 as the SALT I talks were planned between Brezhnev and Nixon. At this same time she married a pianist in the group. The marriage lasted only one and half years, an outcome that was probably foreseeable, given Ponarovskaia's sobbing in the toilet on the day of the wedding. Her husband, Grisha, had been unfaithful with a neighbour, though this turned out to be only one of his failings. He was also, she said, incurably lazy and vulgar.

Undaunted as ever, Ponarovskaia continued her work with Poiushchie Gitary and went off to Dresden in 1975. For two years she had been involved in work on a real generic breakthrough, a musical written for the estrada, known as a *zong-opera*. Entitled *Orpheus and Eurydice*, by Aleksandr Zhurbin and Iurii Dimitrin, it was accompanied not by an orchestra but by the Guitars themselves. The group grew in number to about forty (!) members, yet remained inherently different from a traditional theatrical orchestra.[39] The waif-like nature of the heroine, played by Ponarovskaia, led her to slim further still, so much so that on one occasion she lost consciousness off-stage. Able somehow to withstand such self-imposed pressures, she played the role of Eurydice many, many times. She admits to falling in love with this role and crying on the show's final night.

After *Orpheus and Eurydice* closed, her eagerness to go and compete in the Dresden contest was seen by the ensemble as a desire to go solo.[40] Although the competition was considered unimportant even among the socialist countries taking part, Irina was overjoyed to win first prize. This victory proved a passport to the grander festival at Sopot; it also, as expected, led to her official departure from Poiushchie Gitary. The festival at Sopot was then one of the most prestigious among socialist nations, especially since its Polish location gave it an air of proximity to the West. Ponarovskaia won that contest also –

"proof that in other countries they accepted her a lot earlier and with greater accolade than in Russia."[41]

Suddenly she fell into a fairy-tale atmosphere. "There were autographs requested on the street. There were baskets of flowers set up in her hotel room. She organized a reception in a restaurant for the Soviet delegation, as there was no banquet for the winners ... Ira accepted the congratulations of fellow countrymen. Her dress had an open back, and suddenly somebody delicately touched her shoulder. She turned around and saw a queue of men. Each one went down on his knee and kissed her hand."

On her return to Moscow, however, no one was at the airport to meet her. In her hotel room she found a strange woman busy with her lover. But little by little, as the consequences of Sopot took shape, she became recognized and encountered such depressing rejections less often. She moved to Moscow and was able to perform in a variety concert at the prestigious Rossiia concert hall. She was also invited to take part in a 1978 film, *That Doesn't Concern Me* (*Menia èto ne kasaetsia*), and soon moved on to others such as *Robbery at Midnight* (*Ograblenie v polnoch'*).[42] Despite these successes, the move to Moscow was far from easy, and often she did not have enough money to buy either bread or stockings. Enormous patience was required for her to persevere until the better days of the late 1970s and early '80s, when she began to appear on television almost every month.

Robbery at Midnight certainly had its problems. "Even now I don't know how such an experienced director [Aleksandr Belinskii] could entrust me with the main role in his eccentric musical. In this vaudeville film there were a lot of pranks played and liberties taken that didn't suit everybody. That's probably why the film was shown only on Leningrad TV. Nowadays the things that worried people in the film seem nothing more than a faintly amusing joke. I think *Robbery at Midnight* is a film that would be in keeping with today's cinema."[43] This movie, which has a strong air of the small screen about it, concerns a robbery at a department store. The manager is staying late to do the books when an elderly burglar holds him up at gun point. To their mutual surprise, the two men hit it off – until they find themselves competing for the manager's mistress (Ponarovskaia) who pays an after-hours visit. Ponarovskaia's character here seems very distant from her respectable personality in the press, for she plays a *femme fatale*, moving without effort or conscience between the attentions of the two men. The film says in its conclusion that it has no moral, being a celebration of old-time vaudeville.

One comment by Ponarovskaia about her relationship to directors says a lot about her perceived position in the stage/hall dialogue of estrada. She senses the difficulties of public role-playing: "Things have always been hard for me because viewers relate to me as to something alien, even though I do nothing to encourage that view. It has never been easy for me to win an audience over, as I always seem to everybody to be different. I seem that way to directors, to viewers, to my own mother, although at least *she* now knows who I am in reality."[44]

These pressures of performing and popularity built up and up, to the point where Ponarovskaia collapsed during a November 1979 concert in Kursk. At the hospital it was discovered that her heart had stopped as a result of complications from kidney failure. She still, it appears, continued to have major eating problems, maintaining stubbornly that "excess weight is a problem of the brain."[45] That cultivated extreme slenderness has always been an essential part of her sophisticated blond glamour.

Nearly as big a problem as her health, perhaps, is that of prejudice, associated with her second marriage in 1981 to a black American jazz musician with dual citizenship, born in Moscow; U.S. economic sanctions of the same year can hardly have sweetened the situation. Whilst courting Irina, he told her of his previous wife, neglecting to mention four others before her. The arrival of their son, Anthony, came after Ponarovskaia had tried to adopt a girl, a plan that was scuttled when her husband insisted that the baby be turned over to an orphanage. He then took a lover, which only made things worse. His dual citizenship made it impossible for his wife to get the exit visas she required to perform in Germany and Poland, since officials feared that this international family would never return. Their apartment was broken into, and on one occasion while the couple were being interviewed by the police, they were accused of trading in foreign currency, since there were now relatives in America. Such pressures led to the marriage ending in 1988 and to Ponarovskaia's conclusion after the divorce, "I felt keenly how little a person needs. Just to live. Nothing more."[46]

In 1995 in the magazine *Kul'tura* she spoke angrily about this marriage and the invasion of privacy it led to: "There is a great deal allowed people who love to rummage around in others' lives. I live so quietly that these people try to make a sensation out of anything trivial ... I married a man with differently coloured skin. From that marriage I had a son ... We got divorced, but I spent quite a few years in that situation both sincerely and honestly. They write all kinds of nastiness about me. It hurts, because I don't deserve it, it hurts my mother. May it be on the conscience of those who write it, that's what I reckon."

In January 1986, three months before the Chernobyl' disaster, she was baptized at age thirty-two together with her son in Moscow, a decision taken not only from a growing faith but also in an attempt to improve her son's failing health. Her belief had increased slowly since early days of listening to church choirs. At that time she had started to appreciate the beauty of a church interior and thus her attraction towards the institution had grown.[47] This faith has allowed her some considerable relief from the battering she has taken in the material world. In a 1996 interview with the newspaper *Sobesednik*, she defines the biggest disappointment in her life as the loss of her health, the greatest success as getting it back and her most cherished dream as the elusive ability to *remain* healthy.[48]

Ponarovskaia had also begun to have trouble with her voice, a problem some said had arisen from charity performances near Chernobyl'. By 1988 she was recording concert repertoires on tape, in case her voice gave out completely and she was obliged to lip-sync from start to finish.[49] A letter that year to a national newspaper complained that she performed to recordings whilst on Rotaru's Siberian and Far-Eastern tour: "Does the recipient of such high honours really have such bad taste?"[50] Another rumour was that she had been at the bottle. Ponarovskaia vehemently denied this: "Getting drunk means losing control of yourself. Then you're ashamed of your behaviour, ashamed of your own stupidity. Anything that's shameful is not for me. I won't allow myself to damage my sense of self-worth."[51]

Once again in the summer of 1990 her apartment was burgled when she was on tour, as Ukraine announced its planned sovereignty and Yeltsin dropped out of the Communist Party. The break-in and continued kidney problems led to a bout of depression the following year. Although her situation and presence on the estrada improved as the U.S.S.R. faded away, she nevertheless continued to battle various ailments, again losing consciousness at a 1993 concert in Donetsk. Only a lengthy kidney operation returned her to health. Such an intense schedule allowed her – finally – to acquire a Mercedes. But one month after her release from hospital, she left the car for fifteen minutes to enter a store and came out to discover it was gone.[52] After that disaster she bought herself a considerably cheaper Volga.[53] In a sad interview before the crime in the newspaper *Trud* she talks of that same Mercedes: "They've burgled my apartment but it would probably be hard to take the car. It's in a garage with both blocks and an alarm."[54]

During her extended hospital stays she met a doctor by the name of Dmitrii Pushkar', a future member of the American and European Associations of Urologists.[55] By the end of 1993 their romance had flourished, and whenever possible they combined overseas medical conferences with international tour dates. Once again, though, bad luck returned to claim its own: an early-morning television fitness program which she hosted was cancelled, her son fell ill with asthmatic

For much of her career Ponarovskaia has
subjected herself to dietary torture in
order to look good – most successfully,
as this picture from 1999 shows.

attacks, and on a domestic tour her new car was burnt to a crisp,
perhaps torched by an ill-wisher.[56] In the cause of sanity, Dr Pushkar'
and Ponarovskaia married in June 1995, although the rigours of long-
distance touring and the constant attentions of the singer's male
admirers have done little to make their situation an easy one today.

In September 1997, the 850th birthday of Moscow was celebrated
in New York with a program at Carnegie Hall entitled "America Wel-
comes Moscow." Russian estrada was represented by Irina Ponarovskaia. Looking back on the road that led to this point, she says, "God
sends a tough life to those he wants to test, and an easy one to those
whom he does not. Have I really had only a few tests? I think I've had
enough."[57] Journalists have noticed that Ponarovskaia's private problems have at times been absorbed into her stage persona. In 1990 an
observer commented that "again and again she returns [in her songs]
to the story of a difficult love – a modern woman, living in the modern
world. Sometimes things seemed cramped and uncomfortable. It's
hard for her to battle with loneliness, but she must never give in to it
… It's the same in the songs; in even the most dramatic songs there's
optimism and strength so that you're left inspired."[58]

Such strength is a limited resource, however, and in the careers of Ponarovskaia and Rotaru we start to see the workings of estrada swamping those who try to make estrada work for them.

NATURE OF THE BUSINESS: THE PRESSURES OF ESTRADA

I don't have to please everyone.[59]
Sofiia Rotaru

Only idiots are completely happy.[60]
Irina Ponarovskaia

As early as 1976, Rotaru was concerned that her private expressions on the estrada had snowballed into a public process with no end; the business of being a personality (star) had subsumed the private personality:

I have to find enough strength within myself to get away from the everyday rush. For the last few years I haven't at all belonged to myself. I rush around all kinds of towns from concert to concert, and when I want to get together with my thoughts, to be at home just to think a little about what I'll be singing next, I'm told: "You've got to fly off here and there, sing this and that ..." I'm in tears, but everybody knows that Sofiia will cry a little and, after all's said and done, agree to do it. My indecisive character will be the death of me ... Tell me why there's such a rush all around me? I make a recording at Melodiia, five songs to be done over three hours. Then I listen to it and think: Is that really me? No proper breathing, and a "narrow" voice. I'm ready to drop it all and do these songs over a week, even a month. Am I really reasoning naively? Am I really so very wrong?[61]

Journalists seemed to have equal trouble pinning down the ever-mobile singer: "Getting her at home, in Yalta, turned out to be far from simple. 'Gone off to rehearsals,' 'Doing a concert on a state farm' ... 'Call back in about ten days – she's on tour.'"[62] In an article of *Sovetskaia Èstoniia* in 1990, Rotaru complains that the added burden of foreign tours – in her case, to America, Israel, Australia, and Canada – is worsened by the inability of the U.S.S.R. to advertise its own artists properly, so each Russian-language performer abroad has to "start from ground zero." [63] The business of being a Soviet personality is as geographically limited as the ideology behind it. The public personality is clearly capped, the private afforded no time at all. These socio-political pressures make time spent on stage vitally important in the formation of a subjective *lichnost'*, time of uninterrupted communion of stage and hall, of singer and persona, without the ugly intrusion of the singer/state dialectic that takes up *all* her time off-stage. The significance of estrada as a superior, parallel version of quotidian reality increases along with the pressures upon those who effect that superiority – the singers.

Another new aspect of estrada pressures and the way in which they are discussed by the media is competition or envy between various *lichnosti*. A 1990 interview asks Rotaru how she reacts to a comment by Alla Pugacheva, that nobody except Pugacheva herself is actually producing hit records. "She is a great singer," replies Rotaru diplomatically. "I relate to her statement with a certain lack of understanding." From such delicate thrusts and parries, the pressures of the business in estrada grow with each year to larger, louder dimensions.

These pressures can already be heard in interviews with Ponarovskaia. Musing on her participation in variety competitions as a judge, she says: "I bow before the kids coming into the context of today's estrada, those young people who do so by honest means, by displaying their own talent – and not looking for sponsors ready to buy air time and concert space for performers who know two and a half notes."[64] She herself is neither the talentless protégé of a wealthy sponsor, devoid of all personality, nor the talented protagonist of scandals, the Pugachevian type of persona deliberately woven by an excessively large *lichnost'*. Looking back in 1993, she says, "I've been on the estrada for twenty-three years and can say with pride that interest in me hasn't fallen yet. Sure, I was never a singer with a scandalous reputation or with super popularity, but I always had my public. Stability is many times dearer to me than any fleeting or decade-long success, even. I want to be in this for the long haul – and I've still got something to show, something that'll surprise."

What has conversely surprised Ponarovskaia is the credulity of her audience, its acceptance of an often scandalous stage persona as synonymous with its presenter, the singer. Worse still, audiences often embrace and embellish that stage persona in their minds to the point where it overtakes reality. "Fans sometimes assume things about me that I can only guess about. The only thing you can do is be amazed at their fantasies."[65]

Such amazement in its extreme expression can quickly become despair and then disdain. Ponarovskaia's most biting critique of estrada is "I Don't Give a Damn" (*Mne naplevat'*). She sings of how hard it is "to be completely alone in this evil world" *or* away from her beloved. What spoils the "dialogue" of two people, the simple lyricism that this entire genre has tried to cultivate since the death of Stalin, is the very (public) structure of that genre. Estrada – either as home to large *lichnosti* who have *become* their stage personae or as an industry – ruins the aesthetic or even ethical intent of the songs that it produces. The stage/hall dialogue has produced an unnatural merger of performer and staged persona. Estrada now expects and demands these unnatural dimensions. Ponarovskaia, unwilling to fill boots that big for most of her career, was unable to release albums. In 1996 she did so with *And So My Life Goes By* (*Tak prokhodit zhizn' moia*). It includes the acerbic song referred to above, and attacks the media pressures around her that began in the 1970s and exploded after 1991. Here the rapid fire of (synthesized) horns punctuates vigorous percussion in a way that recalls Utesov's spontaneous, syncopated tomfoolery. The deliberate use of poorly played keyboards and doo-wop backing vocals combines critique and clowning around in a time-honoured fashion.

Мне наплевать, что говорят,
Я не могу другом быть всем подряд,
И не надо, и не надо.
Вам надо знать, чем я дышу,
С кем и куда каждый вечер спешу:
Кто там рядом? Кто там рядом?

[I don't give a damn what they say. I can't be friendly with everyone at once – I don't have to be, I don't have to. You have to know how I breathe, with whom and where I hurry off every evening. Who's that with you? Who's that with you?]

Not only does the media fantasy correspond to fact but the fictions of estrada have become so bold that they cause desperate behaviours. When asked what she thinks about the tendency today of the business to be "self-seeking, to produce hack-work, to look for well-paid criminals," Ponarovskaia blames both "a lack of taste in the public and tastelessness on the stage: they're mutually connected." There is an overt hostility here to the audience, together with a paradoxically desperate desire to please them: "You think it's easy to go on – and especially off – stage to the sound of your own footsteps? Five or six feeble claps in the auditorium, more like slaps to the face – that's worse! I've been through all that but, all the same, I insist that even if at my concerts or the biggest halls three-quarters of the seats are empty, I won't sing cheap stuff!"[66]

Her conflict with the tendencies of modern estrada takes on a moral hue: "The world of estrada is both beautiful and frightening. You need more than a voice and to be attractive. You need a conscience, too."[67] The development of a conscience is linked to the moderation of one's *lichnost'*. Here we see – implicitly – the definition of a process that Ponarovskaia halts in the name of taste and conscience. The grand public workings of Soviet estrada would prefer a *lichnost'* to sacrifice itself, to forget the stage/hall dialogue in favour of the singer/state. The creation of a subjective *lichnost'* between oneself and the audience, or oneself and one's stage personae, can, if one crosses a line (defined by Ponarovskaia's view of conscience), become instead the creation of an "alien, objective" personality designed for public, not private purposes. By this she means that as the hall and stage demand more of each other, the bold roles of the performer become so "stagey" that they no longer have anything to do with the artist. The role overtakes the actor, because the audience *wants* it to. This is the line that Pugacheva will happily cross, displaying an egoism that destroys her quotidian self in favour of her roles.

Although Pugacheva may play up to audience demands, she does not do so out of a P'ekhian "sympathy." She rides the extreme end of the stage/hall dialogue in order to foster the performer/persona discourse, one that allows her later to foist her persona *back upon* the audience in the monologic manner of stardom.

Ponarovskaia suggests a synonymy between egoism, illness, and the lack of a true, balanced dialogue of mutual sympathy. "I think that egoism is caused by not loving yourself. People should look after themselves, after their health, in order not to badly effect the surroundings. When a person's ill, those close to that person suffer no less. Therefore it's easier to be ill yourself than sympathize with another. So to not look after yourself is a great expression of egoism. To not care for your appearance is also egoistic, because you don't realize that it's unpleasant to look at you, that you cause unpleasant emotions in others. You have to love yourself, but not *for* yourself."[68]

The altruistic egoism that Ponarovskaia advocates here, strange as it is, forms a bridge between P'ekha and Pugacheva. The social will soon lessen in favour of the private, and the objectively useful in favour of the subjectively beneficial; but before that happens, the private will rise to meet the challenge of the Soviet estrada juggernaut. A *lichnost'* will grow to a grand, social scale in the 1980s before a truly subjective and self-perpetuating personality is engendered in Pugacheva. Ponarovskaia can hear this juggernaut picking up speed and is already troubled by the processes at hand. A great deal of tension is involved in the shift from public to private, from a widely accepted social stance (the limit of stage/hall) to a lonely and often maligned one (the incipient performer/persona), as Ponarovskaia herself admits. She is not willing to challenge the grand operations of Soviet variety. "If I had to begin life anew, then I'd probably never be a singer again. Not just because it's physically hard – and all the more so for a woman. It's just that there's so much pain, so many obstacles on the way, that sometimes you simply give up."[69] Her surrender is caused in part by being so close to the centre of estrada's increasingly businesslike workings. Rotaru, on the other hand, is seen as inherently free from urban stresses, being from the rue-dappled Carpathians. Soviet perceptions of these two spaces, of the urban Ponarovskaia and the rustic Rotaru, also deserve our attention as influences upon the development of personality.

GEOGRAPHY AS A DETERMINANT OF PERSONALITY: CENTRE AND PERIPHERY

В ее таланте слиты воедино
Мощь голоса и преданность эстраде –
Народная артистка Украины
Поет о Кишиневе в Ленинграде.

[The power of her voice and loyalty to estrada
are merged as one in her talent. The "People's
Artist of Ukraine" sings of Kishinev in
Leningrad.][70]

When Rotaru went to the World Festival of Youth and Students in 1968, she was rigid with fear. Only when she felt herself to be at home in her surroundings did her anxiety recede; suddenly she was "light, free and unfettered. And then she won." These emotional or psychological markers are frequently linked to Rotaru's rustic beginnings in the Soviet press: "The six Rotaru children had fine voices, an extraordinary musical ear ... Everybody sang in the village, for here the very land rears songs. You go beyond its outskirts and all around are hills and forest. The heady vineyards, alive with the sounds of bees calling to the babbling brooks that tumble down into the valley, the ancient Carpathian Mountains, their unique nature and distinctive Hutsul art, all gave Sofiia strength and gave her songs wings."[71] These clichés continue almost ten years later when Rotaru sings two songs that recall "two buckets of water [poured] from a clean earthenware jug, two sunny bunches of grapes, two wings carrying a girl from her village to a twentieth-century estrada lit by spotlights.[72]" Rotaru herself offers a description of how her songs originated in these idyllic surroundings: "There was always a song waiting on the doorstep at home. Half the village can [still] sing, and the other half can play accompaniment. Dozens of marriages are celebrated in the village over autumn at which there is as much music, dancing, and singing as there is at international festivals. My father plays the violin well, sings gently, even though he leads a group of workers in the vineyards from dawn till dusk.[73]"

Rotaru is well aware of her career as a marked deviation from the normal path of a young woman in such surroundings. In particular she draws the distinction between a typical life and her own experience at the outset of matrimony. She is making her commitment to the stage, not a spouse, and thus spoils the idyll.

I wait for that day on tour when I'll turn up in my home village and run out into the courtyard barefoot. I'll feed the chickens and the geese, I'll watch as mother milks the cow. My parents have a complete farm-holding. A great orchard. I love to go fishing. Tonik, my husband, when I first brought him to see our village, doubted that I knew how to fish – so I got out of bed at 4 a.m., dug up some worms and brought back forty carp for breakfast ... It's common practice for a girl in our village to finish school, get married and stay to work on the collective farm. Since childhood, though, I wanted to study music, wanted to become a singer, and my father believed that I'd become a singer, too.[74]

The sense of stability and spatial containment in all Rotaru's stories of Chernivtsi – an idyllic chronotope – are reflected in the interpretation of her work by the Soviet press. There is no modern, ideologically troubling sense of breached boundaries, no Pugachevian rebellious or urban subversion. "This dancing voice, this sung dance – haven't they come down to us as an inheritance from a primitive culture, when melody, words and movement were merged as one (*slity voedino*)?"[75] The political or philosophical connotations of such a spatially "pocketed" cultural expression, of the ethnic songs of Chervona Ruta, are clear when they are termed *in toto* by Soviet critics "ideological or progressive (*ideinaia*) estrada." The progression in actual fact comes not from any sort of real advancement; the implicit thought in the critics' definition is that the best thing for ethnic Ukrainian or Moldovan art to do when it comes to the capital is to do nothing at all. By being "ethnic," by staying culturally committed to the distant villages of Ukraine or Moldova and not making a separatist fuss, Rotaru et al. are being "progressive," aiding the Soviet cause. The rationally conceived immobility of an imperial ideology looks cautiously upon the "peripheral" songs of Rotaru's Ukrainian and Moldovan youth that were "fervent, lyric and passionate."[76]

An indicative song of this passionate lyricism is "Your Traces" (*Tvoi sledy*), with words by Evgenii Evtushenko. The rustic setting of the song is a snowy landscape, far from large social centres of durable political policy. This is the landscape of transience and lonely subjectivity. The speaker has lost his/her other, whose presence and parting is written by footsteps in the snow. The link lost in the material world to absence and distance can be forged anew by memory, tears, and love by one person for another. Spaces in the material world cannot beat this private memory, since there are "no traces that leave no traces." Ubiquitous orchestration, which (together with jazz) marks one of the greatest differences between Soviet and western popular music, is once again evident in this ballad. A private loss is raised by an immaculately dressed orchestra to the universal drama of the song's closing chords, to a final, powerful roll of kettle-drums. The private thought dissolves briefly in a sound that is heard everywhere:

Твои следы
В сугробах у реки.
Как из слюды,
Они тонки.
Чуть подморозило
Два крошки-озера,
И звезды в них дрожат,
Светясь, как угольки.

Возьму в ладонь
Хотя б один твой след,
Но только тронь –
Он просто снег,
Он разлипается,
Он рассыпается,
И вот в руке одна вода,
А следа нет.

Внутри твоих следов лед расставанья,
Но поверни, но поверни следы обратно,
Сквозь чуждые следы, сквозь расстоянья –
По собственным слезам, по собственным следам.

[Your traces in snowdrifts by the river. They are fine, as if made of mica. Barely frozen, two tiny little lakes and stars tremble in them, shining like coals. I take even one trace of you in my hand, I but touch it – it's simply snow, it unsticks and spills. There's just water in my hands, with no traces. There's the ice of partings in your traces, but return, return those traces across the traces of other people, across the distance – return them by your own tears, your own traces.]

Evtushenko's text speaks of a sense of self that exists outside of grand, centralized social schemes, yet it feels no sense of permanence in the world. One factor in the creation of a new *lichnost'* after Èdita P'ekha was how to develop the work of Druzhba, seemingly in an attempt to slow or calm the processes of personality's increasing isolation or independence, born of the stage/hall dialogue and the burgeoning workings of stardom. Estrada wanted to integrate the lonely personality of a solo singer with the more social, new and quickly modish phenomenon of musical ensembles, made often of several people – most of whom could sing.

FROM ENSEMBLE TO VIA: THE SOCIALIZATION (OR DISSIPATION) OF PERSONALITY

In a very early article on Chervona Ruta from 1976, Rotaru remarks that "working in the ensemble I learned how to find something in every song which allows us to express a person's internal world with the greatest depth. Our ensemble's creativity cannot be separated from folk traditions."[77] Those traditions foster a sense of individuality, as one description of a concert explains: "Rotaru presents herself as a unique beauty, one who knows her own worth. Her heroine won't sit to one side waiting for her beloved, won't break her neck rushing after the first man to ask, 'May I have this dance?' She moves bravely into the circle [of male performers] and herself makes a lad happy with her choice. She remains independent, cunning, mocking, chaste, externally carefree, while all the while filled with an expectation of great love in her soul."

Rotaru compared her ensemble with a figure-skating partner. Evdokimenko considered his soloist the bright, concluding stroke in a jointly created painting. At times in interviews she talks of her art as essentially dialogic, in the manner we have seen with P'ekha and others: "A song is a conversation with another person. I look for the kind of song that a listener will believe in at the moment of its performance."[78] As I suggested in my discussion of Il'enkov's philosophy earlier on, it is in this dialogic process that an alternative to entirely material semantics is created. "In each successful song, there is both outward show and a soul. I strive in each song which I perform to see that soul and bring it to my listener. That means trying to create a way or means of being social (*obshchenie*) with people."[79] In 1978 she makes a similar observation, that the image of a song's hero and feelings need in that song to be brought to the listener.[80] What is interesting is how the dialogue or *obshchenie* permitting such images is expressed in the tiny social unit of a musical collective.

When Moscow no longer bothered jamming Voice of America broadcasts and Reagan set off to visit Moscow, new styles appeared within Soviet estrada: in the late 1980s, Rotaru spoke of similar yet new dialogues that needed to be established, all as part of a "democratic" process. "Now [1988] we are experiencing a type of democratic explosion in songs on the estrada. Songs are now more varied than ever before. Lots of styles, directions and searching going on. Searching for one's listener – who, in turn, is looking for and finding a performer to his taste."[81] For Rotaru, her own personal "search" was for a significance beyond material experience, one that could be cultivated in the stage-auditorium dialogue. "A singer, if he wants to be understood, has to find a response in the soul of his listener, he must know well and feel that listener." Such contacts are made ethically: "Goodness opens the heart wide. If a singer knows the cares and feelings of his listeners, then his songs will excite, cheer and make people sad. That's when a unity arises with the viewers in the hall. People are grateful when art helps them see the unusual in the usual, when it helps them to know themselves better."[82]

All well and good, but what happens when the search is on for subjective development within an ensemble? What about "creative individuality and an ensemble, the self-expression of a unique artistic *lichnost'* and a collective?"[83] Ponarovskaia's story answers in part this question, the relationship between being in a collective and then so alone that one relies in the hard times of lonely creativity upon "God [or] ideas from somewhere within me."[84] Rotaru in a similar vein has called naïve the belief that it is easy to work outside of an ensemble and still be popular, as she says of her ex-colleagues in Chervona Ruta, "Where are they now? Practically all without work."[85] Fortunately, Ponarovskaia "loves to be alone." Her faith grants a certain logic to that isolation. At a time in the early 1990s when there was some modishness attached to Christian conversions, she tried "not to advertise my views. Faith went away and deep within [me]." She loses the *obshchenie* of an ensemble but finds a divine, infinitely superior alternative with which to develop her *lichnost'*.

Before Ponarovskaia found herself pondering such matters, she was in the ensemble Singing Guitars. This was a group that helped to institute the phenomenon of VIAs, concisely explained by one well-known Russian journalist.

The first professional pop bands were the Singing Guitars (Leningrad) and the Happy Guys (Moscow). The words "rock" and "beat" were unwelcome, and so these kids (and the dozens of others who flooded into the philharmonias) were officially christened VIA (the initials [in Russian] for vocal/

instrumental ensemble). VIA was a disciplined (or, to be frank, castrated) version of beat music. A VIA band usually had around ten musicians in its line-up (rhythm section, two guitars, organ, some horns and a couple of singers, often with tambourines) and a repertoire including Shadows-style covers of melodies from English and American hits and routine pop tunes with soft electric sound. Dreadfully boring, but it was a stage in our cultural revolution and, in fact, a real sensation in the provinces where people seriously thought that electric guitars were like regular acoustic ones except that you plugged them into the wall like a radio to make them louder![86]

While I would argue that Druzhba were the real instigators of the VIA phenomenon, the writer is correct in defining here the sound of most future VIAs, a sound much closer to the work of Poiushchie Gitary. The increased volume and decreased professionalism of such ensembles caused considerable concern. A primary objection was that although VIAs had several soloists, not all of them had the vocal gifts to deserve a turn at the microphone; even Druzhba came under fire when P'ekha gave up the limelight to another male member of the group.[87]

Poiushchie Gitary's basic composition was four guitars, a piano, organ, trumpet, and drummer. This modern membership was used to produce not only contemporary songs and instrumentals but also reworkings of folk classics. "In their work upon these songs the ensemble did not [however] strive to carefully reproduce the folk manner of singing. In their own modern reading they tried instead to keep the image [*obraz*] or mood of the [original] song."[88] The members of the group were "charming and rhythmic, which allowed them to move freely around the stage. They knew how to use elements of *teatral-izatsiia*, often setting up laconic *mis en scènes* which need light or sound effects, all to create visual images of the songs." Although doubts were often cast over the vocal quality of VIAs (as in the case of Poiushchie Gitary), their musical expertise was conversely felt to be much greater than the quality of their repertoire; they played well – when they tried – but wrote badly.

As noted, the most important event for Ponarovskaia's career after she became soloist for the Singing Guitars in 1972 was the musical *Orpheus and Eurydice*. "It was the first move on our estrada towards a large musical form, an experiment that opened up new possibilities for the art of variety."[89] The scenario, taken from Greek myth, is described by the newspaper *Komsomol'skaia pravda* in 1975 as follows. Eurydice gives Orpheus a song to take to a competition of great singers. Orpheus as a result becomes famous and is idolized, yet he forgets the song given to him by his beloved. Thus the white bird of love dies at Eurydice's feet; Eurydice also dies as a consequence of Orpheus's infidelity to his song and its creator. The work's subject was perceived by the Soviet press to be the "spiritual growth of *lichnost'*, the drama of talent, swapping itself for cheap popularity – but finally [finding] love and self-sacrifice." It was performed to music of "keen and dynamic rhythms, coming from modern estrada songs. The composer [Aleksandr Zhurbin] broadened the palette of the guitar-based ensemble, adding to it on occasion the sounds of a symphony orchestra."[90]

The musical went on – by the time SALT II was signed by Carter and Brezhnev in 1979 – to play more than eight hundred times in different towns around the Soviet Union.[91] Such success inspired another work in the same genre, a rock opera entitled *The Flemish Legend*. The work of the Singing Guitars in these large forms led the newspaper *Trud* to pronounce that "the ensemble has become theatre." It was even suggested by the journal *Sovetskaia èstrada i tsirk* that the VIA rename themselves VIT: *Vokal'no – instrumental'nyi teatr.*

That theatre grew a little too big for its Soviet audience at times, because *Orfei* was criticized – despite its great success – for emotional excess.[92] Theatrical excess was just as salient an issue when Rotaru and Ponarovskaia tried their hands at mastering the aesthetic demands of the silver screen. *Lichnost'* is snowballing in the stage/hall dialogue; not even the mini-society of an ensemble can slow or dissipate it. Will things be any different when these two singers start working in cinema?

PERSONALITY AT THE MOVIES: AFTER ÈDITA P'EKHA

By nature I'm a sincere and open person,
but watching myself on TV I see a happy
woman, one who has absolutely no problems or
whose problems effectively resolve themselves –
and all in a picturesque manner, just like
the movies.[93]

Sofiia Rotaru

A brief overview of Rotaru's career published in 1985 comments in response to the widespread, negative influence of ostentatious *teatralizatsiia* on the Russian stage: "Rotaru does not get dressed up – she instead dresses her songs."[94] The concerns here over attempting to draw a marked line between the stage and quotidian reality are brought to life in an episode regarding the singer's son, Ruslan. As she was performing the famous "Ballad of a Mother" who has lost her son in battle and the chorus rang out in mourning for a certain "Aleksei," Ruslan could not understand for whom his mother was mourning. "The main thing," she remarks, "is that the person and the song are indivisible." Given the hyperbole inherent in such songs, it is not surprising that at times Rotaru has been criticized for excess as she rises to meet the song's heroine in the discourse of performer and persona: "Her openness can transgress into sentimentalism; her air of tragedy into boundless exaltation; her *pafos* into a declamatory pose." This same critic praises, nonetheless, the ability of songs performed by Rotaru, such as "Where Are You, Love?" (*Gde ty, liubov'*) by Il'ia Reznik and Raimonds Pauls, to survive the bad film in which they were showcased.

Two of the wonderful songs, also by Reznik and Pauls, from that supposedly awful film fit our story well. Like the "passionate lyricism" of "Tvoi Sledy," both create a world of immateriality, full of emotions yet devoid of things and people. Lush with horns and strings, their texts tell of the link between songs and the creative yet immaterial world of natural growth. "Early May" (*Nachalo maia*) manages to banish sadness with the power of music, which by its intangible *sounds* becomes a dialogue between the singer and something else, an entity or significance not yet noticed by that singer's lover. He "does not even understand that I love him." Sadness is sent packing to a disco rhythm. Given that style's use of strings in the West, the orchestral traditions of Soviet estrada are easily altered to fit the core structure of bass and hi-hat that guide any disco composition. Despite this apparent nod to western fashion, though, the horn section in Rotaru's song sits strangely between two modes: the traditions of Utesov et al. can be heard staking their claim in the middle of arrangements that suggest, for example, a (very) distant influence of the group Earth Wind and Fire.

Апрель, начало мая –
Струится звонкий дождь
Дождя не замечая
На встречу ты идешь.

[April and early May – the resonant rain pours down, but you go to your rendezvous not noticing the rain.]

The title song of *Where Are You, Love?* also wonders where love or a lover has gone, vanishing without a trace (*bessledno*). She asks that he return his footsteps or traces (*sledy*) to her with love. Only then will there be a union or interaction of some sort that will allow her to believe in the "impossible."

Солнечным днем, солнечным днем, одиноко мне.
В доме твоем, в доме твоем ночь за окнами.

В двери стучу, в двери стучу осторожно я –
Верить хочу, верить хочу в невозможное.

[On a sunny day, a sunny day, I'm alone. In your house, in your house,
there's night beyond the windows. I knock carefully at the doors, at the
doors; I want to believe, want to believe in the impossible.]

This film was released in 1980 and seen by just over twenty-one
million people across the Soviet Union. It is far from bad and of great
use to us. The parallels with Rotaru's own life are obvious. She never
tried to deny such links; in fact, in an interview of early 1981, she
remarks that the overlap of real life and movies made the work
"extraordinarily complicated, and that means it was interesting."[95] Her
life is lived privately, retold publicly, and then re-experienced privately
by the audience. Her life and films are interconnected. If they were
not public, they could not be seen and given private resonance. *Gde
ty, liubov'* is the story of a young woman teaching in a provincial music
school after graduating from a conservatory. She is invited to participate in a musical group, led by the handsome Viktor. This initial
meeting is the impetus for the film's ensuing romance and the great
success that awaits the songs their happy union creates. In September
of that same year Rotaru gave an interview to the magazine *Soviet Screen*
(*Sovetskii èkran*) concerning the film. The interview, writes the journalist, was sought because everyone wanted to know about "an interesting
lichnost' on the estrada, one who has her own particular view of the
world and tries not only to entertain us but first and foremost to
enthral us with the thought and feeling of a real artist."[96]
Rotaru saw at this time two basic ways in which musical estrada and
the movies might be of mutual benefit. The first is what she terms a
film-concert, "a bright spectacle, with no pretence towards an especially profound content or thorough development of the heroes'
characters." Here we can see her concerns about *teatralizatsiia* as
spectacle and little else. The other possibility is an "artistically complete work, one that does not have one-sided personages ... the music
and songs become an element of the drama, have some sense of their
own, contain a well-defined theme and serve to develop certain
images. Sadly there have been few such films thus far." (In fact, in
another interview for *Sovetskaia Rossiia*, Rotaru blames performers if
their audience pays too much attention to the staging of a song. In
such cases, she maintains, the performer is unable to hold the hall's
attention with the songs alone).
The journalist points out that while *Where Are You, Love?* has taken
something of a critical drubbing in some quarters, Rotaru's acting
saves the production. The singer sidesteps pointed questions, hidden

amidst flattery, and says only that her cinematic career is just beginning; another, better film entitled *Soul (Dusha)* is in the works. She emphasizes not her past achievements but her future intent: "The main thing for me as an artist is to share my feelings and thoughts on life with the viewers. It's maximum faith in those who sit either in the concert hall, by their TV, or in a movie theatre."

Elsewhere she talks about *Where Are You Love?* as part of the "difficult process of becoming a singer." An interview in the newspaper *Gudok* allowed her to be a little more explicit, to explain that a film should be supported by, not entirely about, songs. "In this case, the accent was laid [by the director] upon the commercial side of things, on the popularity of the singer [i.e., myself]. The songs were put forward as the main focus at a time when they should have been an addition to the subject, even in musical films such as this. Nobody bothered to find a good director. No, I haven't given up hope on the movies. There just hasn't been any suitable material for me."[97]

When *Dusha* does appear, it also fares poorly with the critics. In the prestigious *Literaturnaia gazeta*, a columnist notes that Rotaru's shift from a folkloric to rock-oriented emphasis is a failure, albeit one to which she is "completely entitled" as an artist.[98] Drawing a comparison between Rotaru and Pugacheva, the journalist remarks that these women are "thoughtful, demanding, and serious artists who have raised estrada songs to the level of a deeply lyrical confession. But why does that mean they have to dramatically lose all sense of measure, the sense of their viewer, or the sense of popularity, when we're talking about a cinematic version of their craft? Why do they have to present themselves before a wide viewership (and both films have had great success) as capricious, hysterical, and crotchety super-divas, all in the style of some *fin de siècle* decadence?" It all boils down to what – in 1982 – is termed "a stereotypical presentation of artistic individuality." Rotaru's personality is now outstripping Ponarovskaia's, amplified as it is by the large dimensions of social art (cinema) to present a sung, lyrical confession. Within the context of cinema the stage/hall dialogue is reaching Pugachevian dimensions.

Rotaru and her performance in *Dusha* received extended investigation in *Sovetskii èkran*. "In the film there are obvious attempts to break the canon of 'films about estrada stars.' This strict canon managed to form as early as the Twenties, with the introduction of sound and the exploitation of 'singing objects' – opera, operetta, estrada, and jazz singers. The 'road to fame' is one way of defining its rather straightforward subject matter. It's used to merge the history or biography of the hero with separate musical numbers."[99] Rotaru herself recognizes the similarity of her life and the heroine's. Cinema magnifies them both and the arbiters of Soviet movie-making are unhappy.

Dusha introduces into generic rigidity discussions of fame's "heavy load, the artist's eternal dissatisfaction, together with an awareness of one's debt before art, the workdays of creativity, full of fatigue, spiritual wounds." That type of excess did not go down well with audiences. Maybe the stage/hall dialogue is feeling the strain as bona fide stardom starts to appear. A woman writing to the newspaper *Sovetskaia kul'tura* after the film's release talks of it "being brought out [of the studio] to the viewers' judgment."[100] That judgment, in her eyes, sits awkwardly between condemning Rotaru for the extravagance of the film – as if she and its heroine were the same person – while simultaneously criticizing the artificial nature of songs inserted in a dramatic tale. The film's "wonderful dresses and extraordinary interiors," as well as Rotaru's car and boudoir, are in bad taste, as if they are real, whereas the songs that appear mid-film appear contrived. The merger of private and public (i.e., artistic) personae is not complete. Almost, but not quite. A full-length review in the same publication a few weeks later saw a similarly disappointing muddle of lyric (emotionally engaging) songs and "unjustified" (unengaging) melodrama.[101]

The "restrained dramatism" one journalist observed in Rotaru, together with the surprising discrepancy between a big, dramatic persona on stage and a small, restrained one elsewhere (in real life) will be resolved in the figure of Alla Pugacheva. Meanwhile, Ponarovskaia sits quietly to one side and has grave doubts about the benefits of what she terms "maximalism." When we also consider how Ponarovskaia views Pugacheva as a singer "who sings a lot about herself," we get an insight into what the latter singer will offer estrada after Rotaru.[102]

Dusha, however, despite its cool reception amongst critics for excessive dramatism and an emphasis upon material well-being in scenes shot in the star's apartment, is still a significant venture in Soviet estrada. Its rejection by the Soviet press can be attributed to the same issues that make it an important film, if we are able to look beyond the chiffon and satin of the singer's surroundings. It is the story of a performer (Viktoriia), who is told that illness threatens not only her voice but her very health. She has trouble respecting doctors' orders that she not sing, because her fans beg her to continue. As her health worsens, she becomes involved with a singer and new ensemble (Mikhail Boiarskii and the group Mashina Vremeni). They inspire her to try a more dramatic, glamorous, even rock-oriented repertoire with a marked tendency towards *teatralizatsiia*. She has at this time a mysterious seaside encounter with an elderly gentleman who tells her that she cannot ignore her fate or calling to realize the "soul" (*dusha*) in her songs. Inspired by these words, she goes on to success at an international festival, though teary-eyed and very ill in the final scenes.

The film echoes unequivocally the type of worldview we saw earlier in the thought of Il'enkov. Rotaru, a singer of some civic importance, has been won over by a screenplay that tells of the spoken or sung creation of a non-material and ethically informed significance. That significance or *dusha* is made in the dialogue between speaker and listener, stage and hall, and represents the naming or claiming of new entities in or above the material world. Viktoriia pushes her (material) body as far as it will go and spends much of the movie wheezing, coughing, and fainting. That extension of material experience to the point where the very integrity of matter itself (health) is endangered produces a spoken, *metaphysical* phenomenon – the soul of her songs. This linguistic claiming or movement of something "else" is amplified again by increased movement around stage, just as we see in the later, bolder songs of *Dusha*. (Interestingly enough, Rozhdestvenskii also contributed material for the film, the words for "My Song" [*Moia pesnia*].)

Dusha marks a new advance in post-Stalinist estrada of Il'enkovian ideas about the creation of an "ideal" within a materialist context. That ideal is of the greatest importance in the creation of a *lichnost'*. Yet the perception by the Soviet press and public of some gap or breach between Viktoriia and Sofiia, between the role and the actress, reduces the social significance of that role, since the film's artifice is revealed. We need a singer who – in the eyes of the public – simply *is* who she appears to be on stage on in her songs. Once again, Pugacheva will be that performer and we will look at the equivalent of *Dusha* in Pugacheva's repertoire to see the true creation of the Il'enkovian ideal on the Soviet estrada.

Rotaru herself would later admit, "I can't say my performances in *Where Are You, Love?* and *Soul* are an unqualified success. I relate very critically to this stage of my work. The screenplays themselves describe me as a beautiful, popular toy, with a no less beautiful entourage. And I *so* wanted to play, that's it, *play*, create the image of a person, a singer according to rules of the art that would be new for me."[103] The restatement in Rotaru's sentence is crucial. Playing – if it works – is creating; to play a person ideally means to create a person. She does not quite pull it off, though, and as a result there remains a discrepancy between Sofiia Rotaru and the woman she plays in her films. When we get to Pugacheva it will be clear what happens when this *does* work.

Ponarovskaia admitted in an interview of 1990 for the magazine *Soviet Trade Unions* that she had long wished for a unified program, like that which the role of Eurydice allowed her, so that she could "show an entire individuality." The relationship of that *lichnost'* to the techniques of *teatralizatsiia* is, however, moot. She doubts that she was ever a true exponent of the staged song, crediting the development of such techniques instead to Pugacheva. She defines her songs as imbued with an "internal drama: an exposition, development and culmination."[104] If our two singers are able to define themselves and performances so simplistically, how do they fare with the simple distinction that structures this book, that of lyric/civic intent?

SOCIETY AND SENTIMENT, TOWN AND COUNTRY

> A civic intent, the impudence of great emotion,
> self-sufficiency, the ability to discover
> the profound significance of a work –
> that's what makes up the basic creative
> significance of Sofiia Rotaru, an artist, singer,
> and woman loved by the people.[105]

An interview with Rotaru and Evdokimenko in 1981 includes a journalist's remark about the shifting generic emphases in Rotaru's career. "Judging by your creative biography, Sofiia, the journey to find 'your' song hasn't been among the easiest. You began with folk melodies, and then became one of the leading performers of civic songs."

Her answer is testament to the tough road ahead in Soviet estrada for purely lyric songs, even in the early 1980s: "I admit that … performing some lyric song or other, I rarely thought much about the profundity of its content. A pretty, decorative melody, tender and heartfelt words and – as they used to say – an 'emotional performance' would all please the listeners. But can you really last very long on the stage with that kind of sung 'baggage'? A song is the soul of the people, and it mustn't just entertain, it must also direct and educate. I'm glad that people of all ages come to my concerts. That's why at those concerts we 'erode' the boundaries of estrada songs, weaving folk and patriotic, lyric and amusing."[106]

Rotaru herself had also questioned emotions in and of themselves in the newspaper *Nedelia* a couple of years prior. "Emotions and expression alone are not really enough for a singer, if her song is going to become genuine art."[107] What is lacking in contemporary estrada, she says, is professionalism. "The elder generation is rarely afforded a chance to instruct its juniors, and there are rarely studies on the problems of estrada and aesthetics, or works on the performers themselves." A 1980 article in the magazine *Musical Life* (*Muzykal'naia zhizn'*) also noticed that Rotaru strove to mix the emotional and ethical in a professional manner. "If one recalls the brightest of Sofiia Rotaru's creative successes, then it'll seem as if they are almost all

connected with songs of a civic content. The theme of one's homeland, love for one's country and the home of one's forefathers, occu-
pies the greatest place in her repertoire; she develops this theme in a
deeply lyrical and extraordinarily sincere manner" – though she does
so only after having learned to overcome the tendency towards emotional excess.[108]

One example of such excess, albeit long since blessed as a classic,
would be the richly orchestrated ballad of 1975 by E. Martynov and
A. Dement'ev called "The Loyalty of Swans" (*Lebedinaia vernost'*). It
tells of two swans, both radiant and happy in their flight above the
material world. The female is shot from the sky, and her mate grieves,
longing for the return of her beauty. Lonely and deprived of a sung
dialogue, he himself can sing no more. He folds his wings and falls
"fearless" from the clouds. The public intent in this otherwise heartfelt
excess comes from the swan's suicidal guilt at not having defended his
mate and from the singer's closing wish that such fidelity "fly into the
bright world of people."

A single drum beat and ominous piano chord create a dramatic
introduction; they set the mark (and volume) which the text will
gradually match. The first line of the chorus slows on each occasion
to emphasize a consequent increase in (and accelerating steps
towards) that pathos. Such changes in tempo and rhythm are under-
scored several times in this personal story, whilst swathed in the sentimental grandeur of strings, in the permanent significance of one
bird's short-lived suffering. The rhythm marks (and is defined by)
discrete, "temporary" units, whereas the sound of violins moves outside
and beyond them.

В небесах искал подругу он,
Звал из гнезда.
Но молчанием ответила
Птице беда.
Улететь в края далекие
Лебедь не мог.
Потеряв подругу верную,
Он стал одинок.

Ты прости меня, любимая,
За чужое зло,
Что мое крыло
Счастье не спасло.
Ты прости меня, любимая,
Что весенним днем

В небе голубом, как прежде,
Нам не быть вдвоем.

И была непоправимою
Эта беда,
Что с подругою не встретится
Он никогда.
Лебедь вновь поднялся к облаку,
Песню прервал.
И, сложив бесстрашно крылья,
На землю упал.

[Forgive me, my dear, for another's evil. Forgive me that my wing did not save our happiness. Forgive me, my dear, that we'll never be together any more in the blue sky as before.

The grief was irreparable, since he could never meet his loved one again. The swan rose again to the sky and broke off his song. And, fearlessly folding his wings, he fell to the ground.]

The importance of looking or seeing ahead as a social imperative is also marked in a brief song written for *Where Are You, Love?* by Robert Rozhdestvenskii called "A Cloud-Letter" (*Oblako-pis'mo*). Rotaru, to a quiet piano accompaniment sings that our lives are short, made of fleeting, unique days. These days, and the years they compose, float like clouds off to "where the ages sleep." The past cannot be recovered; and here is the "essence" of our lives – the constant hoping or yearning for "something until the journey's over." Although Rozhdestvenskii is advocating a general sense of progression, it is done with an emphasis upon individual days, upon nostalgia for unique and passing significances. The primary metaphor is that of roads or wandering, so strong in Soviet romanticism of the 1960s, but now the social becomes the private and personal insecurity is outweighing a public *telos*. There is a problematic positioning of the text between the imperative to go forward and the logical question as to where this might lead.[109]

Several of these problems, either thematic or generic, appear to arise in the minds of Soviet critics from Chervona Ruta's decision to work with folk music. "The hardest thing of all is to find the golden mean: for one thing, to not run up against ethnography, pure and simple. The other danger is to 'over-modernize' the song. Chervona Ruta gets it right."[110] They do so thanks in part to Rotaru's delivery, described as most successful in her "lyrico-dramatic songs, full of deep feeling."

An article of 1984 helps us to understand how and why such dramatic songs are chosen in a way that tries to merge the civic and lyric. A journalist notes that "Rotaru's greatest creative successes are linked with songs that strike a civic note. It's hard to forget her performance of the pathetic 'Ballad of a Mother' by Evgenii Martynov or the kind of musical 'fresco' that is David Tukhmanov's 'My Homeland.'" The singer herself explains, "I needed a song that both passionately and sincerely could praise love for one's country and stir the most sacred civic feelings and patriotism." Such texts required her to "transmit a deep emotional strength."[111] That depth can be damaged by "hackwork" in the field of estrada, which "discredits the song's political and moral idea." Many VIAs, she says, commit this sin by not "thinking their work through, by being slapdash."[112] Avoiding such sins herself, she earns great praise from critics: "The singer has once again proven that on the estrada not only a beautiful voice, a charming way of holding oneself, and fine temperament are important, but first of all [one must stress] human and social activity, a clear civic position."[113] The public spirit is briefly uppermost, and everybody breathes a sigh of relief.

Perhaps the most clearly public song in Rotaru's repertoire is indeed "Ballad of a Mother," otherwise known as "Aleksei … Aleshen'ka," written in 1967. It concerns a mother who like so many other Russian women has waited in vain for her son to come back from the battlefields of World War II. She waits more than thirty years "because she is a mother." One day a documentary film about the war is showing in her village movie theatre and her son appears unexpectedly in some scenes from the front. She cries out to him, trying to shield him somehow, and her instinctual display of love inspires her neighbours to cheer for the boy. Suddenly the scene changes, and because her son when he was last seen was still alive, because he was not filmed at the moment he fell, he remains alive forever. Yet the joy of seeing him exacerbates the mother's yearning for her child.

That element of surprise is emphasized rhythmically in a manner even more dramatic than that of "The Loyalty of Swans." Maternal woes are related without recourse to percussion, but the shared jollity of a movie and the "suddenly" of a son's appearance are each afforded their own rhythmic structure; gaiety turns to awful (and awfully grand) drama.

Трудно было это вспоминать.
Вдруг с экрана сын взглянул на мать.
Мать узнала сына в тот же миг,
И пронесся материнский крик:
– Алексей! Алешенька! Сынок! –
Словно сын ее услышать мог.

Он рванулся из траншеи в бой,
Встала мать прикрыть его собой.
Все боялась – вдруг он упадет,
Но сквозь годы мчался сын вперед.
– Алексей! – кричали земляки.
– Алексей! – просили – Добеги!

Кадр сменился. Сын остался жить,
Просит мать о сыне повторить.
И опять в атаку он бежит.
Жив-здоров, не ранен, не убит.
– Алексей! Алешенька! Сынок! –
Словно сын ее услышать мог.

[It was hard to remember the war. Suddenly a son looked at his mother. The mother knew her son in an instant, and cried in a maternal tone – Aleksei! Aleshen'ka! Son! – as if her son could hear. He rushed from the trenches into battle. His mother stood to shield him. She was afraid that he was just about to fall, but he ran forward through the years. Aleksei! cried the villagers. Aleksei! they begged – You can make it! The scene changed. The son was left to live and his mother asked it be shown again. Alive and well, not wounded, not killed – Aleksei! Aleshen'ka! Son! – as if her son could hear.]

Rotaru claims that she began her singing career at home with pure folk songs, but once she decided to begin performing regularly in public, she needed "more modern rhythms, which is what a student audience expects." Audience expectations over and above those students led her to move on to material such as the "Ballad of a Mother" or "My Homeland."[114]

Rotaru's leaning towards things public vanished after the end of the Soviet Union. Earlier interviews had stressed that her songs could not help but be in some part civic, since she and each one of her listeners were meaningful units of society. In an interview of 1993 Ponarovskaia explains concisely why this shift away from politics took place in the 1990s in the repertoire of both women. "I came to understand that my own interest [in politics] won't change anything. It just tears my nerves to shreds." Such a view does not stop Ponarovskaia calling herself a patriot. But the political situation in Russia has not engendered great freedoms; its economic chaos and political oligarchs now exacerbate a sense of individual, social insignificance.

Despite such social helplessness, another interview with Ponarovskaia points to an opposing, compensatory, and artistic ability in the 1990s to step freely outside certain generic preconceptions in the private world of songs. Songs allow the freedom that daily existence denies: when asked which of the various styles she has tried have remained dearest to her, she replies: "I don't give preference to any one style or genre. Variation is essential. Say you're reading a book and you're following the subject. And suddenly there's an entire chapter given over to a description of nature. What was the point? Perhaps it lets the reader take a break? Or something entirely different – it creates an atmosphere, a mood? Each person will explain it in his own way."[115] Her belief that a performer is generically "free" and that semantics are particular to each and every listener is a radical extension of the stage-hall dialogue we have seen since Èdita P'ekha. The socially useful dimensions of civic songs are being scaled down or collapsing to a lyrical scale, simply because one singer cannot hope to be meaningful in the same way to more than one person. This breakdown of a public dimension leads Ponarovskaia to feel that, unlike Rotaru, she is not responsible for the education or upbringing of her listener: "People should busy themselves with their own upbringing." Rotaru holds onto the civic song; Ponarovskaia wonders about its efficacy, in fact about its entire *raison d'être*.

We have not left didacticism entirely behind, however. Take, for example, the rather asymmetrical relationship of hall and stage Ponarovskaia talks about in 1993. Here she offers a strange view of what it means to be a social singer or just a singer *in* society.

What people see from the hall is a step higher than what I see in the hall from the stage. That's how it should be, anyway. Not in the sense that they can't reach me, but in the sense of the aesthetics of what I do. People sitting in the hall cannot do the same [as I] and therefore there exists for them a moment of admission, perhaps even a moment of education, a little aesthetic university. The hall is the kind of organism that must submit to you. That doesn't mean that I'm after power. My profession simply demands it; otherwise I'll not get things done on stage.[116]

Here the artist contradicts herself. People should busy themselves with their own upbringing, she said a few years earlier, yet she subjects them to a "little aesthetic university." The pedagogical intent of the civic song dies hard! In her equivocation over what – if anything – the stage/hall dialogue means today, Ponarovskaia draws an implicit parallel between Soviet social masses and mass-produced songs, between big politics and big business. Those songs can be "ugly," she says, "but people buy them!" Modern estrada, she believes, has been brought to this state by a lack of care and attention. Another problem is that a natural process of aesthetic development in estrada was retarded by communism – and continues to be held back by capitalism: both ideologies show an unwillingness to embrace novelty, either on political or economic grounds. "There's a category of performers that you just can't get by without – those who break traditions. The public don't understand them. Only their fans flood the TV stations with letters. Those performers don't need to do anything to get on TV. Fame works for them. Usually, [though,] viewers see the same faces and they're happy with them since they know no others, and have nothing with which to compare them."[117]

The complaints voiced by Sofiia Rotaru and Irina Ponarovskaia suggest three things: the nature of estrada is changing, a limit of some kind is being breached, and it unnerves them. The embodiment of a less hesitant transgression of that limit within the female performers of estrada is Alla Pugacheva. Although she was working at the same time as Rotaru and even before Ponarovskaia, the manner in which Pugacheva ultimately altered her craft on the stage and its perception in the auditorium is very much an extension of what we have seen here in Ukraine, Moldova, and Leningrad. If the story of Rotaru and Ponarovskaia is indeed one that can be distilled to a very Soviet dichotomy between periphery and centre, between private and public, then it will come as no surprise to learn that the creation of Pugacheva's persona as an implicit challenge to a materialist worldview takes place in the middle of things, in Moscow itself.

Before, however, we move to the interaction of *lichnost'*, perestroika, and glasnost, we should cast a glance over an equivalent process in male quarters.

7
LEV LESHCHENKO AND VALERII LEONT'EV: TWO NIGHTINGALES

Even now I hear that I'm the "Nightingale of
the Kremlin." What kind of nightingale can
I be if I never sang "Our General Secretary"
and never even had any songs about BAM?
And anyway, I just listened to my own archival
recordings and out of 350 songs,
about 300 are about love.[1]

Lev Leshchenko

The villainous robber Nightingale cried
his bestial cry, his nightingale whistle ...
and all lush grass was intertwined, all azure
flowers were scattered. Dark forests bowed
to the earth, all around fell dead.[2]

The preceding chapter concerned two women; here we turn to two
men. The reason for drawing these gender-specific pairs is to show
that post-Stalinist popular culture, happy though it might often be to
assign matters lyrical to women and those civic to men, in fact experienced an interplay between private and public commitment in the
songs of both male and female performers. Amidst male singers, the
solid, heroic stance of Kobzon shifted considerably to incorporate
both subjectivity and patriotism devoid of political ideology. That shift
increases between the work of Kobzon in the 1960s and Lev Leshchenko in the '70s.

Leshchenko, by his own admission, remains inherently conservative
in his respect for the time-honoured traditions of estrada. Blessed with
a voice as rich as Kobzon's, he has several of the same Soviet classics
in his repertoire but treats them often in a more up-beat fashion, using
the horns and sprightly percussion of '70s pop. What happens after
Leshchenko is Leont'ev. The traditional acoustic instruments are
exchanged for synthesizers, and the foot-tapping jollity of Leshchenko's work becomes bona fide dance music, often heavily influenced by disco. Valerii Leont'ev came from a village in the extreme
north of Russia to change entirely the concept of "male artist" in

estrada, so much so that I have been prompted to draw a parallel with the Robber Nightingale of Russian folklore, whose cry is described in this chapter's epigraph. The shock of Leont'ev results from the fact that whereas Kobzon stood still, Leont'ev dances about; Kobzon sang about the Soviet Union, Leont'ev sings about himself; Kobzon dresses conservatively; Leont'ev encourages the carnivalesque extremes of *teatralizatsiia*. But between the two of them stands Leshchenko, gracefully ceding to the new understanding and new display of "self" upon the Soviet stage.

LEV LESHCHENKO: "SOME KIND OF TRADITIONAL HERO"

Где мой дом родной? Там, где есть друзья.
Где мой дом родной? Там, где счастлив я.

[Where's my native land? The place where my
friends are, the place where I am happy.][3]

Lev Leshchenko was born on 1 February 1942 in Moscow. His father was a professional soldier; his mother died in May 1945.[4] The boy was raised by a foster mother and grandparents in a typically tight-knit community of post-war Soviet society. "If somebody in our courtyard got a bike, then all the kids would take a ride in turn. If somebody got a new suit, all the neighbours would come to see. The joy from each purchase was a common one. If you were hungry, and your parents were still at work, then one of the neighbours would certainly feed you. It was obviously a tough life, yet there was openness and generosity towards one another."[5] He first saw a television in the early 1950s in a neighbour's apartment – children were allowed to come and watch a kids' broadcast once a week, but only if their grades at school were good.[6]

Leshchenko knew from the outset, inspired perhaps by his violin-playing Ukrainian grandfather, the accountant at a sugar factory, that he would be a singer. He joined choral and dramatic clubs within a children's organization, the Pioneers.[7] One day in school he decided to try his luck in front of an audience in the assembly hall. He launched into the Utesov song, "By the Black Sea" (*U Chernogo moria*), but started too high. He could not make it through the chorus, threw up his hands, announced his lack of talent before all present and left the stage, painfully aware of the necessity of taking serious lessons. But by the end of school he was planning a career dedicated to music. In 1959 he tried to get into the operetta division of the State Theatrical

Leshchenko in 1977, when he was
performing songs of considerable
public commitment, albeit in a slightly
more voguish vein than Kobzon

Institute (GITIS). As the entrance exams loomed, he worried that his
desire to emphasize a song's emotional content was not modish
enough to match the new importance of things visual in estrada.
Indeed his traditionalism appears to have tried even the examiners'
patience. They interrupted his reading of Maiakovskii's poem "A
Cloud in Trousers": "OK, that's enough. Can you do anything else?" –
"A fable," replied Leshchenko. "No need, we believe you," came the
hasty response.[8]

He was not accepted, but after another year he tried again; meanwhile he found employment as a metal worker. His second attempt at
passing the exam was no more successful than the first. Despite
thoughts of capitulation, Leshchenko waited yet another year and
went back to GITIS. This time he made it through the initial rounds
of the competition before a most inopportune call came to sign up
for military service. On 20 September 1961 he was taken off – after
the severest of haircuts – to serve as loader in a Soviet tank division.
He was stationed in East Germany only weeks after construction of the
Berlin Wall began. This distant posting curtailed his dream of singing
in the famous Moscow Regional Military Ensemble.

Nevertheless, the army allowed him considerable experience in a
modest, local military ensemble. That experience began when he was

unexpectedly called away from cleaning a machine-gun to be told that he could join the group. He enjoyed great success not only among the rank and file but also with the officers, who would ask him to perform in their dining-hall. Yet he never gave up the dream of entering the Theatrical Institute, and when he returned to a summer 1964 competition of forty-six entrants for each place, he succeeded in entering the musical comedy division.[9] He appears to have pushed his luck somewhat by performing – in Italian – an aria from Verdi's *Don Carlos*; even Leshchenko himself admits that the examiners exchanged doubting glances. When they asked him in addition to read some literature, they remarked that he had a remarkable ability for picking bad poetry.[10]

With acceptance and early studies behind him, Leshchenko married a young woman by the name of Anna Abdalova, all the while singing in the Moscow Theater of Operetta with sufficient success that in 1970 he won a place in the State Television and Radio Choir.[11] In the same year he was supposed to go with a musical group on a southern tour, but the radio station would not allow him to leave. He would shortly be grateful for such interference: the plane carrying his colleagues was destroyed, killing all on board. In 1972 tragedy struck once more. He had requested a new trumpeter for his ensemble, and the new player was due to come to Moscow on 18 May. On that same day, five members of Leshchenko's ensemble were killed in a car crash. During the funeral service a week later, somebody else was being buried nearby – it was the trumpeter, who had never called his new employer in Moscow because he himself had been run over by a bus while buying bread. As Leshchenko himself said, "He was bound to join them [the five others], be it either here or in the next world."[12]

Leshchenko managed to move beyond these terrible events in the same year and win two festivals, the Bulgarian Zolotoi Orfei and the Polish competition in Sopot. He did so with Robert Rozhdestvenskii's song "For That Lad" (*Za togo parnia*), a piece "full of civic pathos." He also cut his first record and within two years would win both the Moscow and Lenin Komsomol prizes.

On the heels of such domestic success, his first trip overseas came in 1973 when the central Soviet concert organization sent twenty Russian artists to Japan to help promote an exhibition called "Soviet Socialist Siberia." Each participant was expected to perform in the pavilion during the day and then give grand concerts in the evening, a typically heavy workload for musicians in a propagandistic role abroad. Another standard practice was a series of ridiculous interviews they underwent prior to such trips to see how well they might represent the U.S.S.R. once abroad: to discover whether they knew the figures for that year's grain harvest, the name of the Communist Party head of Argentina, the number of districts there were in Moscow, and so forth.[13]

In 1976 Leshchenko was again dispatched to spread the word, this time to inspire the Soviet Olympic Team in Montreal. After making their acquaintance with the rowing team and then "boxers, wrestlers, gymnasts, swimmers, and footballers," the musicians went on to sing in the athletes' quarters in the evenings. It all "helped the sportsmen to outdo themselves, find their reserve energy, stay fit, and strive for new heights."[14] Leshchenko would perform a similar duty, together with Iosif Kobzon, for the Soviet team at the Lake Placid Winter Olympics of 1980. But there he was made to feel uncomfortable amongst the American townspeople, given the dark coverage of the Soviets in the local press. Only when impromptu concerts were held in the hotel did the attitude of the U.S. hosts change for the better. Later the same year the Moscow Olympics were held, so once again the power of a bold repertoire was required. Leshchenko sang "Good-Bye, Moscow!" (*Do svidaniia, Moskva!*) at the closing ceremonies, in which he bid farewell to Misha, the event's inflated mascot, and sent him back to his "fairy-tale forest."[15]

The song "Victory Day" (*Den' pobedy*) by David Tukhmanov and Vladimir Kharitonov brought him even greater success. The first time Leshchenko heard the music he found it "exciting from the first few bars."[16] Though one of the most popular songs today about the Soviet experience of World War II, it was written in the mid-1970s and originally rejected by the Union of Soviet Composers for being an excessively cheerful foxtrot having little, if anything, to do with the war. Leshchenko tried to keep the song for himself, but the composer had already offered it to another performer who, in Leshchenko's view, made an unimpressive showing when he debuted the song on a holiday broadcast of the *Little Blue Light* show (*Goluboi ogonek*). Patience solved the problem; the television performance was soon forgotten, and Leshchenko grabbed the song for an important concert at the Ministry of Internal Affairs (the police or *militsiia*). "I waited for a live concert that would be shown on TV, so I could present the work as convincingly as possible."[17]

This powerful song draws not upon the bravery of youthful soldiers but the private memories of ageing, greying veterans. Its poignant combination of joy at a stunning victory and sadness at great loss sounds just as relevant today, when the war itself is something about which many young Russians neither know nor care. In a 1992 article Leshchenko himself says that in the entire textual repertoire of his songs, this is the only one that convinces him that his elderly, post-Soviet audience has not lived in vain.[18]

Этот День Победы
Порохом пропах,
Этот праздник
С сединою на висках.
Это радость
Со слезами на глазах.
День Победы! День Победы!
День Победы!

[Victory Day is soaked with the smell of gun-powder. It's a festival with grey at its temples. It's a joy with tears in its eyes. Victory Day! Victory Day! Victory Day!]

His marriage by now had developed what he called "cracks," and divorce ensued, allowing the singer to join his new love, Irina, whom he had met in a lift of the Pearl Hotel in the Black Sea resort of Sochi. The twenty-four year old was studying in Hungary, at Budapest University. Because she had grown up in Germany, she did not recognize the Soviet superstar in the flesh. This convinced Leshchenko of her sincere emotions when they spoke, and after two years of correspondence and days stolen together during long Siberian tours, they married.

By now Leshchenko was truly famous. "They say that Brezhnev adored his songs and never turned off the TV when Leshchenko was on."[19] He sang for Brezhnev personally at Kremlin banquets on two occasions.[20] Perhaps as a consequence of such high regard, he became an Honoured Artist of the Russian Federation in 1977. The official announcement praised him for his wide and varied repertoire and for his promotion of Soviet songs amongst both young people and the armed forces.[21] Given the wholly socialist context of Leshchenko's career, it is not surprising that prestige won from such awards greatly outweighed any material gain:

I had no perks. It was a humiliating time for me. I could, for example, be called to sing at the dacha of some bureaucrat or other, where they'd lay out a small table for me with a couple of sandwiches and a shot of vodka. I never got anything from the state and had to pay for everything myself. Even then I had to ask for it. For a car, furniture, caviar, kielbasa ... It's a disgusting situation to be in, when you have the chance and money to set up your own life, but you have to bow and scrape everywhere ... Previously, I had a "norm" of sixteen concerts. I wasn't allowed to sing fewer than sixteen. That was called "Not fulfilling the plan." I couldn't do more than thirty-two. That was called "Running after money"... Sometimes we appeared not at the major [sanctioned] venues but somewhere else as well. Then they'd drag us into the procurator's office and say: "What right have you got to do that?!" I remember that for three years they hassled me, Pugacheva, and Rotaru for having performed these so-called concerts on the side. They'd threaten us with prison, so that others wouldn't get the same idea. It was [also] practically impossible to drag a song onto TV that wasn't written by a member of the Composers' Union ... I myself wasn't allowed to step outside the framework of a traditional singer. On stage I had to be an object for emulation. Anything I did that was non-heroic was considered shirking. Why exactly I was chosen for all of this I don't know. Probably the way I looked fit the bill. There were some sort of traditional heroes at that time ... with kind and impartial faces. Mine fit. And then there's the fact that I'm not an anomalous individual. I have an overriding sense of self-preservation. I wanted – and still want – to live, drink, and eat normally.[22]

In 1983, the year that Andropov resigned and a Korean airliner was shot down above Sakhalin in the Far East of Russia, Leshchenko was made a People's Artist of the Federation; but the problems he alludes to continued even into the years of glasnost. At that time "people began to reject everything old. People thought that everything we'd achieved was undeserved or fabricated by a [communist] life that needed a certain kind of artist. Yes, in principle that's the way it was. Our reality moulded us, as did the dominant ideology of the time. But even the most hopeless ideology chooses the most talented people for its prophets. The worst plays were always taken to the best theatres. Bad roles were given to brilliant actors, who salvaged them with their skills ... Even today [singers like myself and Kobzon] show ourselves to be the most professional performers. We've survived even in the current situation."[23] In the same year that he became a People's Artist, the journal *Soviet Estrada and Circus* described Leshchenko's insistence upon sticking to Soviet classics as a "thorny path."[24]

By the mid-1980s Leshchenko had recorded radio and television performances of more than 350 songs. He was touring eight or nine months every year around the Soviet Union. His definition of estrada at this time is of an art that works upon the physical world while aiding the growth of a metaphysical notion. "It goes without saying that estrada songs are a little part of a modern person's spiritual world. But at the same time you can't deny that they influence this world, too, and consequently influence humankind. We have to remember this and awaken in our listeners bright, good, and humane feelings. Works of art have a huge sphere of influence – they can convince and over-throw, extol and destroy, entertain and repel ... That's why we have to always be aware of our responsibility when we go out on the stage."[25]

An off-stage photograph from
1999, showing Leshchenko in
a relaxed moment

Between 1984 and 1985, when Gorbachev and Reagan began their
arms talks, Leshchenko began to feel the influence of perestroika and
the insistent presence of youth upon the estrada. Meanwhile the
requests of those such as Leshchenko, Pugacheva, and Rotaru that they
be paid a fair share of the ticket sales at their concerts were met with
official outrage.[26] These Soviet stars were playing two hundred to three
hundred concerts per year, very often in enormous sports halls. Leshchenko's estimate of the injustice is that he was receiving a salary of 50
rubles per month while the state – quite literally – was reaping millions.

By the time those lingering injustices of the Soviet Union had faded,
Leshchenko celebrated his half-century with a grand program in the
Moscow concert hall Rossiia. His classical good looks were still much
in evidence, his physique still square and solid. On the day of the
concert, *Pravda* likened his long career to that of a marathon runner.[27]
The lasting power of his attraction in 1992 was reflected in that fiftieth
birthday concert, which lasted "five hours without an interval – and
not a single person got up and left."[28] In the following year he makes
reference in an interview to an ongoing project, his experimental
studio or "Theatre of Estrada Performance," which has become enormously time-consuming. Even changing a car tire is a task he can no
longer fit into his schedule, he says; rare free moments in his timetable

are sometimes given over to writing poetry. "It's not that hard to compose, all intelligent people can rhyme a line or two." After a second's thought he adds with a slight smile: "The thing is, though, that the quality varies among them."[29]

Variance from what was normally thought to be an intelligent norm of composition is what defines both the career of Valerii Leont'ev and its relevance for the tradition of Kobzon and Leshchenko. Leont'ev both extends and deviates from the notion of *lichnost'* as propounded by his two distinguished predecessors.

VALERII LEONT'EV: "AN ABSOLUTELY NEW TYPE OF SINGER"

> Leont'ev was lucky in that his entrance onto
> major stages coincided with the moment of
> perestroika – and perhaps even determined it.[30]

Valerii Leont'ev was born on 19 March 1949 in the village of Ust'-Usa, in Russia's extreme north. The family lived there for only twenty days after their son was born; Leont'ev's father was a veterinarian specializing in the welfare of deer and he travelled with the herds across the empty wastelands. Starved of human company, the young boy did not fare well with animals; he was often bitten and butted by the family's dog, goat and cow.[31] However, work in extreme conditions began to tell on Iakov Leont'ev's health and the family transferred in 1966 to the banks of the river Volga, in particular to the Ivanovskaia region north-east of Moscow, where Valerii was able to stay long enough to graduate from school.

In Ivanovskaia dramatic clubs he would often be told, "Stand still!" but insisted upon what were then considered excessive attempts at "depiction."[32] A school friend later recalled that he also wrote and illustrated vigorous, fantastic stories.[33] This avid participation in school plays helped prepare him for a possible future career on the stage, together with whatever records penetrated the deep provinces. Among the singers he heard and admired was Èdita P'ekha. So far was he from the fashions of Western Europe that "word of the Beatles did not make its way to him."[34]

With school behind, the young Leont'ev headed for Moscow with a friend determined – like Leshchenko – to enrol in GITIS. And like another of our seven singers, Rotaru, Leont'ev was bringing a very provincial worldview to the Soviet capital, and suffered great insecurity as a result. "Imagine all those good-looking guys and women. Beautifully dressed. Carrying themselves wonderfully. All of them fashionable

Leont'ev in 1990, encouraging the
resurrection of aristocratic chic as the USSR
began to come apart

and sure of themselves. To look at them, you'd say they were ready-
made stars, fit for a shoot at Mosfil'm or Hollywood. And what hurt
me most of all was that they all spoke properly... [I had] the typical
insecurity complex of a seventeen-year old provincial who, as luck
would have it, finds himself in the capital."[35] Hugely disheartened,
Leont'ev went home even before the examinations were held.

He soon moved from the Volga to Anapa on the eastern Black Sea,
where he had relatives. After working on a building site, he found
employment as greaser in a flax-spinning plant, crawling beneath the
looms to keep them well lubricated.[36] His other jobs included post-
man, electrician, and tailor. Elsewhere in biographical records we can
also find reference to a brick factory.[37] His sister manged to set up
another move in 1968 to the city of Vorkuta inside the Arctic Circle,
where he could work as a lab assistant and then get into the local
scientific institute. Sure enough, after night school studies, he was
accepted by the Vorkuta Mining Institute. He studied as a draftsman,
all the time continuing the amateur dramatic work. It was in Vorkuta
that he staged his first-ever solo concert.

Then, amidst the increasing tedium of technical drawing, a 1972 competition for youth theatre was announced in his far northern Komi republic, though a little further south and away from the ravages of an Arctic climate, in its capital of Syktyvkar. Leont'ev broke a heel-bone in rehearsals, but still managed to limp his way to the competition.[38] Such determination shown by a performer on stage with crutches was enough to impress the jury, and Leont'ev won a place to study estrada in Moscow with fourteen other students.[39] Accommodation was offered only in hotels, which obliged the students to change lodgings every month to avoid the long-term rates. When the director of the Syktyvkar Philharmonia came to visit the students at the end of a year, however, he was so dismayed at their lack of success that he took them all back to Syktyvkar. There they began soon after to work in 1973 with a ready-made estrada group of musicians known as Echo (Èkho).

The first truly professional concert that took place as a result of this return was in December 1973 in the village of Loima, just months before Solzhenitsyn was sent packing from the U.S.S.R. The performance was held in the back of a disused church, and organizers turned up the heating to attract freezing locals to the show. Thus began a series of performances, held for "foresters, geologists, oil and gas workers," as Leont'ev remembers it. In another interview he adds "builders and deer specialists."[40] Soon the tours went so far afield that the performers were away from Syktyvkar for eight or ten months at a time. They lived in hotel rooms or empty railway halls, men in one room and women in another, or at least blankets and curtains dividing them. Water was brought in by the bucket, with snow melted to make tea. The men gathered wood, the women peeled potatoes. In the most distant locations, using the toilet meant going into the snow with two sticks – one to steady yourself and the other to ward off bears.[41]

This work continued for most of the 1970s, until employment was offered in the Regional Philharmonia of Gor'kii. Both Leont'ev and Èkho moved there, if for no other reason than to escape the bears. His more official standing in Gor'kii allowed Leont'ev to enter the First All-Union Competition for songs from all socialist countries, held in Yalta in 1979. Now thirty, he was troubled by his lack of success in the big cities. The rules of the competition obliged him to perform three songs from socialist neighbours, three Soviet, and one brand new. Leont'ev performed a cycle of poems by Rozhdestvenskii, "In Memory of a Guitarist" (*Pamiati gitarista*). Looking back, he recalls his performance invited cruel reviews: "It's an absolute scandal you've sent us, with old curly up there singing, jumping, and dancing about."[42] Old curly, with his astonishing crop of wiry red hair, nonetheless managed to win first prize in the solo singer category. Leont'ev's memories of this victory show an incipient interest in *teatralizatsiia* and the way in which the notions of private and dramatic *lichnosti* are starting to merge. They also reveal how for some audience members the drama of that merged personality was unnerving:

I didn't invent any image for this song. Everything I did was both sincere and true. I mean my own sense of truth, my feelings. It was me. I like to work in a state of rapture, until I'm hoarse, to give my all. I just can't work any other way. Of course I can think up some sort of costume, some details in my behaviour or additions to the scenery ... But you have to put your own truth (*svoia pravda*) into it, as if into a frame. It's simply impossible to force some other nonsense into yourself. What's put there is put there by nature. My style in Yalta was sufficiently unfettered, free, and a mix of various dramatic genres that a lot of specialists didn't accept. I was told later that when it came to the voting, opinions in the jury were divided and they argued until *they* were hoarse. The important thing, though, was the end result. Information about the competition appeared in the papers; it was the first time that the central press had mentioned my name – a little later a record came out.[43]

The victory at Yalta was tempered by the death of Leont'ev's father on the same day. Trying hard to move on after such a blow, the young man put even more effort into his career. He was invited to Moscow television, but since he had neither concert experience in the capital nor sound recordings, he was obliged to sing and dance before the representatives of the studio. Once again, this kind of amateurism was seen as unadulterated provincialism.

Undaunted by such snobbery, Leont'ev asked for a meeting to be set up with the famous composer David Tukhmanov, who was very taken by his skills and effort. Soon afterwards Tukhmanov helped Leont'ev record his song entitled "The Records Are Spinning" (*Kruzhatsia diski*) with the kind of rhythm that allowed him to be more theatrical.[44] Tukhmanov saw in him "a singer combining vocal, thespian, and plastic possibilities, which subsequently blossomed so brightly on stage." They indeed blossomed quickly, since in 1980 he won – with his "thin face and penetrating gaze" – first prize at the Zolotoi Orfei, plus an additional award from the Bulgarian journal *Lada* for the best costumes, sewn by the artist himself. (Here the rules had obliged him to sing two songs, one Bulgarian and one of his home nation.)

Yet again success did not come easily. A few hours before a nation-wide broadcast, Central Television dropped his song about disc jockeys (*Kruzhatsia diski*) from the line-up of 1980's New Year's show, *Goluboi ogonek*, believing the piece to contain obscure references to horses. The theatricality of Leont'ev's television performances often led to their being cut, or re-shot in toned-down formats. The importance of that theatricality is referenced lyrically in several of his songs, for example, "Kabare": "Play louder, music! Fate is the mistress of this cabaret!"

Leont'ev continued to place equal emphasis in his performances upon "vocals, gesticulation and movement … He was an artist unlike any other." He came under more official fire: "No songs in his repertoire about the Party, Motherland, or komsomol. Unsoviet costumes."[45] The various notions of exactly what was unsoviet are nicely condensed in his song "Exemplary Boy" (*Primernyi mal'chik*): "He reads the wrong books, goes to the disco and visits the church on Easter." Leont'ev found it impossible to get concerts scheduled in Moscow, a problem he explains as a fear of freedom: "It seems that those in control of the mass media instinctively sensed in my estrada work an internal freedom. A freedom of thought. Of the spirit. The freedom to look both in life and on stage the way I want to." The distance between stage and private persona virtually vanished as several other regional councils, such as Yalta (ironically), wished to tread the same line as the capital and followed suit with a ban upon Leont'ev. Problems such as these, caused by his ground-breaking developments on the stage, were reflected in the lyrics of his songs, even years later casting professional problems in an existential light: "So many problems. I'm all mixed up! What do I do and how do I go on?" (*Problemy*); "Let each person choose as he wishes" (*Delo vkusa*); "Am I to blame if I'm a black sheep? I was born that way" (*Belaia vorona*).

A brief American article in *Time* that covered the music festival Yerevan-81 included a reference to Leont'ev, likening him to Mick Jagger and to Mikhail Baryshnikov, a taboo personality since his flight westwards. Similar coverage and parallels only worsened Leont'ev's lot. The lyricist Andrei Dement'ev's description of him at this time further explained the singer's problems in terms of *lichnost'*: "Valerii Leont'ev is not only an artistic and creative phenomenon. First and foremost he's a phenomenon of personality … He tried to lay himself bare precisely as a personality and would stand for no compromises." Indeed one journalist had written that "he grips, bewitches, and electrifies an auditorium, forces it to think on his own wave-length. These are things that can only be shouldered by a strong, wilful *lichnost'*." Dement'ev went on to say that "Leont'ev came [to Soviet estrada] and began to break everything … He threw us a challenge … Right away he announced his presence – as a *lichnost'*… I try to imagine, reversing epochs, what would have been if Molotov, Zhdanov, or Stalin would have attended his concerts … In those times he would certainly have ended up as a prisoner. In Brezhnev's time he was seen as a breach of the peace."[46]

At the start of the 1980s plans were made to stage that "breaching" in a framework worthy of its aspirations. In contrast to Moscow's ongoing coldness towards him, Leont'ev found greater sympathy in Leningrad and began to plan a huge *teatralizatsiia* in the city's equally large Oktiabr'skii concert hall. The show's director, Oleg Aver'ianov, spoke of the original grand plans: "We decided that we had to put together a program with ornamentation, specially sewn costumes, and a guest ballet company ... Inside Leont'ev there always lived a show-man; he dreamed of appearing on stage with a ballet, dreamed of a specially created choreography ... It's his soul that dances ... Leont'ev and I for the first time began to create a show with continuous action, with specially written, sung numbers, light effects, and scenery." Certain grand effects, such as pirate ships, live horses, and airplanes on stage, either caused huge organizational headaches or were shelved due to insufficient funds. Despite such hitches, says Aver'ianov, "We eventually did five programs together on the stage of the Oktiabr'skii and, you might say, instituted that kind of genre in Soviet estrada."[47]

A significant influence in Leont'ev's stagey and increasingly popular conception of self was that of Raimonds Pauls, the Latvian composer who was pivotal in the career of Alla Pugacheva. Leont'ev and Pauls met in 1981, at a concert celebrating the pianist's already huge contribution to Soviet variety. As a surprise, Pugacheva brought Leont'ev out onto the stage of Moscow's Theatre of Estrada. The composer later remembered hearing Leont'ev for the first time and immediately considering him a daring performer, "undoubtedly a *lichnost'*."[48]

Leont'ev also entrusted his vocal chords to a Leningrad doctor for a critical 1982 operation. The operation led him to consider further professional training both as a security against future illness and as a ticket to other opportunities in the world of theatre. He entered the Leningrad Institute of Culture, choosing as his future major "Direction of Mass Presentations." Despite the extensive concert experience already behind him, he set off with his old companions, Ékho, to Voroshilovgrad to work with the city symphony. The locals took an immediate shine to their prestigious visitor and nicknamed him, some-what strangely, the Wall of China, because of his long, brick-red hair.[49] However, he was obliged twice a year to return to Leningrad and report on his work in the field of dramatic staging, of large-scale *teatralizatsiia*.

A milestone in this work was the solo program of 1985, *Alone with Everybody* (*Naedine so vsemi*), grand enough to include many actors, ballet dancers, and an entire group of Soviet navy signallers, released from active duty to take part in a "maritime" number! Several of Pauls's songs were included, some with words by Il'ia Reznik: "Verooko" and "Singing Mime" (*Poiushchii mim*). Another evening dedicated to Pauls, this time in Moscow, allowed the singer to appear with ten new songs and finally overcome the unspoken ban from stages in the capital.

Before Pauls had even met Leont'ev, he had heard that "somewhere in the sticks there had appeared an absolutely new type of singer." Now working with this provincial neophyte Pauls says, he was criticized on the grounds that "you're writing such simple, sentimental songs ... But I think that all people are essentially sentimental. Even Mafia bandits. It's exactly sentimental melodies that become the popular ones. And those were *very* sentimental times."[50]

Leont'ev went to perform in the harsher environment of Afghanistan, just as P'ekha (the queen of sentiment) and Kobzon had. Unconvinced by official reports that the so-called war in Afghanistan was merely a local conflict, he asked to be offered a series of concerts in the region. The first thing he saw at Kabul airport in 1985 – moments after arrival – was his aircraft loaded up for the return journey with young Russian corpses. A trip to another terrible locale, Chernobyl', presented equally sad scenes: "Nocturnal, dead villages, a quiet full moon, the complete absence of wind, cats with green eyes sitting on a gate, windows open wide, shutters and doors flung open – and everything overgrown with grass or bushes."

Back in the North, plans began to materialize in 1988 for the staging of what Leont'ev himself called "a musico-dramatic presentation with a running theme." He had dreamed of performing in a drama somehow connected with Kipling's *Mowgli*, but was honest enough to admit that his age made this an increasingly unlikely option. A Leningrad composer approached him with the idea of a musical based instead upon the life of the medieval philosopher Giordano Bruno. The attraction of such a figure for Leont'ev was marked: "His dissent from dogma, his well-defined social, political and moral standpoints. His rebelliousness. His ingenuousness. His fury. His skill in living. He knew how to fight for his idea – and accepted death for it. This is all a logical extension of my efforts to dramatize my material, to join disparate elements in a single show. The drama allows me to live through the life of a specific hero."[51]

The premiere took place in Moscow on June 1988. The troupe, which included the famous artiste Larisa Dolina, had rehearsed (unpaid) in a small room. Only on the eve of the show's debut were the cast allowed to use the stage of the theatre. The prestigious and influential *Literaturnaia gazeta* warmed to the production, praising Leont'ev's ability to raise estrada to the grand and serious level of dramatic theatre without pretensions towards the domain of opera.[52] The *Moscow News* was – to the journalist's own surprise – most impressed by the production and by the use of Leont'ev's personality as a "melan-choly clown."[53] The show went on to play forty-seven times.[54]

Leont'ev had for the sake of his career to be in the "middle of things." After this success in Leningrad, this meant the bureaucratic horrors of finding even the most modest accommodation in the cap-ital. Only with the intervention of the Minister of Culture was he able to get both permission and a place to live in Moscow. But fans soon discovered the address and were knocking on the door at 4 a.m., crying, "Open it up, we wanna take a look at you!" [55] His door and stairwell were so quickly covered with graffiti and trash that a move to the suburbs had to be made. It was hard for him to match the construction of that home to his income, as only from 1990 were performers finally paid a fair wage. Says Leont'ev, "In 1990, the year Yeltsin became president and the Communist Party was reduced to the parliamentary sidelines, market forces appeared ... Censorship collapsed. The public could choose what was interesting or close to them, and production of a different type emerged. The Nineties have been years of conflict between myself and that market."[56]

Despite the new cultural constraints of a music industry based upon money, not ideology, Leont'ev managed to win a prize at the World Musical Awards held in Monaco by Princess Caroline, who was charmed by the Russian visitor. At home, however, life was full of ongoing rather than realized changes. As one journalist says of Leont'ev and post-Soviet reality: "At the forefront [of his work was a new] psychology, both of society and the individual."

Perhaps the biggest event in Leont'ev's career of the 1990s was the stage-show entitled *On the Road to Hollywood* (*Po doroge v Gollivud*): "This performance, in its scale, the seriousness of its staging, the variety of its expressive means, has without a doubt outstripped everything sim-ilar that has ever been done on the Russian estrada." It was so large that *Po doroge* could only be staged in three concert halls: Rossiia (Moscow), Oktiabr'skii (St Petersburg) and Ukraina (Kiev).[57]

The album of the same name was recorded in Los Angeles, a move that reflects the increasingly international work of the singer, who also completed tours in the u.s., Canada, Israel, Germany, and India, to name but five countries. Moscow came to love him, granting him the capital's Government Prize for Literature and Art in 1996, in addition to earlier awards such as the prestigious Lenin Komsomol Prize (1985) and Honoured Artist of the Ukrainian Soviet Socialist Republic (1987). Most important of all, however, is the award that came in the same year as Moscow's gesture of atonement: People's Artist of Russia (1996). It came very late, as readers' letters nine years earlier in an

Leont'ev in 1999, wearing the sort of bright, theatrical costume that
marked a sartorial breakthrough for male performers. His wardrobe and
penchant for dramatic gesture were (and remain) alien to Kobzon's or
Leshchenko's aesthetic.

issue of *Sovetskaia kul'tura* attest. "They're not giving Leont'ev an
honour. But who 'they' are, we've no idea. They do it on the sly,
behind closed doors, answering to nobody except their boss. Is that
really the way it's going to be in the future, or *now,* even?"[58]

Leont'ev is today an extremely active and influential player in Russian estrada. His appearance has altered radically over the years, the
elastic, scarecrow frame now muscular and fit. He has of late gained
a reputation as a sex symbol in an environment that now allows him
to realize the grand dimensions of a staged *lichnost'*. Just as word of
the Beatles came late to his far northern home as a boy, Leont'ev
speaks touchingly of his first encounter with videos in the mid-1980s
and the telling impact of the new technology upon how he might give
a dramatic voice to personality on the stage: "When I got a VCR it
became in the literal sense a little window onto other worlds. I saw
beautiful, manicured people, all very sure of themselves. Bright, brilliant actors. I was suddenly amongst those people that I had never
dreamed of before. I was stunned by the range of expressive means,
by approaches to montage that were new to me, by unexpected ways

of getting a text over. I was stunned by the fantastic technicality of shooting a scene, by the abundance of special effects. Not just a country, but an entire planet opened up, another world."[59]

Given that so many of the stars in Soviet estrada did not write their own material but performed instead the work of others, any discussion of that discovery of *another* world needs to be prefaced by a discussion of which lyricists were favoured. Maintaining an illustrative opposition from earlier in this book, we can see a choice in the work of Leshchenko and Leont'ev between two poets: Rozhdestvenskii or Reznik.

LESHCHENKO AND ROZHDESTVENSKII, LEONT'EV AND REZNIK

I have to go where people are waiting for me.
I have to be where I'm needed and
propagandize as widely as possible the best
songs by Soviet composers. It seems that
I simply don't have the right to restrict myself
to a small audience while [other] people are
calling me to factory shop-floors, to the fields
and construction sites.[60]

Valerii Leont'ev

In a 1973 article that discusses Leshchenko's performance of the Rozhdestvenskii song "For That Lad" (*Za togo parnia*) in Sopot, the singer's *lichnost'* is seen as the perfect complement to the song. Leshchenko's "simplicity and internal virtue" matched the song's theme, that of memory for a fallen soldier. The writer observes that the singer is now beginning to attempt lyrical songs, having feared previously that they might sound rather "loud" in the hands of an exclusively civic singer. However, at this time of incipient experimentation, Leshchenko is starting to move (literally) a little too much across the stage and therefore not look the viewer squarely in the eye.[61]

Leshchenko seems nonetheless to have hit some Polish members of the audience squarely in the heart, since he recalled in the publication *Sovetskaia kul'tura* that after he sang "Za togo parnia" "some Poles came up to me and told me with excitement of their feelings, about the need for songs that remind us of heroes who died for freedom – songs that tell of war to those who never experienced it their own lives."[62]

Prior to 1985, even a performer like Leont'ev had found reason to turn to the civically charged air of a Robert Rozhdestvenskii song twice, in "In Memory of a Guitarist" (*Pamiati gitarista*) discussed above and "The River of Childhood" (*Reka detstva*).[63] Leont'ev has made the more lyrical and logical choice of Il'ia Reznik as a poet many times, on occasion performing works such as "Late" (*Pozdno*), now better known as part of Pugacheva's repertoire.

In beginning with the most overtly civic of all these songs in the repertoire of two men, that is, looking at Leshchenko's use of Rozhdestvenskii texts, it makes sense to choose the grandest, most direct works first: "Ballad of a Banner," "Ballad of Colours," and "Ballad of Immortality." These three poems concern the horrors of war and the deeds of several soldiers who are raised to unimaginable bravery. The bleakness of war inspires something much greater than itself, because these three songs together depict the forward movement in tangible reality (across a battlefield) which is in direct relation to one's progression as a human being. The further and longer you go, the better you are. In the third, culminating text describing the end of (military) movement and the moments prior to an execution at enemy hands, the *song* of a dying man manages to continue beyond the final bullet: beyond the limit of physical movement or experience is music.

A refrain throughout "Ballad of a Banner" (*Ballada o znameni*) insists that the events described did indeed take place "upon the earth," for we are told a tale of almost incredible, superhuman effort. In an uneven military conflict the Soviet banner "withers, rootless" amongst the overwhelmed corpses, but a soldier believed dead still crawls across the devastation to keep it safe. The "Ballad of Colours" (*Ballada o kraskakh*) concerns a woman's two sons, one with red hair ("born of the sun") and one with black (as "the night [of his birth] was so black"). Both are drafted in 1941, but their mother – despite odds of three to one – is lucky enough to get her sons back fit and well. The great difference she sees is the radical change that material conflict brings upon itself: both boys have snow-white hair, bleached by the horrors of the battlefield.

"Ballad of Immortality" (*Ballada o bessmertii*) takes those horrors to their logical conclusion, to death itself. Standing above a grave he has been forced to dig, a Soviet soldier suddenly begins to sing of the construction of a new world, "as though he was resurrected!"

Шептал слова не в такт,
Упрямо повторялся.
И получилось так,
Что он не пел, а клялся!
Литые фразы жгли,
С зарей перемежаясь.
Хорунжий крикнул: «Пли!»
А песня продолжалась.

[He didn't sing the words in sync, and stubbornly repeated them. It happened that he didn't sing, but made a vow! The flowing phrases burned and alternated with the dawn. A Cossack officer shouted: "Fire!" but the song kept going.]

The song has strong christological overtones: "He died that we might not die." The grounding of the logos in real-world, local experience has a counterpart in another Leshchenko song with words by Rozhdestvenskii, "The Pull of the Earth" (*Pritiazhenie zemli*). No matter how high cosmonauts fly, no matter how far their seeking takes them along the romantic roads or ways of Soviet adventure, there is always a pull back to Earth: "We are children of the Galaxy / But most important of all – / We're your children, dear Earth."

The link to Russia informs the flight into space; it does not slow or impede it. The material anchor *allows* a lofty, ideal significance. The effort of making music aids that winged dialogue, just as it does in "We Sing Songs" (*My pesni poem*): "Songs are gradually released like birds." There is another Rozhdestvenskii text, though, this time sung by Leont'ev, that does hold things back. "The River of Childhood" (*Reka detstva*) takes the lyricism evident at times with Rozhdestvenskii and uses it not to suggest the lyric elements in a civic stance but instead hints of how the songwriter's words are used as the starting point for a rapid retreat from (most) things Soviet. The song is one of retrospection, of the desire to go back to one's childhood, just as the song "Ia snova tam, gde lebeda" tells how "a secret path leads into the dreams of childhood." The active military hero is here the passive dreamer, borne along by a river that might help him in his yearning – but then again might not.

И меня река на себе сквозь года
По планете понесла.
Вынесла в моря, взмыла в облака.
Если было мне тяжело, то она
Помогла, как могла,
Добрая река, вечная река!

[The river bore me upon its back through the years across the planet. It bore me out into the seas, washed me up to the clouds. If things were hard, then the river helped as it was able. Kind river, eternal river!]

The Reznik song of Leont'ev's repertoire that is best known today is "Late" (*Pozdno*) in its version by Alla Pugacheva; Pugacheva's husband, Filipp Kirkorov, has recently recorded yet another version. What the text says about spatio-temporal notions is telling: the all-important, cherished progression through the dimensions of Rozhdestvenskii's ballads is here altered. Reznik's text manages to dismiss not only the passage of time but the fact that so much of it was spent wrongly before meeting the one person whose special presence cancels out the rest of the world. As a result of such ideas, the metaphor of the seeker's road is now made "difficult," one of struggle with or against the tangible, social world. That road does not have a specific goal, how-ever; both the strong pull backwards of the past (implicitly bad) and the difficult road forwards are to be ignored in favour of a timeless, immobile love.

Поздно!
Дожди рекою стали
Поздно,
Давно вернулись стаи
В гнезда.
Отшумели наши грозы.
А дорога нелегка,
Нелегка ...
И все же хорошо, что поздно
В твоей руке моя рука!

Поздно!
Теперь нам расставаться
Поздно.
Молвы глухой бояться
Поздно.
Все у нас с тобой непросто –
От былого не уйти,
Не уйти.
И все же хорошо, что поздно
Мы встретились с тобой в пути!

[It's late! The rains became a river too late, the flocks of birds have long since gone back to the nests. Our thunderstorms have passed over. And the road is difficult, difficult ... But all the same it's good that we met each other so late on the road! It's late! Now it's too late for us to part. Too late to fear a vague rumour. Everything between us is difficult, we cannot escape the past, cannot escape. But all the same it's good that we met each other so late on the road!]

Easy though it is to separate two men and two lyricists, a glance should be cast towards exactly how Leshchenko saw room for lyricism in his patriotic songs, how he saw room for a subjective interpretation of Russia in his Soviet repertoire. If such room is there, it will allow us to chart a smoother transition from Leshchenko to Leont'ev.

CIVIC OR PATRIOTIC

[My songs] are of a lofty and civic sound, folk
songs, tender and lyrical, jolly and youthful.[64]

Lev Leshchenko

Revolutions, as long as they don't
play themselves out in my kitchen,
don't really bother me.[65]

Valerii Leont'ev

An early post-Soviet article of 1992 attempts a definition of "patriotic" songs in Leshchenko's repertoire, one that sounds like a need to redefine the civic song of years gone by. "Strange metamorphoses" are said to have taken place in the genre:

It's either excessively in favour [of the status quo] and causes severe trauma [in its audience] like the stamp of a soldier's boot, or else it sounds suspicious when it starts driving everyone away with howling derision. For songs of a "well-defined" position, patriotic [tendencies] can be a means of existence. Here we hear the rustle of our forefathers' cornfields and a pensive rumble from the groves, the roll of rivers and the echo of distant hills ... It goes without saying that a patriotic singer isn't a singing reed. He's prompted not only by nature but by life, too. In his voice are the events he has experienced, history the way he sees it, a dream the way he's realized it. It can hardly go as far as the sterility of having no ideology at all, but he timidly gives voice to one generalized image, that of Russia, of his pain over Russia's woes, pride at its great achievements, and desire to see it prosper.[66]

Here the civic landscape has all the political figures extracted from it; it is landscape pure and simple. It is left for even civic songs to "timidly" suggest the meaning of this empty space or *carte blanche*. Leshchenko's response to that wiping clean, to the end of the U.S.S.R., is dismay: "It's awful, I can't come to terms with it. It's like the destruction of peace at home ... We're all crawling off into little national shells – and that's offensive for Russia, for an enormous, humane, and altruistic organism." He believes that private morality is the one characteristic that will live on amongst those who mourn the collapse of the Soviet Union. A recent song appears to be coming to terms with such awfulness: "Don't be sad that the wind has taken away

197

scraps of old posters. Day replaces night and night replaces the dawn. There's no sadness in my heart" (*Tuzi i kozyri*). Political views have been replaced by quieter retrospection in songs such as "Byli iunymi i schastlivymi": "We were young and happy in that year immemorial. All the girls were pretty and the bird-cherry in bloom."

Leshchenko's attitude to the civic song over the years explains his sadness at his country's demise. In 1979 he was worried about the encroaching popularity of shallow "entertaining" songs that merely copied foreign models.[67] In 1985 he declared that public song was no less than "our contemporary" and must be "as sincere and exciting as the events which it is called upon to engrave."[68] It must transmit the "rhythm and dynamism of today." The connection he saw between civic and patriotic songs was clear even in 1980, when he wrote a report on the *Red Carnation* song festival in Sochi. "Among the many wonderful traditions that help to strengthen the spiritual wealth of our youth, bolstering patriotism is one of the most important. It's a tradition of song festivals dedicated to the great civic thematic."[69] That thematic can be best served by "the art of internal experience," and here we see an inkling of subjectivity in even the most social of Leshchenko's songs. That subjectivity is required to express what he calls, quoting Rozhdestvenskii, "humanity's resonant memory." Private recollections preserve and promote public experience.

If that memory is preserved by fostering traditional songs, says the singer in 1984, then the same songs need a content "that attracts not just with a melody but a word, too ... That content [should] react to the most important events in our country."[70] The only people who can understand the songs or experience complicity are those who took part in these events. In celebrating them, Leshchenko refuses to be seen as either "static or monumental." "He feels light and unfettered on the stage. He not only sings but conducts a sung dialogue with the audience, he tells of his plans." The lyricism of his songs that comes from such a dialogue is said to differ in that he relates the experience of not one but *many* people. "Many people will say – That's about me, about us."

His talk of love, too, is less concrete and more abstracted, making it hard to tell whether the pronouns refers to a pair of lovers or all society: "We wait for spring, we always wait for love" ("Zhdem vesnu"). This ambiguity arises again in the song "Na zemle zhivet liubov'": "Love cannot live on earth without us." It appears that only in Leshchenko's most recent recordings does he reduce his references to tiny, P'ekhian dimensions, scaling down the civic dimensions, employing a direct address to a (private) audience – since only they sympathize: "He who knows how to love will forgive and understand us"

("Zapozdalaia liubov'"). Society shrinks to two people, and "they" become "us."

This wavering between two pronouns in Leshchenko's songs is perhaps rooted in the late 1970s. At this time the composer Aleksandra Pakhmutova commented, "What's attractive in him is the modernity, completeness, and nobility of his lyric hero."[71] The singer himself said, "I'm against a single type of performer on the estrada. A multifaceted, varied singer's a lot more interesting ... I sing songs that correspond to my internal state, to a civic stand ... But if we're talking all the same about my main theme, then that would be my contemporary." An article of 1979 talks of Leshchenko's songs as capturing the "striving of Seventies' youth ... a comprehension of their internal world."[72] The modern citizen is both public and private.

Despite all our efforts at reinterpretation, though, Leshchenko is more a man of public tendencies than anything else, one well described in 1983 as "speaking for all, while knowing how to look into the eyes of each person." Here he is credited with seeing the lyric in the civic and seeing the public "strength and significance" to which the private text can be raised whilst "trying [admirably] to get away from undeviating pathos."[73] In the past few years Leshchenko has indeed been recording some of the more personal songs that were not always seen as suitable in a Soviet environment.

The troubled nature of social themes for male performers after the 1970s is clearer still if we turn to politics and its significance for the two singers of this chapter. Although Leshchenko and Leont'ev have both performed in Afghanistan, their responses to the country are contextualized in different ways. Leshchenko's talk of Afghanistan comes from someone old enough to remember the romance of revolution in Cuba. Leont'ev's perception is evidently more sceptical, given the darker event together with which he often refers to it: Chernobyl'.

AFGHANISTAN, CUBA, CHERNOBYL', AND OTHER EXCURSIONS

> Maybe it's the timeless directive of a real artist –
> to be distant from regimes of various kinds, from
> political and economic commotion. It all helps
> in preserving one's own sense of the universe.[74]

Leshchenko recalls that during a trip to entertain soldiers in Afghanistan he felt completely tongue-tied in his conversations, until a young man asked him to sing "Home of Our Parents" (*Roditel'skii dom*). The song tells of "our" constant yearning for the youthful security of our parents' home; the fact that it is always there leaves us in eternal debt. In a field hospital that text must have had a profound resonance. Looking back on those experiences in a 1995 interview with *Komsomol'skaia pravda*, Leshchenko often mixes the maudlin with tales of adventure in dusty mountain passes: he remembers, for example, the severe bruising he got when his tank almost turned over. The wounded soldier's request is for a song that will take his heart home to Russia, at least for three minutes; the tale of the tank may sound like a moment of bravado from the pages of *For Whom the Bell Tolls*, but given the speed with which the Soviet operation there turned sour, it takes on metaphorical connotations. Afghanistan is more a story of retreat than of advance, and Leshchenko's experience of the country adds to his status as a transitional figure, one working in the vein of Kobzon, becoming famous under Brezhnev and managing to hang on through perestroika and beyond.

Cuba is an equally foreign experience, but one without the forced intrusion of military hardware, an exotic adventure that lends itself to the expansion of Soviet ideology. "I was [in 1978] on Cuba for the first time. I came to the Island of Freedom with a specially prepared program. I'm very nervous but hope to summon all the strength required ... I prepared several things, all absolutely new and even unusual for me. They're done in a modern rhythm ... written by young Soviet composers ... The festival here is, of course, one big holiday, but for each group [taking part] it's a creative marathon too. It's something we're all involved in, something that requires both responsibility and seriousness."[75]

The happy expansion of Russian influence is a subject far from Leont'ev's mind when he writes of Afghanistan in 1986. Interestingly, he links the country with Chernobyl' in several conversations:

We were recently doing some concerts in the Chernobyl' region. People were waiting for us [to play] there, so it was our civil duty to do so. It hasn't been long since our concerts in Afghanistan, either. Do you know what shocked me? Nineteen-year old lads, but what strength, what self-control! What friendship, mutual understanding, courage, spirit of comradeship. They're risking their lives and know it full well. Nobody, by the way, sent us either to Afghanistan or to Chernobyl' – it was our initiative. It's tough there, though, unbelievably tough, and if we could give our lads a few hours of a peaceful life – well, how can you express that in words?[76]

Given the differences, subtle or otherwise, between these two men, we need to look now at where these differences are actually created:

the stage itself. The way in which Leshchenko and Leont'ev discuss their relationship to their audience – military or civilian, Russian or Cuban – is a fundamental element in the transition from a Soviet superstar of the 1970s to one of the '80s.

THE STAGE/HALL DIALOGUE: CHARMING OR CHALLENGING THE AUDIENCE?

> The voice of a singer ... when we know it well,
> it becomes our close friend ... From the very
> first notes of a well-known voice we can say:
> that's Utesov, Shul'zhenko, Kobzon, Pugacheva,
> or Leshchenko. That's how we define the worth
> of a performer.[77]

> I never tried to please everybody.[78]
>
> Valerii Leont'ev

When Lev Leshchenko was voted Most Charming Estrada Singer of 1979, he was asked what made him so popular. He directed the credit squarely at his audience. "Popularity's a fickle thing. To keep the listeners' attention, you have to carefully choose a repertoire that's close to a modern listener. You have to keep learning and looking."[79] As Leshchenko's popularity has continued, while the quality of modern estrada has fallen, he finds himself obliged to extend those thoughts on fame by paraphrasing a well-known saying: a public gets the performers it deserves. "It seems to me that nobody needs quality singing any more. When it comes down to it, you are singing for somebody. That means you have to find the part of the public that will correspond to your conception of a song, spirituality, and aesthetics. You can't get away from that. That's why an artist has to stand somewhat aloof whilst at the same time working for people."

If modern Russian audiences have now tended to choose bad performers, we can better understand Leshchenko's recent pronouncement that "the main thing is not pleasing the audience but being yourself – and leading behind you those who are able. I don't have aspirations to the role of a messiah, but every artist has a little bit of that in him. Only a good, pure, decent heart can influence a person."[80] He goes on, and not for the first time, to quote Pasternak's definition of culture as a sponge. Leshchenko hopes that other singers will gravitate towards a tradition rather than towards him in particular. "We say: Shul'zhenko, Utesov... behind each of these names stands an entire world of songs, indivisible from the singer's *lichnost'*."[81]

What has been lost today from these worlds is the union of singer and listener, the type described in 1979: "I think that a song must become a dialogue with the audience – that's my main demand when I choose a work."[82] Four years later, in two different publications in 1983, Leshchenko is a little more explicit. In one he remarks that "there's a kind of dialogue here: the viewer forms us and we form the viewer. I think that's what constitutes art."[83] In the second he explains the situation in bolder terms: "Before talking with somebody, before you start a serious conversation with somebody, you try to get to know them, their position, interests, so that there's some kind of contact, or points where you come together."[84] Today that major contact, he thinks, is created by videos, but it is of such a different nature that he does not film them himself. The film-stage has replaced the wooden one, and he feels left behind. Leshchenko is worried that compared to a stage's dialogue, a video is much more of a monologue.[85] A video cannot alter itself midstream according to its reception.

His sense of that monologue may well be one dictated by the hard sell of new business. Even at the outset of perestroika Leshchenko felt that the pressure to make money was spoiling the pure contact between audience and performer:

Who cares for the level of an artist's skill? It turns out to be the viewer alone. Philharmonics aren't interested in the quality of estrada concerts; they only want to make money. I had concerts planned in Lviv, just three. I turn up and the director's in a panic. "I've got 16,000 requests here! You've never been here before, you see, and our hall has 800 seats. Please don't be offended, but you couldn't possibly play at the velodrome, could you? There's 3,500 there ... We've already sold all the tickets." I go out to the velodrome. I haven't got speakers powerful enough. There's absolutely no lighting whatsoever. There's no way that kind of concert is going to please either me or the viewers. But what if I refuse? That's an entirely different problem – and the newspapers are absolutely correct when they say that it [big business] is making it hard for us to work normally.[86]

Leont'ev's experience of the stage/hall dialogue is also a transitional one, between a closed ideology and free-market forces: "I'm not saying that the viewers have to love everything I do, but they should at least have an understanding of things, of whether they are enthused or indignant."[87] A song entitled "Prem'era" says to an audience, "You're our viewers and judges." He is aware of what in the past has caused indignation amongst his judges: "extrovert, frank, and unfettered behaviour."[88] An article in the journal *Avrora* in 1985 makes fun of these elements which damaged the stage/hall balance. It emphasizes the "elegance of his figure," the jumping around, and – as if the most salient aspect of his personality – the "uniqueness of his haircut."[89] His poor enunciation and a middling vocal range have also been targets.[90]

A 1993 interview in a national newspaper allows the singer to defend his stance and wildly antagonistic attitude towards the audience as one of "moral freedom. I felt the way I wanted and sang the way I wanted." [91] In songs such as "Bird Song" (*Golos ptitsy*) he tells of wishing liked a caged bird to be freed. By 1995 he expands his memories of his early, spontaneous work on stage to include having "felt" in an unorthodox manner.[92] Feeling oneself to be unorthodox is a process that takes place in the lessening space between a singer's private life and public performance, between the mundane aspects of his or her *byt* and the drama of a staged personality. As we will see in the persona of Leont'ev, the distance between the two lessens. It will vanish altogether in Alla Pugacheva.

PROS AND CONS OF A STAGED OR CINEMATIC PERSONALITY

The art of estrada is one of spectacle, where
movement and a lithesome performance play
an important role ... The modern "theatre of
song" begins with a clothes-hanger.[93]

Valerii Leont'ev

Despite Leshchenko's mildly criticized wanderings around the stage, the real step forward in the notion of *teatralizatsiia* and its consequence for expression of personality is made by Leont'ev. That step takes place both on the stage and the silver screen. In these films we see the continuation of a process begun by the films of Rotaru and Ponarovskaia: the decreasing distance between the actor and the role enacted to the point where it has almost disappeared. "My first encounter with cinema," says Leont'ev, "was the film *At Someone Else's Celebration* (*Na chuzhom prazdnike*). That was in 1982. Then there was *Don't Get Married, Girls* and *How to Become a Star*. In all these films I played myself. I still get scenarios where, let's say, a steamer turns up and there's Valerii Leont'ev playing on board. Screenwriters, sadly, don't have any more imagination."[94] *How to Become a Star* must indeed have been frustrating for Leont'ev. It is an interminable interview between a parrot(!) called Vaka and the singer Leonid Maksimov on the nature of fame in estrada. The meagre wit of such interactions is constantly interrupted by silent skits with numerous clowns and pointless snippets from unrelated performances by Charles Aznavour, Edith

Piaf, Liza Minelli, the Beatles, the Who, and many others. Leont'ev himself performs several numbers, expensively staged indoors or (for moments of simple lyricism) cheaply outside. He is the one reason to suffer the film from start to finish, since he shows here a new approach to *teatralizatsiia*.

The imagination required for a screenwriter to do justice to Leont'ev would be great, since he sees strong – time-honoured – connections between estrada and the circus. Together with Ponarovskaia and Pugacheva, he took part in the one-hundredth anniversary of the Moscow Circus where he played the role of a melancholy clown.[95] In several senses the work of Leont'ev and Pugacheva brings estrada full circle to its pre-revolutionary connections with the big top. It is tempting to draw a parallel between circus, carnival, and the dwindling of Soviet power: "Estrada and the circus combine well." [96] The embrace of a circus's round stage, as it grows, starts to resemble a stadium. Here we see a strange step in the growth of Soviet variety. The demise of the U.S.S.R. ushers in an art form that begs comparison with the relativity of carnival, intolerant as it is of stasis. The playing-out, however, of the personalities of Leont'ev and Pugacheva in a "circus" grows so big that it moves to soccer stadia, and we find ourselves in the realm of imperial circuses, of the grandiose and immobile. The stage/hall dialogue reaches its climax in these venues, leaving or launching the "big" persona in the lonely position of a true star. These dimensions are initially frightening.

"The first stadia were a nightmare for me," Leont'ev recalls. "When I went out, I couldn't see eyes, faces – just some huge mass in the distance. I had no idea who to sing to. Like you're singing into the air, at an empty field. But then I was able to work out a certain internal projection, a way of accumulating a charge of energy and sending it out to the entire space of the stadium … Our time is one of stadium art."[97] In fact by 1990 he says in an Estonian newspaper that "I'm more used to the hard benches or terraces of a stadium than comfortable armchairs."[98] The *need* to make out faces in the crowd shows Leont'ev's desire to stay at least one step from the even larger and entirely imagined audience of a television broadcast, an audience desirous of a pre-recorded song. Television, thinks Leont'ev, offers so many aids and editorial decisions that it can sell a performer with little or no *lichnost'* – only a live performance shows true personality. What worries some critics is the opposite, that using excessive physicality to show "true personality" destroys the "inner meaning" of a song and turns it into mere spectacle.

On the subject of "true personality," the singer holds individuality to be "something given a person from birth, something in his genes.

It's *his* worldview, first and foremost ... Probably each period of our life leaves its trace upon what we're used to calling a soul ... Individuality in art needs work. And, I should add, professionalism" – a quality he defines in the last year of the Soviet Union as indivisible from emotional sincerity.[99] Professionalism also needs money, as Raimonds Pauls pointed out in an interview of 1988. Pauls noted even during perestroika that for Pugacheva and Leont'ev to realize the full extent of their staged repertoires, "you've got to invest something."[100]

The decision to include theatre as an expression of his disconcertingly large personality came "intuitively," Leont'ev says. "In our time it's not enough to just sing: you have to include other means from your artistic armoury – dances, elements of circus and sport ... It's very important for me that when I perform, there's something that you might call the sensation of flying ... everything moves, rushes off and flies as though past me, out of my control."[101] That sense of using and then overcoming the tangible world on stage is applicable even to the microphone cord. "It's a whip or a snake, a rope, you have to fight it constantly. It's alive. The sensation of resistance in the thing is essential." Similarly, discussing *Dzhordano* in an interview of 1990, he talks again of the link between matter and spirit in the context of theatrical or poetic change: "You shouldn't confine yourself to the limits of one genre. That leads to the dying off of some cells and the withering of the soul."[102] Genre and audience expectations are starting to be *detrimental* to the creation of an ideal from sensible matter.

The greatest game played by Leont'ev with sensible reality is in the film *Psychic* (*Èkstrasens*). Here he performs as an extremely stylized Chinese villain (Kitaets), drawing apparently on both Peter Sellers in the western Fu Manchu series and the self-consciously thespian air of David Bowie's film work. The evil of the character he plays is battled twice over by the "good" characters in the film, both by the opposing, positive force of two souls in love and by an individual closing his eyes and affirming out loud, "I am free" (*Ia svoboden*). "It's a fantasy, an adventure of paranormal phenomena in the human psyche, together with an investigation of their possibilities. There I played a villain, an enemy of the human race. In general I'm attracted to extremes, such as extreme altruism or, on the other hand, obvious evil in its human incarnation."[103]

These melodramatic extremes are, in the minds of innumerable Soviet music-lovers, a direct consequence of western influences in Soviet and post-Soviet estrada, all in a way that shifts the socialist metaphor of "seeking" away from Moscow and towards the popular culture of Britain and America. Leshchenko's assertion that all roads lead to Moscow, in the song "I Love You, Capital City" (*Ia vas liubliu, stolitsa*), will soon come under attack, as will the Muscovite dialogue of singer/state.

THE SIGNIFICANCE OF WESTERN ESTRADA AND "SEEKING"

> Songs, just like people, are born, live, and die.
> Yet some of them are eternal.[104]

> The quality of the performance and recording
> are as good as any European equivalent; there's
> nothing specifically Soviet in the sound, and
> that's strange.[105]

During the years of Brezhnev's *zastoi*, when Leshchenko was most popular, the singer was able to find western recordings: Janis Joplin, Bill Haley, Elvis Presley, the Beatles, and Tom Jones.[106] (He said in 1997 that the Welshman was still his favourite singer.) He was even the target of a jibe or two, that he was a little western in his manner.[107] Nevertheless, with the coming of perestroika and the true flood of western culture into Russia, he was left behind as an anachronism. As one journalist points out, being known at that time as the "Nightingale of the Kremlin" was a death sentence in the music industry. When Leshchenko is reminded that while Rotaru and Pugacheva changed their images to match the changing times, he clung to his aesthetic, the singer remarks that by chasing fashion, one can end up "sticking a goat's tail on the back of a bull." This danger is particularly acute in regards to a song's rhythm: "Western songs have one rhythmic structure, whilst ours have a completely different one."[108] Leshchenko sees attempting to sound western as a means of winning a small, young contingent in any hall – but also of losing most of one's long-time audience. That audience was at one time enormous, as he recalls. It was even sometimes too big, and we once again see the conservative, civic singer's uneasiness over the dimensions of the stage/hall discourse's final days:

Unfortunately [at the peak of my career] I had no control over the recordings. They were often handed over [to the media] without my knowledge. Kukharskii, who was then Minister of Culture, came up to me at a reception once and said: "Lev! What are you doing? Yesterday I turned on Channel One, and there's Lev Leshchenko singing. I switch over to Channel Two and you're there as well!" What can you say? That's my job. A lot later I came to understand that there really had been some overkill, so I tried to limit myself and even asked that some old radio and TV recordings be wiped off the tapes – which was done. But now there's the opposite extreme – they don't show me at all.[109]

As the western-sounding pop of glasnost appeared, Leshchenko et al. vanished from television screens for almost two years, and the singer was worried that it might be forever.[110] He soon saw, though, that far beyond the limits of Moscow, in the deep provinces where fashions rarely venture, the new stars were playing to half-empty halls.[111] *Sovetskaia kul'tura* published in 1989 a letter from a seventeen-year old girl who had been a rock fan and shuffled off to a Leshchenko concert out of boredom. She had been bowled over by the performance and promptly wrote to the paper, disputing the claim that Leshchenko was not popular amongst young people.[112] Nowadays the singer is troubled by the tendency of so-called New Russians (*Novye russkie*) to plough money into up-and-coming talentless performers for the sake of a quick return on an investment; he feels these stars will inevitably spoil the public's taste in the provinces and be detrimental to the viewers' sentimental education.

The one western star he feels would not spoil public taste and with whom he compares himself on several occasions is Sinatra. "Had I been born in America, I would have sung country – that's jolly music which needs a good voice. Though I might have sung the kind of music that Frank Sinatra performs. Who knows?"[113] These are the thoughts and choices of a mature man, though, and he understands perfectly well that the young Russian audience of today needs to grow as he himself has done. "In your youth you prefer rhythm and dynamism, but with age you seek something deeper, you seek a more philosophical sound in the music and words."[114]

The early Soviet metaphor of seeking had the tantalizing, implicit meaning that the sought goal was attainable – either close by or soon to be. The sorry state of Russian society and mass culture today has removed that morally validated and culturally imbued destination. "It's very hard for people to orient themselves in this situation. The main thing is that we have no moral immunity, you see?... They instilled in us a sense of what's moral and what's not. People did not educate themselves individually, they didn't create moral criteria for themselves." On the subject of those criteria today, he says, "I'm not a prude, I can watch an erotic film, but in order to watch it you need to work out a certain immunity in yourself."[115]

Compare that with the earlier discussion of his own seeking in an article of 1983. At that time he is on "a tough road of unavoidable losses and gains, all in search of that single intonation without which there is no real dialogue with the public. This is a search for the simplicity, complete freedom, and natural behaviour upon the stage that all result from overcoming a certain dramatic stasis – and then again by overcoming another extreme, that of excessive vanity, of attempts to seem 'unbridled' by using superfluous gestures and pointless movement around the stage."[116] Earlier, in the even more conservative days of 1979, Leshchenko again sees his work in terms of seeking a bridge between extremes or poles: "Together with satisfying the desire of your public, you have to constantly experiment, to look for new paths."[117] This is a process of give and take, dictated by the occasional need to "take a step back" in the name of audience comprehension. "You have to affirm something that's your own, something you sincerely believe in, to master yourself, overcome yourself and put out the most you can – all to win the genuine sympathy of the listeners."[118] Today, with the evanescing of the stage/hall dialogue, there is no sense "of what's moral." Maximalism is the order of the day, as a materialistic worldview replaces a materialist one.

Leont'ev has similar things to say about the post-Soviet situation. He, like Leshchenko, feels the influence of money over talent in today's estrada: "Today everyone who feels like it has started singing. You don't necessarily have to be talented. You need money – and then the chance to be on stage or the radio will appear."[119] Whereas many of Leont'ev's interviews during perestroika stress the need to be a modern singer and concern oneself with relevant, social themes, the awful banality of today's talentless singers and the dark stories of the post-Soviet tabloids have led him to redefine his moral stance of years gone by as "romantic." The socially valid concerns of glasnost now appear outdated and leave the singer in a romantic state of opposition with the younger crowd of 2000. (Hinting at this problem, even articles of the mid-1980s see Leont'ev's "seeking" as a hunt primarily for his sense of self, despite his insistence upon social issues.[120]) Now Leont'ev suggests his music is a step *away* from modern, amoral society: "I'd like to think that listening to my songs, people could forget about … murders, wars, and rising prices." He wishes to steer the Russian listener away from what he has called the "dumping-ground" (*svalka*) of modern music.[121] The sentimentalism that began the snowballing process of a growing, staged *lichnost'* now offers a refuge when the dimensions in which that lichnost' operates are too loud, crude, and void of any ideal significance, based only on money.

This aesthetic "dumping" – often in imitation of the West – Leont'ev views in the same manner as Leshchenko, as the loss of at least one positive aspect of Soviet society, that of morals. As a result Leont'ev's retrospectively defined romantic stance becomes advocacy of an abstract goodness. Soviet socialist sentimentalism becomes sentiment, pure and simple. "My motto is [and always has been] 'increase the amount of good.' I try and stick to that. I've taken all pointedly political songs out of my repertoire – a person needs some breathing room! ... Let people at my concerts remember love, remember goodness in themselves and others."[122] His desire, which he has expressed in similar terms elsewhere, is to "cultivate thoughts of the relationship of man and the universe, thoughts about good and evil, about the need to be more patient towards one another."[123] In 1995 he talks of modern Russian society's moribund "psychic and moral atmosphere."[124] Soviet morality minus the Soviet equals morality abstracted from its historical applicability and safe to discuss in the fickle modishness of post-Soviet estrada.

Morality and the psyche are hardly notions that are often bound together by Soviet syntax, but Leont'ev's implicit suggestion that there is something good that resides in a non-material (even asocial) realm – one of supremely private significance – is a hypothesis which Alla Pugacheva both examines and develops fully. A recent overview of Soviet cinema, published in Moscow, includes the tersest of sentences defining the consequences of Pugacheva's songs. She was "the first Soviet singer to enjoy a scandalous reputation and a talent to threaten the authority of official estrada."[125] Her life and work – given the massive numbers of records she has sold – are of unexpected significance in Russians' self-perception as they move from the stagnation of the 1970s into the final days of the Soviet Union. Her songs share the major tenets of Leont'ev's, but go much further, taking *teatralizatsiia* to its logical extreme. The *lichnosti* of Alla Pugacheva on and off the stage, in and out of the movies, are one and the same.

8
ALLA PUGACHEVA:
REDEFINING ESTRADA

A song has three basic components for me.
The first is probably the character of its
heroine. I want to see in that heroine an
interesting, modern person. After all, when
I sing, I'm no longer Alla Pugacheva but that
heroine, I'm transformed into her. Then, of
course, there's the thought that the song
carries. It must be comprehensible, but not
trivial. It has to excite a lot of people and be
expressed in comprehensible human language.
Last of all there's the basic melody.[1]

Alla Pugacheva

Two chapters in this book are given to Alla Pugacheva, a decision taken
not on the basis of her longevity upon the stage but upon the significance of what she has done, and continues to do, on that platform. A
combination of biography and musical observations is required to do
that significance justice. If there is one moment that defines the initial
rush of Pugacheva into the spotlight and Soviet attention, it is the song
"Arlekino," and as a consequence much attention is paid here to the
way in which it was presented at an Eastern Bloc music festival and
then received by the conservative workings of Soviet estrada. But "Arlekino" was only an introduction to how its performer would change the
relation of civic and lyric songs in the Soviet canon. One vital aspect
of how she did so was to set to music the work of important poets such
as Mandel'shtam, Tsvetaeva, and Shakespeare. Her use of the literary
canon to alter that of estrada illuminates not only the importance of
other poets such as Reznik and the composer Pauls for her career but
also how seamlessly the words and music of those two men dovetailed
with the *lichnost'* that Pugacheva was already fashioning for herself.

ALLA PUGACHEVA:
"GET OFF ME! I'M A SOVIET SINGER!"

She destroyed the established norms, the
standards of our existence. She lived, while

By the early 1980s Pugacheva was unassailable as estrada's primary diva and responded to the duties of her position with increasing flamboyance.

> we – obediently following orders – played a
> role, that of the Soviet woman: the peaceful,
> working woman, without excess or ideas above
> her station, sexually untroubled, politically
> literate, morally upright.[2]

Alla Pugacheva was born on 15 April 1949 to parents who only a year before had lost their first child to diphtheria. Her father, Boris, had dreamed of being a circus artist, but during military service he had been blinded in one eye by a brick splinter shorn from a wall by a stray bullet. Her mother, Zina, had sung in a concert brigade during the war but would later lose her voice. Both parents, engineers by trade, had bid farewell to their dreams of estrada careers and prayed that their daughter would fulfil them instead.[3] Alla's brother was born a year later, in April 1950.

Before Alla was five, her mother had begun music lessons with her.[4] She would place ten matches upon the piano, and move each one from right to left as the exercises were repeated. At these lessons she taught Alla her favourite song, "Autumn Leaves" (*Osennie list'ia*), a piece Alla would later perform on national television – on 1 January 1997 – because even after many years it could "touch the soul of both an adult and a child." The little girl was dragged out to entertain guests on the piano at every opportunity. When they had gone she would compose in private and listen to the family records of Utesov and Shul'zhenko. "But that doesn't necessarily mean that I liked what they sang," she recalls. "I liked *how* they sang. They were never false in front of their viewers or listeners. Everybody sensed what they felt and sang about."[5] The importance of a performer's sensibility also led to the young Pugacheva's love for "sentimental melodies, old waltzes and romances."[6]

She worked hard at school, and later admitted that she regarded her schoolmates as an audience. Though an A student, she would sometimes purposely not do homework, just to give herself the challenge of an impromptu performance when questioned by the teacher.[7] She was equally confident with other children, and when one boy made fun of her father's vision, she threatened to provide him with first-hand experience of blindness. For such behaviour she was soon known as "psycho Pugacheva."[8]

When Alla was fourteen, an odd aspect of Krushchev's Thaw led to searches for Stalinist scapegoats. Boris Pugachev, then director of a shoe factory, was called in on trumped-up charges of economic irregularities. The police trashed the Pugachevs' apartment. He was sentenced to three years, a tragedy explained away by the family as the world's longest business trip. Following much legal wrangling, he was released after one and a half years.

Again, Alla's confidence grew with both her friends and teachers; she went on to get top grades in literature, drawing, home economics and singing. Her friends were sometimes treated to her performances: among her skills were impersonations of other singers, in particular Shul'zhenko.[9] She was soon ready to embark upon the next stage of her parents' plans for her and entered a Moscow musical institute (Ippolitov-Ivanov) to major in choral work and conducting. At this time her intention was to be a pianist and she honed those skills. She would also often hide away in the institute's basement and practice impersonations of Ella Fitzgerald, Louis Armstrong, and Edith Piaf. According to a recent biography, her decision to become a singer resulted from two impulses: the influence of Piaf's records and her own observation that television variety programs were more popular than orchestral ones.[10]

In 1965, at the height of P'ekha's success, the young Pugacheva was discovered by Aleksandr Levenbuk, one half of the comic radio duo Livshits and Levenbuk. They wanted to use Alla for a touring version of their satirical show *Bang-Bang* (*Pif-paf*). Levenbuk had come to the institute looking for some young talent to pad the program, warning contenders that the paying public would expect "a real spectacle."[11] It took considerable convincing for Zina Pugacheva to let her fifteen-year-old daughter go, especially since this was *estrada*, not real music. Early film footage of Alla shows a nervous, red-headed schoolgirl with a winning gap between her front teeth. (Her figure would alter many times over the years, but the gap and the red hair have remained.)

For the show Alla was asked to learn a song called "Robot" that would launch her career, a number so lyrical she cried when she sang it, and "for some reason people liked that."[12] She would later remember the great sense of release from those tears. Pugacheva's private discovery arrived together with a public equivalent of equal importance; that year, 1965, has been defined as the start of an important decade in the history of Soviet estrada:

1965–1975: Start of the period of "stagnation" (*zastoi*) and great falsehood in songs. Formation of a standard in Soviet performers: M. Magomaev, L. Zykina, I. Kobzon. A hybrid of lyrico-civic songs appears in the repertoire of È. P'ekha and M. Kristalinskaia. An increase in the conflict between "official" and "unofficial" music.

1975–1985: The crisis reaches a peak. Of those songs about the distant war, the most often heard is "Small Land" (*Malaia zemlia*), of those dedicated to the heroism of peaceful times the most common is "The Baikal-Amur Railway Line" (*Baikalo-Amurskaia Magistral'*) – "Hear the roar of time: BAM!" It is precisely into these years that the explosion of Pugacheva's success falls, together with that of a clearly expressed opposition: bards, rock groups ...[13]

Pugacheva was soon asked to perform on the national radio show *Good Morning! (S dobrym utrom!)* – something of a risk, given her as yet brief musical education. Here she sang "Robot," and since there were no real distribution networks for records, the song instead proved its popularity in another way; it was sung by amateur performers and customers in restaurants all over the country.[14] At the time of this success in 1965, Pugacheva became a natural contender in *Good Morning*'s listener-supported contest, "Melody of the Month." One of her songs, "How Could I Fall in Love" (*Kak by mne vliubit'sia*), garnered a huge number of votes. When the same thing happened with "Don't Argue with Me" (*Ne spor' so mnoi*), the singer and the songs' composer, Vladimir Shainskii, were asked to step down after accusations of favouritism by the Composers' Union. Pugacheva and Shainskii refused, and the contest was soon off the air for good.

Despite her snowballing success, Pugacheva decided that finishing her education at the institute was of greatest importance. But problems arose when she went off to the teaching practice in the classroom that was a major part of the coursework. Her skirt was deemed too short, her class was poorly behaved, and she was giving low grades to a policeman's son. She was eventually forced to give in and bless the simpleton with better marks, telling the boy sarcastically to "go and please your mother with your success."[15] Even so, she managed to graduate from the institute with top marks in June 1969. She was soon snapped up by a group of estrada and circus performers from Tambov, and then by the makers of a movie to dub the song "My Knight Has Gone" (*Uekhal rytsar' moi*) – though she received no credit for it.

The real shift in her career came between 1969 and 1970 with an invitation to join the ensemble Novyi Èlektron, affiliated with the Lipetsk Philarmonia. She would later call this her first truly professional experience. Musicians at the time had to be linked to a philarmonia or concert organization to win the right to perform. All members of Novyi Èlektron were from Moscow, yet they had sought a trouble-free, provincial affiliation; Lipetsk was a dull town once described as "famous for its huge metallurgical plant, mineral water, and pretty girls."[16] Concerts to indifferent provincial audiences and interminable tours soon became the norm. Without even a tour bus, the band often slept on the same stage where they performed songs such as P'ekha's "Belyi svet" – though the superstitious Pugacheva refused to sing this number ever again after the time at a concert in Perm' when her heel was stuck and then ripped off in a gap between floorboards on stage.[17]

Here the tale turns towards family matters. Pugacheva married Mikolas Orbakas, a Lithuanian from the town of Kaunas; their first child was born on 25 May 1971. Orbakas wanted to name their daughter Kristina, much to the chagrin of Alla, who worried about problems resulting from such a "foreign" name. Zina Pugacheva was still working, and the raising of Kristina was entrusted more to Mikolas's parents, Zenon and Ania, who lived in Kaunas. The little girl became bilingual and was christened in a Catholic church.

Not long afterwards, during a tour in Leningrad in the autumn of 1972, a young lyricist by the name of Il'ia Reznik knocked on the door of Pugacheva's hotel room. When she refused the first song he offered her, he quickly produced another, "Posidim, pookaem," which refers to the key indicator of a deeply provincial accent and means (very) literally, "Let's sit and talk a while, emphasizing the sound 'o' [be it stressed or not]." As the working relationship of Reznik and Pugacheva took shape, touring pressures began to tell on the matrimonial equivalent. By November of 1973 the singer and Orbakas were divorced, just as talk began of her taking part in the Fifth All-Union Contest for Estrada Artists. The finals in October 1974 were broadcast on national TV and attracted great interest because, in the mind of one writer, the quality of other variety shows was so unspeakably dire. Pugacheva chose two songs: "Posidim, pookaem" and a song of the war, "Ermolova s Chistykh prudov."

When the jury began to tally its votes, Pugacheva's lot did not look good. Then, a well-known singer of the '60s, Gelena Velikanova, came to her defence. In what may be an entirely apocryphal account we read:

"Comrades! Respected members of the jury! I want to say a few words about this girl, Alla Pugacheva. How can we award her no place whatsoever? She's so very, very talented! Maybe she has her failings, but she's not like anybody else! Comrades! We'll bear the shameful stigma all our lives of being the ones who gave Pugacheva nothing!"

"But that Pugacheva's so vulgar!" [retorts Utesov, also a jury member.]

"No, she's not vulgar, she's ... colourful [says the leader of the Armenian Estrada Orchestra]. I really liked her, too. And Iosif here agrees with me." [He motions to another member, Iosif Kobzon.]

Even Utesov was convinced to take part in a complete re-vote, according to which Pugacheva was awarded an additional, third place. It was at this competition that two important acquaintances began. Between numbers, wandering the theatre, she first met Raimonds Pauls, and later, after the curtain call, Klavdiia Shul'zhenko came up to the stage and threw the young singer a bunch of roses.

It was also in late 1974 that Pugacheva began her acquaintance with the VIA The Happy Guys (Veselye Rebiata), named after Utesov's musical. They had taken part in a Liverpool contest of bands along with the Rolling Stones and ended up in the top ten.[18] The leader of the group, Pavel Slobodkin, said he had been impressed not only by Pugacheva's ability to perform both classic Soviet and folk-oriented numbers but also by her cutting parodies of P'ekha.[19] She was at this time being spoken of in the Soviet press as a "singer with an excellent voice and undoubted dramatic gift – each of her songs is a little play."[20] Together Pugacheva and Slobodkin hoped to develop that gift and "get away from a certain coldness on the stage, that certain academism" of years gone by.[21] Working with the ensemble, Pugacheva said she felt as if they had been "born together," though by the end of 1976 their aims were noticeably different. Then she started to look for "grander forms" of musical presentation[22] which would give her something "new in the expression of a creative individuality."[23]

At the outset of 1975, plans were being made to send a Soviet contender to the important Zolotoi Orfei competition mentioned so often in this book. The original competitor suddenly found himself embroiled in accusations of homosexuality, and a swift change of candidate was required by the Ministry of Culture. Pugacheva was chosen, albeit with few smiles, and had to quickly find the Bulgarian piece that each performer was obliged to sing. She selected the old song "Arlekino" by Èmil Dimitrov. New words and a new arrangement were created for the competition. She also decided to use a ridiculous laughter she had affected years before for the harlequin's gaiety; she invented the pose of a puppet's arms, broken at the elbow, to suggest a lost, carnival atmosphere. In an interview she would later say that this staging was used to suggest "a circus-like spectacle, a song that allowed me to fill myself with both pain and mockery, both irony and sadness."[24] She remarked elsewhere that "the [text's] hero lived and suffered on the stage just like normal people do ... [It's] about all of us and about me personally."[25] Pugacheva dedicated "Arlekino" to the well-known Soviet clown Engibarov: "He was my favourite clown and even died while working. Just think: he died from laughter. Perhaps I subconsciously dedicated the song to his radiant, smiling memory." Money was collected among her friends to pay for a costume to do justice to the clown's reputation.

The final stages of Zolotoi Orfei took place in a Bulgarian Black Sea resort. Lev Leshchenko and Sofiia Rotaru were among the guests of honour. Of the songs they performed, one journalist has written: "What else was going on around [Pugacheva at that festival]? 'There beyond the Clouds' by Leshchenko ... 'Red Rue' and 'Apple Trees in Bloom' by Rotaru ... nothing but woeful lyrics and the yearning of a heart. And then suddenly there's a breaking of the rules, some pot-shots at the targets ... 'I'm a jester, I'm Harlequin, I'm simply laughter!'"[26] One Soviet newspaper called the song "the daring yet sad confession (*ispoved'*) of a clown ... He's defenseless and hurt, but it is in his power to reveal truths [and] it doesn't matter to whom: to a king, to Hamlet, to a circus gallery."[27]

Her triumph was described as a "spaceship tearing away from everybody else on its way to the stars."[28] The winner's banquet was attended by the Bulgarian Minister of Culture and other dignitaries, one of whom made an indecent proposal to Pugacheva, to which she responded with the clear-cut: "Get off me! I'm not a whore, I'm a Soviet singer!"[29] In another moment of Ponarovskaian experience of the gap between popular and official approval, no one turned out to meet her at Moscow's Sheremetevo airport, and her winning performance, despite the significance of the festival across all of Eastern Europe, was cut from Soviet state television. Her gentle, acoustic songs for the Èl'dar Riazanov comedy *The Irony of Fate* (*Ironiia sud'by*) did little to mitigate the nastiness. An additional problem was that her increasing fame caused tensions and resentment within Veselye Rebiata, and Pugacheva left the group, declaring her desire to work in the vein of western singers such as Barbara Streisand and Sarah Vaughn – or the Soviet Sofiia Rotaru and the comic actress Liudmila Gurchenko, Kobzon's ex-wife.[30]

She decided to enter GITIS in 1977 but had to convince the head of the estrada faculty that a famous singer such as herself had something to gain from further education. GITIS took her on as an extramural student who twice a year would be obliged to give up touring for the sake of exams. She began to study in particular under another well-known clown, Andrei Nikolaev, because "a song shouldn't just be sung, but shown, in order to put on a complete performance."[31] Worried at first by awful tales of her behaviour, Nikolaev was soon won over by her diligence and enthusiasm.

Her graduation presentation at the end of her final year was the show *A Singer's Monologues* (*Monologi pevitsy*), staged in Moscow's Rossiia concert hall. Utesov was head of the examination committee. He sat silently for the whole performance, and word has it that he dabbed his eyes on occasion with a large handkerchief.[32] After all was over, he stood and intoned, "There can only be one grade here. I imagine that there'll be no objections." He congratulated Pugacheva and gave her the diploma.

In 1978 Pugacheva's film *A Woman Who Sings* (*Zhenshchina, kotoraia poet*) was released. The screenplay had been rewritten three times under Pugacheva's orders, since she was the star and wanted a film about herself, not the actual character, Anna Strel'tsova. She admitted even before the film's launch that despite her persona she was in essence playing herself.[33] The authorities were already irritated by the project, because excitement in the press had caused the newspaper *Trud* to print a picture of an interview with Pugacheva five times larger than that of Brezhnev in the same issue.[34] The bosses at the state movie studio of Mosfil'm also objected to the fact that all the songs were about love, with nothing civic in sight.

Not long after the movie, her first album, *Mirror of the Soul* (*Zerkalo dushi*), was released in the stunning quantity of four million copies. Queues formed the instant it appeared in stores.[35] Pugacheva began to dream of a correspondingly grand stage show, despite the private implications of the album's title, a show with "ballet dancers, light effects, and beautiful costumes. I want the audience to see a joyful, beautiful spectacle."[36] The journal *Soviet Screen* awarded her the readers' prize for best actress of 1978 and she was asked to represent the U.S.S.R. at Sopot, since the Soviets had not won first prize there for some while. She decided to perform – despite inflammation of the lungs – "Kings Can Do Anything" (*Koroli mogut vse*), an irreverent song of amorous royalty that had irritated the authorities and was banned from Soviet radio and television.[37] Nevertheless she went to Poland and sang precisely that song "to all of Eastern Europe and the Soviet Union. While bureaucrats in their Moscow offices gripped their hearts, heads, and telephones, the public cried out 'Encore!' to a singer in a Polish resort."[38]

Pugacheva won the Grand Prix, the "Amber Nightingale," and gave her prize money to the construction of a children's health centre.[39] The song bears some likeness to "Arlekino" and given the staginess of both, Pugacheva declared after the competition that "I won't sing this any more. It's not my song ... I don't want to be 'somebody' [such as a harlequin or a king]. I want to be myself on the stage." She was very proud of her Polish triumph, an admission she made "without false modesty."[40] By this time, perhaps, she did not need to be modest: at the close of the 1970s she was lauded as the most popular singer in the U.S.S.R., one who managed to continue all the traditions of Utesov, Shul'zhenko, and Kobzon.[41] A Japanese newspaper listed Pugacheva and Gagarin as the U.S.S.R.'s most famous exports,[42] and the chanteuse became an Honoured Artist of the Russian Federation in the autumn of 1980.[43]

In the last week of December 1981 she performed with Pauls at the Moscow Theatre of Estrada in a program called *The Maestro Is Our Guest* (*U nas v gostiakh maèstro*). Of this broadcast the *Literary Gazette* said in worried tones that Pugacheva was now attempting too much by both performing and presenting the work of such well-established stars, since this type of show – though designed to showcase Pauls's work – was merely an excuse for Pugacheva to gain more airtime. The extension of her staged, "expansive" persona into the real-world role of hostess was not welcome in some quarters. To see Pugacheva behaving on stage as she saw fit before the forgiving times of perestroika was deemed a "vulgar" spectacle.[44] She was now too big for her pantomime boots, yet it was at exactly this time of such troubling tendencies that the creative trio of Pugacheva, Pauls, and Reznik was at its most significant.

Successes with the poet and composer were continued with tours in Australia and Finland (1981) plus Yugoslavia, Romania, Hungary, Italy, and France (1982). Just prior to this wayfaring, Pugacheva had advocated that Soviet estrada was ready to be promoted abroad;[45] it was therefore her performance in Paris that perhaps meant the most to her. This show took place on 28 June 1982 in the Olympia concert hall, and had a special significance because Piaf had sung there.[46] The French press pleased Pugacheva when they compared her to both Piaf and Streisand. Despite such parallels and the temptation to westernize her material, she nevertheless continued to work with a wholly Soviet repertoire.[47]

In 1984 she performed twice in films, in *Season of Miracles* (*Sezon chudes*) and *I've Come to Speak Up* (*Prishla i govoriu*). She was also offered a part in the Anglo-Swedish musical *Chess* but turned it down.

Not only did it involve playing the wife of a Soviet player who defects, but Pugacheva herself would have to work overseas for a year. She considered the risk to any good will between her and the authorities to be too great.[48] *I've Come to Speak Up* had its own problems in choosing a screenwriter until Pugacheva gave the thumbs-up to a familiar name, that of Reznik. He had stayed with her after having problems in finding accommodation in the capital. The two were therefore constantly in adjacent rooms collaborating on a film that had the working title *Alla.*

In 1985 she became a People's Artist of the Russian Federation, an award that suggests the permanent institutionalization of the recipient. At the time, Pugacheva was at the Leningrad Rock Festival, mixing with seminal perestroika musicians such as Boris Grebenshchikov of Akvarium and Kostia Kinchev of Alisa. The next year she began more work in the same vein after meeting the guitarist Vladimir Kuz'min, exponent of what has been called "an estrada version of rock and roll." Although popular in his own right, Kuz'min found Pugacheva's offer of collaboration very attractive, an indication of her clout: "New instruments, recording sessions in a good studio, constant concerts, a good cut guaranteed in advance, trips abroad, and the main thing – an easy existence behind the shoulders of Pugacheva's administrators. It would be a sin not to accept."[49]

One of the most famous songs they recorded together was "Two Stars" (*Dve zvezdy*), written by Igor' Nikolaev, who would subsequently become an important composer for Pugacheva. Kuz'min's most significant concert with her came perhaps with the moment when the hope of perestroika and the hopelessness of the status quo were most keenly felt as incompatible – the disaster at Chernobyl'. Pugacheva travelled to the site to perform before "heroic people,"[50] and a fundraising concert was organized at Moscow's Olimpiiskii concert hall on 30 May 1986.

By the time perestroika had become the death-throes of the Soviet Union in May 1991, Pugacheva was named a People's Artist of the U.S.S.R. and embarked on a new venture: the creation of a perfume – "Alla" – with the French firm Sogo. For two months samples were sent between Paris and Moscow until the singer was happy. The paperwork was also protracted, for it was not until April 1992 that she presented the perfume at a press conference at Moscow's Rossiia concert hall. As an extension of her post-Soviet persona, within a little over a year she had released a glossy magazine dedicated to herself and contemporary estrada, simply and similarly entitled *Alla.*[51]

The major story in the remaining years of Pugacheva's biography is that of her marriage to Filipp Kirkorov. Pugacheva had known Kirkorov, born in 1967, the son of a famous Bulgarian musician, from his early days in estrada, but had not been too approving of his talents: "We have to beat the Bulgarian estrada out of him," she once said.[52] They were married as quietly as possible in St Petersburg in March 1994 by then-mayor Anatolii Sobchak. The couple toured together in Israel; Pugacheva's career came full circle as she became a jury member at Zolotoi Orfei and in July was granted a plaque on the Slavic equivalent of Hollywood Boulevard, Yalta's "Square of Stars."

Not long afterwards Kirkorov took part in the Eurovision song contest but did not do particularly well. At the press conference prior to the event, Pugacheva announced that she would appear the following year herself if her husband did not succeed. She did so in Dublin with the song "Primadonna." As she would later say, "This step stunned everybody, because it was clear that you never win there with a Russian song." After touring the U.S. together in 1995, the couple began to take part in support for Boris Yeltsin's re-election efforts. Pugacheva's career was celebrated in a five-part national television documentary called *Wait for and Remember Me* (*Zhdi i pomni menia*).

In 1997 she brought out a collection of footwear called "Alla Pugacheva" and released a thirteen-CD set of her earlier repertoire, consisting of 211 songs. She helped to celebrate Moscow's 850th birthday, was named Woman of the Year for the second time in a row, and embarked upon a huge tour around all the cities of the erstwhile Soviet Union, an extravaganza concluded with equal panache at a grand party in Moscow in November 1998. What demands our attention now is the manner in which that panache was meticulously composed through the greyest years of the Soviet Union.

WHY SING? "ARLEKINO" — A NEW TYPE OF SONG

> The level of performance in today's estrada
> is a reflection of reality.[53]

With her performance of "Arlekino" at the Zolotoi Orfei in 1975, Pugacheva was pronounced an outstanding "actress of songs."[54] Within two years the significance of that acting was becoming canonized in the Soviet press: "Pugacheva's 'Arlekino' is real theatre, one of both experiences and presentation, a synthetic theatre of estrada. The actress thrilled even the most refined listeners with her virtuoso intonation and the changing palette of her song. It was the quintessence of artistry. The hall at the Zolotoi Orfei exploded with applause."[55]

"Arlekino" marked the beginning of her rejection of "stereotypes of an estrada singer, the unwritten rules about what you can and cannot do on the stage."[56] Suddenly there was an artist who understood that varied songs would require varied treatment, that each song would be different. Yet instead of one's "self" being dissipated over many roles, something comes little by little to join that disparity – a manner of being or delivering information that is created on stage, breaking free of the stage/hall connection. The dialogue at work here is not the civic dialogue of singer/state, nor is it the early, sentimental version of stage/ hall. It is that of quotidian and staged personae, of *lichnost'* as "private sense of self" and "star." The distance between singer and a song's heroine is vanishing. The discourse of hall and stage has prompted such growth of the performer's sense of personality that it swells to huge proportions and is then projected in an unmediated fashion back into the hall, with similar dimensions to that of western fame.

I used to be of the opinion that a song should define the voice it'll be sung with and what image will be created by it. It used to be that I'd sing five songs and you'd get five Pugachevas. But now that I've wised up, so to speak, I see that I have different songs with differing content, but I'll try to keep the timbre of my voice constant in each song ... As a rule, I don't direct myself towards any one listener. If, for example, there are only atomic physicists or first-year students of Moscow's Technological Institute at a concert of mine ... well, of course, that doesn't happen ... there are all kinds people sitting in the hall, and if I start putting together a repertoire based on the taste of any one individual, nobody else is going to find it interesting. Therefore for the most part I sing songs that are close *to me* and which I can carry all the way to a listener. Then it's his business to accept or reject it. Usually, though, a listener will accept a song as long as there's no hint of falsehood in it.[57]

In 1983 Pugacheva would term her reworking of the stage/hall dialogue as "sometimes the contact of like-minded people, sometimes a duel of opponents." The change from a dialogic approach to an increasingly monologic one is part of the intensification of lyricism in her work, the shift to a confessional tone, which can at times lead to her "*dictating* the views of an audience member."[58] By 1982 one journalist had defined this change as "a deeply lyrical art, confessional ... and directed from the depths of a soul into the world,"[59] an art that depends utterly upon a sense of measure. That sense is very unstable, and within four years is prompting review headlines such as "Success or Tastelessness?"[60]

The vector along which the movement from success to tastelessness is drawn finds concise expression in the publication *Teatr* in 1985. The hall/stage dialogue is needed to instigate the smaller, more radical union of singer and her heroine. The singer's personality needs to be popular before (s)he can begin to fashion their significance independent of the crowd: "Any artist has the right to speak from his 'I' and nobody can deny him that. It's another matter, though, how much that 'I,' directed as it is towards the world of people, actually strikes them as interesting. That happens only in one instance – when an artist's work somehow finds a point of contact with the life of society. The more of these meaningful points there are, the clearer that artist's craft is to us, the more we see in his work and the closer we associate it with our own fate. In that way the artist is both clearer and dearer to us."[61]

The beginning of that coincidence or association in Pugacheva's case came with the song "Arlekino," with which she hoped to show the "Gogolian gift of tears."[62] She performed the song in what one journalist who was at the Golden Orpheus remembers as "a long black dress that emphasized and underlined her frailty and femininity. And that's why she shocked [us] with the strength of her feeling and expression." The same journalist notes that Pugacheva did indeed achieve "laughter through tears ... a laughter which is quickly replaced by a tragic intonation as soon as the mask is taken off, because then the heart contracts."[63]

Here there is very little that is made happy or relative by the subversive power of laughter. Pugacheva's harlequin performs in the intermission between fully fledged acts; he does not have the ability of a court jester to cast doubts upon the workings and wisdom of the mighty. Stuck, therefore, in a place of insignificance and self-doubt, the harlequin feels more a Hamlet than an outgoing, adventurous Don Quixote. His laughter and staged persona change nothing, as they are founded on the desperate self-deception of the song's closing cackle.

That desperation is reflected musically by some of the techniques seen with Rotaru: the use of horns for drama and the rhythmic manipulation of the chorus to show a grand entry into that drama. But the clear use of grotesque melodies reminiscent of the big top or a hurdy-gurdy turns joyful pathos into the painted grin of a clown. The music is immediately recognizable as that of the circus, and a traditional estrada orchestra thus undermines its own importance and prestige.

Смешить вас мне с годами все трудней,
Ведь я не шут у трона короля.
Я Гамлета в безумии страстей
Который год играю для себя.
Все кажется – вот маску я сниму
И этот мир изменится со мной,
Но слез моих не видно никому,

Ну что ж, Арелкин я, видно, неплохой!
Ха-ха-ха, ха-ха-ха …

Ах, Арлекино, Арлекино!
Нужно быть смешным для всех!
Арлекино, Арлекино,
Есть одна награда – смех.

[With the years it's harder for me to amuse you; after all, I'm not a jester at a king's throne. So many years I've been playing Hamlet for myself in the madness of passions. Everything simply seems to be – I'll take this mask off and the year will change with me. But my tears are seen by nobody; well – it appears I'm a pretty good Harlequin! Ha, ha, ha! Ha, ha, ha! Oh, Harlequin, Harlequin! You have to be funny for everybody! Harlequin, Harlequin, there's only one reward – laughter!]

In the Soviet magazine *Krugozor* which regularly contained a flexi-disc, Pugacheva presented what she called "one of the possible continuations of 'Arlekino,' my song 'What Do You Mean – Cry? Never!' (*Chto vy, plakat'? Nikogda!*). In essence there's a monological stage in my work. If you take songs from my recent programs like 'A Woman Who Sings' or 'Shakespeare's Sonnet,' then it's clear what we're talking about: big ballads of a confessional nature, poems and tales about myself." [64] The first of these songs, separated though it is from her big, private monologues of the late 1970s, nevertheless helps us to bridge the late and supremely subjective Pugacheva with the early mask or display of "Arlekino." The harlequin's slight and waning hall/stage dialogue quickly becomes the monlogic *lichnost'* on stage.

The song "Chto vy, plakat'?," recorded in 1978, owes both its words and music to Pugacheva. It states her desire never to cry, even in the face of rumours, spasms in the throat, or pain in her heart. The one place tears *are* allowed is the stage. The dramatic tragedy is used to contain the real tears; here we see the beginnings of the truly merged personae of everyday and staged *lichnosti*. They take place (depending on the song's version) to the sound of a single piano or electric organ. The musical personality is stripped down to absolute basics and builds itself anew.

А когда вдруг вспыхнет рампа,
Съем всю тушь, в слезах скользя.
Лишь на сцене плакать можно,
За кулисами – нельзя,
Что вы, что вы, нам – нельзя …

[And when the footlights suddenly come on, I'll swallow the make-up that rolls down in tears. We cry only on stage; we mustn't cry behind the scenes. What do you mean? What do you mean! We simply mustn't.]

CIVIC OR LYRIC —
THE NEW THEMATIC EMPHASES

I try to sing the type of songs where there's a
full correspondence of the melody with the logic
of the text, songs through which I can express
myself, my joyful and sad moments in life.[65]

Alla Pugacheva

It would seem from Pugacheva's biography and texts such as "Chto vy, plakat'?" that the notion of civic songs has been thoroughly dispensed with, but the singer has a final word or two to say about this time-honoured distinction. I mentioned earlier her admiration for "Victory Day" (*Den' pobedy*), when she stressed the great role played by lyric songs at the front in World War II. Now, in the mid-1980s, she shifts the social emphasis from Soviet themes to those of global or supranational significance, "the defence of children, love, work, laughter, beauty, and friendship from nuclear murderers."[66] As the personality fostered by the stage/hall discourse grows to fill stadia, the domestic, moral concerns of Soviet estrada also expand as they are expressed in the increasingly international framework of Gorbachev's period in office.

One of the major ways in which Pugacheva gradually modifies or leaves entirely the domain of civic, social songs is by her very frequent recourse to the metaphor of flight. When asked in a 1987 interview whether she has an *Ex libris* designed yet, she replies in the negative but imagines that if it existed, it would depict an ascent of some description. "I am always flying … in songs like 'Kite' [*Vozdushnyi zmei*] or 'Rise above the Vanity' [*Podnimis' nad suetoi*]. I have dreams of flying, even now … but I don't like it when I go up too high, into space – that's frightening. A little closer to the earth, as high as birds fly … It's only wires that I'm afraid of; they're such a restriction."[67] These metaphors perhaps more than any other define her perception of the risk and gain involved in processes of dramatic innovation. As Pugacheva's lyricist, Reznik has placed upon her lips the call to "ascend above the past" and burn as a "new star" ("Rise above the Vanity" [1979]), or to follow a loved one into the sky as two cranes ("Take Me with You" [1978]). In more mundane terms, he offered her in 1981 the metaphor of love as ascending stairs to an altitude that can be lost at any minute with a concomitant fall into darkness ("The Staircase").

The second of the songs mentioned here, "Podnimis' nad suetoi," was written by Pugacheva and Reznik in 1978 but still holds considerable relevance for the singer years later. It is important in its reinterpretation not only of the Soviet "seeking" metaphor, which is here defined as a private project: the text also suggests an interesting meaning for stardom as an experience *away* from one's normal, social, and vain (!) self, as if there is an inherent selflessness in any (successful) artistic career, especially in the domain of mass entertainment. As we have seen in Rotaru's work, the happy theme of flight or escape is expressed to a disco beat, in this instance embellished by a saxophonist. The rhythm guitar and cymbals are mixed further forward by the producer than in Rotaru's song, stressing the increasing significance in estrada of dance-oriented material.

Просто – вы говорите – в жизни все просто,
Просто считать уже открытые звезды,
Но одну, свою звезду,
Так открыть непросто.
Просто в тени всегда и всюду держаться.
Просто сесть в самолет и в небо подняться,
Но взлететь над суетой
Так порой непросто!

Над дорожной пылью – звездный путь,
Надо только крылья распахнуть,
И взлететь над прежним, над собой,
Загореться новой звездой.
Жить! Гореть и не угасать,
Жить, а не существовать!
Но, однако, уж светает …
Звезды тоже тают, тают …

Просто быть на кого-то очень похожим.
Просто из года в год нам петь одно и то же.
Но свой голос сохранить
Так порой непросто.
Просто считать весь мир простым и обычным,
Просто идти всегда маршрутом привычным,
Но найти свои пути,
Так порой непросто!

[It's simple, you say, everything in life is simple, simple to count stars that are already discovered. But to discover your own stars – that's difficult. It's simple to stand one's ground, no matter where, and to always stay in the shade. It's simple to get in a plane and fly to the sky – but to fly above vanity is difficult at times! Above the dust of roads in a stellar way, you only have to unfold your wings and fly above the past, above yourself, to burn like a new star. To live! To burn and not go out, to live and not just exist! But it is already growing light, and stars also grow dim, grow dim ... It's simple to be very much like another person. It's simple for us to sing the same thing, year after year. But at times it is hard to preserve your voice. It's simple for us to sing the same thing, year after year. But at times it is hard to preserve your voice. It's simple to travel by typical routes, but to find your own roads is at times hard!]

It is in this process of "rising above" the crowds of publicly minded aesthetics that Pugacheva becomes a supremely private performer. When she moves to themes of, say, the aforementioned anti-nuclear stance of perestroika, it is a way of bridging the public and personal. Kobzon's civic songs became patriotic and thus made room for the subjective notions of Russia in Esenin's or Blok's verse. Pugacheva's switch is from a public, Soviet, and overtly political period (through which she simply lived and to which she did not subscribe) to a morally defined one, so on many occasions the notion of "politics" stays close to the idea of personal conviction. "Life has convinced me that you simply cannot remain outside of politics. Each person sings in his own way about what bothers him in particular. One will express his feelings in a more pointed manner, another in a gentler fashion. Nevertheless we all find a common language. We sing on a common theme without repeating one another."[68] The final sentence here does not use the first-person singular pronoun, but its implicit presence undercuts and overshadows the Soviet "we."

At this time of glasnost, Soviet journalists were looking back at Pugacheva's career and admitting that from the outset the U.S.S.R. was perhaps not the easiest place for her to work. "There arose a conflict between the sweep of Pugacheva's creative gift and the objective conditions of its realization. Soviet estrada suddenly turned out to be technically unprepared for the realization of Pugacheva's activity, a reproach that had been audible at the start of the decade, when she complained of poorly trained technicians, stage designers, lighting crews, and special effects experts!"[69]

A combination of these issues – late or post-Soviet politics as private conviction, masquerading as civic duty, all expressed on a grand theatrical scale – came with Yeltsin's re-election campaign of 1996, when a huge tour of superstars was organized around Russia, in a manner reminiscent of the Revolution's agit-trains. Pugacheva's daughter, Kristina Orbakaite, referred approvingly to the entire spectacle as a "propaganda supertour." Although unable to take part herself, Pugacheva nevertheless offered a statement to the newspaper *Rossiiskie vesti* that shows how pseudo-Soviet slogans are still effective in prompting post-Soviet, civic decisions, those made by an appeal to private conviction. The flagging public aim expressed here depends utterly upon private zeal. (Sadly, what we really hear lurking behind the following quote is the *lack* of zeal and an ingrained sense of personal civic ineffectiveness after decades of Soviet social planning.)

In a CIVILIZED country, these acts [of musical support for political parties] are NORMAL! Overseas it's considered typical civic behaviour! Over here we have, along with everything else, loads of spiteful critics, plus other candidates, upset at the lack of attention paid them by [estrada] stars ... What have they got to complain about? Go and find your own artists! Let them propagandize you, like we do President YELTSIN! ... What would I like to tell my friends and colleagues? The simplest of things: "Hey, guys, dear friends, come back victorious! Look after yourselves!" And I'd just like to say one thing to their young fans: "Choose or lose!" What can I add ... I think that although you're young both from the point of view of age and what's written in your passport, you're also entirely adult in your role as a conscious, responsible citizen of your country. Adults decide everything on their own, including the most important thing of all – the choice of their country's fate. So be daring, guys! I'm right beside you![70]

A little over a year later, once Yeltsin's term has lapsed into economic muddle and the dangerous posturing of Moscow's political oligarchy is evident, Pugacheva no longer feels that her bold invitation to Russia's youth has any use or counterpart in modern society. Estrada by 1997 reflects society with its "vanity, nervousness, sensuality, and multicoloured costumes ... Sure, there used to be patriotic themes, but they've vanished together with everything else patriotic in our lives. Perhaps it'll come back again, and then it'll come back in estrada, too!" [71]

USING THE POETIC CANON

Maybe I'll seem a little old-fashioned when
I say this, but I think that each creative person
is an example or guiding light for somebody.
And you mustn't ever forget that.[72]

Alla Pugacheva

In the same way that Pugacheva uses the scale of public spirit or patriotism to draw a proportionally large self-portrait, she employs the received literary canon of other people's poems to amplify her own burgeoning subjectivity. Although the other singers in this book have often relied upon Soviet poets for a different type of text, the writers chosen by Pugacheva suggest a new, foreign, or liberal worldview: Shakespeare, Mandel'shtam, Tsvetaeva, Evtushenko, and Akhmadulina, to name but five. On the first of these she says in an interview of 1978 that "a person can't live in one register of passions and thoughts, a Shakespearean register of tension and depth. That much is obvious."[73] Soviet journalists had frequent doubts about the suitability of popular songs per se as a vehicle for such depth. A 1983 review of her album *This Path Is So Disquieting* (*Kak trevozhen ètot put'*) includes the following cutting observations:

The treatment of Tsvetaeva's and Mandel'shtam's poetry on this album seems very unsuccessful to me (the songs "When I'm a Grandmother" and "I'm No Longer Jealous"). I won't be saying anything new if I remind you that such delicate and inspired poetry is suited less than anything else to adventurous hit records. With regard to that, one shouldn't forget the singer's significantly more successful treatment of Tsvetaeva's poetry in the film *The Irony of Fate* where she performed songs with a great deal more tact and a sense of moderation ... It's a shame that she doesn't try now to make use of the pastel tones of her palette, since they worked so well for her in the film.[74]

With even greater candour, a female journalist for the magazine *Musical Life* in 1984 tells Pugacheva to her face that she feels very uncomfortable hearing the private lyrics of Mandel'shtam sung in an auditorium, "and the more sincerely you sing, the more awkward I feel."[75] Pugacheva, with instant, defensive erudition, refers to Stanislavskii's definition of a theatre curtain as a fourth wall – hence the uneasiness caused by the removal of that wall and an uninhibited view of another person's life. She refers to the rules of stagecraft to defend a song based upon a poem, and indeed her version of one Mandel'shtam text ("Peterburg") has conjured equally dramatic impressions of "a stooped silhouette, slowly swaying to the unhurried rhythm of a barrel-organ with a microphone pushed to her chin, an immobile face with glazed eyes as though drugged, with the heart-rending entreaties of her voice as if from a nocturnal abyss or the horror of premonition." Nevertheless, that writer goes on, despite a full-blooded staging, Pugacheva ultimately "makes no distinction between Mandel'shtam and Reznik."[76]

Does Shakespeare fare any better? If Mandel'shtam is merged with Reznik, then Shakespeare merges with Pugacheva herself, thanks to what she calls herself "the immortal traditions of theatre ... [throughout which] nothing has been interrupted."[77] Those public traditions, filtered through a sung sonnet ("Sonet Shekspira"), are very much an individual performance that strikes in turn an individual chord, as Pugacheva recalls: "Not long ago I got a letter saying that a girl after one of my concerts had gone to the library and asked for a book called *Sonet Shekspira*. She thought that *Sonet* was the poet's name. That's already a plus: she'll be reading Shakespeare. Of course there's no guarantee that I'll please *all* my viewers. Actually, I'm not trying to, but you can be sure that I'm giving my entire soul, all my heart on stage."[78]

Troubled by embarrassing confessional *ispovedi*, by "Shakespeare to a disco rhythm"[79] or the banality that comes from a disregard for the bard's "great severity and ceremonial calm,"[80] the Soviet press by 1985 has concluded that "in one way or another this artist's genuinely artistic confession has begun to be replaced by an individual conversation about herself."[81] Shakespeare has been subsumed in Pugacheva's plans, and simply serves to amplify her lyricism; what looks like a "conversation" is in fact about the performer "herself," the dialogue of singer and the song's heroine. To credit this shift to disco, though, is wrong. The song recalls another western trend – musicals such as *Hair* or *Jesus Christ Superstar* with their choral fortissimo. The music is designed for the heart, not the dance floor. It also fuels subjective feelings, as a textual change in the last line makes clear.

Here is the Shakespearian original:

Then hate me when thou wilt, if ever, now,
Now while the world is bent my deeds to cross,
Join with the spite of Fortune, make me bow,
And do not drop in for an after-loss.
Ah, do not, when my heart hath scaped this sorrow,
Come in the rearward of a conquered woe;
Give not a windy night a rainy morrow,
To linger out a purposed overthrow.
If thou wilt leave me, do not leave me at last,
When other petty griefs have done their spite,
But in the onset come; so shall I taste
At first the very worst of Fortune's might;
And other strains of woe, which now seem woe,
Compared with loss of thee, will not seem so.

And Marshak's version:

Уж если ты разлюбишь – так теперь,
Теперь, когда весь мир со мной в раздоре.
Будь самой горькой из моих потерь,

Но только не последней каплей горя!
И если скорбь дано мне превозмочь,
Не наноси удара из засады.
Пусть бурная не разрешится ночь
Дождливым утром – утром без отрады.
Оставь меня, но не в последний миг,
Когда от мелких бед я ослабею.
Оставь сейчас, чтоб сразу я постиг,
Что это горе всех невзгод больнее.
Что нет невзгод, а есть одна беда –
Твоей любви лишиться навсегда.[82]

And the Pugacheva version from line five (with variants underlined):

И если скорбь <u>сумею</u> превозмочь,
Не наноси удара из засады,
Пусть <u>долгая</u> не <u>разродится</u> ночь
<u>Тоскливым</u> утром – утром без отрады.
Оставь меня, но не в последний миг,
Когда от мелких бед я ослабею,
Оставь <u>меня</u>, чтоб <u>снова ты</u> постиг
Что это горе всех невзгод больнее.
Что нет невзгод, а есть одна беда –
<u>Моей</u> любви лишиться навсегда.

In the Russian versions by Marshak and Pugacheva, the final changed line alone does indeed create a different poem. The Marshak text emphasizes the speaker's need for another's love. That need is expressed by a person who invites cruelty on the part of a lover which in fact does not exist; hence the "if" of the first line ["If you stop loving me …"]. There is a movement here between being pushed and jumping oneself, between being left and being loved. Despite such masochism, the speaker *ends* the poem by describing the awfulness of losing that silent lover's affection. The awfulness of "losing your love" is a psychologically normal and healthy tendency towards being loved rather than loathed; the speaker asks that (s)he be loved, for it is the addressee who is unpredictable. Pugacheva's line expresses fear of "losing *my* [the speaker's] love." Now the problem has become almost paranoiac, at the risk of sounding melodramatic. The speaker herself cannot guarantee that her love will win out over the desire to inflict punishment upon herself.

Her decision to use the verb "to be able" (*sumet'*) in line five in favour of Marshak's "to be allowed" (*dano*) posits this vascillation in an existential, not fatalistic context; in fact the main reason for Pugacheva's insistence upon the use of well-known poetry in her songs is an inherent part of the freely chosen – yet difficult – development of *lichnost'*, of self-awareness and personality.

It's really hard for a singer to remain on the level of great performance if the main idea of a song's theme or thought has been watered down. That's true even in the simplest song. I've heard songs that have a beautiful melody, yet no thought at all. I can't sing them. They make me angry. A song that has a deeply expressed thought counteracts a thoughtless performance; it arranges subtle motifs from our lives which allow a person to hear, as it were, or recognize himself. If all of this is absent, then a singer is a victim of fashion. He sings what people are used to, he sings that which doesn't need soul or self-sacrifice.[83]

Part of this compilation of thoughtful songs involves the poetry of Andrei Voznesenskii. His lyrics for numbers like "Maèstro" and "Song for an Encore" (*Pesnia na bis*) brought "seriousness and good taste" to Pugacheva's repertoire, two attributes which are often seen as lacking.[84] The occasional hyperbole of songs such as "A Million Scarlet Roses" (*Million alykh roz*) and its excessive expression of love is instead seen at times by the Soviet press as a "selflessness of the spirit" that helps to define her lyrical heroine.[85] An artist sells his house and paintings, all to buy an actress a "sea of flowers" for one day before she leaves. The idea of giving all to a chosen elite is clearer still in "Pesnia na bis." The verses are restrained, more narrated than sung, to the accompaniment of disciplined percussion and organ. Only in the chorus do we perceive Pugacheva's signature drama and a strangely brief grandeur of strings (which in later versions of the song is downplayed even more by being synthesized).

Пусть остается в зале
Тот, кто верит, верит и влюблен,
И влюблен, и влюблен.

Я вам спою еще на бис!
Не песнь свою, а жизнь свою!
Нельзя вернуть любовь и жизнь!
Но я артист, я повторю
Свою судьбу на бис,
Пусть голос мой устал.
Знакомые глаза я вижу в зале
Среди тысяч глаз.

Знакомые глаза,
Я обожаю вас,
Я ненавижу вас, знакомые глаза,
Спасибо вам, спасибо вам, спасибо вам.

[May the one who believes and loves, loves, loves, stay in the hall. I'll sing you another encore! Not my song, but my life! You shouldn't return love and life! But I'm an artist and once again I'll perform my fate as an encore, though my voice may be tired. I see familiar eyes in the hall amongst thousands of others. Familiar eyes, I adore you, I hate you, familiar eyes. Thank you, thank you, thank you.]

Two poems by another poet, Osip Mandel'shtam, helped Pugacheva to hone that sense of a chosen audience. Here, however, the tendency is less towards a haughty coterie than the sentimental proximity of performer and listener. A quote from an interview of 1995 looks back on the importance of that relationship; it sets the scene for a brief analysis of Mandel'shtam's poems in Pugacheva's repertoire.

Q: You used to sing to the poetry of Mandel'shtam and Marina Tsvetaeva, but now you sing nothing but commercial texts ...

PUGACHEVA: Life dictates themes and the profundity of texts. Why should I burden and dramatize my lyrics when our entire existence [today] is dramatic enough as it is?[86]

Two of the poems sung by Pugacheva, "Leningrad" recorded in 1977) and "I Am No Longer Jealous" (*Ia bol'she ne revnuiu*) of 1981 show how she employed the poet's drama. The first of these concerns a city which in P'ekha's work we encountered as a civic space made private, since she sang of *her* Leningrad, transformed by her experiences. Here in Mandel'shtam's text we see a city that once again offers something over and above Soviet materialism. (Pugacheva emphasizes this by altering the text to increase the number of first-person pronouns and removing an unwanted reference to mortality.) For both Pugacheva and P'ekha, a song or other form of linguistic expression creates an essential, if not metaphysical dialogue (here a telephone call) between two, not two million people. Paradoxically, that nonmaterial, lyrical experience comes to justify material existence for one person in a city of materialism. This earthbound context is emphasized by the same "organ-grinder" melodies and clumsy rhythm we heard in the contrived jollity of "Arlekino."

Я вернулась в мой город, знакомый до слез,
До прожилок, до детских припухших желез.
Я вернулась сюда, так глотай же скорей
Рыбий жир ленинградских ночных фонарей.

…

Ленинград! Ленинград!
Я еще не хочу умирать,
У меня еще есть адреса,
По которым найду голоса.
Ленинград! Ленинград!
Я еще не хочу умирать,
У тебя телефонов моих номера,
Я еще не хочу умирать.

[I have returned to my city, familiar to the point of tears, of veins, of children's swollen glands. I have returned here, so swallow quickly the cod-liver oil of Leningrad's street lamps … Leningrad! Leningrad! I don't want to die yet, I still have addresses for me to find voices. Leningrad! Leningrad! I don't want to die yet, you have the numbers of my telephones, I don't want to die yet.]

The status of words and things is key also to "I Am No Longer Jealous." In a manner reminiscent of the Shakespeare sonnet, it expresses the desire to give oneself to another while constantly resisting that desire. A struggle emerges between surrender and independence, a struggle conducted linguistically. Once again the speaker seeks (almost!) "torture" in her envious desire to be something or someone else; her words can bring about awful "sacrifice" of herself to another person or notion. By choosing a poem such as this, Pugacheva is both lauding the transformative power of language in her songs while admitting fear in the face of that potential. The atmosphere of power is felt musically in another reworking of disco emphases. Earlier Pugacheva had mixed guitar and cymbals further forward; here the stress is decidedly upon a double bass line, offered by both bass guitar and organ. Thus we have one of the "funkiest" songs in Soviet estrada, especially when stripped down at one point to tom-toms alone.

Я наравне с другими хочу тебе служить,
От ревности сухими губами ворожить.
Не утоляет слово мне пересохших уст,
И без тебя мне снова дремучий воздух пуст.

233

Я больше не ревную, я больше не ревную,
Я тебя зову.
И все, чего хочу я, и все, чего хочу я,
Я вижу наяву.
И все, чего хочу я, и все, чего хочу я,
Я вижу наяву.
Я больше не ревную, я больше не ревную,
Но я тебя зову.

Я больше не ревную, но я тебя хочу,
Сама себя несу, как жертву палачу.
…
Еще одно мгновенье, и я тебе скажу:
«Не радость, а мученье в тебе я нахожу.»

[I want to serve you on a par with others, to soothsay from jealousy and
with arid lips. A word from dried-up lips will not quench my thirst, and
without you the dozing air is empty. I no longer am jealous; I call you. And
everything I want, and everything I want I see in my waking hours. And
everything I want, and everything I want I see in my waking hours. I am
no longer jealous, I am no longer jealous, but I call you … I am no longer
jealous, but I call you, bringing myself like a victim to the executioner …
Just one moment more and I'll tell you "I find torture in you, not joy."]

The drive to self-realization through self-destruction is clear elsewhere, such as in a Tsvetaeva text entitled "Rekviem." Here, though,
we have a situation somewhat different from the competition of matter
and voice and spirit. The inability to change stubborn matter is important enough to be mourned in other texts, for example, in 1978 with
the song "This World" (Ètot mir), which, while it admits that much is
possible in the world, also knows that the earth is neither the product
of one's imagination nor open to corrections and adjustments, once
it has been fashioned in some manner. One acts upon the world once
and once only.

Tsvetaeva's requiem is an extension of that song, as a requiem for
herself; one day she will leave a world that will continue to be wholly
material. She had once loved to watch wood turn to ash in a fireplace,
but as a woman who "knew no measure in anything," she pushed her
own physical state to the same point of (self-) obliteration by her own
pride. There is, nevertheless, in the speed of such an awful decline a
sense of verity, of a game played the right way, so much so that it
inspires love, forgiveness, and faith. That awfulness finds expression
in the boldest and grandest of ballads.

Уж сколько их упало в эту бездну,
Разверстую вдали!
Настанет день, когда и я исчезну
С поверхности земли.
...

И будет всё – как будто бы под небом
И не было меня!

Изменчивой, как дети, в каждой мине,
И так недолго злой,
Любившей час, когда дрова в камине
Становятся золой ...
...

К вам всем, что мне, ни в чем не знавшей меры,
Чужие и свои,
Я обращаюсь с требованьем веры
И с просьбой о любви.
...

За всю мою безудержную нежность
И слишком гордый вид.

За быстроту стремительных событий,
За правду, за игру ...

[So many have already fallen into that distant, yawning abyss! The day
will come when I will vanish from the surface of the earth ... And
everything will be as if I had never existed! I, fickle as a child in every
expression and angry for such a short time; I, who loved the hour when
firewood turns to ash in the hearth ... I, who knew no measure in
anything, turn to you, both friends and strangers, with a demand of faith
and a request for love ... Because of the speed of events that rush by,
because of the truth and the game ...]

The validated linguistic and sentimental movement between matter
and spirit, down and up, whilst "knowing no measure," is here associated with a sincere, childlike "fickleness." Given that Pugacheva is part
of the sentimental tradition of Soviet estrada in which those such as
P'ekha hoped to educate their audience's emotions, what Pugacheva
has to say about children and their linguistic training or reading habits
is of direct relevance to her use of poetry in estrada: "I don't think that
serious works of literature should be kept from children and adoles-
cents. They shouldn't have a reading range that is limited by kids'
literature. The perception of a book at that age is often emotional.

Full comprehension comes later, but if things are dragged on and you read adult books only in your mature years, when your character and way of thinking are already well formed, then new concepts are understood only with great effort and you have to break a lot of habits in order to register those ideas."[87] In 1985 Pugacheva remarked how important the theme of raising children was to her, how important it is for the young "to experiment and not fear mistakes."[88] This latter observation is a step away from the P'ekhian approach, a step completed by 1987. "The young people of today, as they entertain themselves and go through a process of raising themselves (*samovospitanie*), choose their own composers and poets and write their own songs – their own state within the State."[89]

Since *samovospitanie* is discussed throughout this book as work upon the material world, we need to cast an eye over the themes of effort and the subsequent raising of *oneself* towards an ideal.

CHANGING MATTERS: THE HARD WORK OF FOSTERING SOUL AND SPIRIT

> Out into the footlights came a different
> Pugacheva. She was [in 1993] no longer the
> woman who had for years "incited revolt"
> within estrada, sending young people into
> ecstasy with her super-modern rhythms and
> unexpected costumes that shocked anybody
> who was even a little older.[90]

In the magazine *Krugozor* in 1978 Pugacheva noted that in educating or "raising herself" alone, she no longer sought her "own viewer in the hall. The public for me is indivisible. I never forget that each song exists not in the amount of applause but in the number of eyes looking at you. Moreover it's so quiet sometimes that you can clearly hear yourself. And it's then that you hear the echo of your own voice, of your labour (*trud*), nature, and soul."[91] Here we see an explicit connection, akin to the work of Il'enkov, between the manipulation of the material world and the creation of an ideal, supra-material significance. That significance is elsewhere termed a secret, one of private experience: "The greatest secret in art is to be oneself ... On stage it really is more important to 'be' than to 'appear' – but who to be, that's the problem. If an artist is a *lichnost'*, then by remaining himself he brings to the viewers and listeners the truth of art. That's when the greatest secret of all is revealed. The secret that Pugacheva has control

Pugacheva live before an emigré
audience at the Roy Thompson Hall,
Toronto, 2000

over isn't so much in the frankness of her artistic self as it is in the
'game,' the unfettered fantasy, in her artistic metamorphoses."[92]

Those metamorphoses of material and ideal significances are made
possible in one way: through effort, through physical endurance. The
limits of the real world are stretched to reveal something beyond
themselves. "What stuns people is her ability to work," says another
writer. "Behind the apparent ease and simplicity is labour (*trud*),
serious, exhausting labour. Months sometimes go by in the search for
variants of one song's recording. The main thing that she has brought
with herself to today's estrada is an uncompromising nature. It is
exactly this lack of compromise that finds expression in her creative
work. She sings an unusually wide range of songs ... Each song is an
image. An image of Pugacheva herself. Each song is about her, about
what is hers and personal (*lichnoe*), what lives in each of our souls."[93]

In 1983 Pugacheva remarked that she is most happy when physically
exhausted after a concert, when "each drop of blood" has been sacri-
ficed to a performance.[94] A few years later she equates work (on a

horizontal, earthbound plane) with her aforementioned ability to fly (on the vertical).[95] "I don't want to wait until tomorrow, I want [to do things] today and as fast as possible. Everything – and at once. To fly – as never before! To be happy until I'm half-dead. To suffer until stupefied. I don't like doing things by halves."

Such an assault on the physical world no doubt contributed to Pugacheva's temporary retirement from the stage that ended late in 1997. When she returned, she observed that the ability of any artist to create a spiritual significance in the world any more was in doubt:

There are people who still need [on stage] to cry, to lessen their pain to music, who want to lessen their despair with a song, their absolute hopelessness and the dead-end of tomorrow. I could probably fill that niche in estrada, the way that Tania Bulanova filled it at one time for me. A lot of people could do nothing except make fun of her, her tears, as if they were saying, "She hurts but I don't; she's crying but I'm laughing." A full stomach will never sympathize with an empty one. We laugh at a lot of people today. There's a stunning spiritual degradation of feelings, of human relations.[96]

SONGS BY IL'IA REZNIK

The tandem of Pugacheva and Reznik ...
that's a separate theme for an entirely
separate conversation.[97]

The more positive and most popular period of Pugacheva's belief in the transformative, Il'enkovian potential of music is bolstered by the poems of Il'ia Reznik. In an interview with Pugacheva from the newspaper *Trud* in 1981 she represents Reznik as the engineer of some dialogically guaranteed, supernatural significance: "Reznik is a subtle poet who senses well the internal world of people," she says. "In the foreword to his new collection *Monologues of an Artiste* I wrote: 'This is the trusting confession of an estrada artist to a poet, and as a consequence, to a reader as well. Take this confession as carefully as Il'ia Reznik did when he expressed it in his poems and lyrics. I'd like to hope that, having read these lines, many people will reconsider their attitude toward estrada as a "light" genre, so that the monologues of an artist will become a spiritual dialogue with the audience.'"[98]

The significance of this dialogue was great enough for Pugacheva to announce that by August 1983 with Reznik's help, twenty-five songs had been completed. En route to that total, the joint work of Reznik, Pauls, and Pugacheva had also been celebrated with a series of concerts in Moscow's State Theatre of Estrada. Pugacheva maintained that all three of them were bound by a "sacred love for music" which obliged the trio in turn to "give with love all that we can to those sitting in the auditorium. We simply never have a bad audience."[99]

The initial Reznik-Pugacheva collaboration, "Posidim, pookaem," makes a logical first step away from civic grandeur in 1974. Remaining within Soviet canons, Pugacheva looks for a private space and finds it in the idylls of folklore, in the distant villages of far-flung districts – hence her provincial pronunciation of the sound "o" all the way through. (In the early verses of the song, intricate guitar work without a drum to be heard sounds like a harpsichord, adding to the atmosphere of courtly mock-bucolic.) To stretch a point, however, we can see here the motif of an unfulfilled idyll that marks so many of Pugacheva's songs, perhaps the Tsvetaevan non-meeting. The heroine lauds the virtues of her awaited loved one – until she finally gets tired of waiting. Reznik's deflation of expectations in the last line is at least a hint at his subsequent, witty subversion of Soviet songwriting.

Ну, приходи скорей, дружок,
Посидим, поокаем.
…
Хорошо бы, хорошо
Целоваться вволю.
Вот только …
Чё меня ты не нашел, а?
Заблудился, что ли?

Или ты к другой пошел
По траве некошеной?
Хорошо-то, хорошо …
Да ничё хорошего.

[Come at once, my friend; we'll sit and speak the way we do … It'd be so good, so good to kiss to our hearts' content. It's just that … How come you haven't found me, eh? Got lost or something? Or did you go off to another across the unmown grass? It'd be so good, so good … Ah, there's *nothing* good about all of this.]

"People, People" (*Liudi, liudi*), composed by Reznik and Pugacheva together in 1981, shows both the disruption of stage/hall interaction and a reinterpretation of the "seeking" metaphor as utterly lyrical, i.e., devoid of all civic content. The new "road" will be sought since it has nothing to do with the social, cruel crowds of the auditorium, which are guilty of wrecking the balance and respect that once existed between the singer and listener:

Люди, люди, люди,
Ничего со мной не сделать вам.
Люди, люди, люди,
Я не верю больше злым словам.
Ну, зачем словами жечь меня
В огне, в огне, в огне, в огне?
Ну, зачем без спросу в душу лезть
Ко мне, ко мне, ко мне, ко мне?

[People, people, people, there's nothing for you to do with me. People, people, people, I no longer believe evil words. Why do you roast me over the fire of your words? Why do you crawl into my soul without asking?]

Things look worse in some of the songs that Reznik penned for *I've Come to Speak Up* – "Tightrope Walker" (*Kanatokhodka* [1982]), "Sacred Lie" (*Sviataia lozh'*), "That's the Fate I Got" (*Mne sud'ba takaia vypala* [1984–85]) and "Only in the Movies" (*Tol'ko v kino* [1985]). Several filmed versions of these songs include negative portrayals of Pugacheva's fans. Whether the boundary Pugacheva walks in these songs is between stage and audience, self and other, innovation and tradition, independence and subservience, she feels it is well expressed by that metaphor of that female tightrope walker, who is presumed to be brave but must convince herself of the need to chase what Reznik calls the "law of overcoming" (*zakon preodolen'ia*). The harlequin, stuck in subservience to the circus crowd and its whims, is here – at a dangerous height – convinced of the chance for independence.

The song "Sacred Lie" is an extension of this situation, as a vacillation between right and wrong. Truth is perceived as a challenge that calls to the artist, one that may halt her reliance upon the charms of a comforting falsehood. Though it is couched in the vaguest of terms, we see here again the "seeking" metaphor in new, lyric territory.

Святая ложь, пусть даже ты свята,
Твоя мне надоела доброта.
Я тебе не верю!
Зачем ко мне являешься ты в дом?
Зачем сидишь, как гостья, за столом?
Я тебе не верю!
Зачем меня ты бережешь от бед,

А я киваю головой в ответ?
Ты боль больнее делаешь вдвойне,
А истина давно известна мне!

Мне правда горькая сказала: «Не робей!»,
И стала я от этих слов еще сильней!

[Sacred lie, though you may be sacred, I'm tired of your goodness.
I don't believe you! Why do you appear in my home? Why do you sit,
like guests, at my table? I don't believe you! Why do you protect me from
misfortune, and I nod in response? You make my pain twice as bad,
but the truth has long been known to me! The bitter truth said to me:
"Don't be timid!" and I grew even stronger from those words.]

Our lyrical heroine is being defined between dramatically distant
opposites: the height of a tightrope from the sawdust floor, the recti-
tude of a truth versus the "sacred" shelter offered by lies. The songs
"Only in the Movies" and "Photographer" (*Fotograf* [1988]) explain
that celluloid is where such dramatic, illogically extreme opposites and
their transformations take place.

"Photographer" begins as a request that the speaker be filmed in
an apparently happy pose to hide her loneliness. Reznik's words continue the general thematic tendencies of his other songs for
Pugacheva, but late in this text there is a shift towards antagonism,
towards an attack upon one's viewer. Whether this attack comes from
actual hatred or sadness at being obliged to don masks for too long
is a difficult issue to resolve.

Так сними, сними меня фотограф,
Чтоб я даже вызывала зависть
Радостью своей и оптимизмом,
Чтоб никто и не подумал,
Чтоб никто и не поверил
В то, что очень одиноко мне.

[So take pictures of me, photographer, even so I'll cause envy in others
with my joy and optimism. Do it so nobody'll think, so nobody'll believe,
how very lonely I really am.]

Lest we think that Reznik fuels an entirely lyrical emphasis in
Pugacheva's work, we should not forget a post-Soviet text of 1993,
"Russia" (*Rossiia*). Here we see the transformation of politics into
patriotism that is so important for Kobzon's songs. By championing

things lyrical, Pugacheva left behind politics, but patriotism sometimes remains. What is interesting is the way in which her persona and the proud social metaphors of "Rossiia" are similar – both are granted enlightenment in suffering, in the pain that comes from the interplay of free will and fate after release from constraints. It is as if national estrada has created in the dialogues of stage/hall and performer/persona a star so big that (s)he now represents that entire nation. The "seeking" metaphor is therefore easily transposed into the first line of the text. (Although this song is in essence an orchestrated ballad, it differs from the norm in two fundamental ways. First, both strings *and* horns are now synthesized. Second, the bass and more prevalent use of drums in a slower song such as this cannot help but recall how things patriotic or civic filled football pitches only a few years prior, embracing a now-unfashionable rock aesthetic in order to do so.)

Уж сколько дорог мною пройдено
В нелегкой разлуке с тобой,
И вдруг поняла тебя, Родина,
Поняла тебя в этот час роковой.
Душа твоя, как и моя – в ссадинах,
И снова страдает народ.
И новой дороги не найдено,
А старая – в бездну ведет!

Россия! Я верю в твои силы,
Узнаешь ты, где правда, а где ложь …

[So many roads had already been travelled in my difficult departure from you. Then suddenly I understood you, Homeland, I understood you in this fateful hour. Your soul, like mine, is covered in wounds, and once again the people suffer. A new road is not found and the old one leads into the abyss! Russia! I believe in your strengths; you'll find out where there's truth and where falsehood …]

Much reference is made to fate in Pugacheva's songs, a tricky issue not only because of the number of novel choices that she needs to make in redefining estrada but also because throughout her career she offers endless paeans to the value of work, not destiny, as the deciding factor in success. A song written by Reznik and Pugacheva for *I've Come to Speak Up* in 1984–85 defines the issue. The artist feels that she has been fated to *be* a singer; she feels morally bound to perform once placed upon the boards and there – ultimately – *chooses* to see the matter through to the end. "Once again I see the pitiless, cold sword of the executioner above the world. I won't bow my head to the black, enemy force. I'll pardon myself. I'll punish myself."

A few words in summary. In the song "Rossiia," Pugacheva investigates existential issues of self-realization by working within politics as an expression of geographical space. She therefore plays on the boundaries of politics and patriotism in a way reminiscent of Kobzon in order to redefine or abandon Soviet notions of public spirit. Whereas Kobzon remained an inherently civic singer even after he made such a switch, Pugacheva takes a long stride further, beyond geography and into theatrical spaces. The claiming of geographical spaces for civic ends becomes the claiming of the stage for lyrical ones. As a result, *teatralizatsiia* becomes a politically loaded aesthetic. The stage is claimed as perestroika beckons and acts as a podium from which to effect – not reflect – glasnost and all of its implications for a subjective, post-Soviet worldview.

9
ALLA PUGACHEVA:
REDEFINING PERSONALITY

For the first half of their life, individuals work
on their reputations. For the second half, those
reputations work on them.[1]

In this final chapter the geography of Russia is swapped for that of the
stage. The romance of Russia's virgin territory that made geology and
astrophysics such oddly modish disciplines at the time when P'ekha
forged her career is now transferred to the infinitely smaller space of
the estrada itself. The distance between two large and dusty velvet curtains is to be filled with a multitude of new meanings, almost all of
which validate things private at the expense of those public.

Here in the work of Alla Pugacheva, *teatralizatsiia* takes to its logical
extreme the processes set in motion by P'ekha and her student friends
in 1955 at Leningrad State University. The significance of things
staged therefore deserves our attention first, but given that footlights
have long been replaced by flickering movie projectors, we need to
examine how the emphases of *teatralizatsiia* are shifted to the films
starring Pugacheva – all of them enormously successful. What is advocated or created by those films has been a major aspect of her ongoing
reputation; the workings of Pugacheva's often scandalous persona are
clear when we look at them in the context of the waning Soviet *lichnost'*
and the brave alternative proffered by estrada.

What she means as a woman is often interpreted as what is happening to Russian women as a whole; Pugacheva hones a private significance in estrada, but it becomes so popular and important that it has
great public resonance. What she means not only to herself but everybody else speaks volumes about the notion of self in Russia after the
fall of the Soviet Union. Pugacheva as a result reflected perestroika,
glasnost, and so forth, but *created* them too. Hence the attention paid
to several aspects of Russian society in the late 1980s and '90s in the
closing pages of this book. We began with P'ekha two years after the
death of Stalin and will close with Pugacheva's significance for what
"Russia" means over the last two years of the twentieth century. We
look at what it means to be famous and wealthy in a geographic space
so unsure of its import that a lack of identity is transferred to those

within it. Shining as a beacon of subjectivity for over twenty years, Pugacheva's meaning in the grey present is greater than ever.

CHARTING NEW TERRITORY: VULGAR TEATRALIZATSIIA

> I want so much for us to change the way we
> look at estrada! To consider our work nothing
> more than a *product* of today's demands means
> we're surrendering ourselves and others to the
> temptation of a "quiet" life, where any notion of
> creativity is swapped for discordant hack work.[2]
>
> Alla Pugacheva

An early article on Pugacheva in the magazine *Muzykal'naia zhizn'* spoke of a "gypsy" element in her songs, together with a "synthesizing" tendency in her approach to generic differences.[3] Five years later she was being criticized for "trying to join the unjoinable,"[4] yet was praised by a Latvian newspaper for using her "talent, temperament, and charm" to do exactly that.[5] Why the confusion? The answer lies in the violence that Pugacheva did to received notions of *teatralizatsiia*. By 1978 journalists were writing that the "term 'theatre of a song' has become popular. Today's masters are skilled not only in the ways of an actor, knowing how to reveal a song in all its dramatic, conflicting, playful expression but they also have unarguably fine voices."[6] Pugacheva herself expressed the same idea more fully in the same year:

An estrada concert must be a bright spectacle. I'm absolutely convinced of that. *Everything* has to be put into a song. Just as in the theatre, so too in estrada there are sets, light, costumes – and you have to use many means to get the work through to the viewer, whether those means are musical arrangements, special effects, or unexpected turns of musical phrasing. I don't consider the current program "showy"; it's just that you have to keep experimenting, searching for new forms of expression. You may make a mistake – I think, in fact, that I have the right to do so – but you must do your thing. I took a long time to reach this point, and what today seems normal actually shocked a lot of people not that long ago. And we all know how tradition holds sway over us and how strong our inertia can be![7]

Once again the singer defends the extravagance of her stage costumes by explaining the difference between stage and street, between originality (which is good) and vulgarity (bad). Although she would love to be even more extravagant, the cost and paucity of Soviet equipment are insurmountable.[8] Such criticism shows that although Pugacheva from the outset considers theatricality necessary, the public sometimes sees it as excessive or beyond the bounds of good taste. The singer cannot curb or apologize for what she sees as a psychological (or even psychic) necessity. "The main thing is an internal emancipation on stage (*vnutrenniaia raskreposhchennost'*) ... [and] I look in each song for its imagery, its internal drama, I strive for the song's *teatralizatsiia*." [9] That sense of freedom is elsewhere called "an unfettering of relations" with the audience [*raskovannost' obshcheniia*].[10] In several songs Pugacheva has celebrated the stage as a place of liberty, "free as the sky" ("When I Leave" [1985]); on the boards a young girl's dreams can come true of singing about such lyrical commonplaces as "the moon and a nightingale" ("About Estrada" [1977]).

The term *raskovannost' obshcheniia* is moot, though, since what we have is more of an unlimited display *before* the audience, rather than anything in which they actually participate. "In opposition to common sense, to sober and cold logic, she'll plunge you into a world of emotions, not fearing to appear either too shrill or too open. She knows no limit ... she makes no pretence at finesse."[11] Pugacheva herself would admit in an interview of 1982 that "of course freedom and an uncurbed performance are needed [on stage], but from both of them there's only one step to vulgarity and tastelessness – a singer has to sense that limit."[12]

Theatricality and the big, staged personality go hand in hand. If both become unnaturally grand, accusations of tastelessness follow. An observation of vulgarity comes from the auditorium; it is hardly likely to come from the performer! Problems of taste say a great deal about the manner in which Pugacheva's adventures in *teatralizatsiia* refashion or hyperextend the stage/hall dialogue, and she is not about to stop experimenting. "I'm not trying to say that every song has to have all the elements of estrada, including an original genre and choreography – which at times become acrobatics on stage," she says. "The way in which expressive means are employed must correspond exactly to one's emotional character and the imagery or sense of what's being performed. It has to be a rigorously thought-out set and not just a vocal performance alone. That all goes without saying when you consider the work of the best artists in both Soviet and foreign estrada."[13]

An interviewer in 1977 asked Pugacheva if she considered herself an estrada singer. "No," she answered, "I am a musical actress." The periodical *Sovetskaia kul'tura* called her a performer who "does not play or depict a role, but instead experiences the life of a [song's] hero. A song for her is a form of existence in art, a form of self-expression."[14] In describing this new form of expression, Pugacheva returns to the (pre-Soviet) roots of her craft: "Modern estrada develops within the flow of all twentieth-century art, and we've seen on more than one occasion how in each of its aspects there's a tendency to barge into foreign domains – a synthesis of cinema and circus, ballet and painting, drama and music. The same processes are at work in estrada, and that's exactly where the idea of a staged song came from. Without staging, estrada would be feeble or – worse still – dead. When I talk about theatre I mean fairground traditions and puppet shows, which by their democratic nature are closer to estrada. They're all the art of millions."[15]

By the time – in 1985 – we have all those millions squeezed into auditoria, however, the press is worried that Pugacheva's stage is literally too far from the audience, and that the artist's grand theatrical ambitions are increasing the distance, so "in many ways the director Alla Pugacheva gets in the way of Alla Pugacheva."[16] There is too much happening upon a stage which is in turn too big and too far away. Considering her P'ekha-like observation in 1980 that estrada should concern itself with an audience's aesthetic upbringing, the growing distance and dimensions are indeed troubling.[17]

That distance is certainly too great by 1988, when a concert in the Moldovan capital of Kishinev was broadcast at such unfamiliar volume around a stadium that the sound of surrounding traffic was drowned out. "The sound was so tinny, so dead. Where are all the nuances of the performance? There are about 20,000 viewers and the singer herself is somewhere off in the distance, a little bright dot."[18]

We can turn this picture around, however, and look at it from an opposite point of view. Pugacheva has not vanished into nothingness; the entire, stadium-filling spectacle emanates *from* that dot of light. The theatre has grown out of Pugacheva: "There is no theatre of Alla Pugacheva. There is only Alla herself." [19] Alla herself, though, is a two-fold or composite phenomenon: Alla *and* the theatre, the union of singer and sung persona, of two *lichnosti*. The significance of the latter union is made clear in an interview of 1994. "Songs for me are a defence," she says. "Take them away, and who am I?"[20] By 1996 the song's heroine has come to be *bigger* and more real than its performer, as the singer herself admits. "I used to think that I invent the heroine of my songs. I've recently come to understand that my heroine was inventing me."[21]

That process of invention in the late 1970s was termed a "new genre in estrada,"[22] one of "metamorphoses that take place in her voice." [23] What those changes are and how they relate to the differences between real and staged experience confused critics, even in the first few years after "Arlekino":

She wants to – and undoubtedly can – become a great lyrical actress. She has a beautiful voice, rich in overtones, an amazing gift for endurance, dramatic audacity – she has been blessed with a great deal! At a solo concert in the October concert hall [in Leningrad] she spoke about what is sometimes said of her in the press. "Why are you so outrageous?" She explained: "I'm not vulgar, I'm free!" Indeed one senses in her an artistic freedom, that rarest of joys that comes from an unrestrained socializing with any auditorium, for without such socializing there can be no talent. What does she lack? Perhaps taste. Pugacheva hungers for drama.[24]

Here the drama refers to a song of perhaps excessive histrionic intent, "Lovers Don't Give Up" (*Ne otrekaiutsia, liubia*). Exactly this song, believes the journalist, may be a stepping stone to the type of "visual interpretation" that could turn her from a star into the Star of Soviet estrada. This song is once again in the vein of the Tsvetaeva poems that Pugacheva has performed, in the sense that it is apparently part of a dialogue, yet is actually a monologue fluctuating between two views of one person in a moment of self-doubt. A woman who claims she will stop waiting for her lover is hard pressed to convince herself that such a step towards independence is indeed possible.[25] The flip-flopping between two psychological stances is complicated.

Не отрекаются, любя
Ведь жизнь кончается не завтра.
Я перестану ждать тебя,
А ты придешь совсем внезапно.
Не отрекаются, любя.

А ты придешь, когда темно,
Когда в окно ударит вьюга,
Когда припомнишь, как давно
Не согревали мы друг друга,
Да, ты придешь, когда темно …
За это можно
Все отдать!
И до того я в это верю,
Что трудно
Мне тебя не ждать,
Весь день, не отходя от двери.
За это можно
Все отдать!

[Lovers don't give up if they love – life doesn't end tomorrow. I'll stop waiting for you, but you'll come back all of a sudden. Lovers don't give up if they love. And you'll come back when it's dark, when the snowstorm beats at the window, when you remember how long it has been since we warmed one another. Yes, you'll come back when it's dark ... I can renounce everything for that! Until then I'll believe one thing – that it's hard for me not to wait for you – all day, never leaving the door. I can renounce everything for that!]

What Pugacheva says about the origins of such songs as *teatralizatsiia* plots a simultaneous course from singer in the theatre (public) to theatre in the singer (private). In 1979 she is calling upon traditional music forms to find a manner in which to visually express her linguistic drama. "Voice and music are only a part of a performer's ritual. You know those ancient ritual songs? There you have both dance and a form of depiction." [26] Pugacheva sees the major difference between a play and a staged song as the fact that the former takes three hours, the latter three minutes. In the same year she told the newspaper *Literaturnaia Rossiia* that the traditions of folk theatre and puppetry were an important influence upon her type of temporally "compressed" staging. [27]

By 1981 her understanding of the term "a theatre of songs" (*teatr pesni*) moves from social ethnography to something within her own creative work. The public tradition is claimed or usurped by the private singer. When asked to define *teatr pesni*, she does so in terms of her own career: "The term arose, if I'm not mistaken, when each of my songs had a small role, either the role of a harlequin who is painfully sad ... or a dramatic confession like 'Lovers Don't Give Up' ... Today I primarily perform song-monologues. If by 'theatre' people mean dramaturgy, then that's something I can agree with." [28]

Pugacheva is here discussing a switch from various traditional roles or masks to a single, more direct form of expression. An interesting aspect of this switch in emphasis from "folk" theatre to "my" theatre is hinted at in the journal *Avrora* of 1983. The process of increasing fame takes the stage/hall dialogue and replaces it with a self-contained superstar. "The situation seems to be thus: an idol lives in a world where echoes and mirrors rule. He sees his reflection on street posters, on the pages of glossy magazines, even on housewives' plastic bags. When he turns on the radio he hears his own voice, recorded on a radio station a month or even a year ago. Sooner or later he'll get the feeling the world is brimming over with him alone. He no longer winces upon hearing his own name. He is needed by everybody and at the same time lives alone with himself. In the delighted shrieks of his fame he hears only the echo of his own glory – nothing else except that echo." [29]

Another fascinating development in "my" theatre comes in the following year when things get a little out of hand with Pugacheva's

show at Moscow's Olympic stadium: seventy dancers, constantly changing costumes, lasers, dry ice, and air-borne gymnastics. As the political
climate of glasnost begins to emerge, so do grand social themes,
outside of explicitly governmental rhetoric (albeit on the same scale),
themes with which Pugacheva fills her new repertoire. "Quite a few
lyrical songs … but there are patriotic, anti-war, and social songs, too.[30]
The grandeur is acquired by the singer herself, albeit briefly.
Pugacheva's description in 1984 of a "zooming" or telescoping
between stage and hall is a useful expression of the movement between
two extremes described above, the public and private extremes of a
staged performance. "My" theatre is in a state of flux: "My fans write
and say: 'We were initially scared that the field is so big and you are
so small, but as the curtain fell it seemed that the stadium had shrunk.'
I felt that things were the other way around. To start with, I felt big
and the listeners far off looked so tiny, all kinds of tiny listeners. But
then I notice that they're coming up to meet me more and more.
We're drawing towards each other. That's when art comes to life."[31]

Pugacheva makes clearer what she means by this kind of (rather
unwieldy) theatre of "art" or songs in *Literaturnaia gazeta* in early 1985.
She wishes for a theatre that is well equipped with technical wizardry
and seats for perhaps 1,800 viewers.[32] The inherently didactic intent
of Soviet estrada leads her to wonder, now that she is dealing with the
flux of the stage/hall and performer/persona dialogues, how she
might help others do the same. Her private success will be turned into
a public template for others to follow! "My" theatre is being extended
or returned to the "folk" – although nobody is actually asking for it.

At a lengthy press conference a few years later, Pugacheva announced
progress towards the realization of her theatre on Moscow's Kolkhoz-
naia Square (previously known as Theatre Square), though the work
was delayed by the refusal of a bakery operating in the building to
vacate the premises. Whether blessed with four walls or not,
Pugacheva's staged songs hit the road once again in 1997 after a three-
year hiatus. Fifty solo concerts were planned around the cities of the
defunct Soviet Union, with double engagements in the two capitals of
Moscow and St Petersburg.

These plans were discussed at a press conference in November 1997
designed to celebrate a different project, her burgeoning success as a
businesswoman in the world of shoes. Now there was another venture
to accompany her less successful foray into the marketplace with an
eponymous perfume.[33] At the conference she talked again of her
Moscow theatre: "When I spoke about my theatre, I didn't mean my
own personal theatre where I'd perform my own songs. I meant a kind
of synthetic theatre, where my directorial ideal would be realized. A

place equipped with the latest in technical equipment, a place where I could experiment – and to which the Moulin Rouge, Broadway shows, and Vegas spectacles could be invited."

She complained that investors did not really grasp the concept. She was offered $15 million by the state but turned the funds down on the basis that museums and children's shelters would be more deserving recipients of such an enormous sum. While these financial and moral conundrums were slowly resolved, Pugacheva's tour began in Alma-Altai on 3 April. It ended in November 1998 with a huge Moscow party, replete with reports of debauched behaviour. The festivities were documented by, among others, the newspaper *Èkspress gazeta*, and led the editors to conclude: "That's just the kind of person she is – a star!"[34]

THEATRICAL MOVIES AND A COMPLETE SYNTHESIS OF PERSONALITIES

> I feel that cinema is a synthetic art. Its strength
> is the way a whole series of components acts
> upon the viewer: dramaturgy, the actors'
> performances, camera work, the director's
> general concept, music, and so forth. I'm only
> talking about what I know – about songs. Their
> role in a film can be very great indeed.[35]
>
> Alla Pugacheva

In 1978 in the newspaper *Sovetskaia Èstoniia* Pugacheva announced, "I am Boris Gorbonos."[36] Thus she revealed the *nom de plume* and alter ego she had been obliged to adopt as a songwriter, either to avoid the overly easy road an established singer's work might enjoy or – conversely – the prejudices against a female composer. A joke photo session was even set up in 1977 so that Pugacheva could don glasses, a wig, and moustache to pose with a score she was writing.[37]

A film in which she stars, a few months later, entitled *A Woman Who Sings* (*Zhenshchina, kotoraia poet*), pushes this merging of personae even further. Pugacheva becomes the woman she plays – to the point that much of the Soviet public perceived no difference between the actress and what is acted. The critics' usual charges against Pugacheva of tastelessness and excess on the stage are amplified in several reviews of this film. The tale of the heroine Strel'tsova overlaps at several points with Pugacheva's actual biography: in mentions of the Lipetsk Philarmonia, the creation of a musical ensemble, and the story of how the title song's lyrics were re-negotiated with their author. Some viewers saw this fairy-tale of the rocky road to stardom as a pure expression of Pugacheva's materialist yearnings: Pugacheva wants to be rich, glamorous, and famous just as Strel'tsova does. One Tashkent reader of the newspaper *Smena* wrote about exactly the same problems, enduring even seven years later, in Pugacheva's 1985 film, *I've Come to Speak Up*.

Personally I only got one thing out of it – the fact that Alla Pugacheva is always complaining: "I'm tired, I'm tired, I can't go on any more. I've got to smile, sing, and be jolly for them, but I'm so sick and tired of them all." Well, if she's so tired, then why waste her energy on a movie, on concerts? Wouldn't it be better to take a break? But try telling Pugacheva to take a break. You know what she'll say? ... Exactly ... My friend who saw the film before me put it well. "It looks to me as if *I've Come to Speak Up* was filmed by [the Soviet State Travel Agency] Intourist and the House of Models. But for some reason we don't want to show any Russian-made clothing, so we're showing you foreign stuff instead." To be honest, it's a shame that such a good singer agreed to work as a mannequin.[38]

This reader may well be right in conflating actress and heroine. In 1981 Reznik and Pugacheva had already penned a song entitled quite simply "Fatigue" (*Ustalost'*) which expresses in no uncertain terms that she is tired of "getting dolled up in carnival rags." By 1987 Pugacheva talks herself about the merging of "real life" and staged *lichnosti*, the result being the kind of extremes that raise hackles in Tashkent. "I'm convinced that recklessness is a necessary part of a creative *lichnost'*, together with honesty," she says. "I go out on the stage primarily as a normal person, but the artist – if there's one inside me – will come out all the same."[39]

As the myth of Pugacheva began to take shape, certain negative phrases emerged in the state's lexicon used to discuss her: "The star has let herself slip," "big-headedness," "boorishness," "no respect for the public," "poorly spoken," "dissoluteness," and even "anti-patriotism."[40] These problems arose for a singer who had created a conduit of associations between the viewer (living "my life" in the auditorium) and the theatrical dimensions of what is going on in the limelight cast upon the performer (whom I watch on "her stage"). This is now not a dialogue but the one-way movement or projection of a big, staged *lichnost'* into daily life. Pugacheva's films do much to intensify this projection, to give the dullness of her own *unstaged* daily biography as a Soviet citizen an "aesthetic significance [through staged songs] far beyond the social dictates of traditional Soviet entertainment."

"It's not daily life (*byt*) that destroys the spiritual in a person, but precisely the opposite: a battle with objects that leads to the destruction of individuality,"[41] she says. Songs fight back and *use* material, daily life as subject matter for the "spiritual" ideal of a bigger, bolder, and better individuality. The ability of Pugacheva's musical movies to give the things of daily life a huge new significance leads to the oddest of metaphors in a 1993 article in *Smena* comparing her to an "autonomous submarine" moving where no glance is usually cast.[42] The very significance of that submarine's mission, of the path from life to myth, will be so great that by 1994 Pugacheva will be desperate to rid herself of the title "living legend," since its suggestion of a (Soviet-style!) stasis is pure anathema to any notion of creative change or metamorphosis.[43]

Let us look at how these sung changes developed on film. Prior to major cinematic metamorphoses taking place, we begin with the songs Pugacheva recorded for the Èl'dar Riazanov comedy *The Irony of Fate*, in which "beautiful music merged naturally with the lofty poetry of Akhmatova, Tsvetaeva, and Akhmadulina."[44] A little later in the magazine *Soviet Screen* the singer explains in more detail how that music and poetry would then operate in cinema: "There's a certain state of the soul that can only be expressed in song and, moreover, that state demands that a song be found which corresponds to it. So a good director, by introducing music and poetry into a film, will obviously try and follow that natural path. He's already trying to find something worthy of a human soul as soon as he loves a song and respects people. This situation can always be found in a movie ... I'm sure of one thing: songs are the most democratic form of art, the most direct form of address to the human soul."[45]

The film Pugacheva is discussing here is set in Moscow and Leningrad. A young man leaves his (intended) fiancée for a New Year's Eve tipple with friends at a Moscow bathhouse. They become so drunk that they forget which of them has a flight that evening to Leningrad and the young – wrong – man takes the plane. Still in his drunken stupor he gets lost after arriving in the concrete of another Soviet city which appears identical to his own. The buildings, street names, and even door-locks are the same, all of which allow him to hail a cab and travel "home," where he staggers mistakenly into the apartment of a woman awaiting her own fiancé for a holiday meal. As the unexpected visitor sobers up, a relationship develops between him and his unwilling hostess, especially in the face of her boorish boyfriend's violent fits of jealousy. By sunrise the two strangers have fallen in love and realize the degree of self-deception in both of their prior relationships.

The songs in the film, like the screenplay itself, can be seen as a response to the old metaphor of "seeking" or roads noted in this book since the work of Èdita P'ekha. The poems by Tsvetaeva, Akhmadulina, and L'vovskii on which the songs are based have a common emphasis of isolation, of departure or distance. Instead, however, of that departure being made for a known or desired destination, in Èl'dar Riazanov's screenplay we have trains that simply leave and ships that drift, only to pass in the night, as it were. The resulting isolation is actually quite welcome, especially in the Akhmadulina poem "Along My Street" (*Po ulitse moei*), written as a direct appeal for isolation itself:

Даруй мне тишь твоих библиотек,
Твоих концертов строгие мотивы.
И, мудрая, я позабуду тех,
Кто умерли или доселе живы.

И я познаю мудрость и печаль,
Свой тайный смысл доверят мне предметы,
Природа, прислонясь к моим плечам,
Объявит свои детские секреты.

[Give me isolation, the peace of your libraries, the severe motifs of your concerts. When wise, I will forget those who have died or are alive even now. And I will know wisdom and woe, objects will entrust me with their secret sense. Nature will lean upon my shoulder and announce its childlike secrets.][46]

The most significant songs in this discovery of the secrets of the world's "objects" came three years later in *A Woman Who Sings*. They describe – as Pugacheva herself put it – "how a typical woman's success on the stage leads to failure in her private life."[47] This combination of triumph and tragedy evoked parallels with Piaf. The Soviet press in a kinder moment maintained that in these songs "Pugacheva displays her lyrical heroine to us. Her addressee is well defined. It is the hearts and souls of millions of her contemporaries. In this lies the essence of Pugachevamania."[48]

Constructed as a tale of increasing (and increasingly public) self-realization, the essence of the film comes in the title track, the triumph of the Muscovite Anna Strel'tsova at an international music festival. The song is strange, to say the least, expressing the drama of artistry in the face of what we know to be Pugacheva's real-life obstacles, those of the grey, Soviet daily grind or *byt*. It also contains, however, a radically diminished sense of self-determination, with multiple references to "fate" – while paradoxically being an address to fate, in the hope of altering it! Somehow the drama of proud – if not predestined – isolation of the "artist" manages even to incorporate the call of a mother that fate be kind to her children. Given the ubiquitous violence done to metaphors of motherhood by much Soviet culture, it is surprising to see such a call in a film that above all celebrates the stubborn isolation of an artist and her profession:

Судьба, прошу, не пожалей добра.
Терпима будь, а значит, будь добра.
Храни меня и под своей рукою
Дай счастья мне, а значит, дай покоя.
Дай счастья мне! Дай счастья мне,
Той женщине, которая поет.
...
Не приведи судьба, на склоне дней
Мне пережить родных своих детей,
И, если бед не избежать на свете,
Пошли их мне! Мне! Мне! Не детям,
Мне! Мне,
Той женщине, которая ...

[Fate, I ask you not to spare me goodness. Be patient, which means be kind. Care for me and give me happiness beneath your hand, give me happiness, which means give me peace, give it to the woman who sings ... Fate, don't make me outlive my children. At the end of my days, if woes cannot be avoided on this Earth, send them to me! To me! Me! Not to my children, but to me! Me, that woman who ...]

Both song and film were, for Pugacheva, what she called in 1980 a final "rejection of all masks," one of which had been the pseudonym Gorbonos.[49] The expansive melodrama of the song, together with the tenacious intent of its performer in the film to see that drama through to its logical conclusion, led to an interesting parallel which Pugacheva drew. She saw much common ground between herself and Shul'zhenko's stubborn fidelity to songs of love, even during the toughest years of World War II.[50] Such tenacity led the readers of *Soviet Screen* to vote Pugacheva the best actress of 1979, whilst simultaneously censuring her "hysteria and unfetteredness in her relations with the public ... Her sense of measure often lets her down, as does her taste in costumes, sometimes calculated to produce a rather cheap effect."[51]

The later, related film of 1985, *I've Come to Speak Up*, begins with Pugacheva walking towards the camera along a tunnel from the dressing room to the stage of a packed stadium. (Part of the film was shot at an actual stadium show in Yerevan.) In essence it consists of a series of staged songs that have little, if anything, in common. *Literaturnaia Rossiia* criticized the film in a way that shows how the merging of staged and actual personae in estrada movies has reached the point where the excesses of the former are blamed upon the latter, since they are perceived to be one and the same. The same critique also suggests the breakdown of anything resembling a stage/hall dialogue.

We see the following episode. After a concert the heroine is at a gathering in her honour. She is in an expansive evening gown, inside a no less expansive hall. On her shoulders are furs, and around her, as an addition to the gown, are two men. Scene after scene goes by to the accompaniment of a song that tells us of the artist's tough life. The songs tell how that artist is trying to break free from the circle of fans who hound her every step ... Perhaps our musical film is simply unlucky. Or, rather, it is the various musical "stars" in this film who are unlucky. There's some kind of movement back and forth going on, not so much in and out of musicality as in and out of petty vulgarity (*poshlost'*).[52]

Where the audience must take the blame is in its creation of such banal notions of stardom into the hands of which this film plays, the writer maintains: "It's *us* who disseminate such a vulgar, bourgeois notion of a 'star.'" The Soviet audience in its dialogue with state-approved personalities gave birth to a personality that grew of its own accord and was now projecting itself back upon the next generation of Soviet viewers in a way that left the state most uneasy. A writer for the national magazine *Ogonek* referred to the film as "dregs" and could not watch it to the end.

The irony of this situation is that the critics are correct when they claim the personae of *I've Come to Speak Up* are Pugacheva's various modes of self-expression. In the singer's mind, the real and staged personae are one and have grown naturally together. In the same *Ogonek* article the artist defends herself and objects to a general desire in the press that "Alla Pugacheva should stop being Alla Pugacheva." The Soviet media cannot perceive of a *lichnost'* (private sense of self) big enough to match the dimensions of a staged *lichnost'* (or star). As a result, both movies came in for some serious criticism: "Alla Pugacheva deceived her viewers, and did so twice – first of all with the film *A Woman Who Sings* and then with *I've Come to Speak Up*."[53]

Loved or loathed, Pugacheva's film work reveals what she defines in an interview of 1997 as the "essence" of performance, the moment when "on stage the boundary between the [theatrical] game and life is erased. To even die at that moment is happiness. It's extraordinary, something like an orgasm. You have the feeling that you've transgressed something and dissolved in it."[54]

A NOTE ON THE PSYCHOLOGY OF MAXIMALISM

> After their wedding in St Petersburg,
> the newlyweds set off for Moscow. Alla said
> to me: "The people who think that we did this
> for the sake of promotion are idiots."[55]

There is an obvious relationship between the Pugacheva so often embroiled in non-conformist, scandalous behaviour and her passion to ride roughshod over the long-nurtured canons of Soviet estrada. Pugacheva's metaphoric expression of her drive helps to bridge these two aspects of her:

PUGACHEVA: Let's say I've broken though the ceiling with my head, but then it turned out that beneath the roof there's still an attic. In that attic it's dusty, stuffy and tough to breathe. Of course I want to go back down and live quietly, peacefully ... But I want to go for the roof! What do I do? Bash through the ceiling with my head again? What if I don't have the strength?

Q: What's up there, beyond the roof?

PUGACHEVA: The cleanest air of all![56]

Getting to those altitudes was not easy. A writer in 1983 notes that Pugacheva is worthy of journalistic attention "not because she is now the most popular artist in the Soviet Union, but because she's the only woman and only artist in the Soviet Union who is free. That's not empty talk. It's the truth. She doesn't use freedom like the dissidents do in their struggles; she does what the dissidents do not – she says out loud what she thinks, and the authorities begrudgingly allow her to do so."[57] Begrudgingly indeed, as newspapers continue to write of Pugacheva's responsibility as a star. Interestingly, though, by the mid-1980s that responsibility is not specifically political any more. One audience member maintains that "it's important not just to turn up and talk [to the audience], but to turn up and say something profound, touching, or serious. One must penetrate people's souls and force them to think about themselves and life."[59]

There are hints even in the earliest interviews with Pugacheva of future extremes. In 1976 she complained of a lack of "audacity in performers' behaviour on stage or screen." She longed for the "artistry, taste, brilliance, elegance, and temperament" of performers such as Utesov, Shul'zhenko, and Gurchenko to be reinstituted in Soviet estrada.[59] But her own attempts at brilliance and elegance became something of a struggle with a daunting adversary: "The stage for me is something inexplicable," she says in 1978. "I'm drawn to it like a moth to a flame. I sense each entrance on the stage with nausea. I feel really awful. I stand off-stage and pray that 'this' will start and end as fast as possible. A few seconds before going out I feel hope, joy, and a terrible pain, even though each time I am virtually convinced that everything will be fine. I go out on the stage with curiosity. What lies ahead is a complete mystery. Each viewer is a secret!"[60]

UNFIT FOR AN EMPIRE: U.S.S.R. OR RUSSIA?

And so we saw our famous star off [to America] and began to wait for news from overseas with great impatience.[61]

After a concert in Kiev in the early spring of 1978, one Ukrainian journalist was troubled by what he saw as Pugacheva's constant desire to emphasize "I'm not the same as everybody else."[62] In the same year a national Russian music magazine went as far – in oddly approving terms – to call Pugacheva's performance "anti-estrada."[63] Both statements are declarations of difference, reflecting a sense of growing distance between Soviet society and oneself. As Pugacheva's lyricism started to gain a sense of increasing self-worth, it became, perhaps, a little too big for its imperial britches.

Take, for example, this 1987 observation by a journalist from a newspaper of the southern U.S.S.R. He quotes a few lines from the Reznik/Pugacheva song "When I Go Away" (*Kogda ia uidu*):

Когда я уйду далеко-далеко,
не мучайся и не тревожься.
Быть может, вздохнет кто-то
очень легко,
а кто-то заплачет, быть может.

[When I go far, far away, don't torment yourself, don't fret. It just may be that somebody will sigh faintly and somebody might cry.]

"Nevertheless," he goes on, "this admission of inevitable failure in the race for personal (*lichnyi*) leadership does not sound on Pugacheva's lips like a pessimistic tragedy. The *lichnosti* of artists come and go, but art remains. Awareness of one's participation in history gives a sense of calm, of assurance. It would appear that the most existential of Pugacheva's songs are filled with this feeling, not with a sense of helplessness."[64] In the same year *Sovetskaia kul'tura* wondered whether its Soviet readership was troubled by Pugacheva's sense of her own history-making achievements, because the magazine's mailbags were full of imperatives directed toward the singer. "Weed her out!" "Get rid of her!" "Take away her awards!" "Kick her out of the country!"[65]

We have wandered here into territory as far as possible from the gentle, sentimental dialogue of stage and hall in P'ekha's work. By overstepping bounds of decorum, Pugacheva has offended some but increased her worth in the hearts of others. In a 1988 overview of estrada's well-being, of *lichnost'* as created by the processes of staging, shifting emphases in the notion of what constitutes a public person-ality have given rise to suggestions of parallels between Pugacheva and the gruff, hard-drinking bard Vladimir Vysotskii. The stage has begun to usurp reality or is at least accepted by the audience as a second, parallel (and in no way less valid) domain. In a year of increasing freedoms and release from Soviet constraints, those akin to Vysotskii or Pugacheva offer something better on stage. Whether or not that something actually exists is a moot point.

The slogans that Pugacheva's female fans use to greet their idol are extremely interesting. On one banner you might read "Alla We Love You," whereas on another there's "Alla Will Take Revenge For Us." In the latter slogan it is easy to see a psychological state that's associated with the impossibility of being master of one's own fate. Fans of Pugacheva's talent compensate for their own unrealized potential through experiences that border on the relishing of *another* person's success. They write that they love Alla ... but that just means they love themselves first and foremost. For all the incompatibility of the character-masks invented by Alla Pugacheva and Vladimir Vysotskii, they both touch upon the realm of desire and imagination. That desire plays an undoubtedly significant role in our lives. These masks ... represent a certain norm of human relations, one that in [daily Soviet] practice was ruined – and noticeably so. Now, just as in the circus ring, after the [Soviet] abasement of that mask comes its affirmation. An estrada artist's mask is indispensable, primarily because it's an important communicative element, the language in which an artist expresses himself. It also has a significant role to play with its content [not just its form]. Yet one shouldn't look there for what is not. The mask is only an indicator of general hopes, of social tone. A change of masks reflects an evolution in both hopes and society as a whole.[66]

If estrada truly is a vehicle for the expression of hope, then music expresses those hopes before politics spoils or bastardizes them – and thus the Soviet popular song is one step ahead of the Kremlin. Asked in the same year if she believes in perestroika, Pugacheva replies, "I have for a very long time. But something about it has [suffered from being] awfully dragged out, as has my belief in it."[67] The artist is willing to see her *own*, more important version of glasnost as a phenomenon of the 1970s – at least ten years ahead of the state.[68]

Q: We talk about the time of stagnation in our life [under Brezhnev] with some bitterness. For you, though, the last ten to fifteen years have been a time of great recognition …

PUGACHEVA: You can call that political period whatever you want; for a lot of people it was a time of inactivity. In my creative work, though, there was never any stagnation. Quite the opposite: in my musical ensemble for some time now there has been what's now called perestroika. People, artists in particular, can justify their failures and mistakes in the past by referring to the "Stagnation." But what if even now they're doing nothing? That means that their own private stagnation is still going on. I think that this is a case where everything depends upon individuals, upon their psychology, upon how they relate to things. Our society consists of concrete people, of individuals. If each and every one of them does not strive to realize their potential, if they surrender to their opponents when anything new, progressive or vital comes up, there won't be any kind of perestroika whatsoever.[69]

Pugacheva's unwillingness to embrace terms such as perestroika and glasnost in the way the state would like is also reflected in how that same state bestowed its titles, attempting perhaps to atone for its previous disdain. "All those honours and titles which we stick on her look strange and smell a little moribund. Judge for yourselves: what is the title 'People's Artist' [of the U.S.S.R.] worth if it comes with a non-existent union, one that gave it to her whilst cognizant of its demise?"[71] The demise of the political body has allowed for Pugacheva to assess her personality relative to other places and other countries.

A NEW WORLD TO MATCH THE NEW RUSSIA:
BEING ABROAD AND AT EUROVISION

I *myself* was always perestroika and glasnost.[71]
Alla Pugacheva

In 1988 Pugacheva set off to America, initially to a festival in Seattle and later to Carnegie Hall. Here begins the definition of our artist relative to the United States, a process of meaning by which her relationship to the Soviet Union in turn becomes clearer. A revealing remark from a pre-journey press conference shows some anxiety over the indifference that might await her in the New World. The result is two contradictory emotions expressed in the same statement: Pugacheva does not care whether she appears in the U.S.S.R. or in the U.S.A., but – on the other hand – maybe she does. "It's absolutely all the same to me whether I go [to sing] in Sverdlovsk, Kemerovo, or America. There's no difference. There's a big responsibility everywhere. If we're talking about the American trip, then I'll tell you why it's interesting. I'm probably going there for the first and last time ... Six times I got ready to go in the past. Four times I ended up refusing to go myself; two times they turned me down. Cultural relations between the two countries had broken down at that point. And those were the two times when I was really ready, overcome by a desire to conquer the place. But now I'm not going to conquer or even discover America but simply to take a look and show myself a little."[72]

When she came back, her thoughts on how that "showing" went, reported in *Moskovskii komsomolets*, were still cautious:

If I'd been born in America, they'd have known about me for ages – in the Soviet Union, too. But, thankfully, I was born in the Soviet Union, and they're just starting to get to know me in America. It's all a little strange. In 1975, when I sang "Arlekino" at the Golden Orpheus, the first to vote for me were the Bulgarians. ... When I went to Sweden, the Swedes wanted it more than anybody else. They made such a fuss over me. To this day I cannot understand what point there was in making me popular ... Now I have an American opportunity. Once again, it's really only from their side that there's an interest in me being popular in the States. As if they need that! As if they don't have enough singers of their own. Rubbish! Makes no sense whatsoever![73]

Despite the raising of the Iron Curtain, Russian estrada remained throughout the 1990s inherently different from western popular music, as Pugacheva observed. "We've got ourselves an amazing, very special country. The Russian people, who wanted so badly to hear foreign performers all the time, want again to hear Pugacheva, as they've had their fill of the foreigners. No matter how much attention we pay to other countries, no matter how much we speak in English or French, all the same we want [the old Utesov song] 'Poliushko-pole.'"[74] Differences between American and Soviet music were discussed by a U.S. music journalist from *Billboard* and the *New York Post* who at the time of Pugacheva's tour stressed her theatricality and lyricism as the key indicators of her "Russianness."[77] The same areas were stressed in the *New York Times* in reaction to concerts at Queen's College and Carnegie Hall. Loath – as Leont'ev has also been – to sell Slavic clichés to an emigré audience, Pugacheva said at the end of the tour that the best concert had been in Seattle where there were no Russians, allowing her to reach a new and genuinely American audience.

Another experience of the u.s. came in November 1994 when Pugacheva and her husband appeared together at the Taj Mahal casino in Atlantic City. *Trud* criticized her severely for what it saw as the absence of "soul or music," tasteful attire, a bearable volume level, subtle percussion, and all sense of lyricism.[78] An epigram of 1996 recognizes Pugacheva's enduring disregard for those who mock her style of dress:

Чихала на всех
В ком зависть клокочет.
Чем больше успех,
Тем юбка короче.

[She doesn't give a damn for those eaten up by envy. The more successful she is, the shorter her skirt.]

Such an observation may seem a shift towards an utterly western or American perception of mass, popular entertainment, and in fact Pugacheva has a word or two to say about her work relative to that of Madonna: "She brought to puritan America a certain frivolity, freedom, and created a kind of revolution upon the stage. In principle, though – and I sense this strongly – Madonna deep within herself is the biggest puritan of all. She's a remarkable combination of ideas, of self-sacrifice and business ... I was also a symbol of freedom on the stage in my time, of freedom of speech, ease of movement. Nevertheless, in comparison with what's being done now, I'm an absolute angel. So when all is said and done, there's no great distance between us. We'd definitely understand one another."[77]

In 1997 Pugacheva attempted to traverse another "distance" between Moscow and Europe by going to Dublin to take part in the Eurovision Song Contest, a yearly competition of songs offered by the national television networks of Western Europe. "I'll go, knowing in advance that I'll get nothing from it," she said candidly. "That's because it's not a contest of performers, but of songs – and Europe has no need for songs in Russian. Perhaps I'll get our artists to take a look at this teeny-weeny chance of performing one day in Europe ... And you all know it's easier for *me* to do this. A lot of people recognize me already in Yugoslavia, Romania, and Germany."[78]

Pugacheva was right to be modest in her expectations. Although well positioned in the line-up (twentieth in an evening of twenty-five performers) and armed with a truly wonderful song from her own pen, "Primadonna," she finished only in fifteenth place, two places better than her husband had done a couple of years before with a Reznik composition, "Lullaby for a Volcano" (*Kolybel'naia dlia vulkana*). The risk she took at Eurovision in Dublin was only possible thanks to her fame and fortune, built up over the years since "Robot" and "Arlekino."

A NEW WORLD TO LIVE IN:
POST-SOVIET WEALTH AND MEDIA

> I'd really like things to be such in our country
> that an actress could say: "Yes, I am worth
> a great deal, that's right, and in fact I get
> huge royalties ..."[79]

After Pugacheva won the Golden Orpheus with "Arlekino" in 1975 and returned to her hotel room, the phone calls and flowers were overwhelming. It was hard for the young artist to know "what this is – a beginning or a finale, bright though it may be?"[80] Within five years, if not sooner, the question appeared to be answered. *Smena* in 1980 put the sales of her records at 100,000,000, a figure described in another paper as a "virtually astronomical."[81] By 1986 that number had apparently doubled.[82] Such immense sales projected Pugacheva into an entirely new league of performers. What made her the star that she is? In 1982 her popularity is attributed to her "rebellious soul ... which presents to us the kind of life where both sorrow and joy are reason to celebrate ... Her art is one of triumph, raising us in times of trouble and forcing us to be sad in our joy."[83]

A couple of years later Pugacheva is coy in her own definitions of star status. "Popularity is a temporary agreement. On one side there's the people's interest and love, their caring for the artist. On the other there's the artist's huge responsibility before that love, the exertion of all her creative ideas and powers."[84] Meanwhile the press is writing about her "storm of emotions, colours, a literally violent temperament, all emphasized by her unrestrained behaviour on stage ... The immobility of an estrada singer's pose had started to become the singer's common lot ... [but then] Pugacheva destroyed the calm, collected style of estrada performance."[85]

By doing so, she swiftly became famous, a state she said in 1978 she could never get tired of. "One should fight and care for one's popularity. It is gained with so much effort, but probably lost with great ease. For me, popularity is a fragile flower – while at the same time a springboard. By bouncing off it one can move even further."[86] The issue of fame per se over the years gradually comes to be bound so closely to the commercial success or failure of various "theatrical" projects outlined here (such as *teatralizatsiia*) that wealth – the offshoot of fame – comes more and more to define the difference between Pugacheva and her audience. One of the first references to her being financially well off (1992) provides an introduction to a very post-Soviet issue, that of being rich:

Q: You're considered one of the richest women in the country. Does that allow you today to travel abroad without your immersion heater [for boiling a cup of water]?

PUGACHEVA: Of course. It would be embarrassing for me to travel with it today. Naturally there was a time when I used it. But today I consider myself sufficiently wealthy. On the other hand it's all relative. Perhaps in comparison with somebody else I'd be poor. I have exactly enough for myself so as not to feel humiliated. That's sufficient. Anything else is pure vanity.[87]

In a television interview of the same year, however, she says that she "always" travels with that heater, since any income earned from concerts is small, once slices have been taken by the state concert organization and others.[88] With dark humour she notes that losing weight on a foreign tour is extremely easy. In 1992 in the nation's most popular newspaper, *Argumenty i fakty*, she was praised for suffering such expenses and not having milked the state in years gone by for material gain – either by ingratiating herself with the authorities or using tours to Afghanistan to ship in sheepskin jackets in from southern Soviet borders. The paper viewed the step she had taken in establishing her own company to market herself as essential in the early 1990s: "The world of new Russian show-business is even today barely less ephemeral than the mysterious world of perfumes. Income from concerts hardly covers the cost of costumes and transportation. The recording industry agonizes over the inflated cost of producing and distributing records. Any wave of Soviet fashion has long since passed overseas – except in Israel and Brighton Beach. It's [therefore] not hard to understand why Pugacheva is creating the commercial firm Alla, releasing not only a new record but an entire range of cosmetics."[89]

The following year she produced the first issue of her monthly magazine, *Alla*, a large-format glossy publication dedicated to contemporary estrada, with an initial run of 50,000 copies, though it would be several years before the project took off in earnest.[90] Her market and media presence increased with the announcement in early 1994 that Pugacheva, then recently divorced from Evgenii Boldin, was engaged (at the age of forty-four) to the twenty-six year old singer Filipp Kirkorov. The news was broadcast at an award ceremony, where he was being recognized as the best singer of 1992–93, she as recipient of the status "legend."[91] Kirkorov, according to rumour, had been introduced to her at an evening of Reznik's work and had literally thrown himself at her feet, from where he declared his love and begged her to sing a duet. "Grow up some, first of all," was her unromantic response.[92]

Argumenty i fakty made some rather cruel suggestions as to why such a union should have taken place. Among them was the notion that "Pugacheva, having gone into the history books as a Great Actress and a Great Singer, wanted to pick up some points as a woman. It's exactly this kind of marriage that flatters her feminine vanity." Several months later the pair registered their marriage, emerging from the Petersburg registry offices to meet television and newspaper reporters, fans, and a film crew hired by the groom. Among the guests was Mayor Anatolii Sobchak who had helped to reduce red tape. The religious service was conducted in the summer during a tour to Israel.[93] For a singer raised in the respectful atmosphere of Soviet estrada, the new post-glasnost cruelty of the press on her return from Jerusalem upset Pugacheva: "I was generally surprised that people saw our marriage as a kind of self-advertisement. I foresaw that there would be gossip, that everybody would talk about our age difference, but I never expected so much squabbling and malice. We came to see that we have no friends around us." Journalists wondered if the drama, theatricality, and inherent tragedy of songs such as "Ne otrekaiutsia, liubia" would vanish in the haze of Pugacheva's familial bliss.[94] Such speculations did not trouble the singer, confident enough of her achievements not to worry about the vagaries of post-Soviet popularity: "I can tell you in all seriousness that I've been the only star both in Russia and Soviet Union," she said. Nonetheless, the press was right to juxtapose family and infamy, especially given the way post-Soviet Russia now looks back on her career:

Pugacheva emancipated our women, even when feminism was nothing more than a conversation between three lady dissidents. Pugacheva values herself highly and educates the public. She obliges Russian women not to be embarrassed at being short, at lacking long legs, being overweight, elderly or alone … Pugacheva's mini-skirts today are not born of poor taste. They are an essential part of the Pugachevian image, full of reckless daring and a type of heroism. A woman of easy virtue and a difficult fate, she's unrestrained but not debauched, hot-headed but not crude. It's those who've come after her, who've tried her image on for size, who have reduced her to a caricature.[95]

Perhaps at this time, in the mid-1990s, when the burgeoning forces of post-Soviet culture are well under way, Pugacheva felt that a certain closure had taken effect within her career. At a press conference in Alma-Alta, she announced a retreat from concert-performing.[96] Soon afterwards a five-part biographical series summarizing her career, *Wait for and Remember Me* (*Zhdi i pomni menia*), was broadcast on national television.[97] A lengthy review in the magazine *Ogonek* grilled the singer for permitting such a cloying portrayal of her married present at the expense of her more exciting and significant past, which was mostly consigned to the cutting room floor. The same article, nevertheless, provides a telling summation of the singer's career:

You can relate to Alla Borisovna Pugacheva in any number of ways ... but you have to grasp the fact that she's one of a kind and has no equals. There were no dramatic singers before her, and none have appeared since. She has such a free voice, such emancipation and flights into distant realms, epitomized by her super-hits "Arlekino," "Kings Can Do Anything," "Maestro," or "Antique Clock." Neither suppressed Soviet estrada nor its devil-may-care, post-Soviet version have known anything similar. Her voice exploded into the most closeted souls, broke through all boundaries, and seemingly rang out in some infinite space.

Pugacheva shied away from such tributes to her fame; hence the remark in Alma-Alta that an autobiography would to her seem something of a gravestone.[98] A matter which she did want to see closed at this time was her project to produce the fragrance "Alla." She hinted at problems in an interview of May 1996: "I'd rather not talk about it ... Being completely illiterate in the ways of the law and not having consulted with anybody, I signed a contract that means I get virtually nothing."[99] The securities guaranteed by Soviet renown mean significantly less in the rougher waters of Yeltsin's Russia.

Yet another act of summing-up in Pugacheva's career was the 1996 release of a thirteen-CD set covering her repertoire, *The Collection.*[100] Interestingly, she had thought of this compilation at the time of the end of the Soviet Union in 1991 because it "puts a full stop after what I've done ... And a lot has been done." Nevertheless the boxed set did not include her most recent release, "Ne delaite mne bol'no, gospoda" (Don't Hurt Me, Ladies and Gentlemen). The album, which is perhaps her finest ever, was assessed by the magazine *Domovoi* as "epoch-making."[101] In eleven of its eighteen songs Pugacheva is both composer and lyricist. It could well be seen, therefore, as an ongoing move towards the more modern or western model of independent singer-songwriters, and a step away from the creative teams of Pugacheva, Reznik, and Pauls.

Alla Borisovna Pugacheva continues to be of enormous significance to Russian estrada, even in the face of markedly more modish tendencies in both studio material and stage manner. In 1997 a double album entitled *A Surprise from Alla Pugacheva* was released of many of her songs, re-recorded by the stars of today, and performed to the prima-donna herself at a huge gala concert. *Argumenty i fakty* in December 1998 placed her first in a list of the nation's most popular singers. The introduction to a long interview with Pugacheva in June 1998 with the newspaper *Peterburg èkspress* underlines her preeminent role in Russian popular culture, both past and present: "I've got the feeling that Alla Pugacheva has been around forever. Perhaps I just don't remember the time when there was no Pugacheva? Over the last twenty years of her unbroken brilliance upon the stage, she has entered the mind, body, dreams, and life of practically every person inhabiting one-sixth of the earth's surface. Let them talk about the Beatles or Rolling Stones, but we all grew up, our Soviet generations of the Sixties, Seventies, and Eighties, on her songs alone. She sounded loud and clear then, and does so today, from every house."[102]

Yet despite the drama and dizzying melodies of all her hits, Pugacheva remains a mystery to the other five-sixths of the world. A brief 1997 article in the *New York Times* had to start with the simplest of introductions to her, despite her status as the "most popular human being in Russia."[105] It is hard to argue with such an assessment, testament both to the enduring significance of estrada and its ability to express and cultivate positive attitudes in its audience – with growing independence from the very socio-political system that fostered it.

EPILOGUE

Èdita P'ekha seems a woman who tumbled
from comfort into exile. There were foreign
women in the past who travelled all the way to
Siberia for the sake of love. Some did it for
politics. Some did it in search of the exotic.
P'ekha came for the sake of songs. It's as if she
travelled to a village in search of folklore.[1]

One of the most pleasant aspects of writing a book such as this is that I have been able to conclude each chapter with an assertion to the western reader that the careers of all seven performers discussed here are still in full bloom. True, Iosif Kobzon gives much time to the post-Soviet concerns of high business and politics, either in his own name or as supporter of Moscow's Iurii Luzhkov. Èdita P'ekha gives regular concerts at St Petersburg's October concert hall to mark her birthday in the summer and the passing of the old year in the winter. Her gentle, graceful performances continue to remain outside the brash, often scandalous world of modern music. As I write this epilogue, a newspaper on sale in St Petersburg metro stations carries the touching front-page story: "Èdita P'ekha says – 'My Husband's Love Is Infectious!'"[2]

Every New Year's Eve between 1996 and 1999 tens of millions of television sets were switched to the national station ORT for a lengthy musical extravaganza called *Old Songs about What Matters* (*Starye pesni o glavnom*). This program is in many ways the epitome of several emphases in not only post-P'ekhian but post-Soviet estrada. It is a supremely staged presentation of variety's classic songs, re-recorded in a contemporary vein by the stars of today. The studio sets play upon themes of civic importance, but are used as backdrops for purely lyrical texts. The first *Starye pesni* was shot in a mock-up of a collective farm's main yard and included both Rotaru and Leshchenko in a celebration of pre-Thaw popular songs, with all the cast involved meticulously rigged out in period costumes.

The 1960s were the centre of attention in the second *Starye pesni*, with numbers moving between a snow-blown Moscow courtyard and the set of a television show looking much as it would have done on New Year's Eve at the outset of P'ekha's rise to fame. Two of her songs were in fact included: "The White Light Stopped upon You" and "The

Neighbour." The latter was sung by the nymph-like young Ukrainian singer Anzhelika Varum, while the former was injected with a robust degree of passion by the established, self-proclaimed "Empress of Love," Irina Allegrova, playing the role of a woman waiting for the return of a lover. He is shown in the dress of three different generations, all testament to private losses of greater significance for Soviet women than the civic events that might have stolen those men in the first place.

Pugacheva made a guest appearance in the middle of the show, driving into the courtyard to perform her mother's favourite song, "Autumn Leaves." As the reader can already tell, nostalgia was rife, and continues to be so in Russia, to the chagrin of many liberal politicians. Wise grandmothers, however, could tell them that this is nostalgia for one's youth, not for the searing sociological insight of dialectical materialism or the paternal ways of Stalinist agricultural planning. Hence we all sit down and watch estrada on New Year's Eve, not films shot atop Lenin's snow-dappled mausoleum.

The third *Starye pesni* even managed to enliven (or re-invent) the stagnation of the 1970s with the dazzle of disco, heralding the appearance of a latex-clad Leont'ev in a brilliant (though ethnically odd) union of platform shoes and traditional Indian dance. Pugacheva, like any self-respecting legend, paid homage to her own origins, and to the time being celebrated in a sketch that scripted her as a young girl hoping to play songs on her guitar for Riazanov's comedy *The Irony of Fate*.

That legend does indeed live on, and in fact fuels itself with the concert and recording activities of its founders. The strong melodies and safer, if not better, times of the Thaw are reasons for the success of newly founded radio stations such as Retro-Kanal and Nostalgie. But even bad songs are fondly remembered in bad times, and it is not just retrospection that creates the cultural significance of this genre in Russia today. There is a genuine case to be made for estrada as a more important vehicle of private freedom – of *lichnost'* – than literature in the post-Stalinist Soviet Union. With so many records sold and the status of the most popular individual in the biggest country in the world, Pugacheva has both advanced and completed that freedom. Building upon the work of P'ekha and Kobzon and Leshchenko, together with Ponarovskaia, Rotaru, and Leont'ev, she offered a private space where there was precious little, took it on stage, and made it into a fairy tale, which in 1991 became a reality. Russians today are hardly living happily ever after, but they have asked to hear that story told at least 200,000,000 times – and when we consider the miserable income of the typical Soviet worker, we have to admit a figure considerably higher as records are played for and passed on to friends. Numbers that large make hyperbole and the processes of myth-making inevitable.

It seems apt to end an overview of post-Stalinist estrada, therefore, with the best known of all quips about Pugacheva's unreal status in Russian culture, a tongue-in-cheek prediction that encyclopedias will one day begin their entries on an ostensibly more significant *lichnost'* – that of Leonid Brezhnev – by defining his role as "a minor political dignitary in the Age of Alla Pugacheva."

GLOSSARY

The following terms are used on several occasions in this book after their initial translation.

BAM	Baikal-Amur Mainline Railway.
byt	Daily life or mundane existence.
Chervona ruta	Red Rue, Sofiia Rotaru's ensemble.
Druzhba	Friendship, Èdita P'ekha's ensemble.
estrada	Variety or light entertainment.
GITIS	State Institute for Dramatic Art.
Goluboi ogonek	*Little Blue Light* television show.
grazhdanskaia tematika	Civic thematic.
grazhdanstvennost'	Civic spirit.
ispoved'	"Confessional" or deeply personal performance.
komsomol	Young Communist League.
lichnost'	Personality (both "self" and "star").
lirichnost'	Lyricism.
lirika	Lyric.
Melodiia	Melody state record label.
obraz	Image or central symbol of a performance.
obshchenie	Contact of artist with audience during performance.
Oktiabr'skii	October Concert Hall (St Petersburg).
pesnia-perezhivanie	A song of emotion, re-experienced as such on stage.
Rossiia	Russia Concert Hall (Moscow).

samovospitanie	Self-education (as artistic and existential endeavour).
shliager	Hit record, song, or film.
Sopot	A major Soviet estrada festival, and Polish resort.
tea-dzhaz	"Theatricalized jazz" as developed by Leonid Utesov.
teatralizatsiia	The theatricalization or "staging" of a song.
teatr pesni	"Theatre of song" or genre born of *teatralizatsiia.*
Poiushchie gitary	Singing Guitars, Irina Ponarovskaia's ensemble.
Veselye rebiata	*Happy Guys,* a musical comedy of 1934 starring Leonid Utesov; also the name of Alla Pugacheva's early ensemble.
VIA	Vocal-Instrumental Ensemble.
zastoi	The "stagnation" associated with Brezhnev's term of office.
Zolotoi Orfei	Golden Opheus, Bulgarian estrada festival.
zrimaia pesnia	"Visible song"; a song following its *teatralizatsiia.*

NOTES

CHAPTER ONE

1 *Sovetskaia kul'tura*, 1 June 1973, 4.

2 A.N. Anastas'ev, "Èstradnoe iskusstvo i ego spetsifika," in E.D. Uvarova (ed.), *Russkaia sovetskaia èstrada, 1917–1929* (Moscow: Iskusstvo, 1976), 9.

3 D. Remnick, *Ressurection: The Struggle for a New Russia* (New York: Vintage, 1998), 91.

4 A. Kankulov, quoted in È. Chalandziia, "Glazami desiati," *Kul't lichnosti* 2 (1998), 97.

5 Iu. Gladil'shchikov, "Igra v reiting po-nauchnomu," *Itogi*, 23 December 1997, 88–92.

6 J. Brodsky, *Less Than One* (New York: Farrar, Straus and Giroux, 1986), 268.

7 A. Lawton, *Kinoglasnost: Soviet Cinema in Our Time* (Cambridge: Cambridge University Press, 1992), 92.

8 V. Nabokov, *Speak, Memory* (New York: G.P. Putnam's, 1966), 115–16.

9 F. Burlatskii, "Kul't lichnosti: kak èto delaetsia," *Kul't lichnosti* 2 (1998), 98–104.

10 P. Vail' and A. Genis, *60-e: Mir sovetskogo cheloveka* (Moscow: Novoe literaturnoe obozrenie, 1996), 233.

11 I. Kobzon, "Byt' dostoinymi preemnikami traditsii," *Sovetskaia muzyka* 9 (1983), 46.

12 E. Uvarova, *Èstrada: Chto? Gde? Zachem?* (Moscow, 1988), 49.

13 A.N. Anastas'ev, "Èstradnoe iskusstvo i ego spetsifika" in E.D. Uvarova (ed.), *Russkaia sovetskaia èstrada, 1946–1977* (Moscow: Iskusstvo, 1981), 6.

14 E. Kuznetsov, *Iz proshlogo russkoi èstrady* (Moscow: Iskusstvo, 1958), 19.

15 R. Stites, *Russian Popular Culture* (Cambridge: Cambridge University Press, 1992), 16–17.

16 G. Baranova, *Molodye golosa* (Moscow: Molodaia gvardiia, 1966), 94.

17 L. Leshchenko, *Liubov', komsomol i vesna* (Moscow: Znanie, 1985), 63.

18 N. Smirnova, *Mastera sovetskoi pesni* (Moscow: Znanie, 1908), 3.

19 N.N. El'shevskii, "Tsirkovye zhanry na èstrade," in *Russkaia sovetskaia èstrada, 1917–1929*, 281–2.

20 V. Leont'ev, "Èstrada – èto sovremennost'," in *Estrada: Chto? Gde? Zachem?*, 312.

21 V.V. Frolov, "Literaturnaia èstrada," in *Russkaia sovetskaia èstrada, 1917–1929*, 154.

22 Interview with Iu. Semenov, *Smena* 5 (1987).

23 *Vam otvechaet artist* (Moscow: Molodaia gvardiia, 1969), 180.

24 M. Ignat'eva, "Iosif Kobzon," in *Pevtsy sovetskoi èstrady*, ed. L. Bulgak (Moscow: Iskusstvo, 1977), 177. *See also* I. Kuznetsova, "Pesni boitsov i stroitelei," *Sovetskaia muzyka* 2 (1968): 105–7.

25 A. Iurikov, *Skol'ko stoit Valerii Leont'ev?* (Moscow: Sovetskii kompozitor, 1990), 12–13.

26 V. Kuznetsova, "Vyshel avtor na èstradu," in *Èstrada: Chto? Gde? Zachem?*, 223.

27 E. Uvarova, *Russkaia sovetskaia èstrada, 1946–1977*, 492.

28 Frolov, "Literaturnaia èstrada," 157.

29 A.N. Anastas'ev, "Osnovnye tendentsii razvitiia sovetskoi èstrady 20-kh godov," in *Russkaia sovetskaia èstrada, 1917–1929*, 33.

30 Uvarova, "Teatry malykh form," in *Russkaia sovetskaia èstrada, 1917–1929*, 331–2.

31 Anastas'ev, "Osnovnye tendentsii…," 34.

32 Frolov, "Ètsrada v gody grazhdanskoi voiny," in *Russkaia sovetskaia èstrada, 1917–1929*, 48.

33 Uvarova, "Teatry malykh form," 339.

34 O. Brik, *Èstrada pered stolikami* (Moscow/Leningrad: Kinopechat', 1927) 10.

35 Ibid., 23.

36 M. Korotkov, "I serdtse otklikaetsia na pesniu…," *Trud*, 17 January 1988, 4.

37 M.I. Zil'berbrandt, "Pesnia na èstrade," in *Russkaia sovetskaia èstrada, 1917–1929*, 211.

38 Iu. A. Dmitriev, "Èstradnye teatry (Miuzik-kholly)," in E. Uvarova, (ed.), *Russkaia sovetskaia èstrada, 1930–1945* (Moscow: Iskusstvo, 1981), 15.

39 *Ibid.*, 52–3.

40 Zil'berbrandt, "Pesnia na èstrade," in *Russkaia sovetskaia èstrada, 1930–1945*, 128.

41 Zil'berbrandt, "Pesnia na èstrade," in *Russkaia sovetskaia èstrada, 1917–1929*, 235.

42 Frolov, "Rechevye zhanry," in *Russkaia sovetskaia èstrada, 1930–1945*, 78.

43 Uvarova, "Teatry èstrady i minatiur," in *Russkaia sovetskaia èstrada, 1930–1945*, 63.

44 L. Utesov, in T. Didenko, "Podlinnyi èntuziast pesni," *Sovetskaia muzyka* 10 (1978), 32–3.

45 Zil'berbrandt, "Pesnia na èstrade," in *Russkaia sovetskaia èstrada, 1930–1945*, 240.

46 *Neizvestnyi Utesov* (Moscow: TERRA, 1998), 85.

47 Ibid., 80

48 Zil'berbrandt, "Pesnia na èstrade," in *Russkaia sovetskaia èstrada, 1930–1945*, 242.

49 V.B. Feiertag, "Dzhaz na èstrade," in ibid., 279

50 G. Skorokhodov, "On pel serdtsem," in *Neizvestnyi Utesov*, 7.

51 F. Razzakov, *Dos'e na zvezd*, vol. 1, 1934–1961 (Moscow: ÈKSMO-Press, 1998), 8.

52 S. Dreidin, "Tea-Dzhaz," in *Neizvestnyi Utesov*, 61.

53 S. Korev, "Dzhaz-band Utesova v Moskovskom miuzik-kholle," in *Neizvestnyi Utesov*, 63.

54 *Neizvestnyi Utesov*, 78.

55 L. Mariagin, "Moi Utesov," in *Neizvestnyi Utesov*, 53.

56 V. Shklovskii, "Novaia programma Gosudarstvennogo dzhaza-orkestra RSFSR…," in *Neizvestnyi Utesov*, 76.

57 V. Melik-Karamov, "Pesne nuzhen svoi dom," *Literaturnaia gazeta* 5, 30 January 1985, 8.

58 Zil'berbrandt, "Pesnia na èstrade," in *Russkaia sovetskaia èstrada, 1930–1945*, 245–6.

59 *Neizvestnyi Utesov*, 130–1.

60 Razzakov, vol. 1, 12.

61 Ibid., 14–15.

62 Ibid., 16.

63 Shul'zhenko's comment to Alla Pugacheva after hearing the latter sing a patriotic song in private: from the documentary film *Zhdi i pomni menia*.

64 Zil'berbrandt, "Pesnia na èstrade," in *Russkaia sovetskaia èstrada, 1930–1945*, 246.

65 Razzakov, vol. 1, 12.

66 I. Vasilinina, "Klavdiia Shul'zhenko," in *Pevtsy sovetskoi èstrady*, ed. L. Bulgak, 31.

67 Razzakov, vol. 1, 213.

68 Vasilinina, 31.

69 Zil'berbrandt, "Pesnia na èstrade," in *Russkaia sovetskaia èstrada, 1930–1945*, 256.

70 Razzakov, vol. 1, 216–17.
71 *Russkie sovetskie pesni* (Moskva: Khudozhestvennaia literatura, 1977), 76–7.
72 Vasilinina, 35.
73 Zil'berbrandt, "Pesnia na èstrade," in *Russkaia sovetskaia èstrada, 1930–1945*, 256.
74 Razzakov, vol. 1, 222 and 226.
75 *Russkie sovetskie pesni*, 78–9.
76 S. Borisova and I. Iaunzem, "Zhanr obiazyvaet," *Sovetskaia muzyka* 2 (1966), 93.
77 V. Petrov, "Znakomye litsa: Èdita P'ekha," *Gudok*, 13 May 1979.
78 E. Mospanov, "Pesnia ne rasstanetsia s toboi...," *Bytovoe obsluzhivanie naseleniia* 9 (1984), 46–7.
79 A. Trushkin and A. Shumskii, "Rodilas' na Zapade, zhivet v Rossii, a liubit Vostok," *Komsomol'skaia pravda* 4 February 1993, 4.
80 Razzakov, 1: 227.
81 K. Lazarenko, in L. Grechishnikova, *Iosif Kobzon* (Moscow: Glavnoe upravalenie kul'tury Mossoveta, 1985).
82 M. Magomaev, in ibid.

CHAPTER TWO

1 G. Borisov, "Blesk ili svet," *Komsomolets Kubani*, 1 October 1987.
2 W.B. Lincoln, *Between Heaven and Hell* (New York: Viking, 1998), 444.
3 "Iosif Kobzon daet obet molchaniia, khotia emu po-prezhnemu est' chto skazat,'" *Komsomol'skaia pravda*, 26 January–2 February 1996, 4–5.
4 Article by E. Dorozhkin on Kobzon, *Kommersant-Daily* 31 January 1997, 14.
5 I. Kobzon, "Byt' dostoinymi preemnikami traditsii," *Sovetskaia muzyka* 9 (1983), 46–8.
6 L. Luk'ianova, "Pesnia tvoia i moia," *Ogonek* 47 (1978), 32–3.
7 Iu. Dmitriev, "Utverzhdenie sovremennogo geroia," *Muzykal'naia zhizn'* 1 (1973), 22.
8 A. Dement'ev, in L. Grechishnikova, *Iosif Kobzon* (Moscow: Glavnoe upravalenie kul'tury Mossoveta, 1985).
9 *Sovetskaia kul'tura*, 1 June 1973, 4.
10 *Sovetskaia èstrada i tsirk* 11 (November 1980), 26.
11 Ibid., 3 (March 1972), 14–15.
12 U. Ott, *Televizionnoe znakomstvo* (Moscow: Iskusstvo, 1992), 80–106.
13 "Èto zhe radost' bol'shaia – byt' rebenkom, zhenoi Kobzona ...," *Chas pik* 168 (September 1996), 18.
14 T. Maksimova, "Ring posle 'Ringa,'" *Televidenie i radioveshchanie* 9 (1989).
15 Borisov, "Blesk ili svet."

16 T. Cherednichenko, "Alla Pugacheva togda i teper,'" *Sovetskaia èstrada i tsirk* 11 (1991).

17 G. Melikiants, "Videt' zhizn' krasochno ...," *Izvestiia*, 28 July 1984.

18 Iu. Dimitriev and O. Kuznetsova, "Rechevye zhanry," in *Russkaia sovetskaia èstrada 1946–1977*, 86.

19 N. Smirnova, "Pesnia na èstrade," in *Russkaia sovetskaia èstrada, 1946–1977*, 245.

20 *Neizvestnyi Utesov*, 59–60.

21 Smirnova, 246.

22 Smirnova, *Mastera sovetskoi pesni* (Moscow: Znanie, 1980), 13.

23 Cherednichenko, "Èra pustiakov, ili kak my nakonets prishli k legkoi muzyke ...," *Novyi mir* 10 (October 1992), 224–5.

24 I. Reznik, "Starry Summer" (*Zvezdnoe leto*), in *Izbrannoe: Stikhi* (Moscow: Khudozhestvennaia literatura, 1997), 158.

25 R. Rozhdestvenskii, *Razgovor poidet o pesne* (Moscow: Sovetskaia Rossia, 1979), 3.

26 Ibid., 92, and V. Granovskaia, "U nas v gost'iakh maèstro," *Trud*, 13 January 1982.

27 *Sovetskaia kul'tura*, 1 March 1983, 5.

28 *Razgovor poidet o pesne*, 122–4.

29 G.S. Smith, *Songs to Seven Strings* (Indiana University Press, 1984), 28–9.

30 *Razgovor poidet o pesne*, 85.

31 *Sovetskaia èstrada i tsirk*, 9 May 1975, 5.

32 A. Nazaretian, *Ot Leshchenko do Leshchenko* (Moscow: ASLAN, 1994), 86–9.

33 L. Leshchenko, *Liubov', komsomol i vesna* (Moscow: Znanie, 1985), 35.

34 Ibid., 39–41.

35 *Sovetskaia kul'tura*, 14 July 1983, 6.

36 Ibid., 16 January 1973, 3.

37 *Sovetskaia èstrada i tsirk* 9 (1973), 14–15.

38 *Sovetskaia kul'tura*, 29 June 1979, 5.

39 Rozhdestvenskii, *Izbrannye proizvedeniia*, vol. 2 (Moscow: Khudozhestvennaia literatura, 1979), 421.

40 Reznik, *Alla Pugacheva i drugie* (Los Angeles: Arthur/Rey Trading, 1994), 52.

41 Ibid., 32.

42 Cherednichenko, "Alla Pugacheva togda i teper'."

43 "Ikh siiatel'stvo izvolit spet' v den' rozhdeniia," *Moskovskii komsomolets*, 15 April 1995.

44 B. Savchenko, *Dorogaia Alla Borisovna* (Moscow: Znanie, 1992), 28.

45 Reznik, *Alla Pugacheva i drugie* and *Izbrannoe: Stikhi*.

46 *Sovetskaia èstrada i tsirk* 12 (1981), 26–7.

47 R. Pauls, (with O. Goriachev), "Maèstro Pauls nikomu ne pishet," *Argumenty i fakty* 50 (December 1993), 8.

48 V. Granovskaia, "U nas v gostiakh maèstro," *Trud*, 13 January 1982, 4.

49 Reznik, *Izbrannoe*, 270.

50 Ibid., 80.

51 *Alla Pugacheva i drugie*, 178.

52 Ibid., 176.

53 *Izbrannoe*, 183–5.

54 Raimonds Pauls, in *Sovetskaia kul'tura*, 5 January 1984, 4.

55 V. Novakovskii, "Alla Pugacheva," *Komsomol'skaia pravda*, 11 July 1976.

56 V. Tukh, "Arlekino ili teatr pevitsy," *Vechernii Tallin*, 14 July 1977. The cultivated nature of a Tallinn viewer and its consequence for a Russian performer have also been noted by Valerii Leont'ev. See M. Kirsi, "Ia schastliv, chto u menia est' zritel'," *Sovetskaia Èstoniia*, December 28 1986.

57 M. Antsyferov, "Ne imeiu prava oshibat'sia," *Sovetskaia molodezh'* (Riga), 2 October 1977.

58 Iu. Alaev, "I kazhdyi raz, kak v poslednii," *Sovetskaia Tatariia* (Kazan), 21 May 1978.

59 L. Nikitin, "Normal'noe plat'e s rukavami," *Moskovskii komsomolets*, 13 October 1978.

60 Anon., "Rabochee ee mesto – èstrada," *Smena* 16 (1980).

61 V. Karpenko, "Pesnia – zerkalo dushi," *Komsomolets Uzbekistana* (Tashkent), 27 January 1981.

62 I. Rudenko, "Bez strakhovki," *Komsomol'skaia pravda*, 28 August 1983.

63 I. Vasilinina, "Alla Pugacheva … Kakova ona segodnia," *Teatr* 3 (1984).

64 Vasilinina, "Eshche raz ob Alle Pugachevoi," *Teatr* 1 (1985).

65 A. Petrov, "Alla Pugacheva – Pevitsa, aktrisa, kompozitor," *Kul'tura i zhizn'* 12 (1979), 18.

66 M. Barabash (i dr.), "Naedine so vsemi," *Nedelia* 9 (2–8 March 1987), 16.

67 Cherednichenko, "Èra pustiakov," 225. All the same, it has been convincingly suggested that years of women singing folklore on the modern Soviet estrada created a colourful union of the pronoun "we," sanctioned by civic songs, and the "I" of a typical lament. When used in a modern 1970s context, a female singer such as Pugacheva may "embody the union of freedom and unhappiness – the unhappiness of freedom."

68 V.B. Feiertag, "Dzhaz na èstrade," *Russkaia sovetskaia èstrada, 1930–1945*, 279.

69 N. Smirnova, *Mastera sovetskoi pesni* (1980), 6.

70 Ibid., 8–9.

71 Vasilinina, "Klavdiia Shul'zhenko," in L. Bulgak (ed.), *Pevtsy sovetskoi èstrady*, 37.

72 M.I. Zil'berbrandt, "Pesnia na èstrade," *Russkaia sovetskaia èstrada, 1930–1945*, 259–60.

73 Iu. Dmitriev, "Utverzhdenie sovremennogo geroia."

74 R. Zviagina, "Stupeni," *Leninskaia smena* (Gorky), 31 December 1975.

75 B. Serebrennikova, in Bulgak, *Pevtsy sovetskoi èstrady*, 218. See also *Zhdi i pomni menia* and *Ot "Arlekino" do...* for visual examples.

76 È. Kekelidze, "I dykhanie zritel'nogo zala," *Molodezh' Èstonii* (Tallin), 12 July 1977.

77 Smirnova, "Teatr pesni Ally Pugachevoi," *Teatr* 2 (1978).

78 È. Abaidullina, "Laureat mezhdunarodnykh konkursov Alla Pugacheva 'Na stsene – moia zhizn,'" *Na smenu!* (Sverdlovsk), 12 July 1978.

79 M. Ignat'eva, "Vse mogut koroli?" *Sovetskaia kul'tura,* 16 September 1980.

80 Vasilinina, "Eshche raz ob Alle Pugachevoi."

81 Y. Lotman, "Painting and the Language of Theater: Notes on the Problem of Iconic Rhetoric," in A. Efimova and L. Manovich (eds.), *Tekstura: Russian Essays on Visual Culture* (Chicago: University of Chicago Press, 1993), 53.

82 G. Piatigorskaia, "Mif o svobodnom cheloveke," *Teatr* 12 (1990). See also Cherednichenko, "Alla Pugacheva togda i teper'," *Sovetskaia èstrada i tsirk* 11 (1991).

83 Vasilinina, "Klavdiia Shul'zhenko," 45.

84 *Izbrannoe,* 317–18.

CHAPTER THREE

1 Alla Pugacheva, in *Alla* 1 (1991), 2–5 and 16.

2 Èdita P'ekha, in V. Terskaia, "Gospozha pesni," *Daidzhest kuranty,* January (1993), 10.

3 D. Bakhurst, *Consciousness and Revolution in Soviet Philosophy: From the Bolsheviks to Evald Ilyenkov* (Cambridge: Cambridge University Press, 1991).

4 Ibid., 179–80.

5 Ibid., 10–11.

6 E.V. Ilyenkov, *Dialectical Logic: Essays on Its History and Theory* (Moscow: Progress, 1977), 260–1.

7 Bakhurst, *Consciousness and Revolution,* 185.

8 Bakhtin, M., *Problems of Dostoevsky's Poetics* (Minneapolis: University of Minnesota Press, 1984), 98.

9 *Consciousness and Revolution,* 198.

10 *Dialectical Logic,* 8.

11 Ibid., 263–4.

12 Bakhtin, "The Spatial Form of a Character," in A. Efimova and L. Manovich, *Tekstura* (Chicago: University of Chicago Press, 1993), 37–45.

13 *Consciousness and Revolution*, 183–4.

14 T. Cherednichenko, *Tipologiia sovetskoi massovoi kul'tury: Mezhdu Brezhnevym i Pugachevoi* (Moscow: Kul'tura, 1994), 82.

15 W.B. Lincoln, *Between Heaven and Hell*, 351.

16 J. Brodsky, "Reflections on a Spawn from Hell," *New York Times Magazine* 1 (October 1972), 10 and 66–70.

17 Concert program to celebrate Èdita P'ekha's 1998 birthday in the October Concert Hall, St Petersburg.

18 R. Robin, "Stalinism and Popular Culture," in H. Gunther, *The Culture of the Stalin Period* (St Martin's: New York, 1990), 15.

19 V. Dunham, *In Stalin's Time* (Duke University Press: Durham, 1990), 72 and 78.

20 A.M. Etkind, "Psychological Culture," in D.N. Shalin (ed.), *Russian Culture at the Crossroads: Paradoxes of Post-Communist Consciousness* (Boulder: Westview, 1996), 117.

21 Brodsky, *Marbles* (New York: Noonday, 1989), 46.

22 Èdita P'ekha, in *Vam otvechaet artist* (Moscow: Molodaia gvardiia, 1969), 180.

23 B. Slutskii, *Stikhotvoreniia* (Moscow: Khudozhestvennaia literatura, 1989), 133.

24 Èdita P'ekha, *Vechernii Leningrad*, 31 December 1987.

25 B. Groys, "Stalinism as Aesthetic Phenomenon," *Tekstura*, 122.

26 Cherednichenko, *Tipologiia*, 21.

27 P. Vail' and A. Genis, 60-e, 42.

28 M. Èpshtein, *Vera i obraz: Religioznoe bessoznatel'noe v russkoi kul'ture 20-go veka* (Tenafly: Èrmitazh, 1994), 98.

29 M. Kirsi, "Shchedrost' talanta," *Sovetskaia Èstoniia*, 13 January 1990.

30 *Sovetskaia kul'tura*, 11 August 1978, 4.

31 G. Hammarberg, *From the Idyll to the Novel: Karamzin's Sentimentalist Prose* (Cambridge: Cambridge University Press, 1991), 32.

32 *Sovetskaia kul'tura*, 30 July 1987, 2.

33 "S pesnei po zhizni," *Sovetskaia Rossiia*, 2 May 1979, 4.

34 *Dialectical Logic*, 261.

35 A. Erokhin, "I prazdnik, i ispytanie ...," *Literaturnaia Rossiia*, 27 April 1979, 19.

36 *Sovetskaia èstrada i tsirk* 12 (1976), 20.

37 *Dialectical Logic*, 273–4.

CHAPTER FOUR

1 P. Vail' and A. Genis, 233.

2 Ibid. and *Kommersant-Daily*, 31 July 1997, 10a. P'ekha's Polish roots have a lasting (proletarian) charm for Russian readers. See N. Zavadskaia,

"Èdita P'ekha," *Muzykal'naia zhizn'* 16 (1968), 10, and – twenty-seven years later – V. Terskaia, "Èdita, doch' shakhtera," *Smena* (Moscow) 12 (1995), 138–45. The modishness of her accent is often noted. See, for example, V. Solov'ev-Sedoi, "Èdita P'ekha," *Krugozor* 11 (1974), back cover.

3 N. Zavadskaia, *Pevets i pesnia (Metod. sposobie)* (Moscow: Iskusstvo, 1979), 70. Other articles stressing a sung art form above all external phenomena include: N. Bredis, "Marshrutami pesni," *Krugozor* 5 (1981), 15; E. Belostotskaia, "Stala pesnia sud'boiu," *Trud*, 21 January 1982, 4; M. Korotkov, "I serdtse otklikaetsia na pesniu ...," *Trud*, 17 January 1988, 4, and S. Guretskii, "S kem mne spravliat' den' rozhdeniia, esli ne so zriteliami," *Smena*, 29 July 1995, 6.

4 Vail' and Genis, 48 and 126.

5 P'ekha in Sh. Kasumova, "Vy nas prosili rasskazat' ...," *Uchitel'skaia gazeta*, 23 October 1973, 4.

6 V. Zaseev, "Na slabosti – lish' den'!" *Sovetskaia zhenshchina* 2 (1989), 38.

7 Zavadskaia, *Pevets*, 77.

8 N.I. Smirnova, "Pesnia na èstrade," *Russkaia sovetskaia èstrada, 1946–1977*, 271.

9 F. Razzakov, *Dos'e na zvezd*, vol. 2 (Moscow: ÈKSMO Press, 1998), 457.

10 E. Mospanov, "Pesnia ne proshchaetsia s toboi ...," *Bytovoe obsluzhivanie naseleniia* 9 (1984), 46–7.

11 A return visit to France is recorded in O. Petrichenko, "Stil' Èdity P'ekhi," *Ogonek* 40 (1981), 31–2.

12 Zavadskaia, *Pevets*, 58. See also G. George, "Prekrasnaia dama s rozoi," *Televidenie i radioveshchanie* 6 (June 1989), 20–2.

13 Zavadskaia, "Poet Èdita P'ekha," *Kul'tura i zhizn'* 1 (1969), 28–9.

14 E. Ivanova, "Melodiia druzhby," *Smena* 11 (1965), 28–30.

15 È. P'ekha, "Davaite pet'! Davaite druzhit'!" *Avrora* 7 (1978), 39–41.

16 *Sovetskaia kul'tura*, 7 November 1960, 4.

17 Ibid., 22 August 1978, 4.

18 M. Gariaeva, "Vsei dushoiu v pesne," *Nedelia*, 21–27 April 1980, 4–5.

19 V. Ia. Kalish, "Vokal'nye i vokal'no-instrumental'nye ansambli," in *Russkaia sovetskaia èstrada, 1946–1977*, 370.

20 Razzakov, *Dos'e na zvezd*, vol. 2, 460.

21 N. Mikhailovskaia, "Ansambl' Druzhba," *Muzykal'naia zhizn'* 13 (1958), 14.

22 M.W. Hopkins, *Mass Media in the Soviet Union* (New York: Pegasus, 1970), 239–50.

23 G. Zamkovets (ed.), *Moskovskii godudarstvennyi teatr èstrady* (Moscow, 1990), 70–71 and 74.

24 *Vechernii Leningrad*, 24 December 1992, 3.

25 I. Evseeva, "Èdita P'ekha: Menia sovsem ne volnuet konkurentsiia," *Peterburgskii telezritel'*, 10–16 August 1998, 5.

26 Ibid.

27 *Vechernii Leningrad*, 24 December 1992, 3.

28 Èdita P'ekha, in *Vam otvechaet artist*, 178–81.

29 On the post-Druzhba P'ekha, see Zavadskaia, "Èdita P'ekha i ee novye druz'ia," *Muzykal'naia zhizn'* 9 (May 1978), 21–2.

30 *Sovetskaia èstrada i tsirk* 12 (1967) 20.

31 Razzakov, vol. 2, 471.

32 *Sovetskaia kul'tura*, 31 October 1989, 2.

33 V. Terskaia, "Gospozha pesni," *Daidzhest kuranty* 1 (January 1993), 10.

34 Zamkovets, *Moskovskii godudarstvennyi teatr èstrady* (1990), 70–1 and 74.

35 *Sovetskaia kul'tura*, 9 January 1993, 1, and *Kommersant Daily*, 31 July 1997, 10a. See also *Smena*, 4 April 1996, 5.

36 Razzakov, vol. 2, 476. See also N. Ipatova, "Severnoe siianie …," *Smena* 62, 18 March 1995, 1, and "Èdita P'ekha v 'Astorii' …," *Smena* 80, 8 April 1995, 8.

37 K. Kozerogov, "Za god do stoletiia ona vse takzhe moloda i krasiva!" *Chas pik* 140, 31 July 1996, 2.

38 N. Muratova, "P'ekhe ne skazhesh 'Do svidaniia,'" *Chas pik*, 5 August 1997, 2.

39 M. Zaitsev, "U Èdity P'ekhy ukrali 25,000 dollarov," *Sobesednik* 42 (1996), 6–7.

40 "Nemodnoe kino," *OM* (July–August 1997), 33. For P'ekha's attittude towards modern popular music, see A. Gervash, "Na stsene i v zale," *Trud*, 8 November 1988, 4. Her own consistency is discussed in N. Zavadskaia, "Ne izmeniaia sebe," *Muzykal'naia zhizn'* 2 (January 1986), 22–3, and L. Sidorovskii, *Komsomol'skaia pravda*, 21 January 1982, 4.

41 *Sovetskaia èstrada i tsirk* 9 (1982), 33.

42 Lev Leshchenko in *Kommersant Daily*, 2 August 1997, 10.

43 *Sovetskaia èstrada i tsirk* 18 (1972), 18–19. For the development of a "bridge" based upon mail from admirers, see *Sovetskaia kul'tura*, 5 February 1983, 4, and 19 January 1988, 2.

44 I. Gati, "Esli b znali vy, kak mne dorogi …," *Sovetskaia Èstoniia*, 17 March 1978.

45 *Sovetskaia èstrada i tsirk* 10 (1965), 16–18.

46 *Sovetskaia kul'tura*, 18 August 1983, 7.

47 Ibid., 30 July 1984, 2.

48 See also *Televidenie i radioveshchanie* (August 1984), 29. On seeking for songs, see A. Lopukhin and Iu. Filinov, "Pesnia darit radost'," *Komsomol'skaia pravda*, 14 January 1983, 4.

49 *Sovetskaia kul'tura*, 22 August 1981, 5.

50 *Vechernii Leningrad*, 21 March 1990, 4.

51 Ibid., 4 April 1990, 3.

52 Between 1993 and 1994 *Trud* published a similar series of advice arti-
    cles. See 10 April 1993, 7; 10 February 1994, 3; 7 April 1994, 3; 23
    June 1994, 5, and 17 August 1994, 3.

53 Vail' and Genis, 60-e, 53.

54 *Vechernii Peterburg*, 24 December 1992, 3.

55 A.K. Varsobin, "Pesnia sblizhaet narody," *Leningradskaia pravda* 131
    (7 June 1979), 4.

56 D. Barabash and D. Nevelev, "Biletom budet avtograf," *Sovetskaia Rossiia*,
    18 June 1988, 6.

57 *Sovetskaia kul'tura*, 11 September 1984, 5.

58 "Pesnia – dlia afganskikh druzei," *Leningradskaia pravda*, 1 November
    1983, 3.

59 *Sovetskaia kul'tura*, 15 December 1983, 1. See also "Nashi plany,"
    Muzykal'naia zhizn', 10 (May 1984), 9.

60 *Sovetskaia kul'tura*, 9 June 1988, 7. See also V. Svirin, "Do skoroi
    vstrechi," *Trud*, 23 June 1988, 4.

61 Masha Rasputina, *Peterburgskii telezritel'*, 10–16 August 1998, 5.

62 *Sovetskaia Rossiia*, 17 November 1960, 4.

63 Ivanova, "Melodiia Druzhby," *Smena* 11 (1965), 28–30.

64 A. Gervash, "Melodii druzhby," *Trud*, 21 January 1973, 4. Two such
    heroes are depicted in the song "The Boundless Sky," discusssed below.

65 *Sovetskaia kul'tura*, 22 January 1972, 4.

66 Zavadskaia, "Poet Èdita P'ekha," 29.

67 *Vam otvechaet artist*, 178.

68 A. Asarkan, "Ee manera," *Nedelia* 13 (1965), 4.

69 Terskaia, "Gospozha pesni."

70 *Sovetskaia kul'tura*, 11 September 1984, 5.

71 Terskaia, "Gospozha pesni."

72 "S pesnei po zhizni," *Sovetskaia Rossiia*, 2 May 1979, 4.

73 "Voina 'Pustyshkam!'" *Trud*, 21 March 1971, 3.

74 *Sovetskaia èstrada i tsirk* 18 (1972), 18–19.

75 M. Gariaeva, "Vsei dushoiu v pesne."

76 *Sovetskaia kul'tura* 10 June 1977, 8, and *Vechernii Leningrad*, 26 July 1980, 3.

77 G. Mishchevskaia and P. Ermishev, "Èdita P'ekha," in L. Bulgak, *Pevtsy
    sovetskoi èstrady* (Moscow: Iskusstvo, 1977), 187.

78 *Sovetskaia kul'tura*, 22 August 1978, 4, and 5 September 1978, 4.

79 "Nothing" (*Nichego*) by I. Krestovskii and D. Panfilov.

80 L. Makhrasev, *V legkom zhanre* (Leningrad, 1986), 278, quoted in
    A. Kurtsman, *Mark Fradkin* (Moscow: Sovetskii kompozitor, 1991), 97–8.

81 *Sovetskaia kul'tura*, 22 January 1972, 4.

82 Ibid., 11 September 1984, 5.

83 P'ekha's daughter might well sympathize with this working of a mater-
    nal metaphor, given her own experience of post-Soviet estrada: "Doch'

Èdity P'ekhi pala zhertvoi shou-biznesa," *Moskovskii komsomolets*, 6 December 1991, 4.

84 A. Trushkii and Shumskii, "Rodilas' na Zapade, zhivet v Rossii, a liubit Vostok," *Moskovskaia pravda* 22, 4 February 1993, 4.

85 T. Panina, "Da, ona P'ekha," *Sovetskaia Rossiia*, 20 May 1989, 4.

86 V. Andrle, *A Social History of Twentieth-Century Russia* (London: Arnold, 1994), 207.

87 B.A. Anderson, "The Life Course of Soviet Women Born 1905–1960," in J.R. Millar, *Politics, Work and Daily Life in the* USSR (Cambridge: Cambridge University Press, 1988), 203–41.

88 Gariaeva, "Vsei dushoiu v pesne," and *Sovetskaia kul'tura*, 5 September 1978, 4.

89 Gervash, "Melodii druzhby," and *Sovetskaia kul'tura*, 29 August 1981, 5.

90 *Vechernii Leningrad*, 31 December 1981, 3.

91 Mikhailovskaia, "Ansambl' Druzhba."

92 *Sovetskaia kul'tura*, 17 November 1960, 4.

93 *Sovetskaia èstrada i tsirk* 10 (1965), 16–18.

94 Gervash, "Melodii druzhby."

95 S. Borisova and I. Iaunzem, "Zhanr obiazyvaet," *Sovetskaia muzyka* 2 (1966), 91–5. See also *Sovetskaia kul'tura*, 4 April 1972, 3, and 13 July 1972, 2.

96 *Kommersant-Daily*, 31 July 1997, 10a.

97 Sh. Kasumova, "Vy nas prosili rasskazat' …"

98 *Vechernii Leningrad*, 31 December 1970, 3.

99 *Sovetskaia kul'tura*, 22 January 1972, 4.

100 G. Mishchevskaia and P. Ermishev, 187.

101 *Sovetskaia èstrada i tsirk* 18 (1972), 18–19.

102 *Sobesednik* 19 (1996), 10.

103 R. Minasov, "Doch' pol'skogo shakhtera," *Teatral'naia zhizn'* 15 (1965) 23.

104 *Sovetskaia èstrada i tsirk* 10 (1965), 16–18. See also A. Beilin, *Voobrazhaemyi kontsert: Rasskazy o masterakh sovetskoi èstrady* (Moscow: Iskusstvo, 1971), 190–3.

105 *Sovetskaia èstrada i tsirk* 9 (1970), 6–7.

106 Ibid. 18 (1972), 18–19.

107 Mishchevskaia and Ermishev, 183.

108 Sh. Kasumova, "Vy nas prosili rasskazat' …" See also E. Nadeinskii, "Raportuet èstrada," *Muzykal'naia zhizn'* 10 (May 1976), 20–1.

109 *Sovetskaia kul'tura*, 22 January 1972, 4.

110 *Vechernii Leningrad*, 7 March 1990, 4, and *Gazeta dlia zhenshchin* 10 (1993), 1–2.

111 *Kommersant-Daily*, 2 August 1997, 8.

112 *Sovetskaia kul'tura*, 30 March 1985, 5.

113 Mishchevskaia and Ermishev, 183. See also T. Dmitriev, "Razve privy-kaiut k chudesam?" *Televidenie i radioveshchanie* 8 (August 1981), 36.

114 *Sovetskaia èstrada i tsirk* 18 (1972), 18–19.

115 *Sovetskaia kul'tura* 8 (1981), 36.

116 *Sovetskaia èstrada i tsirk* 3 (1973), 24.

117 *Sovetskaia kul'tura*, 29 June 1982, 3.

118 Gervash, "Melodii druzhby," and "Ni dnia bez pesni!," *Leningradskaia pravda* 296, 26 December 1981, 3.

119 *Sovetskaia kul'tura*, 11 September 1984, 5.

120 R. Rozhdestvenskii, *Izbrannye proizvedeniia*, vol. 2 (Moscow: Khudozhestvennaia literatura, 1979), 396–7.

CHAPTER FIVE

1 *Sovetskaia èstrada i tsirk* 10 (1981), 13–14.

2 Ibid., 3 (1972), 14–15.

3 E. Dodolev, "Tot samyi Kobzon," *Moskovskii komsomolets*, 1 February 1992. See also A. Vandenko, "Iosif Kobzon daet obet molchaniia, khotia emu po-prezhnemu est' chto skazat'," *Moskovskaia pravda*, 26 January–2 February 1996, 4–5.

4 G. Rezanov and T. Khoroshilova, "Kobzon oboznachil svoiu nat-sional'nost,'" *Komsomol'skaia pravda*, 14–21 March 1997, 15. See also N. Remizova, "Naposledok Kobzon zapel na ivrite …," *Komsomol'skaia pravda* 14, 25 January 1997, 4.

5 V. Letov, "Ia gorazdo luchshe, chem moia reputatsiia," *Ogonek* 35 (August 1995), 36–8. See also I. Pankov, "Menia obeshchali ubrat' iz ognemeta," *Komsomol'skaia pravda* 17 May 1994, 1–2; S. Govorukhin, "Est' li v Rossii mafiia?" *Argumenty i fakty* 49 (1995), 6 and A. Khinsh-tein, "V otlichie ot menia Iaponchik ne rugaetsia matom," *Moskovskii komsomolets*, 8 July 1995, 1 and 8.

6 For an account of the problems involved see *Kommersant-Daily*, 17 Octo-ber 1997, 7. On a related issue see "Kobzon, ty ne prav," *Smena* 107, 13 May 1995, 3, and L. Kislinskaia, "Protsent tsinizma," *Sovetskaia Rossiia* 11, 28 January 1993, 6.

7 A brief indication of how civic and political goals might overlap is in L. Dneprovskii, "Iosif Kobzon," *Trud*, February 1985, 4.

8 A. Filippov, and V. Gorlenko, "Na samom dele ia – nastoiatel' monas-tyria," *Trud* 15 September 1995, 5.

9 L. Luk'ianova, "Pesnia tvoia i moia," *Ogonek* 47 (1978), 32–3.

10 Dodolev, "Tot samyi Kobzon."

11 A. Pavlova, "Mne vsego-to tridtsat' deviat'!" *Krokodil* 2 (1997), 2–5.

12 F. Razzakov, *Dos'e na zvezd*, vol. 2, 101.

13 Dodolev, "Tot samyi Kobzon."

14 Ibid.

15 Razzakov, *Dos'e na zvezd*, vol. 2, 104.

16 *Sovetskaia kul'tura*, 26 July 1974, 6.

17 *Sovetskaia èstrada i tsirk* 2 (1988), 16–17.

18 L. Luk'ianova, "Pesnia tvoia i moia."

19 Dodolev, "Tot samyi Kobzon."

20 Razzakov, *Dos'e na zvezd*, vol. 2, 107. For an example of one typical (Soviet) year's effort, see "Nashi plany," *Muzykal'naia zhizn'* 4 (February 1986), 10.

21 Ibid., 108.

22 Letov, 1995, "Ia gorazdo luchshe ..."

23 L. Grechishnikova, *Iosif Kobzon* (Moscow: Glavnoe upravlenie kul'tury Mossoveta, 1985), inside back cover.

24 Dodolev, "Tot samyi Kobzon."

25 Razzakov, *Dos'e na zvezd*, vol. 2, 110.

26 "Vsem nam davno izvesten ...," *Argumenty i fakty* 38 (1991), 8.

27 *Kommersant-Daily*, 16 September 1997, 2.

28 "Is Russian Sinatra a Mobster?" *Jewish Bulletin of Northern California*, 19 January 1996.

29 *Kommersant-Daily*, 13 September 1997, 1.

30 Ia. Iur'eva, "Tsar' mafii, legenda èstrady," *Chas pik* 92, 26 May 1995, 2. See also S. Martin, "Grandson of Revolution ...," *Irish Times*, 7 November 1997; "Floating the Virgin," 6 September 1997, and "Mayor's Reign Ends," 8 September 1997.

31 L. McDonnell, "Ambitious Mayor," *OnLine Newshour*, 25 December 1996, and "Russia's Frank Sinatra May Be Denied Visa ...," *Sydney Morning Herald*, 31 October 1997. See also E. Dodolev, "Vragov svoikh druzei ia beru na sebia," *Nedelia* 7 (February 1992), 23.

32 A. Sargin and V. Tsepliaev, "Budu schastliv, esli Dumu razgoniat," *Argumenty i fakty* 39 (September 1997), 11. See also "Otkrytoe pis'mo Prezidentu Rossii," *Moskovskii komsomolets* 151, 11 August 1995, 2.

33 A. Bublikov, 1996 "Polnyi Kobzon: Sviashchennaia korova," *Sobesednik* 39 (October 1996), 4.

34 "I. Kobzon ukhodit s èstrady, no ne so stseny?" *Ogonek* 31 (July 1995), 14.

35 See for example I. Goruinova, "Khochu uiti so stseny krasivo," *Rossiiskie vesti* 11, 21 January 1997, 4.

36 *Kul'tura*, 11 September 1997, 11.

37 Razzakov, *Dos'e na zvezd*, vol. 2, 119.

38 Sargin and Tsepliaev, "Budu schastliv ..."

39 "Is Russian Sinatra ..."

40 "Russia's Frank Sinatra ..."

41 Razzakov, *Dos'e na zvezd*, vol. 2, 119. See also N. Kolesova and I. Goriunova, "Korol' nashikh serdets," *Rossiiskie vesti*, 13 September 1997, 4.

42 I. Kir'ianova, "Kubanskii renessans," *Literaturnaia gazeta* 10, 12 March 1997, 8.

43 V. Gorlenko, "Artist v Rossii bol'she, chem artist ...," *Trud,* 9 June 1994, 7.

44 V. Medvedev and V. Ustiuzhanin, "Dumai Iosif Davydovich," *Komsomol'skaia pravda,* 16 September 1997, 1. In the Duma elections of 1999, Kobzon garnered well over 90 per cent of the votes in the same region.

45 *Kommersant-Daily,* 16 September 1997, 2.

46 Sargin and Tsepliaev, "Budu schastliv ..."

47 *Sovetskaia kul'tura,* 14 February 1994, 7.

48 From promotional material (1997) surrounding Kobzon's grand departure from estrada.

49 *Russkie sovetskie pesni* (Moskva: Khudozhestvennaia literatura, 1977), 216.

50 Ibid., 568.

51 "Victory Day," by D. Tukhmanov and V. Kharitonov (1975).

52 A. Osadchaia, "Poslednii akkord," *Iunost'* 4 (1989), 76–9.

53 *Sovetskaia kul'tura,* 19 February 1994, 7.

54 Ibid., 7 November 1985, 8.

55 *Kommersant-Daily,* 16 September 1997, 2.

56 *Sovetskaia kul'tura,* 10 September 1987, 4. See also E. Zorokhovich, "Chtoby pesniu slushali ...," *Moskovskaia pravda,* 9 September 1987, 1, and R. Guseinov, "Khorkobzonov," *Trud,* 19–25 September 1997, 4.

57 "Èto zhe radost' bol'shaia ...," *Chas pik,* 18 September 1996, 18. See also M. Sadchikov, "Ot Tsedenbala do 'Kèndimena,'" *Smena* (St Petersburg) 3 August 1996, 6.

58 Sargin and Tsepliaev, "Budu schastliv ..."

59 *Sovetskaia kul'tura,* 10 September 1987, 4.

60 "March of Recollection" (*Marsh-vospominanie*), by O. Fel'tsman and R. Rozhdestvenskii.

61 *Russkie sovetskie pesni,* 644–5.

62 Ibid., 581–2.

63 *Russkaia sovetskaia èstrada, 1946–1977,* 179.

64 Kobzon, "Byt' dostoinymi preemnikami traditsii," *Sovetskaia muzyka* 9 (1983), 46–8.

65 *Sovetskaia kul'tura,* 14 August 1969, 3.

66 Iu. Dmitriev, "Utverzhdenie sovremennogo geroia," *Muzykal'naia zhizn'* 1 (1973), 22.

67 Vail' and Genis, 60-e, 126.

68 Ibid., 265–6.

69 A. Pakhmutova, "Izbral pesniu," *Sovetskaia Rossiia,* 11 September 1987, 6.

70 *Sovetskaia èstrada i tsirk* 5 (1974) 27.

71 *Zona BAM: Postoiannye zhiteli* (1987), documentary film directed by M. Pavlov.

72 N. Il'ichev, "Uvlechennost,'" *Sovetskaia Moldaviia*, 5 August 1967.

73 T. Khynku, "Pechal' moia svetla," *Sovetskaia Moldaviia*, 6 March 1983, 4.

74 *Russkie sovetskie pesni*, 375–6.

75 R. Rozhdestrenskii, *Razgovor poidet o pesne* (Moscow: Sovetskaia Rossiia, 1979), 123.

76 Bublikov, "Polnyi Kobzon."

77 *Russkaia sovetskaia èstrada, 1946–1977*, 265.

78 M. Ignat'eva, "Iosif Kobzon," in *Pevtsy sovetskoi èstrady*, L. Bulgak, ed. (Moscow: Iskusstvo, 1977), 170.

79 *Russkaia sovetskaia èstrada, 1946–1977*, 178.

80 "Kontsertnoe obozrenie" (September–November 1984), *Sovetskaia muzyka* 3 (1985), 52–4.

81 O. Sosnovskaia, "Ballada o bessmertii," *Sovetskaia muzyka* 9 (1970), 54–5, and N. Zavadskaia, "Novaia programma Iosifa Kobzona," *Muzykal'naia zhizn'* 14 (1970), 8–9.

82 *Sovetskaia èstrada i tsirk* 8 (1986), 4–5.

83 Ibid., 10 (1981), 13–14.

84 I. Kuznetsova, "Pesni boitsov i stroiteli," *Sovetskaia muzyka* 2 (1968), 105–7.

85 "Èto zhe radost' bol'shaia ..."

86 A. Pakhmutova, "Izbral pesniu."

87 Ia. Iur'eva, "Tsar' mafii ..."

88 O. Sosnovskaia, "Ballada o bessmertii."

89 Kobzon, "Byt' dostoinymi preemnikami traditsii."

90 T. Didenko, "Podlinnyi èntuziast pesni," *Sovetskaia muzyka* 10 (1978), 32–3, and L. Luk'ianova, "Pesnia tvoia i moia."

91 *Sovetskaia èstrada i tsirk* 12 (1977), 23. See also "Afisha nedeli," *Nedelia* #32 (1964), 9.

92 Ignat'eva, "Iosif Kobzon" (1977).

93 *Sovetskaia èstrada i tsirk* 3 (1972), 14–15.

94 "Èto zhe radost' bol'shaia ..."

CHAPTER SIX

1 *Sovetskaia èstrada i tsirk* 10 (1990), 31–2.

2 A. Perevalova, "U Rotaru vse oplacheno ...," *Nedelia* 23 (June 1992), 8.

3 S. Rotaru, "Shest' skripok i tsimbaly ...," *Iunost'* 4 (April 1976), 82–3.

4 F. Razzakov, *Dos'e na zvezd*, vol. 2 (Moscow: ÈKSMO, 1998), 469.

5 B. Sadekov, "Sofiia Rotaru," *Nedelia* 30 (July 1978), 13.

6 "Shest' skripok i tsimbaly."

7 R. Vikkers, in M.V. Uspenskaia, ed., *Pevtsy sovetskoi èstrady* (Moscow: Iskusstvo, 1985), 115–26. See also I. Khmara, "Kharakter u Soni zheleznyi," *Komsomol'skaia pravda*, 22 September 1993, 8.

8 G. Romanova, "Tsvety dlia Sofii," *Sovetskaia Rossiia*, 24 May 1981, 6.

9 N. Bataen, "Chervona ruta – tsvetok schast'ia," *Televidenie i radioveshchanie* 4 (April 1988), 40–1.

10 "Shest' skripok i tsimbaly."

11 *Pevtsy sovetskoi èstrady.*

12 V. Vasilets, "Pesnia ne znaet granits," *Pravda*, 7 October 1976. See also D. Krakaliia, "Dlia pesni rozhdennaia," *Sovetskaia Moldaviia*, 30 November 1974.

13 Razzakov, *Dos'e na zvezd*, vol. 2, 471.

14 "Tsvety dlia Sofii."

15 Ibid.

16 V. Kustov, "Pesni liubvi i vernosti," *Gudok*, 19 June 1988, 4.

17 "Dlia pevtsa i pesni," *Nedelia*, 30 October–5 November 1978, 8.

18 Razzakov, *Dos'e na zvezd*, vol. 2, 471–3.

19 E. Belostotskaia, "Sofiia Rotaru budet pet' v Sopote," *Trud*, 21 August 1974, 4.

20 Razzakov, *Dos'e na zvezd*, vol. 2, 472.

21 For additional context, see L. Kuznetsova, "L'vu sdavat'sia ne pristalo," *Sankt-Peterburgskie vedomosti*, 4 February 1998, 5.

22 Sadekov, "Sofiia Rotaru."

23 Razzakov, *Dos'e na zvezd*, vol. 2, 474.

24 *Pevtsy sovetskoi èstrady.*

25 For a comparision with actuality, see E. Belostotskaia, "Avtopotret," *Trud*, 12 August 1989, 4.

26 Razzakov, *Dos'e na zvezd*, vol. 2, 477.

27 B. Sandratskii, "Sofiia, priezhaite pochashche," *Sovetskaia Èstoniia*, 13 March 1990. See also "Risknu, spoiu po-russki," *Sankt-Peterburgskie vedomosti*, 30 July 1993, 7.

28 Razzakov, *Dos'e na zvezd*, vol. 2, 479.

29 Ibid., 482.

30 A. Perevalova, "Lish' posle shumnogo priznaniia …," *Sovetskie profsoiuzy* 11/12 (1990), 82–4.

31 V. Nabokov, *Speak, Memory* (New York: Putnam's, 1966), 25.

32 Ibid., 27.

33 A. Perevalova, *Irina Ponarovskaia: Biografiia* (Moscow: Zakharov, 1998), 11.

34 A. Muskatblit, "Rabota, poiski, somneniia," *Iunost'* 9 (1979), 95–7.

35 *Irina Ponarovskaia*, 15.

36 "Rabota, poiski, somneniia."

37 *Irina Ponarovskaia*, 29.

38 "Rabota, posiki, somneniia."

39 M. Provorov, "Obratnyi put' poterian," *Iunost'* 5 (1976), 107–9.

40 On Ponarovskaia and the nature of work in a collective, see A. Moskusenko, "Podsnezhnik dlia Iriny Ponarovskoi," *Rossiiskie vesti*, 18 March 1995, 16.

41 *Irina Ponarovskaia,* 49. See also *Krugozor* 1 (1977), 11, 12, and 14.

42 See also L. Burova, "Esli by on ee ne potseloval ...," *Èkran i stsena,* 20–27 February 1992, 14; V. Bereslavskii, "Zvonkii golos Iriny," *Nedelia* 38 (September 1976), 4, and "Po rasskazam O. Genri," *Televidenie i radioveshchanie* 6 (1982), 25.

43 I. Abel', "Podozhdem prem'ery," *Televidenie i radioveshchanie* 11 (November 1988), 27–8.

44 *Sovetskaia èstrada i tsirk* 10 (1990), 31–2.

45 *Irina Ponarovskaia,* 67.

46 Perevalova, "Lish' posle shumnogo priznaniia ..."

47 I. Kabak, "Pevitsa v mirskoi suete," *Argumenty i fakty* 47 (November 1991), 6.

48 *Sobesednik* 25 (1996), 5. See also V. Kravtsov, "Vzgliad s portreta," *Pravda* 63 (April 1992), 4.

49 *Irina Ponarovskaia,* 125.

50 Ibid., 95.

51 *Sovetskaia kul'tura,* 18 October 1988, 1.

52 *Irina Ponarovskaia,* 100.

53 M. Margolis, "Khochu bezhat' na dlinnuiu distantsiiu," *Daidzhest Kuranty* 36 (September 1993), 7.

54 A. Petrov, "Mir èstrady i prekrasen, i uzhasen," *Trud,* 12 February 1994, 7.

55 "Rabota, poiski, somneniia." See also A. Maliugin, "Èlegantnaia zhena doktora," *24 chasa,* 26 November 1996, 6.

56 *Irina Ponarovskaia,* 139.

57 "Lish' posle shumnogo priznaniia ..."

58 *Sovetskaia èstrada i tsirk* 10 (1990), 31–2.

59 Rotaru, in *Pevtsy sovetskoi èstrady.*

60 Ponarovskaia, in A. Petrov, "Mir èstrady ..." See also I. Stessel' and A. Boichuk, "Èta neprostaia èstradnaia zhizn,'" *Pravda Ukrainy,* 2 August 1987, 4.

61 "Shest' skripok i tsimbaly ..."

62 Romanova, "Tsvety dlia Sofiia."

63 Sandratskii, "Sofiia, priezhaite pochashche."

64 Margolis, "Khochu bezhat' ..."

65 Kabak, I. "Pevitsa v mirskoi suete."

66 Muskatblit, "Rabota, poiski, somneniia."

67 Petrov, "Mir èstrady i prekrasen ..."

68 A. Perevalova, "Irina Ponarovskaia," *Nedelia* 30 (July 1993), 3.

69 *Sovetskaia èstrada i tsirk* 10 (1990), 31–2.

70 Ibid., 3 (1977), 33.

71 Vasilets, "Pesnia ne znaet granits."

72 *Pevtsy sovetskoi èstrady.*

73 Ibid. See also G. Pavlenko, "Sestra moia, zhizn'!" *Sovetskaia Moldaviia*, 24 March 1985; I. Lepsha, "Poiut sestry Rotaru," *Pravda Ukrainy*, 26 October 1979; "Sofiia Rotaru," *Televidenie i radioveshchanie* 11 (November 1984), 29, and G. Dolzhenko, "A gde mne vziat' takuiu pesniu?" *Pravda Ukrainy*, 1 January 1986, 4.

74 "Shest' skripok i tsimbaly."

75 *Sovetskaia èstrada i tsirk* 12 (1982), 16–18.

76 *Moskovskii komsomolets*, 17 July 1976.

77 Vasilets, "Pesnia ne znaet granits."

78 V. Lapin, "Kogda poet dusha," *Pravda Vostoka*, 27 September 1981, and "Poet Sofiia Rotaru," *Pravda Vostoka*, 19 October 1975.

79 M. Levitin, "V pesne – moia dusha," *Sovetskii èkran* 17 (1981), 12–13.

80 Sadekov, "Sofiia Rotaru."

81 Kustov, "Pesni liubvi i vernosti."

82 Bataen, "Chervona ruta – tsvetok schast'ia."

83 N. Zorkaia, "Kazhdyi, pravo, imeet pravo," *Sovetskii èkran* 23 (1982), 12–13.

84 Margolis, "Khochu bezhat' ..."

85 *Sobesednik* 9 (1996), 12.

86 A. Troitsky, *Back in the USSR* (London: Faber and Faber, 1988), 28. See also V. Zak, "Poiushchie gitary," *Muzykal'naia zhizn'* 6 (1968), 19.

87 N. Zavadskaia and E. Nadeinskii, *Muzykal'naia zhizn'* 17 (1976), 18–20.

88 *Sovetskaia èstrada i tsirk* 3 (1978), 18–19.

89 Iu. Klimov, "Chto na èstrade?" *Pravda*, 15 July 1976.

90 A. Petrov, "Volnuet i segodnia," *Krugozor* 5 (1976), 14–15.

91 Iu. Smelkov, "Opera na èstrade," *Trud*, 24 June 1979, 4. See also V. Vishnevskii, "Orfei, Èvridika ...," *Komsomol'skaia pravda*, 17 August 1975, 3; "Èta udarnaia slabaia dolia," *Muzykal'naia zhizn'* 17 (1976), 18–20, "Gitary poiut o Flandrii," *Muzykal'naia zhizn'* 4 (1980), 6–7, and E. Èpshtein, "Irina Ponarovskaia," *Muzykal'naia zhizn'* 15 (1981), 22–3.

92 A positive assessment of that same excess can be found in Iu. Smelkov, "Liubov'iu rozhdaetsia pesnia," *Komsomol'skaia pravda*, 29 August 1981, 4.

93 I. Abel', "Podozhdem prem'ery."

94 This is, however, a moot point, as a remark of 1981 shows: "I have a rule: new song – new costume." G. Romanova, "Tsvety dlia Sofii."

95 *Sovetskaia kul'tura*, 13 February 1981, 4.

96 Levitin, "V pesne – moia dusha."

97 Kustov, "Pesni liubvi i vernosti."

98 V. Ivanova, "Kreslo no. 13," *Literaturnaia gazeta*, 4 August 1982, 8.

99 Zorkaia, "Kazhdyi, pravo, imeet pravo."

100 *Sovetskaia kul'tura*, 25 June 1982, 4.

101 Ibid., 27 July 1982, 5.

102 A. Petrov, "Ia ne liubliu èstradnyi mir," *24 chasa*, 8 February 1996, 2.

103 *Sovetskaia kul'tura*, 13 September 1984, 5.

104 Petrov, "Ia ne liubliu ..."

105 Lapin, "Kogda poet dusha."

106 Romanova, "Tsvety dlia Sofii."

107 T. Kareva, "Zvezdy sovetskoi èstrady," *Sovetskaia zhenshchina* 9 (1981), 27.

108 E. Èpshtein, "Glavnaia tema," *Muzykal'naia zhizn'* 28 (October 1980), 29.

109 For Ponarovskaia and the same metaphor, see Petrov, "Moi mir – muzyka," *Kultura i zhizn'* 1 (1985), 17, and G. Kachuk and A. Perevalova, "Vslukh o sokrovennom," *Nedelia* 3 (1995), 8.

110 E. Nadeinskii, "Poet Chervona ruta," *Muzykal'naia zhizn'* 4 (February 1975), 19.

111 *Sovetskaia kul'tura*, 13 September 1984, 5.

112 Ibid., 18 October 1984, 4.

113 Ibid., 30 July 1985, 5.

114 M. Istiushina, "Prinosit' liudiam radost'," *Moskovskaia pravda*, 13 March 1979.

115 Perevalova, "Lish' posle shumnogo priznaniia ..."

116 Perevalova, "Irina Ponarovskaia."

117 Perevalova, "Plat'e na bulavkakh," *Nedelia* 25 (1989), 19.

CHAPTER SEVEN

1 Razzakov, *Dos'e na zvezd*, vol. 2, 467.

2 From a folk epic "The Nightingale Robber." For an interesting description of what makes Leont'ev a "different" type of singer, see V. Kuznetsov, "Takoi nestandartnyi Valerii Leont'ev," *Sankt-Peterburgskie vedomosti*, 3 June 1995, 5.

3 "Gde moi dom rodnoi," by M. Fradkin and R. Rozhdestvenskii.

4 L. Leshchenko, *Liubov', komsomol i vesna* (Moscow: Znanie, 1985), 7.

5 O. Saprykina, "Ia chuvstvuiu, chto nuzhno narodu," *Komsomol'skaia pravda*, 31 March 1994, 3.

6 *Liubov', komsomol i vesna*, 9.

7 L. Melik-Nubarova, "Kryl'ia pesni," *Pravda*, 4 May 1983.

8 *Liubov', komsomol i vesna*, 13.

9 Razzakov, *Dos'e na zvezd*, vol. 2, 462.

10 *Liubov', komsomol i vesna*, 22.

11 For an assessment of Leshchenko at this time see E. Èpshtein, "Vstrecha cherez dvenadtsat' let," *Muzykal'naia zhizn'* 1 (1971), 18–19.

12 Razzakov, *Dos'e na zvezd*, vol. 2, 463.

13 P. Ermishev, "Lev Leshchenko," *Studencheskii meridian* 5 (1980), 31, and inside back cover.

14 *Liubov', komsomol i vesna*, 51.

15 T. Rymshevich, "Lev Leshchenko," in M.V. Uspenskaia, ed., *Pevtsy sovetskoi èstrady* (Moscow: Iskusstvo, 1985), 105–14.

16 *Liubov', komsomol i vesna*, 52. See also E. Belostotskaia, "Lev Leshchenko," *Trud*, 28 August 1984, 3, and E. Èpshtein, "Preodolenie rubezhei," *Muzykal'naia zhizn'* 1 (January 1978), 21.

17 A. Nazaretian, *Ot Leshchenko do Leshchenko* (Moscow: ASLAN, 1994), 52.

18 V. Chikin, "Spet' zhizn'," *Sovetskaia Rossiia* 22 (February 1992), 4.

19 Razzakov, *Dos'e na zvezd*, vol. 2, 466.

20 Saprykina, "Ia chuvstvuiu, chto nuzhno narodu."

21 *Sovetskaia èstrada i tsirk* 1 (1978), 21.

22 Razzakov, *Dos'e na zvezd*, vol. 2, 466–7.

23 Saprykina, "Ia chuvstvuiu, chto nuzhno narodu."

24 *Sovetskaia ètrada i tsirk* 11 (1983), 3–5.

25 *Liubov', komsomol i vesna*, 63.

26 Nazaretian, *Ot Leshchenko*, 51.

27 A. Balebanova and A. Riabtseva, "50 ne 50," *Pravda*, 1 February 1992, 2.

28 Nazaretian, *Ot Leshchenko*, 57.

29 "Chtoby vyzhit', prikhoditsia krutit'sia," *Smena* (Moscow) 8 (1993), 102–7.

30 A. Iurikov, *Valerii Leont'ev* (Moscow: Zakharov, 1998), 41–2.

31 Iu. Mikhal'tsev and V. Shakhidzhanian, "Trinadtsataia stupen'," *Ogonek* 40 (1986), 17–18. See also R. Sergazieva, "Kogda stanovish'sia sam sebe pamiatnikom ...," *Rossiiskie vesti*, 16 March 1993, 8.

32 N. Samoilova, "Neuspokoennost' i poisk," *Uchitel'skaia gazeta*, 29 January 1985, 3.

33 "Trinadtsataia stupen'."

34 *Valerii Leont'ev*, 11.

35 Ibid., 12.

36 A. Petrov, "Valerii Leont'ev," in *Pevtsy sovetskoi èstrady* (Moscow: Iskusstvo, 1991), 213–30.

37 A. Salbiev, "Valerii Leont'ev," *Televidenie i radioveshchanie*, 2 February 1985, 28–9.

38 *Kul'tura*, 6 March 1993, 9.

39 Iu. Aleksandrov, "Prem'ery Valeriia Leont'eva," *Gudok*, 14 September 1985.

40 Samoilova, "Neuspokoennost' i poisk."

41 *Valerii Leont'ev*, 21.

42 Ibid., 24. See also V. Pervukhin, "Èkzamenuet pesnia," *Komsomol'skaia pravda*, 11 January 1980, 4.

43 Ibid., 26.

44 Petrov, "Valerii Leont'ev."

45 *Valerii Leont'ev*, 35–6. Today he buys those costumes in Los Angeles and New York.

46 Ibid., 41–2.

47 Ibid., 53–5.

48 R. Kalnynysh, "Rozhdenie obraza pesni," *Televidenie i radioveshchanie* 3 (March 1988), 40–1.

49 *Valerii Leont'ev*, 57.

50 Ibid., 60–1.

51 Ibid., 72–3. See also A. Shunavikin, "Nel'zia 'opuskat' planku,'" *Trud*, 6 August 1988, 4.

52 "Koster Dzhordano," *Literaturnaia gazeta* 30 (July 1988), 8.

53 Iu. Saul'skii, "Poiski zhanra," *Moskovskie novosti*, 17 July 1988, 15.

54 S. Sukhaia, "Valerii Leont'ev po doroge v Gollivud," *Trud*, 25 March 1995, 5.

55 *Valerii Leont'ev*, 97. See also "Kritik – èto ne tot, kto nyriaet k artistu pod odeialo," *Rossiiskie vesti*, 6 March 1997, 4.

56 Ibid., 98.

57 See, for example, "Polnolunie – otvet Maiklu Dzheksonu!" *Chas pik* 42 (October 1993), 12; L. Sorokina, "Po doroge v Gollivud," *Moskovskaia pravda*, 31 May 1995, 6, and S. Guretskii, "Ves' v chernom V.L. spel 'muzyku chernykh,'" *Smena* 62 (March 1995), 5. The financial and structural difficulties in hosting productions of this size are noted by M. Sadchikov, *Smena* (St Petersburg) 66 (April 1994).

58 *Sovetskaia kul'tura*, 16 April 1987, 6.

59 *Valerii Leont'ev*, 140.

60 È. Zabavskikh, "S pesnei – v dorogu!" *Smena* (Moscow) 23 (1981), back cover.

61 *Sovetskaia èstrada i tsirk* 9 (1973), 14–15.

62 *Sovetskaia kul'tura*, 7 September 1972, 4.

63 On Leon'tev and things civic, see, for example, M. Antonov, "Znako-mye imena," *Trud*, 16 February 1986, 4.

64 L. Melik-Nubarova, "Lev Leshchenko," *Krugozor* 9 (1983), 12.

65 Leont'ev in M. Raikina, "Lunnyi P'ero na zheltom," *Argumenty i Fakty* 34 (September 1992), 5.

66 Chikin, "Spet' zhizn'."

67 I. Volodina, "Priz na èstrade," *Nedelia* 3 (1979), 7.

68 Rymshevich, "Lev Leshchenko."

69 L. Leshchenko, "Zvuchashchaia pamiat' chelovechestva," *Sovetskaia muzyka* 5 (1980), 92–7.

70 E. Belostotskaia, "Lev Leshchenko," *Trud*, 28 August 1984, 3.

71 N. Alekseeva, "Poiu o sovremennike," *Ogonek* 19 (1977), 32–3.

72 P. Ermishev, "Pesni L'va Leshchenko," *Televidenie i radioveshchanie* 10 (1979), 40, and back cover,

73 *Sovetskaia èstrada i tsirk* 11 (1983), 3–5.

74 Kuznetsov, "Takoi nestandartnyi."

75 *Sovetskaia kul'tura*, 28 July 1978, 4.

76 "Trinadtsataia stupen'."

77 M. Fradkin, "Moia professiia – pesnia," *Krugozor* 11 (1978), 10.

78 "Valerii Leont'ev," *Sovetskaia zhenshchina* 5 (1990), 39.

79 Volodina, "Priz na èstrade"; Volodina, "Priz za obaianie," *Nedelia* 3 (1979), 7.

80 A. Nakhalov, "Lev Leshchenko èpokhi Lady Dèns," *Moskovskie novosti*, 22–29 January 1995, 1 and 7.

81 N. Bataen, "Pesnia dlia vsekh," *Televidenie i radioveshchanie* (September 1983) 30–1.

82 *Sovetskaia kul'tura*, 29 June 1979, 5.

83 Ibid., 14 July 1983, 6.

84 "Pesnia dlia vsekh."

85 "Chtoby vyzhit', prikhoditsia krutit'sia."

86 *Sovetskaia ku'tura*, 6 February 1986, 4.

87 Samoilova, "Neuspokoennost' i poisk." See also I. Khmara, "K schast'iu, ia nadoedaiu sebe bystree, chem zriteliam," *Izvestiia*, 21 December 1993, 7.

88 M. Barabash et al., "Naedine so vsemi," *Nedelia*, 2–8 March 1987, 16.

89 V. Volin, "My s vami gde-to vstrechalis'," *Avrora* 5 (1985), 152–7. That jumping and energy are in fact celebrated in several songs, such as "I'm Energetic" (*Ia zavodnoi*), or "Zelenyi svet" – "Why was the light green? Because he's in love with life!"

90 N. Zavadskaia, "Sovershenoletie," *Muzykal'naia zhizn'* 18 (1980), 22–3, and E. Nadeinskii, "Vospitanie prekrasnym," ibid. 15 (1981), 22–3.

91 I. Khmara, "Vse begut, begut, begut … a on ne speshit," *Komsomol'skaia pravda*, 30 October 1993.

92 S. Sukhaia, "Valerii Leont'ev po doroge v Gollivud." See similarly titled article by S. Biriukov, in *Trud*, 26 March 1996, 8.

93 L. Leont'ev, "Èstrada – èto sovremennost'," in E. Uvarova, *Estrada: Chto? Gde? Zachem?* (Moscow, 1988), 312–20.

94 M. Raikina, "Valerii Leont'ev," *Sovetskii èkran* 2 (1989), 29.

95 "Chto takoe novogodnii atraktsion?" *Televidenie i radioveshchanie* 1 (January 1982), 48.

96 "Èstrada – èto sovremennost'."

97 Ibid.

98 M. Kirsi, "Shchedrost' talanta." *Sovetskaia Èstoniia*, 13 January 1990.

99 V. Lozhkina and M. Filatova, "Artist," *Televidenie i radioveshchanie* 12 (1990), 44–5.

100 Kalnynysh, "Rozhdenie obraza pesni."

101 Petrov, "Valerii Leont'ev."

102 *Sovetskaia èstrada i tsirk* 2 (1990), 10–14.

103 N. Bobrova, "Kazanova, poiushchii sam po sebe," *Moskovskii komsomolets*, 5 August 1995, 2 and 7. On a related issue see A. Nikolaev, "Pevets

Leont'ev uletaet v kosmos," *Argumenty i fakty* 47 (November 1997), 19, and O. Svistunova, "Trinadtsatogo v 13:13," *Moskovskaia pravda*, 14 September 1991.

104 L. Shugalo, "Chuvstovat' vremia, v kotorom zhivesh'," *Televidenie i radioveshchanie* 5 (May 1987) 28–9.

105 D. Lovkovskii, review of Leont'ev's "Noch'," *Èkho planety* 36 (September 1993), 16–17.

106 Saprykina, "Ia chuvstvuiu, chto nuzhno narodu." See also T. Zhurbinskaia, "K novym beregam," *Muzykal'naia zhizn'* 13–14 (July 1992), 7, and D. Tukhmanov, "Solovinaia roshcha," *Krugozor* 4 (1977), 14.

107 *Sovetskaia kul'tura* (June 1979), 5.

108 Saprykina, "Ia chuvstvuiu, chto nuzhno narodu."

109 "Chtoby vyzhit', prikhoditsia krutit'sia."

110 Nakhalov, "Lev Leshchenko èpokhi Lady Dèns."

111 Iu. Geiko, "L'va Leshchenko chut' ne zastrelili v Solov'inoi roshche," *Komsomol'skaia pravda*, 1 February 1997.

112 *Sovetskaia kul'tura*, 11 May 1989, 4.

113 Nakhalov, "Lev Leshchenko èpokhi Lady Dèns."

114 Bataen, "Pesnia dlia vsekh."

115 "Chtoby vyzhit', prikhoditsia krutit'sia."

116 *Sovetskaia èstrada i tsirk* 11 (1983), 3–5. See also E. Zabavskikh, "S pesnei – v dorogu!" *Smena* (Moscow) 23 (1981), back cover, and L. Melik-Nubarova, "Lev Leshchenko," *Krugozor* 9 (1983), 12.

117 *Sovetskaia kul'tura*, 29 June 1979, 5.

118 Ibid., 14 July 1983, 6.

119 Khmara, "Vse begut, begut, begut … a on ne speshit."

120 *Sovetskaia èstrada i tsirk* 8 (1986), 8–9.

121 D. Radyshevskii, "Perezhevannoe nevkusno," *Moskovskie novosti*, 16–23 July 1995, 14. For more on Leont'ev and seeking, see T. Sashko, "Put' k uspekhu," *Kul'tura i zhizn'* 8 (1980), 35.

122 M. Kirsi, "Shchedrost' talanta." See also L. Sorokina, "Dusha dolzhna imet' ostrovok dlia peredyshki …," *Rossiiskie vesti*, 29 October 1993, section 4 ("Retsept").

123 M. Kirs (sic), "Ia schastliv, chto u menia est' zritel'," *Sovetskaia Èstoniia*, 28 December 1986.

124 Sukhaia, "Valerii Leont'ev po doroge v Gollivud."

125 M. Utevskii, *Domashniaia sinematkia* (Moscow: Dubl'-D, 1996).

CHAPTER EIGHT

1 N. Zavadskaia, "Radosti i trevogi," *Muzykal'naia zhizn'* 16 (August 1984), 8–9.

2 I. Vasilinina, *Alla Pugacheva* (Moscow: Sovetskii kompozitor, 1991), 34.

3 U. Ott, *Televizionnoe znakomstvo* (Moscow: Iskusstvo, 1992), 87.

4 A. Stepovoi, "Veselyi Arlekino," *Studencheskii meridian* 10 (1976), 24–5.

5 G. Skorokhodov, "Fenomen Pugachevoi," *Zvezdy sovetskoi èstrada* (Moscow: Sovetskii kompozitor, 1986).

6 A. Petrov, "Alla Pugacheva – pevitsa, aktrisa, kompozitor," *Kul'tura i zhizn'* 12 (1979), 16–20.

7 Vasilinina, *Alla Pugacheva*, 8.

8 A. Beliakov, *Alla, Allochka, Alla Borisovna* (Moscow: Zakharov/Vagrius, 1998), 25.

9 Ibid., 32.

10 Ibid., 40–1.

11 Stepovoi, "Veselyi Arlekino."

12 S. Parkhomovskii, "Novye imena," *Trud*, 14 September 1975, 4.

13 B. Savchenko, *Dorogaia Alla Borisovna* (Moscow: Znanie, 1992) 39.

14 Beliakov, *Alla, Allochka*, 55.

15 Ibid., 85.

16 Ibid., 98.

17 "Novogodniaia elka nedeli," *Nedelia* 12 (1975), 12.

18 V. Bystrov, "Zolotoi Arlekino," *Chernomorskaia zdravnitsa* (Sochi), 12 July 1975.

19 Beliakov, 136.

20 T. Butovskaia, "Èto nezharkoe èstradnoe leto," *Muzykal'naia zhizn'* 18 (1974).

21 R. Zviagina, "Stupeni," *Leninskaia smena* (Gorky), 31 December 1975.

22 B. Sadekov and A. Shaguliamov, "Alla Pugacheva," *Nedelia* 49 (December 1976), 13. For a useful assessment of Pugacheva in 1976, see E. Ogon'kova, "Znakom'tes'," *Kul'tura i zhizn'* 9 (1976), 46.

23 È. Borina, "God spustia," *Uchitel'skaia gazeta*, 13 November 1976, 4.

24 Beliakov, 140–1. See also M. Èlina, "Alla Pugacheva," *Studencheskii meridian* 7 (1977), 23.

25 Vasilinina, *Alla Pugacheva*, 15.

26 Savchenko, *Dorogaia Alla Borisovna*, 18.

27 Bystrov, "Zolotoi Arlekino."

28 N. Zavadskaia, "Vstrecha s 'Zolotym Orfeem'," *Muzykal'naia zhizn'* 16 (1975).

29 Beliakov, *Alla, Allochka*, 143.

30 B. Sadekov and A. Shaguliamov, "Alla Pugacheva."

31 N. Alekseeva, N. "Svoia pesnia," *Ogonek* 11 (1977), 32–3.

32 Beliakov, *Alla, Allochka*, 161.

33 S. Parkhomovskii, "Znakomye imena," *Trud*, 8 January 1978, 4.

34 Beliakov, *Alla, Allochka*, 173–4.

35 Petrov, "Alla Pugacheva – pevitsa."

36 Parkhomovskii, "Znakomye imena."

37 As if to hide such troubles, Pugacheva said in a 1978 interview with *Gudok* that "Arlekino" had begun her "wonderful" relationship with television (19 November).

38 Beliakov, 189.

39 "Gran-pri – Alle Pugachevoi," *Sovetskaia zhenshchina* 12 (1978), 12.

40 *Literaturnaia gazeta*, 1 January 1979, 8.

41 Petrov, "Alla Pugacheva – pevitsa."

42 A. Erokhin, "I prazdnik i ispytanie," *Literaturnaia Rossiia*, 27 April 1979, 19.

43 *Muzykal'naia zhizn'* 20 (October 1980), 3.

44 Iu. Bogomolov, "Telegosti i telekhoziaeva," *Literaturnaia gazeta*, 10 November 1982, 8.

45 M. Shpagin, "Rabochee mesto – èstrada," *Smena* 16 (1980), 24–6.

46 T. Mikhailova, "Tri trevozhnykh dnia, tri schastlivykh dnia," *Muzykal'naia zhizn'* 19 (1982), 22.

47 I. Rudenko, "Bez strakhovki," *Komsomol'skaia pravda*, 28 August 1983, 4. The article makes an interesting contrast with another of 1996 by the same author, "Pro Allu," *Komsomol'skaia pravda*, 10 December, 4.

48 Beliakov, *Alla, Allochka*, 233–4.

49 Ibid., 254.

50 "Pust' sbudetsia, o chem mechtalos'," *Gudok*, 31 December 1986. See also "My zhelaem schast'ia vam!," *Sovetskaia zhenshchina* 12 (1986), 3.

51 An interesting and early post-Soviet portrait of Pugacheva is in N. Dobriukha, *Rok iz pervykh ruk* (Moscow: Molodaia gvardiia, 1992), 287–98. On the issue of personality and perfume, see V. Vernik, "Pugacheva stala poklonnitsei shveitsarskogo parfiuma," *Nedelia* 9 (March 1993), 13.

52 Beliakov, *Alla, Allochka*, 317. See also M. Sadchikov, "Filipp Kirkorov – Alla Pugacheva: Gor'ko? Gor'ko!" *Smena* 48 (March 1994), 1; "Marsh Mendel'sona milee vsekh khitov," *Smena* 47 (March 1994), 1–2, and the slightly earlier "Tili – tili – testo, Filipp i Alla – zhenikh i nevesta," *Smena* 11 (January 1994), 12.

53 S. Matvievskii, "Ia koroleva plebeev," *Argumenty i fakty* 49 (December 1997), 3.

54 Zviagina, "Stupeni."

55 B. Serebrennikova, *Pevtsy sovetskoi èstrady* (Moscow: Iskusstvo, 1977).

56 È. Kekelidze, "... I dykhanie zritel'nogo zala." *Molodezh' Èstonii* (Tallin), 12 July 1977.

57 M. Antsyferov, "Ne imeiu prava oshibat'sia," *Sovetskaia molodezh'* (Riga), 2 October 1977.

58 A. Chudinovskikh, "Pesnia-ispoved'," *Vechernii Sverdlovsk*, 5 July 1983, and L. Nikitin, "Rekviem po Borisu Gorbonosu," *Moskovskii komsomolets*, 13 October 1978.

59 A. Demidov, "Alla Pugacheva," *Teatral'naia zhizn'* 21 (1982).

60 "Udacha ili bezvkusitsa?" *Smena* 5 (1986).

61 I. Vasilinina, "Eshche raz ob Alle Pugachevoi," *Teatr* 1 (1985).

62 A. Stepovoi, "Veselyi Arlekino."

63 N. Zavadskaia, "Vstrecha s 'Zolotym Orfeem.'"

64 A. Gal'perin, "Kryl'ia pesni," *Krugozor* 4 (1978), 9–10.

65 Borina, "God spustia."

66 G. Melikiants, "Videt' zhizn' krasochno," *Izvestiia*, 28 July 1984.

67 Iu. Semenov, "Alla Pugacheva," *Smena* 5 (1987).

68 E. Bovkin, "Pesnia ob ediniaet liudei," *Izvestiia*, 16 September 1987.

69 Iu. Sushkov, "Èstrada – dom dlia druzei," *Trud*, 12 November 1981, 4.

70 V. Chebotarev, "Golosui – i pobedish'!" *Rossiiskie vesti* 120, 29 June 1996, 7.

71 *Rossiiskaia gazeta*, 28 November 1997.

72 V. Kuznetsov, "Byla vesna i bylo leto," *Sankt-Peterburgskie vedomosti*, 24 September 1994, 7.

73 Iu. Alaev, "I kazhdyi raz, kak v poslednii," *Sovetskaia Tatariia* (Kazan), 21 May 1978.

74 A. Kolosov, "Kak trevozhen ètot put'," *Moskovskii komsomolets*, 29 April 1983.

75 Zavadskaia, "Radosti i trevogi."

76 "Otkrytoe pis'mo," *Teatral'naia zhizn'* 6 (1986).

77 S. Stavitskaia, "Glavnaia pesnia," *Sovetskaia Èstoniia* (Tallin), 21 July 1978.

78 L. Nikitin, "Normal'noe plat'e s rukavami," *Moskovskii komsomolets*, 13 October 1978.

79 V. Kichin, "Shekspir v ritmakh disko," *Literaturnaia gazeta*, 7 October 1981.

80 Demidov, "Alla Pugacheva."

81 Vasilinina, "Eshche raz ob Alle Pugachevoi."

82 S. Marshak, *Sobranie sochinenii* vol. 3 (Moscow: Khudozhestvennaia literatura, 1969), 96.

83 L. Dorosh, "Chelovechestvu khochetsia pesen," *Vechernii Kishinev*, 31 December 1979.

84 Kolosov, "Kak trevozhen ètot put'."

85 Vasilinina, "Alla Pugacheva: Kakova ona segodnia," *Teatr* 3 (1984).

86 Vasilinina, "Eshche raz ob Alle Pugachevoi."

87 "Mesto knigi," *Literaturnaia gazeta* 49, 5 December 1984.

88 V. Melik-Karamov, "Sud'ba-pesnia," *Nedelia* 30 (1985), 11.

89 M. Shaikevich, "Neskol'ko slov po povodu …," *Televidenie i radioveschanie* 6 (June 1987), 29–30.

90 B. Metlitskii, "Fenomen Pugachevoi," *Sankt-Peterburgskie vedomosti* 179 (August 1993), 8.

91 Gal'perin, "Kryl'ia pesni."

92 I. Chereiskii, "Teatr pesni Ally Pugachevoi," *Moskovskaia pravda*, 10 January 1978.

93 Iu. Filinov, "Zhenshchina, kotoraia poet," *Komsomol'skaia pravda*, 2 November 1979, 4.

94 Rudenko, "Bez strakhovki."

95 S. Vlasov, "Kto razgonit tuchi?" *Ogonek* 11 (March 1987), 17–18.

96 *Rossiiskaia gazeta*, 28 November 1997. In the newspaper *Chas pik* she referred to come-back tours by Tom Jones and even Elvis Presley as proof that a return from silence to prior renown was possible: S. Guretskii, "Filipp voshel v komnatu …," 6 September 1995, 16. Ta'tiana Bulanova is a hugely successful singer from Petersburg and arguably the major exponent of grand ballads in the style of Pugacheva's work from the 1970s. Bulanova, in fact, recently recorded a marvellous version of her mentor's "Ne otrekaiutsia, liubia."

97 "Ikh siiatel'stvo izvoliat spet' v den' svoego rozhdeniia," *Moskovskii komsomolets*, 15 April 1995. See also O. Iakubov, "Kazhdyi kontsert – prem'era," *Pravda vostoka*, 25 August 1983.

98 Iu. Sushkov, "Èstrada – dom dlia druzei."

99 V. Granovskaia, "U nas v gostiakh maèstro," *Trud*, 13 January 1982, 4.

CHAPTER NINE

1 Iu. Iuferova, "Alla Pugacheva obuet vsiu stranu," *Izvestiia*, 23 January 1997, 5. For a similar thought re P'ekha see A. Ivanov, "Èpigrammy," *Moskovskii komsomolets*, 9 August 1967.

2 B. Novakovskii, "Alla Pugacheva," *Komsomol'skaia pravda*, 11 July 1976; my italics.

3 N. Zavadskaia, "Vstrecha s 'Zolotym Orfeem,'" *Muzykal'naia zhizn'* 16 (1975).

4 "Rabochee ee mesto – èstrada," *Smena* 16 (1980).

5 V. Berzinysh, "Talant, temperament, sharm," *Golos Rigi*, 8 July 1981.

6 N. Smirnova, "Teatr pesni Ally Pugachevoi," *Teatr* 2 (1978).

7 È. Abaidullina, "Laureat mezhdunarodnykh konkursov Alla Pugacheva: 'Na stsene – moia zhizn','" *Na smenu!* (Sverdlovsk), 12 July 1978.

8 L. Nikitin, "Normal'noe plat'e s rukavami," *Moskovskii komsomolets*, 13 October 1978.

9 B. Tukh, "Arlekino, ili teatr pevitsy," *Vechernii Tallin*, 17 July 1977.

10 N. Smirnova, "Teatr pesni Ally Pugachevoi." The applicability of staged songs for television in the following year is discussed in S. Stavitskaia, "Zrimiaia pesnia," *Sovetskaia Èstoniia*, 14 January 1979. See also "Glavnaia pesnia" by the same author and in the same paper, 21 July 1978.

11 A. Demidov, "Alla Pugacheva," *Teatral'naia zhizn'* 21 (1982).

12 "Pozhivem – ulsyshim …," *Avrora* 2 (1982).
13 M. Vartanian, "Alla Pugacheva: Kazhdyi den' – otkrytie," *Komsomolets* (Yerevan), 4 August 1978.
14 M. Ignat'eva, "Vse mogut koroli?," *Sovetskaia kul'tura*, 16 September 1980.
15 Ibid.
16 I. Vasilinina, "Eshche raz ob Alle Pugachevoi," *Teatr* 1 (1985).
17 "Rabochee ee mesto – èstrada."
18 M. Goler, "Strasti po … stadionu!" *Sovetskaia Moldaviia*, 14 October 1988. If we are hinting at Pugacheva's fondness for things Soviet at times, an article of 1995 is especially interesting: O. Gerasimenko, et al., "Poidet li Alla Pugacheva za suprugom v kommunisticheskii rai?," *Komsomol'skaia pravda*, 28 June.
19 A. Chernigovskaia, "Teatr odnogo aktera," *Vechernii Leningrad*, 3 April 1990.
20 "Ia ne pevitsa," *Argumenty i fakty* 43 (1994), 3.
21 V. Gavrilov and A. Gasparian, "Alla Pugacheva stala zhadnoi, no na ovoshchakh poka ne èkonomit," *Moskovskii komsomolets*, 27 September 1996.
22 I. Chereiskii, "Teatr pesni Ally Pugachevoi," *Moskovskaia pravda*, 10 January 1978.
23 A. Babadzhanian, "I masterstvo i vdokhnovenie," *Krugozor* 11 (1977), 9–10.
24 L. Genina, "S pesnei – naedine," *Sovetskaia muzyka* 3 (1978), 23–8.
25 For a tongue-in-cheek assessment of such vacillation, see T. Aref'eva, "Diktator so slabostiami / Alla ne ustala," *Krest'ianka* 6 (June 1995), 44–5. See also Iu. Bogomolov, "Alla Pugacheva vsegda prava?," *Sovetskii èkran* 9 (June 1989), 13.
26 A. Petrov, "Alla Pugacheva – pevitsa, aktrisa, kompozitor," *Kul'tura i zhizn'* 12 (1979), 16–20.
27 A. Erokhin, "I prazdnik i ispytanie," *Literaturnaia Rossiia*, 27 April 1979, 19.
28 Iu. Suhkov, "Èstrada – dom dlia druzei," *Trud*, 12 November 1981, 4.
29 N. Prokhorov, "Tetrad' pisatelia Nikolaia Prokhorova," *Avrora* 11 (1983), 130–3.
30 Iu. Gladil'shchikov, "Nado li pet' na stadione," *Sovetskaia Rossiia*, 11 July 1984, 4, and L. Semenova, "Prishla i govoriu …," *Leningradskaia pravda*, 17 July 1984, 4.
31 Gladil'shchikov, "Nado li pet' na stadione." See also Gladil'shchikov's related article of 1987, "Rekviem po èstrade," in *Literaturnaia gazeta* 37, 8.
32 V. Melik-Karamov, "Pesne nuzhen svoi dom," *Literaturnaia gazeta*, 30 January 1985, 8.

33 *Rossiikaia gazeta,* 28 November 1997.

34 *Èkspress gazeta,* 47 (November 1998), 6–7.

35 "Kak taina," *Sovetskii èkran* 16 (1977), 12–13.

36 S. Stavitskaia, "Glavnaia pesnia," *Sovetskaia Èstoniia* (Tallin), 21 July 1978. See also "Alla Pugacheva v roli kompozitora," *Literaturnaia gazeta,* 4 September 1985, 6.

37 Skorokhodov, *Zvezdy sovetskoi èstrady.*

38 "Èkran i stsena," *Smena* 11 (1986).

39 M. Shaikevich, "Neskol'ko slov po povodu …," *Televidenie i radio-veshchanie* 6 (1987).

40 G. Piatigorskaia, "Mif o svobodnom cheloveke," *Teatr* 12 (1990).

41 Ibid.

42 "Novosti semeistva Pugachevoi-Presniakovykh," *Smena,* 24 March 1993.

43 V. Bochkarev, "Ot chego ustala Alla," *Moskovskii komsomolets,* 26 January 1994.

44 È. Borina, "God spustia," *Uchitel'skaia gazeta,* 13 November 1976, 4.

45 "Kak taina," *Sovetskii èkran.*

46 The notion of singing one's way through life is discussed in S. Stavitskaia, "Ne pesniu poiu a zhizn' poiu …," *Sovetskaia Èstoniia,* 16 September 1981.

47 S. Parkhomovskii, "Znakomye imena," *Trud,* 8 January 1978, 4.

48 Petrov, "Alla Pugacheva – pevitsa."

49 "Rabochee ee mesto – èstrada."

50 "Poslednii raz v dekabre," *Ogonek* 1 (1993), 3.

51 A. Konnikov, *Mir èstrady* (Moscow: Iskusstvo, 1980), 50–1.

52 V. Ivanova, "Pesnia! Pesnia! Pesnia!" *Literaturnaia Rossiia,* 18 October 1985, 19. Readers' responses to the article can be found in the December 6 issue, 20.

53 D. Vdovin, "Èto znachit – padat' i vzletat'," *Sovetskii èkran* 2 (1988), 12–14.

54 I. Grigor'ev, "Mart. Angelikos," *OM* (May 1997), 105–7 and 158–9.

55 M. Sadchikov, "Alla i Filipp tseluiutsia vovse ne raz v godu," *Smena* 62, 18 March 1995, 2.

56 I. Rudenko, "Bez strakhovki," *Komsomol'skaia pravda,* 28 August 1981.

57 For the fuller context, see P. Leonidov, *V. Vysotskii i drugie* (New York: Russian Publishing, 1983).

58 "Udacha ili bezvkusitsa?" *Smena* 5 (1986).

59 Borina, "God spustia."

60 Parkhomovskii, "Znakomye imena."

61 A. Gasparian, "Amerikanskii shans," *Kul'tura i zhizn'* 3 (1989), 17–18.

62 L. Petrova, "Esli dolgo muchit'sia …," *Rabochaia gazeta* (Kiev), 11 February 1978.

63 N. Zavadskaia, *Muzykal'naia zhizn'* 5 (1978).

64 G. Borisov, "Blesk ili svet?," *Komsomolets Kubani* (Krasnodar), 1 October 1987. There appears to be a slight mistake on the part of the journalist. The actual lyrics to the song read: "When I go far, far away, neither tormented nor fretting …"

65 M. Ignat'eva, "Ot imeni i po porucheniiu …," *Sovetskaia kul'tura*, 5 December 1987.

66 Iu. Bogomolov, "Èstrada v maskakh," in *Èstrada v maskakh* (Moscow: Iskusstvo, 1988).

67 A. Gasparian, and Iu. Konstantinov, "Ia edu ne pobezhdat' Ameriku …," *Moskovskii komsomolets*, 31 August 1988.

68 "O sebe, zriteliakh i tvorcheskom dolgoletii," *Argumenty i fakty* 20 (1988).

69 Ibid.

70 V. Bochkarev, "Ot chego ustala Alla."

71 V. Mostovets, "Amerika otkryvaet Pugachevu," *Èkho planety* 29 (October 1988), 39–42.

72 Gasparian and Konstantinov, "Ia edu ne pobezhdat' Ameriku."

73 Gasparian and Konstantinov, "Appetit prikhodit vo vremia edy …," *Moskovskii komsomolets*, 14 October 1988.

74 "Ia ne pevitsa," *Argumenty i fakty* 44 (1994). Leonid Utesov (in 1937) was one of several Soviet performers who recorded "Poliushko-pole."

75 Mostovets, "Amerika otkryvaet Pugachevu."

76 A. Tul'chinskii, "Million, million, million …," *Trud*, 1 December 1994, 5.

77 Grigor'ev, "Mart. Angelikos."

78 Ibid. See also the strangely titled article by G. Sapozhnikova, "Ia ne dumala, chto 'Evrovidenie' prineset mne takoi uspekh!," *Komsomol'skaia pravda*, 7 May 1997, 1, and last page. A more sobering account is offered the day before (!) by the same journalist on the newspaper's front page.

79 "Ia koroleva plebeev," *Argumenty i fakty* 49 (December 1997), 3.

80 B. Novakovskii, "Alla Pugacheva," *Komsomol'skaia pravda*, 11 July 1976.

81 "Rabochee ee mesto – èstrada," and V. Karpenko, "Pesnia – zerkalo dushi," *Komsomolets Uzbekistana*, 27 January 1981.

82 "Alla Pugacheva otvechaet," *Teatral'naia zhizn'* 24 (1986).

83 Demidov, "Alla Pugacheva."

84 S. Kalenikin, "O vremeni, o zhizni, o liubvi," *Meditsinskaia gazeta*, 13 January 1984.

85 I. Vasilinina, "Kakova ona segodnia," *Teatr* 3 (1984).

86 A. Sherel', "Teatr Ally Pugachevoi," *Televidenie i radioveshchanie* 11 (1978), back cover.

87 O. Saprykina, "Chto skazala Alla Pugacheva o vnuke i o sebe," *Komsomol'skaia pravda*, 23 January 1992, 4.

88 U. Ott, *Televizionnoe znakomstvo* (Moscow: Iskusstvo, 1992), 80–106.
89 A. Troitskii, "V dukhe Ally," *Argumenty i fakty* 25–26 (June 1992), 7.
90 V. Vernik, "Zhurnal Pugachevoi i 'Pokolenie-93,'" *Nedelia* 52 (December 1993), 4.
91 M. Sadchikov, "Tili-tili-testo, Filipp i Alla – zhenikh i nevesta," *Smena* (St Petersburg) 11 (1994), 19.
92 A. Liubiashchii, "Zachem Vam, Alla, shum skandala?," *Argumenty i fakty* 5 (February 1994), 1 and 11.
93 A. Shumskii, "My poniali, chto vokrug nas net druzei," *Domovoi* (1994), 27. See also *24 chasa*, 6 October 1994, 11.
94 M. Sadchikov, "Alla Borisovna posle svad'by pomiagchela," *Komsomol'skaia pravda*, 11 August 1994, 4, and I. Grigor'ev, "Mart. Angelikos."
95 T. Moskvina, "Drama zhenskoi potentsii pered litsom muzhskoi impotentsii," *Chas pik*, 29 October 1994, 3.
96 O. Pshenichnyi, "A. Pugacheva ukhodit v zasluzhennyi otpusk," *Ogonek* 33 (August 1995), 12, and È. Stradin, "Koroleva pesni osvobodila p"edestal," *Rossiiskie vesti*, 21 December 1995, 8.
97 V. Matizen, "Prosto Alla," *Ogonek* 52 (December 1995), 76–7.
98 "Skol'ko lits u Ally Pugachevoi," *Trud*, 12 August 1995, 2.
99 A. Uglanov, "Svita, svita, koroleva znamenita," *Argumenty i fakty* 22 (May 1996), 3.
100 Gavrilov and Gasparian, "Alla Pugacheva stala zhadnoi."
101 A simultaneous assessment of her real-world popularity at this time can be found in "Alla Pugacheva – na trone khit-parada," *Rossiiskie vesti* 41 (March 1996), 3.
102 *Peterburg Èkspress*, 24 June 1998, 16–17.
103 A. Stanley, "Russia's Biggest Singer Is Invisible in West," *New York Times*, 23 April 1997. See also "Famous Name a Boon for the 'Other' Alla Pugacheva," *St Petersburg Times*, 24 July 1998, 16. The "supernatural" dimensions of Pugacheva's fame find strange expression in M. Sadchikov, "Alla Pugacheva prozrela bez doktorov," NLO 8 (August 1998), 17.

EPILOGUE

1 A. Perevalova, "Orkhideia sovetskoi èstrady," *Nedelia* 8 (February 1993), 8–9.
2 For equal banality, see articles such as M. Bogdanova, "Èdita P'ekha spit s otkrytoi fortochkoi," *Moskovskii komsomolets*, 7 March 1996, 2, or N. Shmitko, "Zvezda v semeinom inter'ere," *Smena*, 6 March 1997, 6.

SOURCES

PERIODICALS

Materials from the following newspapers and magazines (1955–99) were used in the writing of this book.

24 chasa
Alla
Argumenty i fakty
Art-fonar'
Avrora
Bytovoe obsluzhivanie naseleniia
Chas pik
Chernomorskaia zdravnitsa (Sochi)
Cosmopolitan (Russia)
Daidzhest Kuranty
Domovoi
Èkho planety
Èkran i stsena
Èkspress-gazeta
Financial Times
Gazeta dlia zhenshchin
Golos Rigi
Gudok
Irish Times
Iunost'
Izvestiia
Jewish Bulletin of Northern California
Kaleidoskop

Kavkazskaia zdravnitsa (Piatigorsk)
Kazakhstanskaia pravda (Alma-Alta)
Knizhnoe obozrenie
Kommersant-Daily
Komsomolets (Rostov-na-Donu and Yerevan)
Komsomolets Kubani (Krasnodar)
Komsomolets Uzbekistana
Komsomol'skaia pravda
Krest'ianka
Krokodil
Krugozor
Kul'tura i zhizn'
Leningradskaia pravda
Leninskaia smena (Alma-Alta and Gor'kii)
Lesnaia gazeta
Literaturnaia gazeta
Literaturnaia Rossiia
Meditsinskaia gazeta
Molodezh' Èstonii
Molodezhnaia gazeta (Frunze)
Molodoi Leninets (Volgograd)
Moskovskaia pravda
Moskovskie novosti
Moskovskii komsomolets
Muzykal'naia zhizn'
Na smenu! (Sverdlovsk)
Nedelia
New York Times
NLO
Novosti Peterburga
Novyi mir
Ogonek
OM
Peterburg Èkspress
Peterburgskii kur'er
Peterburgskii telezritel'
Playboy (Russia)
Pravda
Pravda Ukrainy
Pravda vostoka
Ptiuch
Rabochaia gazeta (Kiev)
Rabotnitsa
Rossiiskaia gazeta

Rossiiskie vesti
Saint Petersburg Times
Sankt-Peterburgskie vedomosti
Smena (Petersburg and Moscow editions)
Sobesednik
Sotsialisticheskaia industriia
Sovetskaia Belorussia (Minsk)
Sovetskaia Èstoniia
Sovetskaia èstrada i tsirk
Sovetskaia Kalmykiia
Sovetskaia kul'tura
Sovetskaia Moldaviia/Moldova
Sovetskaia molodezh' (Riga)
Sovetskaia muzyka
Sovetskaia Rossiia
Sovetskaia Tatariia (Kazan')
Sovetskaia zhenshchina
Sovetskie profsoiuzy
Sovetskii èkran
Stroitel'naia gazeta
Studencheskii meridian
Sydney Morning Herald
Teatr
Teatral'naia zhizn'
Teleman
Televidenie i radioveshchanie
Trud
TV *Park*
Uchitel'skaia gazeta
Vecherniaia Alma-Alta
Vecherniaia Moskva
Vecherniaia Perm'
Vechernii Kishinev
Vechernii Leningrad
Vechernii Sverdlovsk
Vechernii Tallin
Znamia iunosti (Minsk)

FILMS

Brillianty dlia diktatury proletariata (1975), dir. R. Kromanov
Chuchelo (1983), dir. R. Bykov
Dusha (1981), dir. A. Stepanovich
Èkstrasens (1992), dir. G. Glagolev

Gde ty, liubov'? (1980), dir. V. Gazhiu

Ironiia sud'by (1975), dir. È. Riazanov

Kak stat' zvezdoi (1986), dir. V. Aksenov

Menia èto ne kasaetsia (1976), dir. G. Rappaport

My iz dzhaza (1983), dir. K. Shakhnazarov

Na chuzhom prazdnike (1981), dir. V. Laptev

Neispravimyi lgun (1973), dir. V. Azarov

Ne khodite, devki, zamuzh (1985), dir. E. Gerasimov

Ograblenie v polnoch' (1977), dir. A. Belinskii

On svoe poluchit (1992), dir. V. Riabtsev

Prishla i govoriu (1985), dir. N. Ardashnikov

Sezon chudes (1985), dir. G. Iungval'd-Khil'kevich

Sluzhebnyi roman (1977), dir. È. Riazanov

Sud'ba rezidenta (1970), dir. V. Dorman

Veselye rebiata (1934), dir. G. Aleksandrov

Zhenshchina, kotoraia poet (1978), dir. A. Orlov

Zona BAM: Postoiannye zhiteli (1987), dir. M. Pavlov

CONCERT FOOTAGE
AND OTHER VIDEO MATERIALS:

Miscellaneous

Goluboi ogonek (from ORT archives. Refashioned in recent years with contemporary artists on RTR)

Pesnia goda 1972, 1973 and 1974 (2 vols.)

Pesni 80-kh godov (2 vols.)

Pesnia 88

Pesnia 94: Final (2 vols.)

Pesnia 95: Final (2 vols.)

Pesnia 96: Final (2 vols.)

Pesnia 97: Final (2 vols.)

Pesnia 98: Final (2 vols.)

Pesnia 99: Final (2 vols.)

Soiuz, 15–25

Starye pesni o glavnom (three editions: 1996, 1997, and 1998. A fourth, live edition was staged in Moscow, 1999)

Kobzon

Dva roialia

Iosif Kobzon: Iubileinyi tvorcheskii vecher

Iosif Kobzon: Proshchal'nyi vecher (5 vols.)

Staraia kvartira (RTR)
Subbotnii vecher s Iosifom Kobzonom

Leont'ev

Valerii Leont'ev, i shou balet Todes
Valerii Leont'ev: Izbrannoe
Valerii Leont'ev: Na ploshchad' zvezd
Valerii Leont'ev: Po doroge v Gollivud
Valerii Leont'ev: Polnolunie
Valerii Leont'ev: Rozhdestvenskie vstrechi

Leshchenko

Lev Leshchenko: 50 ne 50 (2 vols.)
Lev Leshchenko: Imeniny v Solov'inoi roshchi
Ot Leshchenko do Leshchenko
Vecher posviashchennyi 25-letiiu tvorcheskoi deiatel'nosti L'va Leshchenko (2 vols.)

P'ekha

Nam rano zhit' vospominaniiami
Sorok let s vami

Ponarovskaia

Poet Irina Ponarovskaia, 1994

Pugacheva

Alla Pugacheva. Ot Arlekino do ... (2 vols.)
Izbrannoe: Live Concert
Ne delaite mne bol'no, gospoda ...
Novogodnii akraktsion (ORT archives)
Rozhdestvenskie vstrechi
Siurpriz ot Ally Pugachevoi
Zhdi i pomni menia (5 vols.)

Rotaru

Iubileinyi kontsert: 25 let
Liubi menia
Monolog o liubvi

SOUND RECORDINGS

Miscellaneous: Recent and Relevant Compilations of Classic Estrada

The sound recordings below are all long-playing records, unless specified. They have been supplemented by the enormous archives of the Moscow author and journalist Valerii Safoshkin, who provided me with a multitude of album-length "programs." These consist of rare recordings, singles, flexi-discs, and other elusive items. Rather than burden the reader with such exhaustive listings, I have instead appended to most of the discographies here only a brief reference to the total number of Mr Safoshkin's materials which are now part of my own collection.

Should western readers wish to investigate these songs for themselves, a reasonable number of old recordings are now available as re-releases through émigré record stores in New York, Los Angeles, and other cities with sizable Russian communities. Films and concert footage may also be purchased in this way, thus avoiding the problems of conversion to North America of video format. The last couple of years have seen an explosion of free audio files available on the Russian web. Since, however, the sites offering such recordings are becoming increasingly commercial, their content (and existence) depends upon the moods and health of the market. It is best, therefore, to use any of the major Russian search engines as a means of staying in touch with material to be downloaded, be it contemporary or archival.

David Tukhmanov: Belyi tanets. Luchshie pesni 70-kh i 80-kh gg (L-Junction: 1997)
David Tukhmanov: Kak prekrasen ètot mir (L-Junction: 1997)
David Tukhmanov: Pritiazhenie zemli. Luchshie pesni 70-kh i 80-kh gg (L-Junction: 1997)
Desiat' pesen o Moskve (Soiuz: 1997)
Èto zdorovo! (Melodiia: 1996)
Glavnoe, rebiata, serdtsem ne staret' (M.A.Y. 1995)
Ia tebia podozhdu (Melodiia: 1996)
Kak molody my byli: Pesni Aleksandry Pakhmutovoi (Melodiia: 1995)
Khit-parad 70-kh: vypuski 1, 2 & 3 (Zmeya/ Melodiia: 1998–99)
Khit-parad 80-kh: vypusk 1 (Zmeya: 1999)
Koroleva krasoty (Melodiia: 1996)
Lebedinaia vernost': Pesni Evgeniia Martynova (Melodiia: 1997)
Million alykh roz: Pesni na stikhi A. Voznesenskogo (Melodiia: 1995)
Mnogoe v zhizni byvaet (Melodiia: 1996)
Pesni sovetskikh kompozitorov: 1. Pesni ob otechestvennoi voine; 2. Russkaia narodnia pesnia (Melodiia)
Russian Collection: V.I.A. 70-kh. Luchshie pesni 1971–81 (vol. 5 [JMG: 1996])
Russian Collection: V.I.A. 70-kh. Luchshie pesni 1969–80 (vol. 3 [JMG: 1996])
Russian Collection. Zolotoi shliager 70-kh. (vol. 4 [JMG: 1996])

Russian Collection. Zolotoi shliager 80-kh. (vol. 6 [JMG: 1996])
Siurpriz ot Ally Pugachevoi (double album [Soiuz: 1997])
Sochi 67 (Melodiia: 1967)
Sovetskie pesni (Melodiia)
Starye pesni o glavnom 1[1996], *2* [1997] *and 3* [ORT:1998]
Ty ne pechal'sia (Melodiia: 1995)
Vernis': Populiarnye pesni 60-kh godov (Melodiia: 1994)

Kobzon

Beloe solntse (Zeko: 1997)
Evgenii Zharkovskii: Pesni (Melodiia: 1973?).
Ia – artist (Zeko: 1997)
Ia obiazatel'no vernus' (Zeko: 1997)
Krugozor 1966 no. 2. Pochta golubinaia.
Krugozor 1966 no. 3. Doroga.
Krugozor 1968 no. 2. Dorogi.
Krugozor 1968 no. 7. Doverchivaia pesnia.
Laskovaia pesnia (Melodiia: 1982)
Liricheskie pesni (Akkord: 1964?)
Liustry starinnogo zala (Solo Florentin: 1996)
Mne doverna pesnia (Solo Florentin: 1996)
Ne pokidaet nas vesna (Solo Florentin: 1996)
Noch' svetla (Zeko: 1997)
Pesni Bulata Okudzhavoi (Melodiia EP) Polnochnyi trolleibus.
Pesnia ne proshchaetsia s toboi ([double album] Melodiia: 1987)
Pesni Oskara Fel'tsmana (Melodiia EP). Podskazhi mne/ Ia sam po sebe
Pobeda ostaetsia molodoi (Melodiia: 1983)
Russkoe pole (Zeko: 1997)
Sredi mirov (Zeko: 1997)
Tango, tango, tango (Melodiia: 1980?)
Vyidu na ulitsu (Zeko: 1997)
Vy pomnite (Zeko: 1997)
Zlatye gory (Zeko: 1997)
Zvezdy na nebe (Solo Florentin: 1996)
plus 144 songs from the Safoshkin archives

Leont'ev

Dialog ([with Pauls] Melodiia: 1984)
Doktor-Vremia (Melodiia: 1995)
Greshnyi put' (Melodiia: 1990)
Kazhdyi khochet liubit' (VL Studio: 1999)

Kanatnyi pliasun (ARS: 1999)
Nenagliadnaia storona/ Bredu po zheltym sklonam (single: 1980)
Noch' (Moroz/SNC: 1993)
Po doroge v Gollivud (Apex: 1995)
Polnolunie (ZeKo)
Prem'era: Pesni Aleksandra Morozova (Melodiia: 1984)
Santa- Barbara (Dana: 1998)
Tam, v sentiabre (ZeKo:1996)
plus 64 songs from the Safoshkin archives

Leshchenko

Aromat liubvi (Soiuz: 1996)
Den' pobedy: Pesni o Velikoi Otechestvennoi voine: Zapisi 1946–80gg (Melodiia)
Evgenii Zharkovskii: Pesni. Morskaia pamiat' (Melodiia: 1975?)
Lev Leshchenko (Melodiia)
Mir grez (ORT: 1999)
Skol'ko v mire dorog. My pesni poem (Melodiia)
Vospominanie ([double album] Soiuz: 1996)
plus 47 songs from the Safoshkin archives

P'ekha

Ansambl' Druzhba (Akkord: 1963?)
Ansambl' Druzhba i Èdita P'ekha (Melodiia: 1968)
Èdita P'ekha. (Akkord: 1964)
Èdita P'ekha (Melodiia. 1965?)
Èto zdorovo! 60-e. (KDK/Azart: 1997)
Ia vas liubliu (Zeko: 1994)
Krugozor 1965 #5. Mama
Krugozor 1968 #8. Ogromnoe nebo.
Krugozor 1968 #11. Veriu.
Krugozor 1969 #6. Liubov'
Moim druz'iam (Melodiia: 1987)
Pochuvstvui, dogadaisia, pozovi (Melodiia: 1986)
Tem, kto liubit P'ekhu (Korporatsiia: 1996)
plus 148 songs from the Safoshkin archives

Ponarovskaia/Poiushchie Gitary

Poiushchie Gitary (EP). Provody / My rasstalis' / Karlsson / Net tebia prekrasnei
Poiushchie Gitary (Melodiia)
Poiushchie Gitary (PG/Korporatsiia: 1996)
Tak prokhodit zhizn' moia (IP:1996)

Pugacheva/Veselye Rebiata

Alla Pugacheva (Melodiia)
Alla Pugacheva poet pesni M. Min'kova (Melodiia: 1983)
Arlekino ([single] Melodiia) plus Posidim, pookaem/ Ty snish'sia mne
Belyi sneg (ABP: 2000)
Da! (Extraphone: 1998)
Diskoklub 2 (Melodiia PG: 1981)
Druzhit' nam nado (Melodiia PG: 1980)
Ia bol'she ne revnuiu/ Beda ([single] Melodiia: 1981)
Izbrannoe ([double album] AP Production: 1999)
Kak trevozhen ètot put' ([double album] Melodiia: 1982)
Kollektsiia (General: 1996) Thirteen albums: *Po ostrym iglam iarkogo ognia; Akh, kak khochetsia zhit'; I v ètom vsia moia pechal'; Tol'ko v kino; Èto zavtra, a segodnia ...; Bilet na vcherashnii spektakl'; Vstrechi v puti; Na doroge ozhidanii; Razmyshleniia u kamina; Èto bylo odnazhdy; Baryshnia s krest'ianskoi zastavy; Alla Pugacheva v Stokgol'me; Pesni na bis*
Liuba-Liubov' (Melodiia EP/PG) Ukhodilo leto/ Shkol'naia pora/ V podslednii raz
Minutochku!!! (Melodiia PG: 1987)
Muzykal'nyi globus (Melodiia PG)
Muzyka sovetskogo kino (1981)
Ne delaite mne bol'no, gospoda (Soiuz: 1995)
Ostorozhno, listopad! (MP: 1999)
Podnimis' nad suetoi (Melodiia: 1980)
Prishla i govoriu (Melodiia: 1987)
Schast'ia v lichnoi zhizni! Pesni I. Nikolaeva (Melodiia: 1986)
To li eshche budet (Melodiia: 1980)
Zerkalo dushi (Melodiia: 1978)
plus 178 songs from the Safoshkin archives

Reznik and Pauls

Akh, vernisazh, akh, vernisazh (Melodiia: 1995)
Billiardnye shary (General: 1995)
Brilliantovye khity I. Reznika (Soiuz: 1996)
Cinema: Muzyka i melodii iz kinofil'mov (JSP: 1995)
Dalderi (Melodiia: 1983)
Isa pamāciba mīlēšanā (Melodiia EP: 1980)
Muzyka ia kinofil'ma "Dvoinoi kapkan" (Melodiia: 1985)
Pesni (Melodiia: 1985)
Pesni I. Reznika: Kaif (Jeff: 1993)
Pesni k spektakliu "Sherlok Kholms" (Melodiia: 1981)
Maèstro (Melodiia: 1997)

Raimonds Pauls (Melodiia: 1969)
Riadom so staroi pesni (Melodiia: 1985)
Zilie lini (Melodiia EP: 1970)

Rotaru

Chervona Ruta (Melodiia: 1996)
Gde ty, liubov' ([double album] Melodiia: 1981)
Khutorianka (Bekar/ Soiuz: 1995)
Lavanda
Liubi menia (Extraphone: 1998)
Monolog o liubvi (Melodiia: 1987)
Muzyka sovetskogo kino (1986)
Poet Sofiia Rotaru (1973?)
Sofiia Rotaru (1976?)
Sofiia Rotaru: Zolotoe serdtse (Melodiia: 1988)
Sofiia Rotaru: Zolotye pesni 1985–95 (Bekar/ Soiuz: 1995)
plus 159 songs from the Safoshkin archives

Shul'zhenko

Klavdiia Shul'zhenko (New York: Alma [two cassettes])
Klavdiia Shul'zhenko (six cassettes)
Nemnogo o sebe (Melodiia: 1994)
O liubvi ne govori (Melodiia)
Pesni proshlykh let (Melodiia)
Pesni, rozhdennye voinoi (RCD: 1995)
Poet Klavdiia Shul'zhenko (Melodiia)
Recordings of the Late Forties (Melodiia)
Tol'ko odin den' (Melodiia)
Ty pomnish' nashi vstrechi? (RCD: 1995)
Vernost' (Melodiia)
plus 142 songs from the Safoshkin archives

Utesov

Akh, Odessa moia (Kominform: 1996)
Doroga na Berlin (Russkii disk: 1995)
Dorogie Moskvichi (Kominform: 1996)
Gop so smykom (Kominform: 1995)
Gosudarstvennyi èstradnyi orkestr RSFSR (Melodiia)
Limonchiki: 1933–1937 (I&S)
Lunnaia rapsodiia (Kominform: 1996)

Odesskii port (Kominform: 1997)

Ot vsego serdtsa (Melodiia)

Para gnedykh (Kominform: 1995)

Poet Leonid Utesov (Akkord)

Poliushko-pole (Kominform: 1995)

U Chernogo moria (Kominform: 1996)

Zapisi 30-kh i 40-kh godov (Melodiia)

Zapisi 40-kh godov (Melodiia)

Zhdi menia (Kominform: 1996)

plus 256 songs from the Safoshkin archives

INDEX